CHRIST ALONE

THE UNIQUENESS OF THE GOSPEL
AND ITS IMPACT ON THE WORLD

Global Implications of Biblical Doctrine
Volume Two

Faculty of
THE MASTER'S ACADEMY INTERNATIONAL

General Editor Mark Tatlock

Xulon
PRESS

Christ Alone
The Uniqueness of the Gospel and Its Impact on the World
by The Master's Academy International

Printed in the United States of America.

ISBN 9781498496292

www.xulonpress.com

ACKNOWLEDGEMENTS

A book like this one—made up of essays from over 20 different authors from nearly as many countries—is truly unique, and completing such a work requires significant contributions from many people. A special thank you goes to Aaron Darlington, whose mind and pen worked tirelessly to contribute to each essay and provide cohesion to the entire volume. Another thank you goes to Bryan Tahmisian, whose careful attention and management helped bring the whole project to completion. In addition, I am indebted to our faithful team of content editors: Dr. David Deuel, Dr. William Barrick, Dr. William Webster, Dr. Brad Klassen, and Chris Burnett. I am also indebted to Sam Hanchett and Vadim Chepurny for their translation work, as well as to Mark Scarborough, Dan Powell, and John Azar for their assistance regarding Muslim theology. I'm grateful for the individual contributions made by Cameron Buettel and Josh Slocum, as well, and for all the copy editing work done by Joel Wilcox, Randy Ferreiro, and Adam Silva. Finally, I thank the authors not only for their contributions to this book, but more significantly, for their fervent dedication to the Lord Jesus Christ and His Great Commission. The words on these pages represent decades of service by these men to our Lord, and for that I am most profoundly appreciative. It is a deep and abiding blessing to serve the Lord together with them.

Mark Tatlock
President, The Master's Academy International

TABLE OF CONTENTS

FOREWORD

The apostle Paul, assigned by God to preach the mystery of the
gospel to the Gentiles, expressed this responsibility as preaching
Christ, Christ alone, and Christ crucified (Colossians 1:26–29). Paul
fully comprehended that it is Christ who is the theme of Old Testament
prophecy and necessarily the theme of New Testament preaching. For
Paul the entire missionary enterprise is aimed at fulfilling God's ultimate purpose: that His Son be worshipped by those from every tribe,
tongue, and nation. This is the ultimate destiny for those who believe.

Paul's priority, therefore, was preaching a biblical Christ and so
must ours. So, I would say to every preacher, every evangelist, and
every missionary that the benchmark of legitimate ministry is their
devotion to the biblical teaching of the person and work of Christ.
If there is any diminishing or deviation from proclaiming the true
Christ, they are in violation of the purpose of God as revealed in the
Scriptures. If the theme of the Bible is Christ, then the legitimacy of
Christian missions is tied inextricably to a consuming preoccupation
with enabling the lost to know all that has been revealed about Christ—
to understand His full glory with a view to worshiping Him, honoring
Him, and loving Him.

The apostle John warns that there will be many antichrists. This
is the strategy of Satan to confuse and mislead those who are lost. He
intends to keep them in darkness by sophisticated imitations which
appeal to man's self-centeredness. Antichrists, who are fashioned in
the image, not of the true God but of man, offer works-centered religious systems. These systems keep sinners enslaved, believing they
are genuinely following Christ. The closer we come to the end of the

age, the more pseudo-Christs and false Christs will appear. In every age, there are extensive and effective lies about the Lord Jesus Christ.

Many preach Christ, but they preach a false Christ, violating the features of a biblical Christology. If you fail to love the true Lord Jesus Christ, 1 Corinthians 16:22 clearly states you're cursed. Every man must be believe in the biblical Christ, not a Christ of their own imagination; not the Jesus of liberalism, not the Jesus of liberation theology, not the Jesus of the prosperity gospel, not the Jesus of Mormonism, not the Jesus of Islam, and not the Jesus of Catholicism. This deadly practice has even found its way, amazingly, into evangelicalism. The confusion that comes from this is worldwide; it's global.

We are here to declare what the true church has declared through all its history—Christ as revealed in Scripture. We must get it right about Christ. Salvation comes by believing in Christ. The apostle John makes it perfectly clear that his gospel account of the life of Christ was written so that we "might believe that Jesus is the Christ, the Son of God, and that believing have life in His name" (John 20:31). He would later write, "every spirit that confesses that Jesus Christ has come in the flesh is from God" (1 John 4:2). When you hear a true Christology, you have a messenger from God. "And every spirit that does not confess Jesus is not from God; that is the spirit of antichrist, of which you have heard that it is coming, and now it is already in the world" (1 John 3:4). That's the test. Christology is the test. If your Christology is aberrant, you're not a true messenger from God.

I am grateful for the men who teach in the pastoral training centers affiliated with The Master's Academy International. Their daily commitment is to equip church leaders around the world to faithfully declare the biblical Christ. These men minister in the immediate contexts of dominant false religions and faulty teaching propagated by Western missionaries. Their students are committed pastors, honing their exegetical skills to accurately preach Christ. It is my great joy to observe their faithfulness to the truth and regularly hear testimony of the gospel impact they are having.

This volume illustrates the necessity of a sound Christology, for a sound Christology will inform a sound missiology. This is the great need in missions today and these men's work is essential, assuring that the church which bears His name will faithfully proclaim the saving truth of Christ alone.

John MacArthur

INTRODUCTION

I n the following statement, Philip Jenkins provides the chief lie promoted by religious pluralism as it relates to Christianity:

> We cannot be too precise about defining Christianity. Ever since the movement began two thousand years ago, the range of groups defining themselves as followers of Jesus has always been very diverse, and we should acknowledge and accept a broad range of self-conceptions. [1]

He goes on to state:

> A Christian is someone who describes himself or herself as Christian, who believes that Jesus is not merely a prophet or an exalted moral teacher, but in some unique sense the Son of God, and the messiah. Beyond that, we should not inquire into detailed doctrine, whether for instance a person adheres to the Bible alone, accepts the Trinity, or has a literal belief in Jesus' bodily resurrection. The vast majority of self-described Christians worldwide do in fact meet most of these criteria for membership in

---

[1]   Philip Jenkins, *The Next Christendom: The Coming of Global Christianity* (Oxford: Oxford University Press, 2002), 88.

the faith, but for present purposes, we cannot label
as heretics those who do not.[2]

While one might expect this from an ecumenical author, these
very assertions are increasingly expressed within the ranks of evangelical missiologists.

Christ Alone, the second volume in the Global Implications of
Biblical Doctrine series, addresses aberrations within the teaching
of major world religions *and* within the contemporary evangelical
church as to the person and work of Christ. The authors make efforts
to identify and correct erroneous departures from the true gospel,
while seeking to reclaim the centrality of Christ Jesus in all missions
endeavors. These authors serve as TMAI faculty members, training
national pastors in multiple and diverse cross-cultural contexts. The
common thread shared by all is a clarifying call to uphold biblical
orthodoxy in gospel content and gospel methodology, believing this
will serve the global church best as it seeks to faithfully fulfill the
Great Commission.

This book is centered on the themes of Christ, with a broader
consideration given to those aspects which also regard salvation
(soteriology), man (anthropology), and sin (hamartiology). These
doctrines comprise the heart of the missionary message and must
be understood accurately by both the preacher and the prospective
convert. While these doctrinal tenets are largely debated within a
Western context, the focus of this series is the particular implications
of these doctrines in the international ministry context. In every culture, there are not only local indigenous belief systems, folk religions,
and religions brought by colonial powers, but also there are growing
influences from secular humanism and liberalism. The gospel around
the world is under assault, and churches in each setting face the challenge to correct these unbiblical teachings. In many cases, it has been
the influences from the West, brought to bear by evangelical missionaries, which have imposed pragmatic and faulty evangelistic strategies. This is often seen in missionary efforts that stem from Arminian
theological traditions, which will be shown by several authors.

---

[2]   Ibid.

While pastors and missionaries have the great responsibility of teaching a biblically accurate view of Christ, man, sin, and salvation, they also equip their congregations to rightly apply these truths to correct any errors that may still linger in their own thinking. The desire of the authors here is to assist the reader in understanding the prevailing threat(s) that exist to a proper Christology and soteriology in their cultural setting, and to guide believers to understand how the person and work of Jesus Christ is sufficient to combat those threats.

In approaching this volume, the authors were asked to consider the following:

1. In what specific areas does accurate teaching on the person and work of Christ confront the dominant cultural and/or religious teaching in your context?
2. Are there historical denominational influences in your country that have influenced a faulty or inaccurate soteriology?
3. What Christological and soteriological threats exist in your cultural and regional context as a result of a non-biblical worldview?

The results of their research and writing provide us insight into how the doctrine of Christ has been rejected, wrongly interpreted, or stands as a direct apologetic to the major faith tenets within their home country. While each essay does not exhaust the variations of where a biblical Christology is diminished, they do offer specific case studies that alert the reader to the vital importance of biblical doctrine in the life of the Church. Moreover, these studies call for the need to be faithful to the one true Christ revealed in Scripture. Essays written by our faculty in Italy, Spain, and Honduras expose the erroneous teachings of Roman Catholicism and provide insight into its historical and contemporary efforts, both of which threaten the true gospel of Christ alone.

Our faculty serving Russian-speaking populations in the United States address the impact of the Eastern Orthodox Church, mirroring many of the same excesses and creedal errors of Catholicism, but explaining its differing perspective on justification. Our faculty in Russia provide a careful analysis of the destiny of the unevangelized, exposing the dangerous notions that face the Russian evangelical church today. These increasingly popular unbiblical notions pose direct assaults on the historical significance of Christ's incarnation, the necessity and sufficiency of His atoning work, and the importance of the proclamation of His death and resurrection.

Faculty members serving in a post-communist setting, such as the Czech Republic and Ukraine, provide insight into the harmful effects of humanistic worldviews. These worldviews elevate man's ability to advance his own eternal destiny and minimize the need there is for Christ. A clear proclamation of the sinfulness of man and the cross of Christ is of paramount importance, especially where atheism poisons a society's conception of Jesus from childhood, or where doctrinal concession has informed pragmatic missiological practices that overshadow the preaching of Christ alone.

Our faculty in the Balkans address a variety of weighty topics, such as Bible translation in Albania, an interaction between Christ and Islam, and religious pluralism in Croatia. In a South African context, the implications of how a society understands and receives Christ are illustrated by a careful examination of orality, authority, and the resulting cultural views of mediation. And our faculty training Chinese pastors in Southeast Asia provide a biblical perspective on suffering with a personal touch, highlighting the mostly unknown (in the West) testimony of pastor Lee Tian En.

Finally, essays addressing false representations of Christ in Mexico and the Philippines identify where biblical teaching about Christ has been exchanged for syncretistic or heretical views. The false claims of Apollo Quiboloy, for example, who considers himself to be the modern realization of Jesus Christ, illustrate the reality that antichrists exist today and deceive millions of people. These essays, like all of the essays, labor to show that the one and only Lord Jesus Christ of the Scriptures alone is worthy of our utmost admiration, honor, and praise.

It is not lost on the authors that this work is being published on the 500th anniversary of the Reformation. The Reformers recognized the critical threat to genuine Christianity, and gave their lives to correct the unbiblical dogmas that diminished the exclusive person and work of Jesus Christ. Their corrective and defiant actions, based on convictions forged by accurate interpretation of the Bible alone, birthed a movement of thinking and teaching that exalts the unique and glorious identify of our Lord Jesus Christ. They rightly affirmed *Solus Christus*, Christ alone. May the ongoing labors of the men who train and study through TMAI training centers across the globe accomplish in our lifetime the most important thing required of our generation: to proclaim and preach Christ faithfully. To Him alone be the glory!

Mark Tatlock
President, The Master's Academy International

Between God and Men: Proclaiming Christ as Mediator in Light of the South African Concept of Mediation

Charlie Rampfumedzi and David Beakley

Christ Seminary, South Africa

[Editor's Note: One of the greatest challenges to pastoral training in cross-cultural settings involves overcoming the various worldview grids through which information is filtered. At its core, a worldview is built upon a person's understanding of God, man, sin, and salvation. Therefore, it is vital that ministers of God's Word not merely seek to change a person's worldview but also to confront concepts within that worldview that are at odds with God and the means of salvation provided in His Son. This first essay is especially instructive in providing an analysis of the South African concept of mediation, and in demonstrating the need for such a concept to be challenged by the biblical claim that Christ Himself is the only mediator between God and men.]

Introduction

Western Authority and the Written Law

European societies are largely based on the authority of written law, having descended from Greek and Roman cultures that functioned according to written contracts and decrees.[1] From a spiritual standpoint, the Jewish Torah and Christian Bible were the framework for objective truth as these two religions were incorporated into Western culture. However, during the Middle Ages (ca. AD 550–1350) many of these societies began depending less on the written law of Scripture and more in the magisterium of the Roman Catholic Church. As the people became separated from the Scriptures, they developed a desperate need for a visible spiritual mediator and intercessor between them and God. The Protestant Reformation's call for *sola scriptura* in the 16th century was a call to break the stronghold of man-made authority and false mediation.[2] Once Scripture was available in both print and sermonic form, and the people were taught that they were responsible for pursuing their own salvation through Jesus Christ, the true church naturally responded and grew. But, what about the places where the written law, or written authority, was not present and was not part of an existing worldview?

African Authority and the Oral Law

In Africa, unlike Europe, written law and written history did not play a role in society. The African people on the whole neither invented nor implemented an alphabet for the art of reading and writing.[3] Instead, all necessary information was passed on from person to person, generation to generation, by word of mouth.[4] The result

---

[1] Some examples include the collection of French law known *as Répertoire de la législation du Notariat,* the English Magna Carta, and, when the Europeans migrated to the Americas, the United States Constitution.

[2] Martin Luther sounded the alarm from Scripture itself by appealing to Romans 5: "There [in Romans 5] we clearly see that Christ is established as our mediator. When I do not use Him as such, but rather seek another mediator, I dishonor Christ, despise His blood and shove this mediator out of the way, apart from whom I can never be saved." (Martin Luther, *Festival Sermons of Martin Luther,* trans. Joel Baseley, [Dearborn, Michigan: Mark V Publications, 2005], 53.)

[3] Until the middle of the 20th century, only a few West African countries had produced creative writing in European languages. In South Africa, Xhosa literature began a bit earlier in the 19th century, and that mostly by foreign (Western) missionaries, who were concerned more with moral edification and the propagation of Christianity. This was largely due to the efforts of Western Protestant missionaries who reduced the local language to a written form and then translated biblical passages and works like *The Pilgrim's Progress.* See Albert S. Gérard, ed., *European Language Writing in Sub-Saharan Africa* (Budapest: Akadémiai Kiadó, 1986), 17, 168.

[4] John S. Mbiti, *Introduction to African Religion,* 2nd ed. (London: Heinemann, 1975), 4.

is that historical truth and law were never codified in or transmitted through a written source but were arbitrated by human mediators. Thus, people, not written documents, held authority and played the role of mediators within African society.

The same is true for spiritual truth. African spiritual authority relates to the societal concept of *ubuntu,* a kind of humanism common among many African peoples.[5] According to *ubuntu,* "There is God in a human being."[6] In other words, the truths about God and the laws from God do not reside in a written document but in the African people, whether it be an individual authority figure or a group of elders. Because divine truths are communicated to the people through authority figures rather than the written word, the community leader assumes the role of spiritual mediator between the individuals of the community and the creator God.

When Two Authority Structures Collide

The spiritual leader's mediatorial function in the community had long existed before missionaries came to Africa. When Western missionaries flooded into the continent and evangelized many villages during the modern era, many Africans accepted Christian doctrine but never adopted a new worldview relative to spiritual authority.[7] Because of the humanistic value system of *ubuntu,* which endows spiritual authority to the community leader by way of oral tradition, the doctrinal teachings of the missionary were seen to be as valid as Scripture itself. It became natural for the Africans to associate mediation with their new authority figure.[8] Each community with a

---

[5]   The South African Nobel Laureate Archbishop Desmond Tutu describes *ubuntu* as: "[The] essence of being human. It speaks of the fact that my humanity is caught up and is inextricably bound up in yours. I am human because I belong." <http://www.buzzle.com/editorials/7–22–2006–103206.asp>.

[6]   According to Mfuniselwa John Bhengu, as discussed in Christian B. N. Gade, "What is *Ubuntu?* Different Interpretations from South Africans of African Descent." South African Journal of Philosophy 31 (3):489 (2012). Trace Bhengu's original thought in M. J. Bhengu, *Ubuntu: The Essence of Democracy,* (Cape Town, South Africa: Novalis Press, 1996).

[7]   David Beakley, "Influence and Authority in an Oral-Oriented Culture" in *The Implications of Inerrancy for the Global Church.* (Maitland, Florida: Xulon Press), 204–208. Also see Wilbur O'Donovan's comments in *Biblical Christianity in African Perspective* (Ilorin, Nigeria: Nigeria Evangelical Fellowship, 1992), 5.

[8]   The problem of combining unbiblical worldviews with Scripture is not a problem of the past. Rather, syncretism is still rampant today among many African peoples. In fact, because of

missionary now had a "true" mediator living and breathing right in front of them.

The purpose of this essay, then, is to explore the difficulties in having the truth of the mediatorial work of Jesus Christ penetrate the African worldview and to provide some missiological solutions to the problems. First, we will demonstrate that the concept of a mediator is well established in South African thought, though the truth of a single mediator between God and man (Jesus Christ) is largely unknown and misunderstood. Second, we will provide a case study from Acts 8 to show that such challenges have always existed among fallen humanity. Then, we will examine the mediatorial role of Jesus Christ, providing a testimony to illustrate its truth. Finally, we will provide some cogent missiological recommendations for breaking through the South African worldview to proclaim Jesus Christ as the sole mediator between God and man.

The Mediator Is an Established African Concept

Traditional Beliefs and Practices

The Supreme Being (God) is perceived as being far distant and beyond the reach of ordinary Africans, which makes direct communication and relationship with God impossible. Africans are led to believe that they need the help of a mediator in order to approach God. According to social customs, a person of lower status may only approach someone of a higher status through the efforts of a mediator,[9] so both human and spiritual intermediaries may be necessary to approach God.[10] Such mediators include ancestors, traditional doctors, medicine men, seers, diviners, priests, prophets, rainmakers, kings, and ritual elders, among others. Details concerning some of these mediators follow:

---

cultural pride and an undue respect for African traditional religions, Africa today is fertile soil for universalism. See Tokunboh Adeyemo, *Salvation in African Tradition,* (Nairobi, Kenya: Evangel Publishing House, 1997), 13.

[9] In South Africa, this person who fills this role in a village is called an *enduna*.

[10] Mbiti, 68. O'Donovan opens up his discussion on permissible mediators between God and man: "Mediators are very important in Africa. Many practices are built around the function of a mediator." (Wilbur O'Donovan, *Biblical Christianity in African Perspective,* [Carlisle, UK: Paternoster, 1992], 258.)

Ancestors are highly admired spiritual beings from whom South Africans derive their identity, life, and right to exist. These spirits play a major role in the daily life of most South Africans. Their duty is to mediate between God and the tribe, bind the community together, provide for daily needs of the tribe through rain and fertility, and preserve the customs of the tribe.[11] They may be called on for the occasion of a birth, marriage, sickness, or family reunion, and they are invoked for bringing rain, favorable hunting, and victory in war.[12]

Traditional doctors supposedly mediate between man and the spirits of the deceased in order to discover the cause of someone's sickness, difficulty, or death.[13] Once the direct cause of a personal calamity has been discovered, the diviner then mediates between the victim and the ancestors for a favorable solution. Divination might also involve placing curses on the person, who may have been the cause of the problem. In South Africa, traditional doctors are accepted by the government as legitimate health care practitioners.

Priests, as official servants of a god, offer sacrifices as the ancestors' representative.[14]

Other important intermediaries include men who go between the king or chief and the common people, relatives who negotiate the bride price in a wedding, and persons who mediate between two parties with legal or familial disputes.

Religious Beliefs and Practices within African Independent Churches

Many African Independent Churches (AIC) in South Africa emphasize the role of mediators but do not teach the sole mediation of Jesus Christ.[15] Instead, the bishops or priests are considered to be

---

[11] Piet Meiring, *A World of Religions: A South African Perspective*, (Pretoria, South Africa: Kagiso Publisher, 1996), 14.

[12] E. G. Parrinder, *African Traditional Religion*, 3rd ed., (London: Sheldon Press, 1962), 62.

[13] See O'Donovan, 242.

[14] See Parrinder, 101.

[15] The African Independent Church is an African-initiated church started in Africa by Africans and not by missionaries from another continent. In South Africa alone, the latest assessment revealed that there are no fewer than six thousand denominations falling within this religious institution, operating in a strange way within the Christian context. African Independent Churches can lay claim to approximately 11 million adherents in South Africa alone. These people represent nearly thirty percent of the total African population in the country, and forty percent of its total Christian community.

the true mediators between God and men. Barnabas Lekganyane, the current bishop of the Zion Christian Church (ZCC), is often called "Mediator,"[16] and his duties include revealing God's will to man and communicating with lesser gods or ancestral spirits. In the ZCC and other AIC churches, the bishop or pastor possesses the authoritative word of God since he speaks to God and receives messages from Him. As explained above, these practices naturally arise from a societal milieu in which truth has been transmitted for centuries by authority figures rather than by written documents. The bishop or pastor is seen as the spiritual authority, divine truth is mediated by him, and only through him is a relationship with God possible.[17]

Christ as Mediator Is Not Sufficiently Established

Though the concept of mediation is well established and widely attested in South Africa, relatively few South Africans have come to know the only *true* mediator between God and man, Jesus Christ. Among many ethnic groups, Jesus is simply unknown.[18] He is not found or mentioned in their tribal or clan meetings, and He is noticeably absent in the elementary stories shared by the elders around the fire or in their initiation schools.[19] Though mediators of all kinds abound within their cultural and religious strata, any true understanding of how God has revealed Himself to man or how man might have a relationship with God is sadly absent.

---

[16] A.J. de Visser, *Kyrios and Morena, the Lordship of Christ and African Township Christianity,* (South Africa: Gezina, 2001), 108.

[17] Devastating consequences of this kind of misplaced authority are seen throughout the country, with pastors abusing this position for personal gain or requiring church members to demonstrate their faith and obedience by performing bizarre acts, such as eating grass, snakes, or rats. This is has been widely reported throughout the media in South Africa. For one such reference, see <http://citizen.co.za/news/news-national/423976/pastor-mnguni-makes-congregation-eat-snakes/>.

[18] This is true in spite of the fact that the gospel first reached Ethiopia soon after the founding of the church (Acts 8:22) and that, according to Eusebius, the apostle Mark planted churches in Alexandria, Egypt. See Eusebius, *The Church History,* 2.16, trans. Paul L. Maier, (Grand Rapids, Michigan: Kregel, 2007), 64.

[19] Though the author has a degree of personal experience, these claims are corroborated by the fact that there are virtually no articles to document or support any kind of understanding of the person and works of Jesus Christ among ethnic groups with African traditional religious backgrounds. See de Visser, 61.

To compound the problem, even within the religious circles of syncretistic African "Christianity," Jesus is not truly known. Within the AIC, for example, the name of Jesus is familiar but often insignificant in practice, for many of these churches do not teach that Jesus is the sole mediator between God and man, that He is the Word of God who alone reveals God to man, or that He is our great High Priest who alone represents man to God. Instead, many of the pastors of these churches claim these prerogatives for themselves.

Initial Challenges in Proclaiming Christ as Mediator

Because many South Africans traditionally, culturally, and religiously depend on a variety of spiritual mediators, the proclamation of Jesus as the *exclusive* mediator between God and man presents a serious challenge. It is difficult to understand and even harder to swallow, especially in light of the typical South African worldview. Evangelists and missionaries need to understand the African concept of mediation and recognize that mere profession of Jesus' name does not necessarily indicate that a person has learned to trust in Christ's mediation alone. Furthermore, they need to know how South Africans from oral-based societies are prone to understand authority (i.e., in the *messenger*, rather than the *message*). It might surprise Western readers that these challenges have existed from the very beginning. It will be instructive, therefore, to consider two biblical cases from Acts 8 that highlight the same kinds of challenges that exist in African contexts today.

The Case of Simon the Magician

In Acts 8:4–24, Luke describes the ministry of Philip as a preaching ministry throughout Samaria (vv. 4–5), which was accompanied by signs and wonders to substantiate the gospel message (vv. 6–8). In the midst of Philip's evangelistic ministry came Simon, described as a former practitioner of magic and possessor of some powers to perform magic arts. He was essentially a mediator between the people and the spirit world, and thus they called him "the Great Power of God" (vv. 9–10). Yet, while the community was astounded with the experience of Simon's apparent power, many were convicted by Philip's words of truth, believed, and were baptized in the name of Jesus (vv. 12, 16).

Even the great Simon believed and was baptized. Nevertheless, when he saw that many people had received God's Holy Spirit through the human act of laying on hands, he tried to negotiate a price with the apostles to give him the same power (vv. 17–19). In doing so, he showed his true colors. He had not submitted to the authority of the *message* but rather was impressed by the perceived authority of the *messengers* (i.e., mediators). He coveted the powerful signs and miracles that were intended to validate the gospel message. He had no need for the mediator Jesus Christ; instead, he wanted to *be* the mediator who could give or withhold the Holy Spirit for personal gain.

The actions and motives of Simon unfortunately typify many of the leaders of the AIC in South Africa. These leaders are widely recognized by the locals to be the power of God, considered by the people to be mediators between God and man, vested with supernatural power and authority. They command great respect and obedience from their congregants. But Peter saw right through Simon the magician, as his strong rebuke indicates. He saw that Simon's heart was not right before God, that he was full of wickedness, in the gall of bitterness, and in the bondage of iniquity (vv. 21–22). In other words, Simon was no mediator; rather, he was still in desperate need of one for the forgiveness of his own sins.

The Case of the Ethiopian Eunuch

Following the account of Simon in Acts 8, we are introduced to an African who did not know Jesus. Luke identifies this African as an Ethiopian eunuch, a court official of Candace, Queen of the Ethiopians. This royal figure had an immense responsibility of stewardship over the queen's treasury (8:27). Although he was African, he had traveled all the way to Jerusalem to worship. Like Simon, he was interested in religion but still condemned in his sin.

After an undoubtedly rich experience in Jerusalem, we find him reading the book of Isaiah with no understanding (vv. 28, 30–34). The Holy Spirit sent Philip to address the man's understanding of what he was reading (vv. 29–30), to which the eunuch responded in verse 31, "Well, how could I, unless someone guides me?" The eunuch's response is telling, for he was not looking for a man to follow, nor was he looking for content that might match oral tradition. Rather, he was longing for the exposition and understanding of the very words in the scroll before him. He wanted to understand the content of Scripture.

The words themselves were so critical to the eunuch that he posed an interpretive question to Philip in verse 34: "Please tell me, of whom does the prophet say this? Of himself or of someone else?" In response to Philip's exposition of the messianic text, with the clear gospel presentation of the substitutionary atonement of Jesus Christ on behalf of sinners, the eunuch was granted the understanding that he sought (vv. 35–38). After the eunuch was baptized and had demonstrated saving faith (vv. 37–38), Philip was immediately snatched away by the Spirit, never to be seen again by the eunuch. Of particular note to the question of South African authority is that the eunuch "went on his way rejoicing" from that moment forward (v. 39). He placed no trust in Philip but rather placed all his trust in the gospel truths about Christ that he had read and now understood. That Philip left his presence was of no consequence. He was left with the Word alone, and for this, he rejoiced. Conversion is genuine when it does not depend on the messenger but responds entirely to the message of Jesus Christ.

These two biblical pictures from Acts 8 underscore the stronghold of one's worldview and the power of God to change it. South Africans need true biblical knowledge of the person and works of Jesus Christ in order to comprehend that He is the only Mediator between God and man. Only Christ has the power to save the sinner. Like the Ethiopian eunuch, the South African today must trust not in the preacher but in the gospel, and not in the personal revelations of authority figures but in the revelation of Jesus Christ in Scripture.

Biblical Revelation of Jesus Christ as Our Sole Mediator

Many New Testament passages declare the truth of Jesus Christ as sole mediator between men and God. It will be profitable to examine passages from 1 Timothy and Hebrews.

Jesus Christ Is a Superior Mediator because He Is Fully God and Fully Man
1 Timothy 2:5–6. In perhaps the clearest text on the topic, Paul explains that God provided His Son as the perfect ransom for sinners.

All prior mediators in Israel's salvation history pale in comparison to the power and the purity of Jesus Christ.[20] The Son of God was perfectly righteous and holy, an unblemished sacrifice (1 Pet 1:19). In addition to being the Son of God, Jesus Christ is also designated as "the man Christ Jesus." In this way, Jesus Christ supersedes even Moses, Israel's mediator of the written Law of God.[21] Peter Lewis comments on the superior faith established through the superior Mediator: "Indeed where Christianity is concerned, the place of Jesus Christ as the one mediator between man and God is absolutely fundamental and is its chief distinguishing feature. To be a Christian is to know God in the Mediator, to be right with God by the Mediator, and to live for God through the Mediator."[22]

Jesus Christ Alone Is Both Sinless Sacrifice and High Priest

Hebrews 8:6. Jesus Christ is explicitly declared as the unique mediator between God and men specifically because His covenant is based on better promises than the covenant established through Moses' mediation.[23] The new covenant provides for a sacrifice "once for all" (Heb 10:10, 14) that is able to save forever those who draw near to God through Him (Heb 7:25).

Hebrews 9:14–15. The previous chapter's theme of the "better covenant"[24] is foundational for this text. Because Jesus Christ "offered Himself without blemish to God" He in His sacrificial death presented an acceptable sacrifice to God.[25] In this way, He provided atonement even for sins committed under the first covenant. Jesus

---

[20]   Peter Lewis, *The Glory of Christ*, (Chicago, Illinois: Moody Press, 1997), 232.

[21]   In Exodus 20:19, the people cried out to Moses, "Speak to us yourself, and we will listen; but do not let God speak to us, or we will die." In this way, the people were pleading for Moses to be their mediator. Also, Galatians 3:19 indicates that the Law came through Moses, "the agency of a mediator." That mediator was Moses. Hebrews 3:3 states that Jesus is "counted worthy of more glory than Moses."

[22]   Lewis, 231.

[23]   The term for "better" (*kreittonos*) is a comparative adjective which compares the new covenant (Jer 31:31) with the "old" Mosaic covenant. It is not used to demean the old covenant but is used to show that the new covenant is "more prominent," or "higher in rank." The old covenant did not bring life, where the new covenant brings eternal life through the holy and pure blood brought by the sacrifice of God's Son, Jesus Christ.

[24]   Ellingsworth sees the topic of a "better covenant" as the theme of all of Chapter 8. See Paul Ellingsworth, *The Epistle to the Hebrews*, (Grand Rapids, Michigan: Eerdmans, 1993), 459.

[25]   F. F. Bruce, *The Epistle to the Hebrews*, (Grand Rapids, Michigan: Eerdmans, 1990), 222.

Christ thus holds the right and responsibility to establish fellowship between God and sinners.

Hebrews 10:19–20. The boldness[26] with which all believers in Christ enter into fellowship with God today is set in contrast with the numerous restrictions that God placed on Israel to prevent full, direct access to God.[27] Whereas God previously allowed limited access to His presence through the high priest, now the Christian has full access because Jesus has eternally and perfectly become our great High Priest. Jesus Christ serves as a bridge between God and men because He is both God and man and thus holds the proper credentials on both sides of the bridge.[28] Because He is qualified to mediate, His mediation is sufficient, and there is no need for any other human to act in such a capacity. Reconciliation and fellowship with the transcendent God is now made immanent through the mediation of Jesus Christ, and all who belong to Him may boldly enter the presence of God without fear of inadequacy.

Hebrews 12:24. Jesus Christ is the mediator of the New Covenant, which is a "better" covenant because of His "sprinkled blood." Here Jesus' blood is compared to the blood of Abel who offered a "better sacrifice" than his brother (Heb 11:4). Similar to how Melchizedek was the first man to be called a priest in Scripture,[29] Abel was the first man to offer an acceptable sacrifice to God. Since Abel's acceptable sacrifice preceded that of the Levitical sacrifices, it was superior to the human priesthood. Since the sacrifice of Jesus Christ "speaks better" than that of Abel, it is both superior to the first sacrifice and superior to all subsequent sacrifices which came from the Levitical priesthood.[30]

---

[26] The word *parresian* conveys the idea of "boldness" or "being outspoken in public."

[27] F. F. Bruce, 249.

[28] K. J. Pali, "Christ as once for all sacrifice: a cultural reading of Hebrews," *Acta Theologica*, Vol. 34 n. 1, (Bloemfontein: Jan. 2014), a paper presented in the Department of Practical Theology, University of Free States.

[29] Cf. Psa 110:4; Heb 5:6, 20; 7:14–17. Note that Jesus Christ is not compared to the priests in the Levitical system but is superior to them "according to the order of Melchizedek." Jesus' priesthood, like Melchizedek's, did not derive from a bloodline. Furthermore, all priestly activity prior to that of Jesus Christ was temporary due to the sins of the priests (Heb 5:3–6).

[30] Ellingsworth, 682.

The Context of the Book of Hebrews

The context of the epistle to the Hebrews addresses the problem of many African Independent Church members today who, like the Jewish Christians in first-century Jerusalem, are tempted to regard the ancient rituals of their people as worthy substitutes for the biblical Jesus. In times of trial and stress, they forget the value and superiority of Jesus Christ as mediator and sacrifice over all the temporary "shadows" of their cultural religious system. The death of Jesus Christ inaugurated the new covenant of which only Jesus Christ, the unblemished Son of God, could be the sole mediator. By offering His blood once for all as the Chief High Priest, Jesus entered heaven itself and opened the way for repentant sinners to have loving fellowship with the Father.

On the basis of the perfect mediatorial role of Jesus Christ, the true African believer must recognize that his ancestors were no more than imperfect and sinful human beings, who themselves needed a Savior. Likewise, bishops and pastors are imperfect human beings, who also need a Savior. None of these African figures can carry out the mediation of Jesus Christ according to the testimony of 1 Timothy and Hebrews. In fact, the African role as intermediary is null and void in virtue of Jesus' once-for-all offer of redemption through His blood. Jesus Christ even now sits at the right hand of God, interceding for His own.

A South African Case Study on Spiritual Authority

An aunt in many African ethnic groups is an extremely important person. She is often revered for her portfolio and responsibilities, which in a royal family, would include advising the current chief or king on traditional and customary matters and acting as intermediary during marriage negotiations and dispute resolutions. The aunt's mediatorial status is important in spiritual matters, as well. She will often act as the family priestess, offering libations on behalf of the family in times of sacrifices.

The author's widowed aunt is a sister to the chief of a village in South Africa. When she joined the ZCC (the largest AIC in South Africa), she was recognized as a prophetess and served as a key figure in one of the village branches. She entrusted herself and her children to the rituals and instructions prescribed by the bishop for salvation. Through her influence, she managed to recruit her mother and her brother, the chief, to the ZCC, and so the royal family as a whole placed their hope of eternal life in the bishop of the ZCC.

After some time, an African evangelical pastor led an outreach in the village. Through God's leading, the author's cousin repented of his sin and was saved, though for the time being he remained in strict obedience to his mother and the ZCC. A while later, the same evangelical pastor sought lodging in the aunt's house for the night. In the evening, the preacher led the family in a gospel-focused devotion from Psalm 91. After everyone had gone to bed, however, the aunt woke up, rushed into her son's room, and asked that the pastor be summoned. As soon as he came, she confessed that she had been greatly convicted by the Word of God, that she had become aware of the darkness that gripped her soul, and that she believed the truth about Jesus Christ. She repented that very moment from her sinful practices and took all her ZCC uniforms and associated relics to be burned in the middle of the night.[31] What is astounding about the aunt's story is that the Spirit of God granted to her repentance and faith not through a "revival," a manifestation of power, or any suggestive manipulation, but through the very simple teaching about the person and works of Jesus Christ. The gospel is indeed the power of God for salvation to all who believe (Rom 1:16).

At great cost, the author's aunt left the ZCC and her traditional role as family priestess, never to return to her demonic practices. She was baptized and became a member of the Baptist church in the very same village. Despite enduring painful insults and criticisms from family members and people that she had once led to the ZCC, her faith remained steadfast. Even now into her eighties, she continues to serve not man but the God-man Jesus Christ, in whom she finally found true reconciliation to God.

Conclusion

Westerners often associate the blessing of God with their societal empires and economic successes, a heritage heavily influenced by

---

[31] Note a similar response by the Ephesians in Acts 19:18–20, who repented of their witchcraft.

Greek philosophy and Roman law. Sub-Saharan African societies do not share this heritage and, because of their history of oral tradition, have only recently begun to adopt the idea of a "written law code" for moral, legal, and spiritual authority. But is the Western pedigree really a blessing that provides spiritual advantage? It seems best to conclude that all people (Western or southern African) are dead in their sins and alienated from God and that the only way to bring life is not through education or "civilization," but by the power of God through the mediation of Jesus Christ.

Westerners are "educated" and have a "civil" society, but they are also highly independent and self-reliant and thus, sadly, have little recognition of their own need for a mediator. Though South Africans have not long benefitted from objective law codes and principles passed on through writing, they have preserved over the centuries a few concepts that are worth noting. First, virtually every South African is brought up with an understanding of the existence of God, and second, virtually every African recognizes the need for a mediator in order to commune with the transcendent God.

Educating Africa with more "civilized" church polity or leadership will not resolve Africa's sin problem but may exacerbate the overall problem of authority by introducing yet more mediators into the community. With the significance that power plays in the African mindset, Christianity is viewed either as a religion of the West and is interpreted through a haze of cultural overlays, or is whatever the spiritual leader says it is.[32] The power to overcome the deadly effects of sin rests in God alone through the supreme mediation of Jesus Christ as made known in Scripture. Now is the time to re-evangelize African "Christians" with the exclusive Reformation claims of faith being informed by Scripture alone and coming through faith alone, by grace alone, in Christ alone to the glory of God alone. And for South Africans, there is no greater call than that from Norvald Yri:

> One thing is obvious: the dividing line between different systems of hermeneutics is not a geographical line between Europe and Africa; in fact the time is past when one can divide Western Christianity and

---

[32] Cornelius Olowala, "The Person and Work of Christ" in *Issues in African Theology*, (Nairobi: East African Educational Publishers, 1998), 155.

African Christianity in this way. The theological and hermeneutical dividing line is faith in Christ versus faith in tradition, self, or ideology.[33]

And with this clarity of thought that dispels any "cultural" sensitivities or need for special contextualization, Yri concludes with this:

> The classical Christian view of salvation then, is that salvation is not found independently of Jesus Christ. And faith in Christian terms is faith in Jesus Christ. *This attitude is not a Western imperialistic or discriminatory attitude. This is clearly what is taught in God's special revelation in the Judeo-Christian context and culture—a culture that is much closer to African milieu than European....* This is the message Luther rediscovered five centuries ago. It is a message Africa needs to discover now, more than ever.[34] [emphasis added]

The search for specialized contextualization approaches with more nuanced "cultural" sensitivities is, on the basis of the authority problem in Africa, a futile search. Pastors, missionaries, and Christian workers in the sub-Saharan African church would do well to maintain the following priorities as they establish biblical churches with God-honoring leadership:

1. Challenge the African Worldview

Evangelistic endeavors provide a key initial opportunity for learning about how the community's beliefs are shaped. Once the local worldview is assessed, it must be challenged on the basis of Scripture. Otherwise, many "Simons" may emerge, who do not adopt the biblical worldview but become armed with spiritual knowledge to be used for their own gain. Throwing biblical tools and exegetical methodology at Africans is hopelessly insufficient without taking

---

[33] Norvald Yri, "Luther Speaks to Africa" in Issues in African Theology, (Nairobi: East African Educational Publishers, 1998), 189–190.

[34] Ibid., 190.

the time and effort to build trust and thoroughly investigate local beliefs. From this perspective, evangelism is only the beginning of the assessment—discipleship will deepen one's insights into the cultural mindset tremendously.

2. Preach Expositionally

The priority of the expository preaching of the Word of God cannot be overstated. All South African pastors, missionaries, and theologians must carefully and constantly repeat that it is God to whom we listen, not to man. God speaks through Scriptures, and He speaks to all peoples of all cultures today. The epistle to the Hebrews in particular draws an excellent parallel to the southern African worldview. The concepts of *ubuntu,* community, mediation, sacrifices, and communal spirituality are deeply embedded in the southern African cultural framework and comfortable concepts to revere, but believers must be continually reminded that the death and resurrection of Jesus Christ makes Him superior to all forms of idolatrous mediation by imperfect human beings, whether they be dead ancestors or living leaders.

3. Emphasize Regeneration

Emphasis on the new birth will communicate the necessary connection to Jesus Christ, the perfect Mediator. While we have changed our headship from Adam to Jesus Christ, this can also be seen as changing blood lines from being a child of wrath to a child of God. We are not saved on the basis of taking an oath or stating a belief in the objective truth in the gospel and work of Jesus Christ. Although our faith is the means of our salvation, our salvation is totally based on the fact that God brings life to the dead, mediated through the perfect work and sacrifice of His Son, Jesus Christ. In essence, God makes us new (2 Cor 5:17). The presence of the Holy Spirit proves we are of new lineage, and the new birth effectually brings the believer out of the darkness of the domination and blind allegiance to his culture's norms and taboos. It is what changes men like Zacchaeus, the apostle Paul, and the Ethiopian eunuch, and what differentiates them from men like Simon Magus, Demas, and Judas.

Transformation begins not with obedience to a written law code, or even to the Scriptures, but with the Law that is written on our hearts (Rom 2:15). If churches and mission endeavors in Africa would begin to adopt these principles stated above, then perhaps we could see the next wave of reformational transformation in the church in sub-Saharan Africa. Transformation into a biblical world-view and life of submission to the lordship of Jesus Christ once began with an Ethiopian eunuch. With this emphasis on understanding and penetrating the African worldview, it can circle back around with renewed vigor.

SHOULD WE TAKE THE ROAD BACK TO ROME? AN ANALYSIS OF ROMAN CATHOLIC ECUMENICAL TRENDS

Massimo C. Mollica

Italian Theological Academy, Italy

[Editor's Note: There is a strong impetus within evangelicalism today to view the Roman Catholic Church in friendlier terms. Some would even consider them partners in the gospel. But can Roman Catholic and Protestant soteriology be reconciled? Has the Roman Catholic Church changed its position in the past 500 years? And how should Protestants today react to recent ecumenical trends developing within the Roman Catholic Church? This essay, coming from our training center at the heart of the Roman Catholic world itself, provides excellent analysis to help Christians navigate these important questions.]

Introduction

After years of study and deep reflection on the message of the gospel, Luigi Desanctis escaped from Rome on September 11, 1847, making his conversion to the evangelical faith public. He explained, "God is my witness that I am not lying: the only purpose of my abandoning the Roman Church was the salvation of my soul, and the only motive was the corruption of that Church that I abandoned."[1] What makes this conversion impressive is that he was an examiner of the Catholic Inquisition and professor of theology at a university in Rome.[2] His words give us cause for reflection in light of ecumenical discussions between the Roman Catholic Church (hereafter the RCC) and Evangelicals. Desanctis was convinced that the only safety for his soul was outside of the walls of the RCC. Is it safe for evangelicals today to consider ecumenical unity with the RCC? This question is even more important given that in 2017, the Lutherans and the RCC will jointly commemorate the 500th anniversary of the Reformation. They say:

> Catholics and Lutherans realize that they and the communities in which they live out their faith belong to the one body of Christ. The awareness is dawning on Lutherans and Catholics that the struggle of the sixteenth century is over. The reasons for mutually condemning each other's faith have fallen by the wayside.[3]

Is it then safe for us today to consider gospel unity with the RCC?[4] To answer this question, we must proceed with discernment. Five hundred years ago, the Protestant Reformation created a historic division in the Western Church that was over the essence of the gospel itself. The anniversary of the Reformation gives us an opportunity to explore the answers to two related questions that will in turn assist in reflecting on the safety of gospel unity with the RCC.

---

[1]   Tito Chiesi, *Lasciò la Chiesa per seguire Cristo: La vita e l'opera di Luigi Desanctis (1808–1869)* (Mantova, Italy: Passaggio, 2014), 35 [translation mine]. In referring to corruption in the Church, Desanctis intends both doctrinal and moral corruption.

[2]   As an examiner, he was responsible to examine various books and their authors to see if they were orthodox or heretical from the Roman Catholic perspective.

[3]   "From Conflict to Communion: Lutheran-Catholic Common Commemoration of the Reformation in 2017," Vatican Website, sec. 238. http://www.vatican.va/roman_curia/pontifical_councils/chrstuni/lutheran-fed-docs/rc_pc_chrstuni_doc_2013_dal-conflitto-alla-comunione_en.html#New_challenges_for_the_2017_commemoration_.

[4]   It is not the purpose of this essay to explore what the Evangelical approach should be regarding collaboration with the RCC to fight against social ills of our time, like abortion and threats to the institution of marriage. This essay focuses on whether or not there are grounds for gospel unity such that Evangelicals and Catholics belong together in the Body of Christ and could thus participate in common projects for world missions and evangelization.

First, what are the theological and historical underpinnings of ecumenism that brought about the change in the RCC? Second, is there enough convergence between Rome's gospel and the biblical gospel to suggest that we are in a new era where Christian unity should be pursued with the RCC?

What Is Ecumenism?

Before delving into these questions, a more basic question must be answered. What is ecumenism? In recent decades, as a result of the Second Vatican Council (1962–1965), there has been a transformation of attitude within the RCC toward Christians who are outside of the Church, which has led the RCC to seek to unify various branches of Christianity, both on an individual and ecclesiastical level. The best place to start when seeking to understand the Ecumenical movement is Vatican II's decree on ecumenism, *Unitatis Redintegratio* (Latin for "Restoration of Unity"). In this document, the burden, the meaning, the means, and the final goal of ecumenism are laid out. The decree opens:

> The restoration of unity is one of the principal concerns of the Second Vatican Council. Christ the Lord founded one Church and one Church only … . Everywhere large numbers have felt the impulse of this grace, and among our separated brethren also there increases from day to day the movement, fostered by the grace of the Holy Spirit, for the restoration of unity among all Christians. This movement toward unity is called "ecumenical." Those belong to it who invoke the Triune God and confess Jesus as Lord and Savior, doing this not merely as individuals but also as corporate bodies.[5]

---

[5] Second Vatican Council, *Unitatis redintegratio* [Decree on Ecumenism], Vatican Website, November 21, 1964, sec. 1. http://www.vatican.va/archive/hist_councils/ii_vatican_council/documents/vat-ii_decree_19641121_unitatis-redintegratio_en.html. In reference to the Reformation, the Council recognizes that "in subsequent centuries much more serious dissensions made their appearance and quite large communities came to be separated from full communion with the Catholic Church" (sec. 3).

According to Vatican II, the unity for which Christ prayed for his disciples (John 17:21) is the unity of the one Church (the RCC) to which belong all those who affirm the Trinity and Jesus as both Lord and Savior. Those who affirm these truths but are outside of the RCC are referred to as "separated brethren." This sin of separation was something that happened in the past such that "the children who are born into these Communities and who grow up believing in Christ cannot be accused of the sin involved in the separation, and the Catholic Church embraces upon them as brothers, with respect and affection."[6] Through kind-spirited dialogue, fair representation, mutual prayer, and discussion, the Council proposed to seek unity with these once excommunicated brethren because they are not enemies, but "separated brethren."[7]

It is evident from the preceding statements that Vatican II marked a substantial development in the posture of the RCC toward Christians, who did not belong to its institutional jurisdiction. The well-known dictum from Cyprian, a third-century bishop and martyr, that "outside the Church there is no salvation" (*Extra Ecclesiam nulla salus*) had governed the RCC for centuries.[8] Both the Council of Trent (1545–1563) and the First Vatican Council (1869–1870) anathematized those who were outside of the RCC's doctrinal confines. As a result, history is stained with the blood of those who were tried and killed as heretics by the RCC, both in- and outside of Italy.[9]

---

6   Ibid., sec. 3. The Council of Trent saw the separation over the doctrine of justification as a "grievous detriment to the unity of the Church," and consequentially strictly forbade that anyone believe differently from the doctrine of justification explained in that same Council. (Session 6, January 13, 1547, Decree concerning justification, intro, in *Canons and Decrees of the Council of Trent*, trans. H. J. Schroeder (Charlotte, North Carolina: Tan Books, 2011), 29).

7   *Unitatis redintegratio*, sec. 4 states, "The term 'ecumenical movement' indicates the initiatives and activities planned and undertaken, according to the various needs of the Church and as opportunities offer, to promote Christian unity."

8   Cyprian, *The Epistles of Cyprian*, 72.21. This position is historically traceable throughout various papal documents and Roman Councils. For example, *Unam Sanctam*, the papal bull by Pope Boniface VIII in 1302, Trent in 1547, and Vatican I in 1870 all made similar statements about the necessity of the RCC and its sacraments for salvation. For further examples, see William Webster, *Roman Catholic Tradition: Claims and Contradictions* (Battle Ground, Washington: Christian Resources Inc., 1999), 68–71.

9   Regarding the impact that the anathemas of the RCC had, Leonardo De Chirico states, "Before the Second Vatican Council, non-Catholic Christians, and in particular, Protestants, were considered to be 'heretics.' The excommunications and the anathemas against Protestants pronounced by the Council of Trent caused the Protestant Reformation to

However, Vatican II apparently signaled a new era in the Protestant-Roman Catholic relationship, as though the anathemas had faded into the past in favor of the phrase "separated brethren." Fifty years have elapsed since Vatican II. Many efforts at dialogue and discussion have occurred between the RCC and the Evangelical world.[10] These dialogues have led to the point mentioned above where the Lutherans and the RCC will declare the Reformation over in their joint commemoration of its anniversary.

The Historical and Theological Context of Vatican II

In order to discern whether or not gospel unity with the RCC is advisable, Vatican II must be understood in its broader historical and theological context. The history of the RCC can be broken down into three general eras.[11] First, there was the imperial era, starting with the fall of the Roman Empire. Leonardo De Chirico states:

From the ashes of the Roman Empire rose the imperial church that assumed a pyramidal institutional structure, clothing it with Christian language and symbols. The imperial hubris of Roman Catholicism (that is, its desire to be both church and state) is its original sin which has never been seriously questioned."[12]

This imperial notion is woven into the fabric of what it means to be the RCC. The wedding of both imperial and spiritual power is nowhere more clearly stated than in the 1302 papal bull, *Unam Sanctam* where Pope Boniface VIII states:

---

be considered heresy and the evangelicals were stigmatized with the name 'heretics.' In countries with a Catholic majority, this title has heavily conditioned evangelical witness and has often fueled strong discrimination against evangelicals." "Il Vaticano II, banco di prova della teologica evangelica," *Studi di Teologi: Il Vaticano in ottica evangelica*, IFED, 25/2, no. 50 (February 2013): 121. [translation mine]

[10] For an excellent overview of these dialogues, see De Chirico's *Evangelical Theological Perspectives on Post-Vatican II Roman Catholicism*, Religions and Discourse, vol. 19 (Bern, Switzerland: Peter Lang, 2003), 119–164.

[11] I am indebted to Leonardo DeChirico, the pastor of a Reformed Church in Rome and a scholar of Roman Catholicism. He used this helpful historical breakdown in a debate with another evangelical leader Giovanni Traettino in April, 2016 at the annual assembly of the Italian Evangelical Alliance.

[12] De Chirico, "Evangelicals and Catholics: A New Era?" *Vatican Files*, May 1, 2016, http://vaticanfiles.org/2016/04/124-evangelicals-and-catholics-a-new-era-4/.

> Therefore, both are in the power of the Church, namely, the spiritual sword and the temporal sword; the latter is to be used for the Church, the former by the Church; the former by the hand of the priest, the latter by the hand of princes and kings, but at the nod and sufferance of the priest. The one sword must of necessity be subject to the other, and the temporal authority to the spiritual ... For truth being the witness, the spiritual power has the functions of establishing the temporal power and sitting in judgment on it if it should prove to be not good ... Furthermore, that every human creature is subject to the Roman pontiff,—this we declare, say, define, and pronounce to be altogether necessary to salvation.[13]

Second, there was the oppositional era which includes both Trent, Vatican I, and the years before Vatican II. In this era, the RCC opposed all those who disagreed with their teaching, thus defining saving faith and its content according to the RCC. It is well known that Trent tragically cemented the sacramental system of the Middle Ages into the Catholic understanding of salvation and also anathematized the biblical gospel.

Vatican I cemented the RCC itself as an institution, reasserting papal rule and declaring the infallibility of the pope.[14] Vatican I teaches (in the same trajectory of the 1302 Bull by Boniface VIII), that "hierarchical subordination and true obedience" to the Roman Pontiff are a duty.[15] In fact, according to Vatican I, "all the faithful of Christ must believe that the holy Apostolic See and the Roman Pontiff possess the primacy over the whole world."[16] Vatican I is clear

---

[13] Boniface VIII, *Unam sanctum*, November 18, 1302, in Philip Schaff, *A History of the Christian Church* (Grand Rapids, Michigan: Eerdmans, 1910), 6:26.

[14] First Vatican Council, Session 4, July 18, 1870, First Dogmatic Constitution on the Church of Christ, Chapter 4, in Philip Schaff, *The Creeds of Christendom* (New York: Harper & Brothers, 1890), 2:270.

[15] Ibid., Session 4, Chapter 3, 2:262.

[16] Ibid., Session 4, Chapter 3, 2:262–263.

that if one does not embrace the Council's teaching on the pope, they are anathematized.[17]

In this same era, the Marian Dogmas were also solidified. In 1854, in the papal bull *Ineffabilis Deus,* Pope Pius IX declared under the alleged inspiration of the Holy Spirit, the doctrine of the Immaculate Conception. Mary, from conception, was kept free from the stain of original sin. Pius IX says that if one thinks otherwise, he has "made shipwreck concerning the faith, and fallen away from the unity of the Church."[18] In 1950, the doctrine of the Assumption of Mary was dogmatically and authoritatively defined by Pope Pius XII in the apostolic constitution *Munificentissimus Deus.* This doctrine states that Mary was assumed into heaven, body and soul, without dying.[19] If one denies or questions this, "he has fallen away completely from the divine and Catholic faith."[20] If anyone changes it or opposes it, they will "incur the wrath of Almighty God and of the Blessed Apostles Peter and Paul."[21] In this second general era, the RCC drew distinct lines as to what must be believed, opposing all who would dare contradict it.[22]

During this oppositional era, starting in the early 1900s within Evangelical Christianity in Europe, there were various attempts to find a broad ecclesial unity around the gospel and mission.

---

[17] Regarding Vatican I, De Chirico explains, " ... Vatican I creates a desert around the church, burns up the ground around it, cuts ties with the world, and creates a state of continual belligerence. Was this a strategic choice worthy of being called "catholic"? Maybe it was Roman, too Roman, but hardly Catholic" [translation mine]. ("Il Vaticano II," 114) [translation mine]. Interestingly, Vatican I was brought to a premature finish due to the Italian armies invading Rome, armies that united the Italian peninsula as a country for the first time since the fall of the Roman Empire. This invasion, ironically during Vatican I, took political power away from the Vatican at the same time the Council was trying to consolidate its institutional authority.

[18] Pius IX, *Ineffabilis deus* [Decree on the Immaculate Conception of the Blessed Virgin Mary], December 8, 1854. in Philip Schaff, *The Creeds of Christendom Church* (New York: Harper & Brothers, 1890), 2:212.

[19] Pius XII, *Munificentissimus deus* [Apostolic Constitution Defining the Dogma of the Assumption], November 1, 1950, sec. 44, http://w2.vatican.va/content/pius-xii/en/apost_constitutions/documents/hf_p-xii_apc_19501101_munificentissimus-deus.html.

[20] Ibid., sec. 45.

[21] Ibid., sec 47.

[22] For a helpful explanation of what saving faith is, according to historical Catholic councils and documents, see William Webster, *Saving Faith: How Does Rome Define It?* (Battle Ground, Washington: Christian Resources Inc.), 1997.

Representatives from the Vatican were invited to be involved in these dialogues.[23] The Vatican, however, was not interested in dialoguing about unity at the invitation of evangelical organizations. Pope Pius XI, in his 1928 encyclical, *Mortalium Animo,* condemned the evangelical ecumenical efforts, calling out Protestants who refused to submit to the pope. He stated, "It is clear that the Apostolic See cannot on any terms take part in their assemblies, nor is it anyway lawful for Catholics either to support or to work for such enterprises; for if they do so they will be giving countenance to a false Christianity, quite alien to the one Church of Christ.[24] Pius XI refused any kind of unity in which a Protestant would engage with the RCC as equals because "the union of Christians can only be promoted by promoting the return to the one true Church of Christ of those who are separated from it."[25] Pius XI continues, "In this one Church of Christ no man can be or remain who does not accept, recognize and obey the authority and supremacy of Peter and his legitimate successors."[26] It is plain to see that the theological presupposition entering into Vatican II was a unity that maintained the primacy of the RCC and the papacy because evangelicalism was ostensibly a false Christianity.

This leads to the third era, "the era of compliant and captivating Catholicism." Perhaps because of the RCC's loss of political power in Italy in the 1860s or because of the isolation and marginalization the church faced in the oppositional era, Vatican II exhibited a monumental shift in tone or posture to a more pastoral approach.[27] This can be observed in Pope John XXIII's opening address to Vatican II in 1962. In the section "How errors must be fought," he states, "That being so, the Catholic Church, raising the torch of catholic truth by

---

[23] In 1914, 1919, and 1927, Pope Benedict XV declined an invitation for Catholic representatives to participate with one Christian ecumenical group known as "Faith and Work." In 1925, another Christian group named "Life and Order" also had an invitation declined. De Chirico, *Quale unità cristiana? L'ecumenismo in discussione.* Caltanissetta (Italy: Alfa & Omega, 2016), 37.

[24] Pius XI, *Mortalium animo* [Encyclical on Religious Unity], January 6, 1928, sec. 8, http://w2.vatican.va/content/pius-xi/en/encyclicals/documents/hf_p-xi_enc_19280106_mortalium-animos.html.

[25] Ibid., sec. 8, 10

[26] Ibid., sec. 11

[27] De Chirico, "Evangelicals and Catholics."

means of this Ecumenical Council, desires to show herself to be the loving mother of all, benevolent, patient, moved by mercy and goodness toward the brethren who are separated from her."[28] Errors are no longer fought through anathemas but through mercy and patience.

Through this more softened approach, the RCC sought to become the protagonist of ecumenism. Rome's desire to see a unified Christianity flowed out of its self-understanding as the one true Church of Christ and the means of God's salvation. As *Unitatis Redintegratio* confirms:

> Nevertheless, our separated brethren, whether considered as individuals or as Communities and Churches, are not blessed with that unity which Jesus Christ wished to bestow on all those who through Him were born again into one body ... For it is only through Christ's Catholic Church, which is "the all-embracing means of salvation," that they can benefit fully from the means of salvation.[29]

Dialogue with other Christians and other religions is a means to the end of bringing separated brothers back to communion with the Mother Church in order to enjoy the full benefits of salvation and unity. While Protestants enjoy a degree of God's grace because of shared doctrines and shared history, they do not experience the fullness of God's grace that is found in the RCC.[30] The shared elements actually belong to the RCC in the first place and are therefore, "forces impelling toward catholic unity."[31]

Doctrinal change and repentance is not the goal of their ecumenism. The RCC has no intention of being moved from its position. The RCC believes it is inseparable from the biblical gospel because

---

[28] John XXIII, "Solenne apertura del Concilio ecumenico Vaticano II," October 11, 1962, sec. 7.3, https://w2.vatican.va/content/john-xxiii/it/speeches/1962/documents/hf_j-xxiii_spe_19621011_opening-council.html. [translation mine]

[29] *Unitatis redintegratio,* sec. 3.

[30] Second Vatican Council, *Lumen Gentium* [Dogmatic constitution on the Church], November 21, 1964, sec. 15, http://www.vatican.va/archive/hist_councils/ii_vatican_council/documents/vat-ii_const_19641121_lumen-gentium_en.html.

[31] Ibid., sec. 8.

it cannot be wrong. That is, at no point in history, would it ever be necessary to separate from it because of gospel infidelity. Vatican II states it this way: "We believe that this unity subsists in the Catholic Church as something she can never lose, and we hope that it will continue to increase until the end of time."[32] The final goal of ecumenism is Roman Catholic unity, when "all Christians will at last, in a common celebration of the Eucharist, be gathered into the one and only Church in that unity which Christ bestowed on His Church from the beginning."[33]

While it is right to observe the contradiction between Vatican II's calling Protestants "separated brethren" and the preceding Church councils that anathematized them, it is also critical to observe that the shift in tone at Vatican II is a strategic choice to bring all Christianity under the jurisdiction of the RCC. Dogmatic condemnations and rigid declarations are not winsome and will push people away. Thus, the RCC opts for the motherly language of mercy and dialogue because it is more compelling. Therefore, ecumenical dialogues are the natural outflow and method of their catholicity, their mission in the world, in order to bring about this papal unity. As De Chirico states:

> Indeed, the dimension of fellowship with Rome and that of submission to Rome are inseparable and indissoluble aspects of the ecumenical vision of Catholicism. You cannot have one without the other. You cannot be cum Petro [with Peter] unless you are sub Petro [under Peter]. The fact is, we are talking about Catholicism, of course, but the kind of Catholicism that remains, down to its core, roman, papal, marian, and vatican. The ecumenical openness is therefore targeted at the catholicization of all of Christianity. It is the Catholic system that requires it and it is the Catholic system that has the resources to accomplish it.[34]

---

[32] *Unitatis redintegratio*, sec. 4.

[33] Ibid.

[34] De Chirico, "Il Vaticano II," 122. [translation mine]

The ecumenical posture of the third era must be understood on the backdrop of the imperial era and the oppositional era of the RCC. When Vatican II speaks of uniting all Christians under the Vatican and when they speak of obedience to the Roman Pontiff and his jurisdiction, it is hard not to perceive the continuing imperial and oppositional tone that characterized the first two eras, especially given the fact that "the Roman Catholic Church is not a simple denomination. It is a church-state, with a monarch, political claims, and an army."[35] Imperialism and opposition are imbedded into the DNA of the RCC through the infallible and authoritative statements of the first two eras. One must recall Boniface VIII's statement in 1302 "that every human creature is subject to the Roman pontiff,—this we declare, say, define, and pronounce to be altogether necessary to salvation." These historical and theological underpinnings of the ecumenical movement strongly warn evangelicals that unity with Rome would come at the high price of gospel compromise. It should therefore be adamantly avoided.[36]

Understanding Ecumenical Efforts since Vatican II: The Joint Declaration

Having examined the theological and historical backdrop to ecumenism, it must be discerned whether there is enough convergence

---

[35] Leonardo De Chirico, "Roman Catholic Ecumenism: Let the Italian Evangelicals Speak," *Vatican Files,* July 23, 2014, http://vaticanfiles.org/2014/07/84-roman-catholic-ecumenism-let-the-italian-evangelicals-speak/.

[36] For other Vatican documents regarding Ecumenism after Vatican II, see the 1993 "Directory for the Application of Principles and Norms for Ecumenism." See also Pope John Paul II's 1995 encyclical *Ut Unum Sint* ("That they may be one") which reaffirms and advances the vision of Vatican II. Yet an interesting development can be noted in this encyclical. *Ut Unum Sint* goes a step further than Vatican II. John Paul II says that brotherhood has been rediscovered as a result of ecumenical dialogue (sec. 42). However, in the same paragraph, he also underscores that, while the change of attitude is encouraging, the Churches and Ecclesial Communities are not in full communion with the Catholic Church. "Full unity will come about when all share in the fullness of the means of salvation entrusted by Christ to his Church" (sec. 36). Specifically, a visible head is the foundational piece of Christian unity. "This designation is the best possible safeguard against the risk of separating power" (sec. 88). *Ut Unum Sint* also affirms the vision that the Eucharist is the highest sacramental expression of unity as its common celebration signals that all obstacles to ecclesial communion have been overcome (secs. 23, 40, 45). (*Ut Unum Sint* [Encyclical Letter on Commitment to Ecumenism], May 25, 1995, http://w2.vatican.va/content/john-paul-ii/en/encyclicals/documents/hf_jp-ii_enc_25051995_ut-unum-sint.html).

between Rome's gospel and the biblical gospel to suggest that unity should be pursued. In order to answer this question, one must take into account one of the most notable examples of ecumenical efforts between Protestants and the RCC, the 1999 *Joint Declaration on the Doctrine of Justification* (hereafter the *JD*) by the RCC and the Lutheran World Federation. It is because of this document that Lutherans and the RCC will commemorate the Reformation together in 2017.[37]

The principal statements in the *JD* that give pause for reflection are "Together we confess: *By grace alone,* in faith in Christ's saving work and not because of any merit on our part, we are accepted by God and receive the Holy Spirit, who renews our hearts while equipping and calling us to good works"[38] and "... *Through Christ alone are we justified,* when we receive this salvation in faith" [emphasis added].[39] Considering that the *five solas* have been the distinguishing marks of the Reformation, how is the RCC's seeming rapprochement with *solus Christus* and *sola gratia* to be understood? Before getting into specifics, it is helpful to keep the following observations in mind while reflecting on the *JD*.

The document must be read in its ecumenical context. This means there is an extra effort on the part of both parties to avoid inflammatory language.[40] Both churches recognize that excommunications stemming back to the time of the Reformation are substantial barriers to unity in the present generation. New understandings and dialogue have led them to believe that there is enough convergence on the doctrine of justification to say "the corresponding doctrinal condemnations of the sixteenth century do not apply to today's partner."[41] Notwithstanding this newfound convergence, the *JD* says, "the churches neither take the condemnations lightly nor do they disavow

---

[37] See "From Conflict to Communion" for details regarding the 2017 joint commemoration.

[38] Lutheran World Federation and the Catholic Church, *Joint Declaration on the Doctrine of Justification,* October 31, 1999, sec. 15, http://www.vatican.va/roman_curia/pontifical_councils/chrstuni/documents/rc_pc_chrstuni_doc_31101999_cath-luth-joint-declaration_en.html.

[39] Ibid., sec. 16.

[40] David Estrada, "The Joint Declaration on the Doctrine of Justification," *Christianity & Society* 11, no. 1 (January 2001): 12.

[41] *Joint Declaration,* sec. 13.

their own past."[42] This means that the substantial difference between 1999 and the sixteenth century is that there are no excommunications in the current generation, without saying much about change in doctrinal conviction. Furthermore, as an ecumenical document, there is an elasticity in the vocabulary that is used. Extra effort is made to use language that both sides can agree with, without giving precise theological exposition of what one means by that language.[43]

It is most important to keep in mind that in 2000, the year after the *JD,* then-Cardinal Joseph Ratzinger (later Pope Benedict XVI from 2005–2013), issued the Declaration *Dominus Iesus.* This document reaffirms that ecumenical dialogue is necessary for evangelizing the outside world. However, this openness to dialogue does not mean that the RCC has changed its self-understanding. Therefore, the *JD* of 1999 hardly represents any shift in Roman Catholic theology. *Dominus Iesus* is clear that one cannot experience the fullness of God's grace and salvation apart from the Church, which is the "universal sacrament of salvation."[44] Therefore, the *JD* must be read so as not to compromise historical Catholic teaching on the subject. Rather, we must seek to see how Roman Catholic theology has the flexibility to use these Protestant phrases, but invest them instead with their own definitions and understandings. With these observations in mind, we are now prepared to understand the usage of the more Protestant-sounding terms, as well as the *JD*'s teaching on justification.

---

[42]   Ibid., sec. 7.

[43]   According to De Chirico, in the interest of ecumenical unity, the hermeneutical approach to the excommunications is guided by the thought that profound and mutual misunderstandings existed surrounding key words. These misunderstandings have only been further compounded over the centuries as a result of the different meanings of the words in Latin and other European languages ("La giustificazione come questione ecumenica irrisolta," *Studi di Teologi: La giustificazione per fede oggi* IFED, 27/1, no. 53 (January 2015): 102).

[44]   The Declaration states, "Above all else, it must be *firmly believed* that 'the Church, a pilgrim now on earth, is necessary for salvation: the one Christ is the mediator and the way of salvation; he is present to us in his body which is the Church'... The Church is the "universal sacrament of salvation," since, united always in a mysterious way to the Saviour Jesus Christ, her head, and subordinated to him, she has, in God's plan, an indispensable relationship with the salvation of every human being" (Joseph Cardinal Ratzinger, *Dominus Iesus* [Declaration on the Unicity and Salvific Universality of Jesus Christ and the Church] August 6, 2000, sec. 20, http://www.vatican.va/roman_curia/congregations/cfaith/documents/rc_con_cfaith_doc_20000806_dominus-iesus_en.html).

Sola Gratia

How can the RCC affirm the phrase "Together we confess: *By grace alone*, in faith in Christ's saving work and not because of any merit on our part, we are accepted by God" [emphasis mine]? This is unraveled in two ways. First, one must observe that they have linguistically stretched the meaning of *sola gratia* to conform with their sacramental understanding of grace. When a Roman Catholic uses the word "grace" in relationship to justification or salvation they do not mean the unmerited favor of God to unworthy, hell-bound sinners. What is meant is that grace is a redemptive power that is infused into the believer, channeled through the sacraments (in particular, water baptism, the Eucharist, penance, confession, and last rites) in which there is a cooperation between man and God.[45] According to the 1995 *Catechism of the Catholic Church,* "the Church affirms that for believers the sacraments of the New Covenant are necessary for salvation."[46] This is because "the sacraments confer the grace that they signify."[47] So, when the *JD* states, "We confess together that all persons depend completely on the saving grace of God for their salvation,"[48] it means people depend completely on the saving grace of God as mediated through the sacraments.[49]

A second help in unraveling the *JD*'s teaching on grace is to actually examine the current practice of the RCC, rather than just reading words in an ecumenical document. In 2000, the year following the

---

[45] The *CCC* says that grace is "favor, the free and undeserved help that God gives us to respond to his call to become children of God" (sec. 1996). The *CCC* continues, "The grace of Christ is the gratuitous gift that God makes to us of his own life, infused by the Holy Spirit into our soul to heal it of sin and to sanctify it." (sec. 1999). Paragraph 2000 further elaborates, "Sanctifying grace is an habitual gift, a stable and supernatural disposition that perfects the soul itself to enable it to live with God, to act by his love." *Catechism of the Catholic Church* (New York: Doubleday, 1995).

[46] Ibid., sec. 1129. These sacraments of salvation are instituted by Christ (sec. 1117), for the church (sec. 1118), conferred by the ordained Catholic priest (sec. 1120). Trent states, "If anyone says that the sacraments of the New Law are not necessary for salvation but are superfluous, and that without them or without the desire of them men obtain from God through faith alone the grace of justification ... let him be anathema" (Session 7, March 3, 1547, Canons on the sacraments in general, Canon 4, 52).

[47] CCC, sec. 1127. See also Trent which says "If anyone says that grace, so far as God's part is concerned, is not imparted through the sacraments always ... let him be anathema" (Session 7, March 3, 1547, Canons on the sacraments in general, Canon 7, 52).

[48] *Joint Declaration*, sec. 19.

[49] De Chirico, "La giustificazione," 109.

JD, the RCC celebrated the year of the Jubilee, notorious for its granting of innumerable indulgences throughout the year. It is well-known that the sale and granting of indulgences were the provoking cause of the Reformation as is evident in Luther's Ninety-five Theses, many of which discuss purgatory and the abuse of indulgences.[50]

Similarly, the year of 2016 was declared to be an extraordinary Year of the Jubilee in which, once again, innumerable indulgences were granted. This is the very year before the joint commemoration of the Reformation's 500th anniversary. In the papal bull of indiction for 2016, *Misericordiae Vultus,* Pope Francis discusses the granting of indulgences and states that "Reconciliation with God is made possible through the paschal mystery and the mediation of the Church."[51] Francis concludes the Bull by exhorting the Catholic faithful to turn to Mary, "so that she may never tire of turning her merciful eyes upon us, and make us worthy to contemplate the face of mercy, her Son Jesus." It is hard to see how one could say in the *JD* that we are accepted by God through grace alone, yet still say that reconciliation comes through the Sacrament of the Eucharist and the mediation of the Church which grants indulgences *and* that Mary needs to make us worthy to contemplate the mercy of Jesus Christ. This confirms the conclusion above that the RCC has linguistically stretched the meaning of *sola gratia* to conform with their sacramental understanding of grace.

In light of the ongoing practice of granting indulgences, one must remember that this practice exhibits in a unique way the sacramental system of the RCC, thus actually contradicting *sola gratia.* The Church, as mediator, is able to dispense from the treasury of merits in order to bring forgiveness, expiation, and placation of divine justice for the temporal punishments for sin. The *Manual of Indulgences,* reprinted in Italian in 2016, contains the text of Pope Paul VI's 1967 apostolic constitution, *Indulgentiarium Doctrina,* which states:

---

[50] De Chirico notes that indulgences are the very point "in which synergistic, sacramental, and ecclesiocentric theology was concentrated" ("La giustificazione," 110). [translation mine]

[51] Francis, *Misericordiae vultus* [Bull of Indiction of the Extraordinary Jubilee of Mercy], April 11, 2015, sec. 22, https://w2.vatican.va/content/francesco/en/apost_letters/documents/papa-francesco_bolla_20150411_misericordiae-vultus.html.

> For this reason there certainly exists between the
> faithful who have already reached their heavenly
> home, those who are expiating their sins in pur-
> gatory and those who are still pilgrims on earth a
> perennial link of charity and an abundant exchange
> of all the goods by which, with the expiation of all
> the sins of the entire Mystical Body, divine justice
> is placated. God's mercy is thus led to forgiveness,
> so that sincerely repentant sinners may participate as
> soon as possible in the full enjoyment of the benefits
> of the family of God.[52]

This concept of the exchange of the church's merits or goods which leads to expiation of all sins and the placation of divine justice, which in turn induces God's mercy to forgive sins and affords us the full enjoyment of salvific benefits is clearly not what is intended in *sola gratia* in a biblical sense, undermining the all-sufficient work of the Lord Jesus Christ on the cross and his sovereign grace to sinners who deserve his judgment.

Solus Christus

Having seen that the *JD*'s teaching on grace does not exhibit a new coherence between Protestant and Catholic teaching on the nature of God's saving grace, we now turn to the doctrine of *solus Christus*. When a Protestant affirms *solus Christus*, the doctrine that is being affirmed is that salvation is found in Christ alone.[53] In the *JD*, the RCC says that through Christ alone are we justified. As one reads through various Catholic documents, the RCC never avoids affirming that Christ is the one and unique mediator. In fact the *JD* states, "Lutherans and Catholics share the goal of confessing Christ

---

[52] Paul VI, *Indulgentiarum doctrina* [Apostolic Constitution], Vatican Website. January 1, 1967, sec. 2.5. https://w2.vatican.va/content/paul-vi/en/apost_constitutions/documents/hf_p-vi_apc_01011967_indulgentiarum-doctrina.html.

[53] *Solus Christus* means that only Christ's once-for-all time sacrifice for sins can propitiate and expiate sins. This also means that He is the only mediator between God and man who can accomplish reconciliation. There is no other religious leader, saint, or any other man or woman who has ever lived who can save man from his sins or participate in this salvation (Acts 4:12). Only Jesus through His perfect life and death provides an all-sufficient righteousness and sacrifice for all who believe.

in all things who alone is to be trusted above all things as the one Mediator."[54]

The RCC, however, understands this much differently than a Protestant. *Lumen Gentium* states, "The unique mediation of the Redeemer does not exclude but rather gives rise to a manifold cooperation which is but a sharing in this one source."[55] This means that in an addition to Christ's unique mediation, there are multiple mediators that cooperate with him and find their source in him. The RCC adds Mary; it adds itself as the sacrament of salvation, along with the saints as those capable of interceding for us in heaven, and those ordained through the sacrament of holy orders (i.e., the priests) who can perform the Mass.[56]

There are at least two fatal flaws in the Roman Catholic understanding of the uniqueness of Christ's mediation. First, the logic of having multiple mediators that derive from one source is simply neither compatible with biblical teaching nor implied by what the authors of Scripture intended. The verse cited by both Protestants and Catholics is 1 Timothy 2:5, which states, "For there is one God, *and* one mediator also between God and men, the man Christ Jesus." Is 1 Timothy 2:5 compatible with the idea of other sub-mediators, like Mary and the Church? No—there is one mediator between God and man in the same way that there is also only one God. The RCC does not teach that the oneness of God can give rise to a manifold cooperation of sub-gods. If there can be no sub-gods, then there can be no subordinate mediators. "One" should be understood numerically, that is, *one* mediator and *one* God, in contrast to *manifold* mediators or *manifold* gods. As can be expected, Vatican II attempts to qualify the subordinate mediatorial role of Mary, *Lumen Gentium* states:

> Taken up to heaven she did not lay aside this salvific duty, but by her constant intercession continued to bring us the gifts of eternal salvation ... Therefore the Blessed Virgin is invoked by the Church under

54 *Joint Declaration*, sec. 18.

55 *Lumen Gentium*, sec. 62

56 *Lumen Gentium* says, "the priest alone can complete the building up of the Body in the Eucharistic sacrifice" (sec. 17)

the titles of Advocate, Auxiliatrix, Adjutrix, and Mediatrix. This, however, is to be so understood that it neither takes away from nor adds anything to the dignity and efficaciousness of Christ the one Mediator.[57]

However, it is not simply a question of adding to or taking away from the dignity and efficacy of Christ's work.[58] It is a question of numerically adding to Christ. If there are other mediators, then there is not just *one* mediator, no matter how one logically arranges their subordination to a principal source.

The second fatal flaw has to do with the fact that the RCC sees itself to be the continuation of the incarnation of Christ.[59] This mystical union between Christ and the church derives from the Augustinian idea of *totus Christus* (whole Christ) which suggests that the entirety or wholeness of Christ consists of both body and head. The head is Christ in heaven, the body is the church on earth. The two cannot be separated since they form the whole Christ. The use of "Christ-alone" must be understood in light of this. They believe they are the presence of Christ on the earth in such a way that they cannot be separated from Christ. *Lumen Gentium* says, "Christ, present to us in His Body, which is the Church, is the one Mediator and the unique way of salvation."[60] So, logically, in the Roman Catholic mindset, to say Christ alone saves is compatible with the church mediating

---

[57] Ibid., sec. 62

[58] Despite Vatican II's qualification of Mary's subordinate role, it is evident that throughout history Mary is not subordinate to Christ. William Webster explains, "This is clear from the following parallels between the Lord Jesus and Roman Catholic teaching on Mary: Christ was immaculately conceived—as was Mary; Christ was sinless—so was Mary; Christ accomplished a work as redeemer and mediator—as did Mary; Christ was assumed body and soul into heaven—likewise Mary; Christ is the source of life—so is Mary; Christ is Lord and King—Mary is Queen and Sovereign; Christ is the mediator in dispensing grace—so is Mary; Christ is an object of prayer and trust and supreme devotion—so is Mary." Thus, Webster rightly concludes, "Mary has often displaced Jesus as the true object of worship and devotion" (*The Church of Rome at the Bar of History*, 88).

[59] For a more in depth understanding of this concept see Pope Pius XII's 1943 encyclical *Mystici Corporis Christi*. For evangelical interactions on the subject, see De Chirico, *Evangelical Theological Perspectives*, 246–283 and Gregg R. Allison, *Roman Catholic Theology & Practice: An Evangelical Assessment* (Wheaton, Illinois: Crossway, 2014) 56–66.

[60] *Lumen Gentium*, sec. 14.

salvation, because, in a mystical sense, they are Christ. Therefore, the use of terms like "Christ alone" and "one mediator" in the *JD* should not be understood as if the RCC now supports the Protestant understanding of *solus Christus*, but rather, for the sake of ecumenical unity, they have introduced their extra-biblical theology into the concept of *solus Christus*.

Justification by Faith

Having removed some of the consternation that could be created by an evangelical reading of the *JD*, we are now ready to offer some assessments regarding the overall teaching of the *JD* on justification by faith. The *JD* states that "the post-Vatican II ecumenical dialogue has led to a notable convergence concerning justification, with the result that this *Joint Declaration* is able to formulate a consensus on *basic truths* concerning the doctrine of justification" [emphasis mine].[61] It is evident once again that the document is carefully crafted in order to find common ground. Yet in reality, it actually exhibits continued divergence on some of the most basic truths of doctrine of justification that led to the Reformation. Three shortcomings are sufficient to demonstrate this point.

The Definition of Justification. First, the most glaring omission is a lack of any discussion on the meaning of the word *justify*. In the section on the "Biblical Message of Justification," there is some theological discussion, and typical verses are cited, but there is no attempt to give the precise meaning of what justification actually means. The closest definition given is in paragraph 11, where it says, "Justification is the forgiveness of sins (cf. Rom 3:23–25; Acts 13:39; Lk 18:14), liberation from the dominating power of sin and death (Rom 5:12–21) and from the curse of the law."[62] "Liberation from sin" is conflated with justification, forensic terminology is missing, imputation is absent, and there are no explanations of justification as a legal declaration. This is typical of the RCC as is seen in Trent, which said that justification "is not only the remission of sins but

---

[61] *Joint Declaration*, sec. 13.

[62] *Joint Declaration*, sec. 11.

also the sanctification and renewal of the inward man."[63] The RCC continues to use biblical terms like "justification," but continues to define them in an unbiblical way, describing justification as a process by which the sinner, through the help of God's grace, becomes more righteous.[64] From a Protestant perspective, it appears as though the biblical understanding of justification has been compromised.

The Ground of Justification. The *JD* discusses the imputation of sin as something both Lutherans and Roman Catholics would agree upon, but the imputation of righteousness, the ground of justification, is not affirmed by the RCC.[65] This is because Trent officially condemned the truth of imputed righteousness[66] and also clearly stated that the single formal cause of justification is not the righteousness by which God is righteous, but the righteousness of God which is infused into the believer.[67] In the Roman Catholic section of the *JD*, being made righteous is "the renewal of the interior person through the reception of grace imparted as a gift to the believer."[68] For the Lutheran on the other hand, righteousness before God in Christ is granted through the declaration of righteousness.[69] There is no real

---

[63] Council of Trent, Session 6, January 13, 1547, *Decree concerning justification*, chap. 7, 33. Cf. *CCC*, sec. 1989.

[64] Trent officially condemns those who do not view justification as a process when they say, "If anyone says that the justice received is not preserved and also not increased before God through good works, but that those works are merely the fruits and signs of justification obtained, but not the cause of its increase, let him be anathema" (Session 6, January 13, 1547, *Canons concerning justification*, canon 24, 45). Cf. *CCC*, sec. 1989.

[65] *Joint Declaration*, secs. 22–24.

[66] "If anyone says that men are justified either by the sole imputation of the justice of Christ or by the sole remission of sins, to the exclusion of the grace and the charity which is poured forth in their hearts by the Holy Ghost ... or also that the grace by which we are justified is only the good will of God, let him be anathema" (Council of Trent, Session 6, January 13, 1547, *Canons concerning justification*, canon 11, 43–44).

[67] Trent states, "the single formal cause is the justice of God, not that by which He Himself is just, but that by which He makes us just" (Session 6, January 13, 1547, *Decree concerning justification*, chap. 7, 33).

[68] *Joint Declaration*, sec. 24

[69] *Joint Declaration*, sec. 23. Declarative language is used only in the Lutheran section, but even here, it seems as though the forensic character of justification and the imputation of righteousness is softened by unclear explanations. See Thomas R. Schreiner, *Faith Alone: The Doctrine of Justification*, Kindle ed. (Grand Rapids: Zondervan, 2015), 419.

consensus on this *basic truth* of whether the ground of justification is imputed righteousness or infused righteousness.

The Instrument of Justification. A final shortcoming has to do with the *basic truth* of the instrument of justification. The Lutherans affirm justification by faith *alone*.[70] The Catholics affirm the importance of faith but refuse to affirm *faith alone*.[71] The RCC affirms that "Persons are justified through baptism as hearers of the word and believers in it."[72] Like they did at Trent, the RCC of today holds to its sacramental understanding of salvation with baptism being the cause of justification. Trent stated, "The instrumental cause [of justification] is the sacrament of baptism, which is the sacrament of faith."[73] Furthermore, the RCC affirms that the "justification of sinners is ... being made righteous by justifying grace."[74] As has been demonstrated, justification is for the RCC the *process* of being made righteous. Trent also taught that faith cooperating with works increases one's righteousness and thus further justifies the sinner.[75] Once again, the *JD* exhibits a divergence rather than a consensus on the basic truths of justification.

These three shortcomings lead to an important conclusion. A more loving and friendlier tone, no matter how well-intentioned, cannot erase the Reformation if there is no real consensus on these three basic truths of justification.[76] There is no substantial difference

---

[70] Joint Declaration, sec. 26.

[71] Of course the RCC could not affirm *faith alone* because the Trent says, "If anyone says that justifying faith is nothing else than confidence in divine mercy, which remits sins for Christ's sake, or that it is this confidence alone that justifies us, let him be anathema" (Session 6, January 13, 1547, Canons concerning justification, canon 12, 44).

[72] *Joint Declaration*, sec. 27. Lutheran belief in baptismal regeneration makes them susceptible to confusion with the RCC on this particular point.

[73] Council of Trent, Session 6, January 13, 1547, Decree concerning justification, chap. 7, 33. Cf. *CCC*, sec. 1992.

[74] *Joint Declaration*, sec. 27.

[75] Trent states, " ... they, through the observance of the commandments of God and of the Church, faith cooperating with good works, increase in that justice received through the grace of Christ and are further justified" (Session 6, January 13, 1547, Decree concerning justification, chap. 10, 36). Cf. *CCC*, secs. 1990–1992.

[76] Over 240 German Lutheran theologians saw the *JD* as a compromise of the gospel (Schreiner, *Faith Alone*, 414).

between the *JD*'s understanding of justification and the teaching of Trent, which means the RCC continues to diverge from the gospel.

Concluding Implications

Where does this leave us regarding gospel unity with and under the RCC? The Bible says that the ground for unity is not just the truth of who Jesus is, but the truth of how Jesus saves. In Galatians 1:9, Paul states, "if any man is preaching to you a gospel contrary to what you received, he is to be accursed!" The Galatians were faced with the Judaizers in their midst who distorted the gospel by teaching adherence to the Old Testament customs as a prerequisite for justification, especially circumcision (Acts 15:1). No doubt these men, being part of the church, had an orthodox understanding of the person of Christ. However, they were to be rebuked and accursed because they added to faith. Scripture teaches us to take seriously any deviation from or addition to the doctrine of justification by faith alone. Vatican II calls for unity under the pope among Christians who profess the Trinity and those who confess Jesus to be Savior and Lord. Their understanding of the person of Christ may appear orthodox on paper; however, the RCC, in its addition of extra-biblical doctrines to the gospel, is actually saying "no" to the gospel itself, fundamentally denying the biblical doctrine of justification by faith. Therefore, Protestants must not unite with Rome. To do so would pervert the gospel and bring the condemnation of our Lord Jesus Christ.

Of utmost importance is that this generation strive for a robust understanding of the biblical doctrines of salvation, especially that of justification by grace alone, through faith alone, in Christ alone. This doctrine, in a particular way, is the foundational piece for the message that the true church of Jesus Christ believes and preaches. If this doctrine is perverted or compromised, the church crumbles, there is no gospel to proclaim, and missions become a useless effort. There are millions of people all over the world from many different cultures within the system of the RCC, each with differing degrees of understanding of Church teaching and different levels of faith and adherence to Church beliefs and traditions. There is no salvation for those who believe in the teaching of the RCC. Roman Catholics must be encouraged to a deeper understanding of the biblical gospel and to evaluate its coherence with the teaching of the RCC. Roman

Catholic countries like Italy are a mission field to be reached. For the sake of our Lord and for the sake of the lost, this generation must then labor, like the Reformers 500 years ago, to protect, clarify, and proclaim the true gospel in all of its glory.

THE DANGER OF KARMA AND THE DOCTRINE OF CHRIST

Samuel Williams

Pastoral Training Seminary, India

[Editor's Note: India is one of the most pluralistic and multi-ethnic countries in the world. False religion is promoted across the landscape as counterfeit gods are on display on nearly every street corner and in every village. Amidst the spiritual confusion, clear thinking is needed. This essay aims to expose one of the key tenets of Hindu thought, karma, *and to contrast its damning implications with the light of the gospel of Jesus Christ.]*

Introduction

India is a diverse country of stark economic contrasts. Mumbai, the commercial capital of India, boldly displays this disparity. Chatrapati Shivaji International Airport is a $3 billion state of the art facility with 750 hectares of air-conditioned terminals filled with the best of first-world retail outlets and luxuries.[1] Adjacent to this modern utopia is Dharavi, Southern Asia's largest slum, with one million inhabitants. Here, whole families sleep on concrete floors in tin huts, with only one toilet for every 1,440 people. It is evident that the people living in such squalor could have a better life if just a fraction of the investment used to build the airport was used to their benefit. While project proposals for the development of the slum

---

[1]   Chatrapati Shivaji International won the "Best Airport in India and Central Asia" at the Skytrax 2016 World Airport Awards.

abound,[2] a culture of apathy dissolves any actual progress. A large part of this attitude can be traced to the reality that most slum inhabitants are from a lower caste or have non-Hindu roots. It is believed that they should live in such conditions because of their karma.

The Hindu Doctrine of Karma

The Hindu idea of karma[3] is a non-negotiable core belief in a religious system that otherwise largely defies doctrinal definition. This term appears briefly in Hindu texts such as the *Rig Veda*[4] and the *Brahmana*,[5] while the *Upanishads*[6] contain a fuller description of the karma ideology with application to real life. For instance, in *Chandogya Upanishad* 5.10.7, it is said that living a good life will result in rebirth as a *Brahmin* (the highest caste), and a bad life in rebirth as a dog or pig.[7] The *Kaushitaki Upanishad* 1.2 further warns that bad deeds can lead to rebirth as a worm or insect.[8] Reincarnation and the cycles of rebirth are therefore the outworking of bad karma in a fatalistic loop (*samsara*).[9] For the *Nyaya* school, one of six orthodox schools of Hindu philosophy, karma is the means by which the existence of the gods is manifested—namely, through the perpetual experience of consequences in one's actions and ultimately in one's multiple lives.[10] The doctrine of karma is the Hindu

---

[2]   Many of these projects are actually motivated by the high real estate value and profit potential of the land occupied by this slum. See http://www.nytimes.com/2011/12/29/world/asia/in-indian-slum-misery-work-politics-and-hope.html?_r=1&hp

[3]   *Karma* comes from the Sanskrit *kri*, meaning "work" or "deeds."

[4]   A collection of religious hymns in Sanskrit (1200–1500 BC).

[5]   Text and commentary on the Vedas (700 BC).

[6]   Philosophical Hindu writings (700 BC).

[7]   Charles Johnston, *Chadogya Upanishad, Translation and Commentary* (Kshetra Books, 2016), 160.

[8]   Yuvraj Krishnan, *The Doctrine of Karma* (Delhi: Motilal Banarsidass Publishers, 1997), 21.

[9]   C. Norman McClelland, *Encyclopedia of Reincarnation and Karma* (Jefferson, North Carolina: McFarland, 2010), 240.

[10]   C. Sharma, *A Critical Survey of Indian Philosophy* (Delhi: Motilal Banarsidass Publishers, 1997), 209.

worldview's answer to the problem of evil. The question is answered with a sense of fatalism and works-oriented living.[11]

The Moral Fallout of Karma

False teaching that arises from the wisdom of man will always promote pride and selfishness (2 Pet 2:10–11; see also Col 2:8, 23). Such is the case with the application of karma in the culture and life of India. The Hindu system contradicts the gospel and God's plan of salvation in Christ in at least three ways, leading to absolute moral degradation.

Karma Denies Sin and the Need for Repentance

The idea of karma obscures truth, especially in the area of morality. For instance, it is said that the reason a man might be born in poverty is that he committed some crime in a previous life. Yet he will never come to know what his specific "sin" was, nor should he, because repentance is not the goal of karma. Rather, every person must accept his or her lot in life. By looking at the present life through the lens of past actions with a view to the next life, the actuality of the present life is obscured. Thus it does not take long for the Hindu search for salvation to degenerate into moral relativism.[12]

The Hindu worldview demands that followers trivialize the world and their actions in it. As venerated Hindu guru Sathya Sai Baba[13] expressed, "The world is an illusion, do not put your trust in it."[14] *Moksha,* or the liberation of the soul (*atman*), involves escaping this world and not focusing on it. Moksha may be considered the chief goal of man because if and when it is reached, the chains of karma will be forever broken, and the atman may finally unite with Brahman, a blissful merging with the ultimate being. However, Sai Baba's teaching on self-denial (asceticism) was ironically self-

---

[11] McClelland, *Encyclopedia of Reincarnation and Karma,* 141.

[12] Vishal Mangalwadi, *When the New Age Gets Old: Looking for a Greater Spirituality* (Downers Grove, Illinois: InterVarsity Press, 1992), 79.

[13] For an excellent Christian analysis of Sai Baba and other gurus, see Mangalwadi, Vishal, *The World of Gurus: A Critical Look at the Philosophies of India's Influential Gurus and Mystics* (Chicago, Illinois: Cornerstone Press, 1987).

[14] V. K. Gokak, *Sri Sathya Sai Baba* (New Delhi: Abhinav Publications, 1975), 229.

serving, as he allegedly sexually exploited several of his male devotees.[15] A moral vacuum is thus created in the karma cycle of suffering through birth, death, and rebirth. Moral relativism results wherever sin is not defined by Scripture (1 John 3:4).

Karma Undermines Compassion and Service toward the Needy

Without the moral foundation of Scripture, the Hindu follower has no basis for offering genuine service toward others. To attempt to relieve a sufferer of a burden is an obstruction of justice, a work *against* karma, interfering with the prison of bad karma from a previous life. For a sufferer to experience relief through another's interference might actually result in yet another cycle of reincarnation and another unpleasant (or even worse) life. To offer service, according to the Hindu worldview, may be no service at all.

Thus, the shackles of karma can and often do lead to unspeakable tragedy. For example, when a female child is born to a rural Hindu family, it is preferable for her to die than to be raised to adulthood. Her placement in the family is considered bad karma because her parents must bear the additional financial burden of her dowry if and when she marries. Some years ago, a Christian nurse, the sister of a seminary student in Goa, was asked by a Hindu doctor to discard a newborn girl in the garbage on behalf of the parents. Yet because she was informed by the Bible, her conscience would not allow her to participate in the murder (see Jas 1:27). She brought the child to the seminary leadership. By the grace of God, they were able to facilitate an adoption with another family unable to have a child of their own. Gospel compassion such as this is learned from Christ (1 John 4:19) but has no real place in the fatalism of karma.

Karma Contradicts the Serious Reality of Death and Hell

The Hindu worldview opposes and thereby dismisses the seriousness of death and judgment,[16] which have been appointed once

---

[15] See questions raised in the BBC article from April 24, 2011, http://www.bbc.com/news/world-south-asia-13180011. One of the young men who reports having been victimized by the guru was American Tal Brooke, who spent nineteen months as a private devotee of Sai Baba. Brooke later fled and was led to faith in Christ. See Tal Brooke, *Avatar of Night: The Hidden Side of Sai Baba*, (Createspace Independent Pub, 2015).

[16] Mangalwadi, *When the New Age Gets Old*, 196.

and for all by a holy God (Heb 9:27). In Hinduism, each individual determines their future by their works, yet the cycle of reincarnation is virtually endless. If samsara is indeed a fatalistic loop, then judgment in hell—the conscious torment of the soul in a body suitable for eternal suffering—is pointless. The final and sure judgment of hell is replaced with a slowly purging punishment until the individual is absorbed in the divine consciousness and granted eternal rest. Moksha is thus the Hindu concept of eternal salvation, and it is eventually available to all. There is therefore no real accountability for one's actions in this life because there is no individual judgment for one's deeds in this life. As a result, the Hindu follower does not feel the real and serious weight of sin. Where there is no sense of guilt, there is no sense of need for a savior. What the Christian calls sin is, in the Hindu mindset, merely a step on karma's gradual path of reform, which all sufferers will eventually find.

Inadequate Responses to Karma

Hindu philosophy has gained widespread acceptance in the West through the New Age movement and many Hollywood stars who have given it a popular voice.[17] Today's philosophical melting pot has produced some ecumenical approaches to Hinduism, karma, and reincarnation that have entered mainstream culture. One popular teacher of ecumenical Hinduism is Deepak Chopra, who claims:

> Jesus raised the topic of Karma when he said, "as you sow, so shall you reap," and he touched on the world as illusion when he said, "Be in the world, but not of it." These are familiar sayings, into which Jesus delved more deeply that people realize. He may not have used the Sanskrit word Karma, but there is abundant evidence that he had already incorporated the lessons of Karma into his worldview.[18]

---

[17] For instance, see Shirley MacLaine, *Out on a Limb* (New York: Bantam, 1983).

[18] Deepak Chopra, *The Third Jesus: How to Find Truth and Love in Today's World*, (Random House, 2008), 50.

Some teachers in the church have incorporated a form of this philosophy in their teaching, using adages like "what goes around comes around."[19] This idea—that good deeds endlessly cycle in a community—is contrary both to a biblical view of man's total depravity (Rom 3:10) and the nature of Christian kindness (Matt 5:38–48). The truth of Scripture cannot be mixed with false karmic ideology.

This ecumenical approach has had an influence on evangelistic methods in India.[20] For instance, certain mission groups have begun promoting an "insider movement" of outreach to Hindus. They encourage evangelists to Hindus to wear monastic robes, practice Hindu rituals, and make pilgrimages to Hindu religious sites.[21] When people show an interest in Christianity, they are encouraged to do so as practicing Hindus, or *Jesu Bhaktas*.[22] These methods seriously endanger the contrast that should be evident between the gospel of Christ and Hindu philosophy. Borrowing from Hindu doctrine and practice only moves one further away from biblical Christianity.

The Christological Response to Karma

Nothing could be further from the gospel of Jesus Christ than the Hindu concept of karma. The Bible teaches that man is cursed by God for his sin, with the consequences being suffering, broken relationships, toil, and death (Gen 3:16–19). The reality of sin points to human frailty and, rather than resulting in fatalism, allows the sinner to look to God alone for redemption through the seed of the woman (Gen 3:15). The curse of sin is meant to bring us to our knees in helplessness, without hope in our goodness or works, so that we would hope in God alone. The Bible offers three key correctives to the fatalism of karma that are rooted in the suffering of Jesus Christ, the Savior of sinners.

---

[19] http://www.lightsource.com/ministry/daily-hope/devotionals/daily-hope-with-rick-warren/every-person-is-worthy-of-respect-daily-hope-with-rick-warren-dec-3–2015–11745445.html.

[20] Robin Boyd, *An Introduction to Indian Christian Theology*, (Delhi: ISPCK, 2004), 266.

[21] S. Guthrie, *Missions in the Third Millennium: 21 Key Trends for the 21st Century* (Waynesboro, Georgia: Paternoster, 2000), 106–07.

[22] http://www.christianitytoday.com/ct/2013/january-february/hidden-history-of-insider-movements.html. For a sympathetic survey of the Hindu insider movements see, Herbert E. Hoefer, *Churchless Christianity* (Pasadena, California: William Carey Library, 2001).

Suffering Is Designed to Draw Us to Christ in Worship

In John 9:1–3, the disciples of Jesus fell into a very pharisaical way of thinking, seeking to blame a young man's congenital blindness on the man's or his parent's sinfulness. According to the rabbinical worldview, suffering was always caused by sin. Some rabbis even taught that it was possible to sin in the womb.[23] While it is true that suffering is a general result of the curse of sin, not all personal suffering should be seen as directly resulting from personal sin.

John Calvin wisely comments, "We do wrong in this respect, that we pronounce condemnation on all, without exception, whom God visits with the cross or with tribulation."[24] In response to the disciples' question of whether the young man's blindness was the result of his or his parents' sin, Jesus answers in verse 3 with the emphatic "Neither." Jesus rejected a cause-and-effect, "what goes around comes around" kind of morality in the context of the young sufferer. Jesus instead revealed the purpose of God for his suffering, that "the works of God might be displayed in him." Calvin points out that Christ intended by these words to encourage his disciples to expect of a miracle. But at the same time Christ reminded them in a general manner that this must be abundantly exhibited in the theater of the world, as the true and lawful cause, when God glorifies His name. Men have no right to complain about God when He makes them the instruments of His glory in either way—whether He shows Himself to be merciful or severe.[25]

The suffering of man is a backdrop to the theatre of God's glory in redemption. Suffering should drive men to humble themselves before Christ's grace and redemption, just as it ultimately did for the man who at the end of a redemptive process saw Jesus with clear vision, believed in Him, and worshiped Him (9:38).

No One except Christ Jesus Has Righteousness before God

Another nail in the coffin of karmic thinking is the contrast between self-righteousness and divine righteousness in the Person

---

23 See D. A. Carson, *The Gospel according to John*, Pillar New Testament Commentary (Grand Rapids, Michigan: Eerdmans, 1991), 362.

24 John Calvin and William Pringle, *Commentary on the Gospel According to John*, vol. 1, electronic ed. (Bellingham, WA: Logos Bible Software, 2010), 364.

25 Calvin and Pringle, 367.

of Jesus. The Bible teaches that man is entirely unable to achieve righteousness in the eyes of God. In Philippians 3:7–9, Paul reveals that his utmost goal is to be fully united to Christ (v. 9). However, his deeds were not sufficient in themselves to bring him into the eternally peaceful presence of God. He references the religious practices that could count as "gain" (v. 7), which in his context were the highest expressions of pharisaical righteousness that anyone in his day could attain (vv. 4–6; compare Gal 1:13–14). Yet Paul viewed his best attempts at righteousness as a loss to him, as little other than rubbish or dung, futile in "view of the surpassing value of knowing Christ Jesus [his] Lord" (Phil 3:8 NASB). This hero of faith considered his former self-righteous life as effectively worthless in spiritual terms.

The overwhelming worth of Christ's perfectly righteous life and obedient suffering and death before God is not only the divine standard for righteousness, but also the divine means for righteousness to all who come to Christ by faith. In Philippians 3:9, Paul teaches that Christ's perfect life and death earned the righteousness of the repentant sinner who now "may be found *in Him,* not having a righteousness of [his] own derived from the Law, but that which is *through faith in Christ,* the righteousness which comes from God on the basis of faith" (NASB). Faith is therefore not a work we offer to God (Rom 4:4–5). The point of contrast between sinner and Savior is crucial. Paul realizes that he is bankrupt of any real righteousness as derived from the religious Law. The spiritual debtor has to flee from his religious world view to find refuge in the righteousness of Christ, which is divinely imputed to sinners through faith (Rom 5:16–19).

The lie of self-righteousness is that the ultimate liberation of the soul will come from one's own righteousness. One should not think that his righteous deeds will please God when done apart from faith in Jesus Christ and His righteousness. The self-righteous mindset is an offense to God worthy of eternal wrath (Rom 2:5–8). To the one who clings to his moral deeds with the hope of the eventual liberation of the *atman,* his sense of moral rectitude must truly be abandoned as "dung." While works can never absolve the sinner of his debt of death before God, only Christ and His righteousness can.

No Present Suffering Is Comparable to the Suffering of Christ for Sinners

The crucial question in salvation, is "How can sinners be made right with God?" Romans 3:25 provides the answer in one weighty word: propitiation. This word alludes to the mercy seat of the Old Testament Israelite sacrificial system in connection with the Day of Atonement (Heb 9:5; cf. Exod 25:17–22; Lev 16). In the New Testament, the term *propitiation* denotes the offering of Christ as a satisfaction for sin because He absorbed the blunt force of God's wrath destined for sinners (1 John 2:2; cp. Isa 53:4–6, 8). In Romans 3:25, the phrase "God displayed publicly" indicates that God the Father was pleased to crush His Son (Isa 53:10) so that He could justify and spare the eternal souls of the sinners He had elected to salvation (Eph 1:4–7, 5:25–27; Heb 2:10–13).

God is not the distant "god" of karma who lets justice play out in the lives of men in a detached way. Because of His abundant mercy, He frees sinners from condemnation and endures religious pluralism with remarkable patience (Acts 14:16) so that man might be led to repentance. The God of the Bible even amply testifies to His goodness by providing the means for human life despite man's idolatrous response (v. 17). The humbling thought thus emerges: no sufferer in this life yet experiences the degree of suffering that he actually deserves, which he will experience forever in hell if Christ is not his Savior. In light of the biblical witness of both God's goodness toward the sinner and the incomparable degree of suffering awaiting the unrepentant, any amount of human suffering may be seen from a renewed perspective. In fact, the reality of suffering is the grounds for considering the greater suffering of Christ and the offer of refuge in Him (Acts 17:30). The gospel is therefore the only lens through which one may rightly view the broken and suffering world, a world that is still under the kind and forbearing guidance of God.

Implications for Evangelism to Hindus

To evangelize Hindus, then, the Christian must address the core dogmas of karma and samsara (reincarnation). These speculative elements of the Hindu worldview construct a fortress that must be torn down through the wisdom and mercy of Christ (2 Cor 10:5). In order to lay a new foundation for truly saving faith, the missionary must emphasize and exalt the gospel over the false ideologies, which trap Hindu followers in their sin.

Emphasize the Uniqueness of the Gospel of Christ

The first lie of the Hindu system of karma relates to the extent of salvation. Since salvation in Hinduism is the inevitable result of good works, irrespective of one's faith or religion, positive actions will bring a person to a better next life. Hinduism teaches that all roads lead to the same mountaintop and that all religious efforts will result in reward. Salvation through karma is therefore universal salvation for all.

Karmic inclusivism can seem disarming at first when the Hindu claims to accept the good in Christianity without sensing the need to obey Christ. But the reality is that Hinduism and Christian truth are diametrically opposed. Christ has nothing in common with the prince of this world and his schemes. The gospel has no common ground with *karma*. In our evangelism, we must establish the biblical truth of Isaiah 64:6:

> For all of us have become like one who is unclean,
> And all our righteous deeds are like a filthy garment;
> And all of us wither like a leaf,
> And our iniquities, like the wind, take us away.

Every man must confess the confession of a sinner. The sinner must come to understand that all he can produce are external acts of spurious righteousness, while the heart is filled with the weight of iniquity. Only when we realize that sin is in our nature and that we ourselves cannot eradicate it will we forsake self-righteousness and look to Christ for salvation from sin.

Exalt Sovereign Grace over Human Ability

Until human works are seen as morally bankrupt in the sight of the Holy One, salvation will be a man-centered endeavor. The Hindu plan of salvation is at best viewed as a cooperation between men and the divine, insofar as karma, however impersonal, divinely guides imperfect man toward a higher version of self. But on the contrary, only when man understands the depths of his sin will he lift his eyes to the true God who alone performs saving action. There is nothing that we can offer to God except for our sin, and sin is no gift worthy of God. In Jeremiah 13:23, God declares to sinners:

> But there is little hope for you ever doing good,
> You who are so accustomed to doing evil.
> Can an Ethiopian change the color of his skin?
> Can a leopard remove its spots?

Yet it is the kindness of God through Jesus Christ's righteous life and blameless death to make a way to holiness to unworthy man. Titus 3:3–6 declares the full participation of the Triune God on behalf of the sinner:

> For we too were once foolish, disobedient, misled, enslaved to various passions and desires, spending our lives in evil and envy, hateful and hating one another. But "when the kindness of God our Savior and his love for mankind appeared, he saved us not by works of righteousness that we have done but on the basis of his mercy, through the washing of the new birth and the renewing of the Holy Spirit, whom he poured out on us in full measure through Jesus Christ our Savior.

He alone gives repentant sinners all they need in the life and death of Christ (Col 3:3). Charles Spurgeon offers a fitting thought on the singular, sovereign design of the Savior:

> If any man be saved, he is saved by Divine grace, and by Divine grace alone; and the reason of his salvation is not to be found in him, but in God. We are not saved as the result of anything that we do or that we will; but we will and do as the result of God's good pleasure, and the work of his grace in our hearts.... God is always first in the matter of salvation. He is

before our convictions, before our desires, before our
fears, before our hopes.[26]

Conclusion

The doctrine of karma produces hopelessness and fear. The Hindu
has no idea whether his present life is achieving any tangible step
toward ultimate peace. In fact, he has no real basis for understanding
the suffering and evil in and around him, even though he might receive
some feigned solace in the idea of a more promising life cycle to come
based on his ethics today. Hinduism, like any atheistic or polytheistic worldview, sticks the suffering sinner in an ideological prison in
which the hope of eternal life is a distant possibility, far out of reach.

The doctrine of karma also produces a damnable arrogance in the
face of the one true God. The Hindu who denies a sovereign, personal
deity also denies any personal responsibility for sin before the righteous Judge. While the Hindu cannot discern the true path of salvation
without the sovereign enabling of divine grace through the Holy Spirit,
he already understands that he is not presently at a place of human per-
fection over his weaknesses and errors. In this sense, his conscience
should drive him to his knees to God—not another life—for help.

Only the gospel of Christ can bring grace and truth like a light to
the blind eyes of the sinner (John 1:4–5). In the wake of the harmful
teaching of karma, the Christian who encounters a Hindu follower
must emphasize that the personal God is offended by sin, yet wants a
relationship with the sinner. Real fellowship with the Divine is available here and now through the mercy of God in Christ Jesus toward
every sinner who would repent and believe.

The exclusivity of the deity of Jesus Christ and the true path of
salvation through His death on the cross are stumbling blocks to the
Hindu, who conducts himself according to the impersonal, inclusive
doctrine of karma. Yet Christ is the only way out of sin and away from
eternal judgment at the conclusion of this life (John 14:6; Acts 4:12; cf.
Heb 9:27). To the Hindu who is bogged down by a seemingly pointless
struggle against sin and suffering, Jesus Christ alone offers a distinct
and radiant hope—the liberation of the soul now and forevermore.

---

[26] C. H. Spurgeon, "Sovereign Grace and Man's Responsibility," in *The New Park Street Pulpit Sermons*, vol. 4 (London: Passmore & Alabaster, 1858), 338.

Poisonous Pragmatism: The Harmful Effects of Western Missiological Trends on the Churches in Ukraine

Igor Bodun

Irpin Biblical Seminary, Ukraine

[Editor's Note: Western missionaries have done much good for the cause of Christ around the world, but it would be wrong to assume that everything that has been done is positive. Some missionary efforts and trends may actually do longstanding harm to foreign churches. Coming from the perspective of a Ukrainian national pastor and teacher, this essay provides many gems of historical and biblical insight, together with a sober reminder that missionary methodology must center on Christ alone.]

The Contemporary Decline in Proclaiming the True Gospel

For Ukrainian evangelicals, the last decade was marked by the gradual decline in proclaiming the message of salvation in Christ alone. This has occurred after a long period of gospel success, when churches had qualitative and quantitative spiritual growth[1] in spite

---

[1] "Ukraine is also known as the "Bible belt" of the former Soviet Union; evangelical Christianity is stronger there than in any of the other ex-Soviet republics, making up at least three percent of the population. Ukraine enjoys full religious liberty, churches are growing,

of many years of Orthodox and Communist oppression. Above all, this decline has touched the churches of the Ukrainian Baptist Union, which is the largest Protestant denomination in Europe.[2]

Before the USSR collapsed in 1991, Soviet Ukraine was the home to the second-largest Baptist community in the world after the United States. When the Iron Curtain fell, all evangelical churches in Eastern Europe obtained long-awaited religious freedom and got unprecedented opportunities to preach Christ and fulfill His great commission more effectively (Matt 28:19–20). During the time immediately following (1991–1997), a huge number of unbelievers had a tremendous interest in Christianity, which is described by contemporary historians as an "evangelical explosion,"[3] or as the "frantic evangelism phase."[4] The collapse of the Soviet Union happened so suddenly that post-Soviet evangelicals were not ready to go out onto the boundless missionary field of Ukraine. They were unready, and it was caused primarily by a lack of two essential elements that had not been allowed to germinate in the Soviet Union. The first was a lack of the practical experience of evangelism outside the walls of the church. The second was a lack of finances for the work. At that time, many missionaries from the West flooded Eastern Europe and enthusiastically offered their evangelizing *methods* and *money* to the churches. These two things dramatically broke open the once-closed conservative door by allowing questionable evangelistic

---

and a large number of indigenous mission societies have sprung up there" (Raymond P. Prigodich, "Ukraine," in *Evangelical Dictionary of World Missions*, A. Scott Moreau, Harold Netland and Charles van Engen, eds., [Grand Rapids, Michigan: Baker, 2000], 979).

[2]   The Ukrainian Baptist Union is the largest Protestant denomination in all of Europe, and is recognized as the fourth largest Christian Church in Ukraine, after: (1) The Ukrainian Orthodox Church-Moscow Patriarchate; (2) Ukrainian Orthodox Church-Kievan Patriarchate; and (3) Ukrainian Catholic Church. (Walter Sawatsky, "Ukraine," in *The Encyclopedia of Christianity*, Erwin Fahlbusch and Geoffrey William Bromiley, eds., [Grand Rapids, Michigan: Eerdmans, 2008], 5:585.)

[3]   Michael Rowe, *Russian Resurrection*, (London: Marshall Pickering, 1994), 229–38. For example, evangelicals could go outside and simply yell, "Jesus loves you" and gather a crowd of people that would take all of the gospel tracts they had. One in five people would come to church the next day, and half of them would come forward and repent. (John White, "Three Periods of Awakening in Eastern Slavic Lands," in *Theological Reflections*, [Odessa, Ukraine: EAAA, 2013], 252.)

[4]   W. W. Sawatsky, "Return of Mission and Evangelization in the CIS (1980s–present): An Assessment," *Mission in the former Soviet Union*, W. W. Sawatsky and P. F. Penner, eds., (Schwarzenfeld, Germany: Neufeld-Verlag, 2005), 99.

strategies and philosophies for church growth into the post-Soviet church. Mostly, this was done with a sincere desire to help the local churches; however, the Ukrainian churches were seriously infected with American religious *pragmatism*.[5] This pragmatism had already killed many evangelical churches in the West, and now it became an obstacle for the strength and vitality of post-Soviet churches.[6]

Certainly, the Western missionary activity did many positive things in Ukraine. It supported the national pastors, expanded the church work, developed national theological training, built new church buildings, and printed a lot of Bibles and useful Christian literature. However, too often it was guided by pragmatic methods. Such pragmatic philosophy brought only temporary "results," and very soon it caused the gradual decline that made even the most ardently evangelical communities weak and worldly.

Now, Ukrainian evangelical churches are in serious trouble, and many of the pastors do not understand the real reason for this decline. A closer look at the present state of the churches through a biblical lens shows the dangerous consequences of pragmatism. Very sadly, the new foreign methods of evangelism have caused believers to minimize the significance and power of preaching Christ alone. Today, many Ukrainian Christians believe more in methods than in the power of God unto salvation. Different strategies for attracting unbelievers to Christ has caused many to prioritize worldly methods and cast away Christ and theology from the church. New conceptions of church planting have moved many weak churches to the point of

---

[5] For a pragmatist, an idea is said to be true if it works. A course of action is right if it brings desired results (Norman L. Geisler, *Baker Encyclopedia of Christian Apologetics*, [Grand Rapids, Michigan: Baker, 1999], 666). If there is a common religion to be found within the Western world, it surely is pragmatism—the religion of "What works?" (Gray E. Gilley, *This Little Church Had None*, [Carlisle, Pennsylvania: EP Books, 2009], 93).

[6] John McArthur shared his impressions of his first trip to the former Soviet Union, specifically to Ukraine and Russia. He noted the strength and purity of the ministry in the evangelical churches there. He said: "During my earliest visit to that part of the world, I was so absolutely amazed to see the strength and vitality of evangelical churches there. Their worship services were the very picture of austere simplicity—just the preaching of the Word and the celebration of the ordinances, totally devoid of the flash and entertainment being touched as essential tools for the times by all the 'experts' back home." He concluded: "I was convinced that even the weakest of their churches could teach evangelicals in America a lot about the biblical approach to church growth" (John MacArthur, *Ashamed of the Gospel: When the Church Becomes Like the World*, 3rd ed., [Wheaton, Illinois: Crossway, 2010], 15–16). However, to our deep regret, the situation in Ukraine has changed for the worse.

death when these little communities were neglected by the leaders of the Baptist Union in pursuit of quantitative growth.[7]

The time has come to disperse the darkness of pragmatism and to light a fire of a "new Reformation" by reviving orthodoxy in gospel content and methodology in missions work. The next part of this essay evaluates the former success of evangelical ministry in Ukraine, the preconditions that made it vulnerable to decline, and the harmful effects of Western pragmatism that have pushed that decline. To say it simply, pragmatism has hidden the Person of Christ and the core of the gospel. When Christ and His Word were in the center of ministry, the churches and their ministries were fruitful. When pragmatism was put at the center, however, the fruitfulness was largely eliminated.

This research focuses primary attention on the situation in the Ukrainian Baptist Union, although it recognizes the fact that the same situation is observed in virtually all evangelical churches throughout the former USSR. The essay does not contend that everything that came in the post-Soviet time from Western evangelicalism was bad or that there was not any real help from the West to preach the true gospel of Christ. We pay a tribute to the support of those Western evangelical churches and missions that did not build their ministry on pragmatism, but on biblical strategies. The unfortunate fact remains that they are in the minority.

The Period of Gospel Success

Looking back at the history[8] of the Ukrainian Baptist movement, we are reminded of the period of effectiveness and success of the gospel when the person of Christ and His Word were at the center of the mission. Although under Soviet rule it was not permitted to preach Christ or engage in any kind of missionary methods outside the walls of the church, we find that, in spite many difficult circumstances, even the "weakest" preaching of the gospel was constantly

---

[7]   The decline is clearly visible by reducing the number of local churches and the number of converted–baptized people. In 2005, there were 2,782 churches in the Baptist Union, whereas by 2015 the number of churches reduced to 2,284. In 1990 (a year before the collapse of the USSR) there were 988 local churches in the Union, which baptized 6,612 new members; in 1999 and 2000 the churches baptized 10,621 new members; in 2015, 2,284 local churches of the Union baptized only 3,402 new members.

[8]   Since its beginning at the middle of 19th century.

bearing abundant fruit. At that time, the only source for the preaching of the gospel was Scripture (the written Word), and the only center of the gospel was Christ alone (the Incarnate Word). If contemporary pastors and missionaries emulated this historical period, they would see an indisputable effectiveness of the true gospel that has rarely been seen in the last few decades.

The Start of an Evangelical Awakening

The evangelical awakening in Ukraine started in the middle of the 19th century. It occurred a millennium after Ukraine had officially adopted Christianity,[9] and it had a few important precursors. The first precursor was the missionary activity of the German Baptists and Western European settlers populating the southern part of Ukraine after they obtained land during the reign of the Catherine II and the subsequent Russian tsars.[10] The settlers had the opportunity to share the gospel with ordinary Ukrainians, who had been born into the Orthodox Church but were not truly born again until then. This missionary influence gave impetus to a further awakening and caused many people to read the Bible and live according to the gospel of Christ.

The second precursor was the wide distribution of Bibles among the Russian- and Ukrainian-speaking people in their native languages.[11] After the 19th century, Ukrainians finally had access to the written Word, and many people came to the Lord after they read the

---

[9]   Although Ukraine officially adopted Christianity in 988, it did not bring a spiritual awakening. When the formal separation of church on the East and West occurred in 1054, the adoption of Christianity in Ukraine was conducted not only under the auspices of the Eastern Church (Orthodox Church), but under the leadership of the Western Church (Roman Catholic Church) as well. These two traditions for centuries killed all possibilities (by their traditions, dogma, opposition, and political influence) for spiritual awakening in Ukraine.

[10]   П. Яроцький, ред., *Протестантизм в Україні*, Історія релігії в Україні, том 5 (Київ: Світ знань, 2002), 296; С. Н. Савинский, *История евангельский христиан-баптистов Украины, России, Белоруссии 1867–1917* (Санкт-Петербург: Библия для всех, 1999), 92–104.

[11]   The British Bible Society made a significant contribution. Until the mid-18th century, Ukrainians did not have the Bible in the plain language. Traditionally, the Orthodox Church used the Bible in Old Slavonic language, and the Catholic Church used the Latin translation of the Bible, both of which were totally incomprehensible for most people; Яроцький, ред., *Протестантизм*, 298.

Scriptures.[12] Consequently, they left their Eastern Orthodox faith, began to live according to the gospel, and shared it with their relatives, friends, and neighbors.[13] In the second half of the 19th century, almost all converted believers had been active national missionaries. Initially, they preached the gospel in their villages, then throughout the southern region, then to the whole Ukraine, and even to Russia and Belarus.

Multiplying of Evangelicals

Preaching the gospel awakened many sinners to be reconciled to Christ despite many external obstacles.[14] From the beginning of the 20th century, the evangelical Baptist churches were growing until the harsh Stalinist repressions of the 1930s.[15] This time was characterized by an increase in missionary activity and the success of the gospel.[16] One historian wrote that the "evangelical movement spread spontaneously in Ukraine. Church meetings utterly overflowed; there were crowds near the church buildings. Masses of sinners converted to Christ and were baptized, and the evangelical churches grew like in the apostolic times."[17] Historian Andrij Yurash said that in the beginning of the 20th century approximately five percent of all

---

[12] All pioneers of the Ukrainian revival (at the end of the 19th century) were also the first native preachers of the gospel in Ukraine; among them the first Ukrainian native "Baptist" Ivan Onyshchenko (he was converted to Christ and baptized in 1852), Gerasim Balaban (converted c. 1855), Michael Ratushniy (converted c. 1856), Uhim Tsimbal (converted c. 1856), and Ivan Riaboshapka (converted c. 1865). Й. Іваськів, *Український народ і християнство*, (Харків: Глобус, 2005), 200–27.

[13] According to the history of the Baptist movement in Ukraine, the first native evangelical church appeared in Osnova village in Odessa Oblast in 1852. This church was planted after a family read the Bible. Initially, one family (the family of Ivan Onyshchenko) used to read the Bible at the table in the family circle. After a while, the circle expanded, and the house was no place to accommodate the audience. Many sinners sincerely turned to the Lord. Julia Kruedener and Anna Lion, *Evangelist John Onyshchenko,* (Morris Plains, New Jersey: All-Ukrainian Evangelical Baptist Fellowship, 2002), 29–32.

[14] A foreign reader has to know that Ukrainian and Russian evangelicals experienced religious persecution from the Russian Orthodox Church up to the Soviet era. This was followed by the atheistic persecution of the Soviet period.

[15] For example, at the start, in 1884 about 24,700 new believers had been baptized just in the Kyiv region; Іваськів, *Український народ*, 233.

[16] С. И. Головащенко, сост., *История евангельско-баптистского движения в Украине*, Материалы и документы (Одесса: Богомыслие, 1998), 65–66.

[17] L. Zabko-Potapovich, *The Life of a Church*, (Winnipeg, Manitoba: Doroga Prawdy, 1977), 12.

Ukrainians were Baptists.[18] In 1927, a senior leader of the Baptist Union, P. V. Ivanov-Klyshnikov, in his article in the journal *The Baptists of Ukraine,* happily reported that over the preceding sixty years (from 1867 to 1927) the Baptist churches "were replenished by hundreds of thousands the newly redeemed members."[19] Remarkable is that this multiplying was not a result of any "special" contemporary evangelizing methods but was a consequence of the faithfulness to Christ and His Word.

Endurance of the Gospel in Spite of Severe Obstacles
Since 1927, evangelicals began to experience the great pressure of the Soviet atheistic regime that aimed to completely eradicate the church from the country.[20] Consequently, during the reigns of Stalin, Khrushchev, and Brezhnev, thousands of evangelical preachers and pastors were poisoned, tortured, and killed because of their faith in God.[21] Thousands of evangelical churches were closed by force. It was forbidden to preach the Bible outside church buildings. Children of Christian parents were not allowed to attend church. Quite often, believers were fined because of their faith. However, as always, when they shared the gospel of Christ even in these humble circumstances, it had success. The severe obstacles could not destroy the message about Christ. On the contrary, it only purified and strengthened their faith in Christ. Amid such struggle, the Baptists lived out their witness, and their churches showed greater spiritual vitality and high rates of numerical growth.[22]

---

[18]   Andrij Yurash, "Ukraine," in *Worldmark Encyclopedia of Religious Practices*, Thomas Riggs, ed., (New York: Thomson Gale, 2006), 3:503.

[19]   П. В. Иванов-Клышников, «Наше шестидесятилетие 1867–1927», *Баптист Украины,* №9, (Харков, Украйна : ВСОБ, 1927), 1–4.

[20]   С. Н. Савинский, *История евангельский христиан-баптистов Украины, России, Белоруссии 1917–1967* (Санкт-Петербург: Библия для всех, 2001), 111–12.

[21]   According to information that was declassified from the KGB archives, during the Stalinist regime in the 1930s, near 25,000 Baptist pastors were arrested in the USSR. Of this number, 22,000 were killed or died in prison camps; Леонид Коваленко, *Облако свидетелей Христовых* (Киев: Центр христианского сотрудничества, 1997), 14.

[22]   H. Leon McBeth, *The Baptist Heritage: Four Centuries of Baptist Witness,* (Nashville, Tennessee: Broadman, 1987), 805.

Vulnerabilities to Western Pragmatism

Religious pragmatism among Ukrainian evangelicals did not appear out of the blue. Before 1991, there were some preconditions that made the churches of the Ukrainian Baptist Union defenseless against the pragmatism that arrived shortly after the dissolution of the USSR. Because of these, Western pragmatism was adopted without much resistance. The previous success of the gospel did not protect the churches from the future infusion of pragmatism because of these preconditions, which were like a time bomb waiting to explode in the following decades.

The Weakness of the National Theological Schools

Throughout the Soviet era, it was forbidden for the Baptists to organize theological seminaries and to develop any theological training.[23] As a result, almost all pastors were far removed from such disciplines as exegesis, systematic theology, and biblical languages. This had an influence on the development of practical theology. Although the Soviet Baptists usually held to the Baptist traditions and creeds, this was not enough to enable them to preserve the purity of the gospel and to confront the new challenges of the future. This superficial knowledge of the Bible set up the Ukrainian church for the future intrusion of pragmatism in the area of gospel proclamation.[24]

Doctrinal Diversity within the Union

In 1944–5, the Baptist Union was forced to integrate with other Christian confessions that held to different doctrinal views. At that time the Soviet government had strictly forbidden them to raise any kind of criticism or disagreement against the theological differences within the Baptist Union.[25] Five years before the collapse of the Soviet Union, Baptist historian Leon McBeth wrote:

---

[23] In the late 1960s, Soviet Baptists were allowed to have only one distinctive theological school in Moscow. This education was superficial. Furthermore, the distinctive courses were not available to the majority of pastors and did not provide the proper level of theological education.

[24] The subjectivism is related to pragmatism because it works according a subjective human perception that might be far from the objective biblical truth.

[25] Since 1991, the Pentecostals, the Mennonites, and the Evangelical Christians have left the Baptist Union and took a portion of the church members from the Baptist churches.

Ultimately the All-Union Council contained four distinct denominational groups: the Baptists, who were probably most numerous at first; the Evangelical Christians; the Mennonites; and the Pentecostals. Not surprisingly, such a diverse grouping, formed more from government pressure than church desires, continues to reveal tensions and disagreements.[26]

This forced confessional "unity" led to the development of two features that created fertile ground for the adoption and proliferation of pragmatism. First, it led to religious pluralism and doctrinal tolerance within the Union. For many years before pragmatism came, the Baptist Union had been trained to keep silent and not to show any disagreement against opposing doctrinal views.

Second, the forced union with the Mennonites, the Pentecostals, and the Evangelical Christians,[27] led to Arminianism,[28] the general soteriological position of the Baptist Union, since it was the traditional view of the new, non-Baptist majority.[29] These three denominational groups held to conditional election and libertarian "free will," and brought them into the Baptist Union. Consequently, the infiltration of Arminianism opened the door for future pragmatism in evangelism. As American pastor John MacArthur notes:

> Pragmatism's ally is Arminianism, the theology that denies God's sovereign election and affirms that man must decide on his own to trust or reject Christ. That places on the evangelist the burden of using technique that is clever enough, imaginative

---

[26] McBeth, *The Baptist Heritage*, 813.

[27] This is the name of an evangelical movement in Ukraine and Russia that was organized by Ivan Prokhanov in 1908. Unlike the Baptists, the Evangelical Christians held to Wesleyan-Arminian theology, and were more concerned with the "simple" preaching of the gospel based on pietistic motives.

[28] Arminianism is especially attractive to believers coming out of an Eastern Orthodox background, in which works and human effort are stressed.

[29] The Reformed Calvinistic view of soteriology was the official opinion of Ukrainian Baptist Churches from the 19th century to 1984. It was based on an accepted Baptist Creed prepared and published by two respectable Baptist leaders: Vasili Pavlov (1854–1924) and Nikolai Odintsov (1870–1939).

enough, or convincing enough to sway a person's decision. The *content* of the message is thus subjugated to the issue of how it is packaged.[30]

Material Poverty of the Evangelicals

The financial position of evangelical believers under the Soviet regime was radically different from the position of believers of the capitalist West. Throughout Soviet history, evangelicals were forced to live at poverty level. Living a hard life under socialism, they were not allowed to get a higher education, occupy high positions, or take lucrative jobs. At that time, most Soviet people lived in poverty, and the evangelicals were often the poorest of the poor. Usually, the Baptist pastors and leaders of the Baptist Union were financially poor and did not have enough resources to sustain their families. In most cases, the Soviet regime prohibited them from receiving any kind of financial support.

After the fall of the USSR, Western evangelical churches and missions offered their support with money together with their evangelistic methodology. Since that time, many local churches and church leaders have received Western support of various kinds: humanitarian aid, money for the building new churches, and financial support for national pastors and missionaries. Frequently, this aid influenced the doctrinal loyalties of the Ukrainian Baptist leaders. Those who closely collaborated with foreign churches might obtain the material means to build luxury homes, to buy expensive cars, to give their children a Western education, or receive money for living expenses. It may seem strange to some, but such cooperation and financial aid opened the way for Western pragmatism and tied the hands of many Baptist pastors.

The Continuing Harmful Effects of Western Pragmatism

Twenty-five years after the start of pragmatism, it is now necessary to recognize the "bitter fruits" it has brought to the evangelical churches in Ukraine. These fruits have become clearly visible, particularly in the last decade. They are "bitter" because the pragmatic

---

[30]   John F. MacArthur, *Our Sufficiency in Christ*, (Dallas: Word Publishing, 1997), 152.

methods have removed from many churches any real sense of the gospel. Sadly, now most believers do not understand the content, the center, the purpose, or the power of the true gospel of Jesus Christ. The fruits of pragmatism are ongoing, like a nuclear explosion, the effects of which last a long time. Attempts to preach the gospel through pragmatic methods led to the most painful consequences, which demonstrate the progression of religious pragmatism.

Underdeveloped Doctrine

At first, pragmatism led to underdeveloped doctrine in the church. When it came to missionary work, it minimized theology and popularized new methods. Most of the evangelistic methods, strategies, and programs were seeking to bring sinners to God without causing discomfort by biblical teaching or to create a comfortable environment to develop friendships. This does not mean that there was no respect for the Bible, but the Bible was not perceived as the standard for any kind of methodology for missionary work. One national researcher of the Western evangelistic methods of the post-Soviet era concluded:

> We have to admit that bringing of the long-awaited good news for the countries of the former Soviet Union has become the greatest failure of the Church in the 20th century... . We are deeply convinced that the main reason for the failure of the "traditional" methods of evangelism is that they are not biblical... . We consider that the failure of evangelism in Eastern Europe is a modern warning to Western missions.[31]

Unfortunately, everything turned out according to the Western scenario. A whole generation of believers has grown up in the churches where the Bible has not been systematically preached and taught. Pragmatism ruled over doctrine. As a result, most of the people who have come to the evangelical churches since 1991 have a very poor knowledge of the Scriptures. Therefore, they are

---

[31] Сергей Головин, *Мировоззрение — утраченное измерение благовестия*, (Симферополь, Україна: Диайпи, 2008), 8–9.

highly susceptible to following false teachings or falling away from the faith. Most Ukrainian Baptists follow the church traditions but are weak in biblical doctrines. When they try to preach the gospel, it usually does not expose the gospel message but a bundle of logical arguments. Most of those who were saved under pragmatic methods and teaching are not able to live according to the gospel and do not know how to preach it.

Anthropocentrism

The religious philosophy brought by Western evangelicals has taught the post-Soviet believers to place man, his features, and his needs in the center of evangelizing methodology. First, anthropocentrism locates a sinner in the center of the gospel. As such, the methods become humanistic and revolve around what sinners need to find fulfillment. Second, anthropocentrism locates the minister in the center of gospel methodology, putting undue stress on his own ingenuity and ability to winsomely draw a person to Christ.

But God has established the gospel in such a way that He is at the center of it. Any attempts to put man at the center lead invariably to preaching a false gospel, with Christ insufficiently emphasized. Only God Himself and His Sovereign salvific purposes are at the center (1 Cor 8:6). The fallen sinner cannot be the center of the gospel. He must hear the gospel message and obey it, recognizing his own sinfulness and insignificance (1 Tim 1:15). Any anthropocentric methods could not open the veil of salvation for those people "who are perishing" and for whom "our gospel is veiled ... that they might not see the light of the gospel of the glory of Christ" (2 Cor 4:3–4). A preacher of the gospel should not think of himself as a spiritual guru, but as a lowly ambassador for Christ, making an appeal for the fallen sinners to be reconciled to God through Christ (2 Cor 5:20).

Pursuit of Quantity over Quality

The pragmatic pursuit of quantity in missionary work has reduced the quality that is required by God in His Word. Foreign evangelical missionaries and missions cooperating with national churches have taught them to measure the success of their ministry by focusing on the number of people reached and converted. Furthermore, their financial dependence on the Western supporters motivates them to aim for numbers of churches planted, believers baptized, or kids "saved" at summer camps. Unfortunately, many pastors today are inclined to evaluate the success and quality of their ministry based on these numbers. Those who pursue such quantitative indicators may be tempted to use various worldly methods to attract and hold the attention of unchurched people. Eventually, the churches are filled with secular people, who separate themselves from fellowship life and live according to their individual standards. Usually, such people want the church to continue the use of the same pragmatic methods used to draw them in and do not have appetites for sound theology.

Sometimes, pragmatism causes church leaders to start new churches by artificially dividing existing churches in order to show Western sponsors quantitative church growth. Also, quite often, the pursuit of numerical growth causes a "silent battle" between churches due to envy and competition.

Every missionary who gets financial support, as well as the church or agency that provides this support, must be aware of the temptations and troubles that might be caused by the financial dependence. Remember, the gospel does not need the human pursuit of numerical growth; rather, the ministry is dependent on God's sovereign activity. Church history abounds with examples of spiritual awakenings and quantitative growth that was done by God through godly ministers (e.g., Acts 2:44–47). The key to church growth is the miraculous work of the Holy Spirit that He accomplishes through Christ's servants who live like Jesus "in a manner worthy the gospel of Christ" (Phil 1:27). God's servants should pursue the spiritual quality of His ministry, knowing that the true gospel "is constantly bearing fruit and increasing" (Col 1:5–6).

Emphasis on "Effective" Methods

During the last twenty-five years, pragmatism has gradually and quietly tamed the Ukrainian believers. Perhaps it sounds funny, but for many, the preaching of the gospel is synonymous with a professional concert, a youth club, a children's camp, a playground, humanitarian aid, clowns, balloons, an English class, or street cleaning. While these are positive things, a frenzy to produce the right "effect" may at times obscure the real mission. Today the official position of the Ukrainian Baptist Union is "to search for effective methods for evangelism."[32] Significantly, many evangelical churches have become activity-driven rather than Christ-centered. Emphasis on effective methods has paved the way for two unhealthy trends that should be mentioned: the social gospel and ecumenism.

The Social Gospel

The emphasis on "effective" methods gives rise to and motivates people toward the social gospel. The social gospel has shifted the mission of the church away from making disciples and toward the "transformation of society." Today this is the most popular method to attract masses to Christian meetings. The leaders of the Baptist Union call on and motivate all the churches to influence society through social work.[33] Today, the social activity is perceived as a sign of a good evangelical church. Even the government of Ukraine encourages Baptists and other Protestants to contribute to the solution of social problems. The situation is further stimulated by the low social position of people, by political problems, and by the war with the Russian aggressors.

Certainly, Christian compassion is a companion of the gospel. But, any one virtue must not supplant the explicit call for the church to make and teach disciples. Compassion ministries may help people, but they do not inherently lead them to the Savior. Although the Bible supports social justice and Jesus Himself demonstrated the virtue of compassion, the social gospel may change the center of the biblical gospel when the main motivators of the church's mission are material and social needs. To our deepest regret, the social gospel may lead to busyness about many things to the neglect of the most important thing: the proclamation of Jesus Christ for the forgiveness of sins.

---

[32] Валерій Антонюк, ред., *Євангельські християни-баптисти: історія і сучасність,* (Київ: ВСО ЄХБ, 2012), 54.

[33] Регіональна конференція служителів. Березень 2016. «Церква, яка впливає на суспільство». Тема 4. Критерії успішності у благовісті (Сергій Мороз). http://ecbua.info/index.php?option=com_content&view=article&id=3992%3Aregonalna-konferenczya-sluzhitelv-berezen-2016-lczerkva-yaka-vpliva-na-susplstvor-tema-4-kriter-uspshnost-u-blagovst-sergj-moroz&catid=13%3As-&Itemid=53&lang=ua

Ecumenism

Emphasis on "effective" methods has also given birth to ecumenism. Just such a practice was proposed in 1992 by the *Billy Graham Evangelistic Association,* which was accepted by the post-Soviet Baptists as the most authoritative Western mission. However, Billy Graham's ecumenical approach has provided a model of denominational tolerance for the national church leaders. During the great crusade to Moscow in 1992, Baptists were forced to cooperate with the Pentecostals in the work of mass evangelism.[34] In 2007, the *Billy Graham Evangelistic Association* initiated a "Festival of Hope" in the capital of Ukraine, involving the Baptist Union, the Pentecostals, and the Charismatic churches working together. This pluralistic ecumenical spirit has spurred on some pastors to greater cooperation with other denominations and even cult groups. It laid a dangerous precedent for pragmatic approaches where the end justifies the means. In 2012, the Ukrainian Baptist Union officially participated in a big evangelistic project that included Pentecostals, Charismatics, Messianic churches, and Seventh-day Adventists. This project further blurred important doctrinal distinctions.

In spite of everything, the power of the gospel is in Christ alone. This power of salvation dictates the implementation of methods, and not vice versa. The true gospel is "the power of God" (Rom 1:16) which indicates that salvation is the work of the Triune God. The Scripture depicts God the Father as the ultimate source, planner, and initiator of salvation (Eph 1:3–6), who predestined the elect sinners to "become conformed to the image of His Son" (Rom. 8:29). God the Son provided complete redemption through his atoning death (Eph 1:7–12). God the Holy Spirit applies, makes effective, and preserves the redemption of Christ to those who believe (Eph 1:13–14).[35] Every pastor and missionary is called to the accurate preaching of the Word despite the fact that sinners "will not endure sound doctrine" and "will turn away their ears from the truth" (2 Tim 4:3–4). The minister of God must "do the work of an evangelist" (2 Tim 4:5),

---

[34] Джон Поллок, *Жизнь Билли Грема* (Киев: Христианский центр «Возрождение» ЕХБ, 2006), 291–99.

[35] Bruce Demarest, *The Cross and Salvation*, (Wheaton, Illinois: Crossway, 2006), 44.

despite the fact that other teachers will try to attract their audience by cunning methods and replace Christ with erroneous substitutes.

American pastor David Doran helpfully emphasizes the supremacy of God in missions. The practical implications of God-centered missions are that: (1) the priority of missions must be faithfulness to God and His Word, not numerical growth; (2) the promotion of missions should be based primarily on God and His Glory, not man's needs; (3) the practice of missions must be directed and informed by Scripture, not traditions or trends; and (4) the power for missions must be divine, not human.[36]

Conclusion

Looking at the contemporary Ukrainian Baptist Union, the time has come to awaken and to uncover the threats of religious pragmatism. It is necessary to accept the prediction made by John MacArthur that "the poison of religious pragmatism is now an enormous *global* problem,"[37] and "he who marries the spirit of the age soon finds himself a widower."[38] The decline of the gospel message in evangelical Churches in Ukraine is the most vivid proof of this. The once-fertile spiritual field has gradually turned into a spiritual desert directly impacted by religious pragmatism. This pragmatism has infiltrated the Ukrainian evangelical church just as it has the Western churches. The gospel of Christ has declined because of the popularity of a false gospel.

The failure of evangelism in Eastern Europe is a modern warning to Western missions and for those who work on the foreign fields of evangelism. This period of decline raises an alarm for all national church leaders and for the foreign missionaries. At the very beginning of the 20th century, an American pastor named Andrew Murray drew the attention of Western evangelical missionaries to the problems of international missions. Even then, he noted the dependence of missions on the following key factors: (1) the state of the church;

---

[36] David M. Doran, et. al., *For the Sake of His Name: Challenging a New Generation for World Missions,* (Allen Park, Michigan: Student Global Impact, 2002), 61–67.

[37] MacArthur, *Ashamed*, 18.

[38] Ibid., 22.

(2) the love of Christ as our motivation; (3) the deepening of the spiritual life; (4) the power of believing prayer; (5) the power of the Holy Spirit; and (6) godly leadership.[39]

We pray for a new revival in Ukraine, but that revival will only happen when Ukrainian believers imitate and preach Christ alone. May the Lord use this research to open the eyes of many national pastors, western evangelical missionaries, and churches regarding the dangers of pragmatism, which have contributed to the decline of the salvific message of Christ.

---

[39]   Andrew Murray, *Key to the Missionary Problem*, 2nd ed., (Fort Washington, Pennsylvania: Christian Literature Crusade, 1993).

RECLAIMING THE FORGOTTEN CHRIST IN THE CZECH REPUBLIC

Lance Roberts and Marcus Denny

Czech Bible Institute, Czech Republic

[Editor's Note: A post-Christian society is not merely one that is characterized by atheism, agnosticism, or secularism, though it is that; rather, it is one that is rooted in the history, culture, and practices of Christianity *while largely forgetting or rejecting* Christ. *This essay tells the tale of the Czech Republic's abandonment of Christ and discusses what must be done to see Him reclaimed. It will resonate with and give hope to every believer who yearns to see Jesus Christ reclaimed throughout the post-Christian world.*

Introduction

By all appearances, few countries from the former Soviet bloc have rejuvenated as quickly as the Czech Republic. With a growing middle class, a massive influx of tourism, and a key location at the very heart of Europe, the Czech Republic is advancing on the European stage. But beneath its physical, first-world appearance lies a country in deep spiritual poverty. Centuries of Roman Catholic domination and persecution, followed by decades of atheistic communism, have salted the entire land, leaving behind a poisoned soil in which, spiritually speaking, little will grow.

This is a long fall from the spiritual and theological heights to which these regions had risen. The lands now making up the country of the Czech Republic were once flourishing with the gospel, experiencing their own reformation, even before Luther and Calvin came on the scene. Men like Milíč of Kroměříž, whose powerful preaching shook up Prague, pointed the multitudes away from the corrupt clergy and back to the saving power of God's Word. Milíč regarded the Scriptures as containing all that is necessary for salvation and taught that the elect of God are saved by the Holy Spirit through the preaching of God's Word.[1] Among those affected by his preaching were hundreds of prostitutes and unprincipled men whose transformation was so great that a brothel was turned into dormitories for them. Their sacrificial service and ministry throughout the city was known by all, and their center of ministry became known as "New Jerusalem."[2]

In 2015, the Czech Republic remembered the 600th anniversary of the martyrdom of Jan (John) Hus, appointed preacher of Bethlehem Chapel in Prague, who was burned at the stake for espousing the doctrines of Wycliffe and confronting the abuses of the Catholic Church. Lesser-known men such as Petr Čelčický, Jeroným of Prague, and John Amos Comenius (the father of modern education) also were mightily used to proclaim Christ in the lands now known as the Czech Republic.

Yet where is Christ preached now? Where are the Bethlehem Chapels with their thousands longing for the preached Word? Where are the converted brothels, vibrant ministries, and Christ-exalting churches? They are all but extinct. With the exception of a few statues bearing the image of these pre-Reformers, and the chapel where Hus and others preached, little if any remnants of such reformation or revival are visible today. Catholicism again and again decimated these lands physically and spiritually. And any hope of revival that had arisen after the fall of communism is quickly being squelched by a form of "godliness" that denies the true saving and sanctifying power of Jesus Christ.

---

[1]   See Matthew Spinka, *John Hus' Concept of the Church* (Princeton, New Jersey: Princeton University Press, 1966), 14–15.

[2]   Ibid., 15.

How did this great fall come about? How was the living Christ replaced with an imposter? More importantly, how can Christ once again be set before this people that He might be preached, believed upon, and glorified? Addressing these questions is the aim of this essay. Our purpose, therefore, is first to survey misleading depictions of Christ, both past and present, that have helped lead to the current deadness of this country. Having accomplished this, we then hope to offer the means by which Jesus Christ may once again have the proper place in the minds of His people and at the center of His church.

Misleading Depictions of Christ in the Atheist Czech Republic

The Czech Republic is not unique in its faulty portrayals of Christ. However, it is unique in how some of the faulty caricatures of Christ have arisen. A brief survey of Czech Republic's spiritual landscape helps to piece together how we got to where we are today.

Historical Erosion of the Biblical Christ

Christianity was introduced to the Czech Republic when Byzantine missionaries Cyril and Methodius arrived in the 9th century. Following this period, Catholicism rose to prominence as Bohemia became part of the Holy Roman Empire, with Prague eventually becoming its capital.[3] Near the end of the 14th century, the Great Schism initiated the start of the Bohemian Reformation. This created many problems at the University of Prague, as the Czechs and Germans took different sides. The Czechs sided with Gregory V, who later sent a papal bull to stop the preaching at Bethlehem Chapel and to burn Wycliffe's writings. The fiery preacher Jan Hus ignored the bull and continued preaching. Hus's passionate, truth-centered preaching would not be stopped by a papal bull. Later in 1412, Hus was forced to leave Prague as his preaching against the corruptions of the church, indulgences, and the pope left Prague under an interdict[4] so long as he was there.

---

[3] Howard Kaminsky, *A History of the Hussite Revolution*. (Eugene, Oregon: Wipf & Stock, 1967), 7.

[4] A censure or prohibition to keep the faithful from participation in holy ceremonies involving worship.

The Emperor Sigismund promised Hus safe passage to come to Constance, Germany in 1414, to defend his views and settle the controversies. However, Hus was never given a chance. He was immediately arrested and charged as a heretic. In a letter to the University of Prague a few days before his death, he wrote, "The Council desired me to declare the falsity of all of my books and each article taken from them. I refused to do so, unless they should be proved false by Scripture."[5] One week later, as he was tied to the stake at which he was burned, he declared, "I have never thought nor preached save with the one intention of winning men, if possible, from their sins. In the truth of the gospel I have written, taught, and preached today I will gladly die."[6]

The death of Jan Hus brought about the Hussite movement, which arose in opposition to the burning of Hus at the stake. The movement eventually led to separation from the Roman Catholic Church. Over the next 200 years, much of Bohemia forsook Catholicism and embraced the teachings of the Czech Reformers, but the Protestant Revolt ended on November 8, 1620, at the battle of White Mountain.[7] This decisive battle became a great turning point in Czech history.

Following the Protestants' defeat by the Imperial army at White Mountain, a manifesto was issued by the emperor, ordering the exile of all Calvinistic ministers and those of the Moravian Brethren.[8] On June 21, 1621, twenty-seven Protestants were executed outside the town hall to strike terror in the hearts of the people. In 1622, Ferdinand, King of Bohemia and Holy Roman Emperor, made it his aim to convert the Bohemian people back to the "true faith" of Catholicism. Two years later in 1624, a decree was passed, ordering all non-Catholic priests to leave the country, with all churches to be immediately placed under the supervision of Catholic priests and bishops.[9]

---

[5]   Herbert B. Workman, *Letters of Jan Hus* (London: Hodder and Stoughton, 1904), 268.

[6]   Ibid., 279.

[7]   "The whole action lasted an hour and ended in the total defeat of the Bohemians ... it has been estimated that about 10,000 men of the Bohemian army, and probably 4,000 of the Imperial, were left upon the field of battle." Ibid., 411.

[8]   Frances Gregor, *The Story of Bohemia* (Cincinnati, Ohio: Cranston & Curtis, 1895), 414.

[9]   Ibid., 418.

The process of re-Catholization continued with priests refusing to marry couples, beating people, and imprisoning them. In Prague, a greater part of the population refused to be converted, and four of the most prominent citizens were sent into exile as an example of what could happen to the rest. The process continued as the Czechs refused to convert to Catholicism. People were harassed, driven from their homes, hanged, beheaded, broken on the wheel,[10] and mutilated. Over thirty-six thousand families fled as refugees to other countries.[11]

After 160 years of oppressive Catholic rule, Emperor Josef II issued the Edict of Toleration, allowing non-Catholics the freedom of religious belief and assembly.[12] Czech Protestants took advantage of the opportunity and began public worship. However, Jozef left one caveat, namely, that Protestants could only choose from either the Augsburg or the Helvetic Confession as their statement of faith.[13] Nevertheless, Czechs were zealous for freedom after years of oppression.[14]

Looking back, the role of the Roman Catholic Church in the process of establishing the Czech nation is evaluated as rather negative.[15] In the 19th century, Czechs viewed their national greatness not as being connected with Catholicism, but rather with their Hussite predecessors.[16] It was during this time that Enlightenment ideology made its way into Czech society. In 1867, a new liberal constitution was established for the Cisleithan Regions that cover most of modern-day Czech Republic. This new constitution made way for a secularized state. In 1918, religious pluralism and freedom of confession

---

[10] A form of torture where the victims' bones were broken with a cart wheel.

[11] Ibid., 418–19.

[12] Jiří Otter, *Through Prague in the Footsteps of the Czech Reformation* (Prague: Kalich, 2006), 119, 143.

[13] Ibid., 144.

[14] "The first toleration congregations in Prague did not have an easy beginning. Austrian authorities were alarmed by the unexpected number of registered Protestants whose count soon rose to 80,000. Therefore, they tried, in every way possible, to obstruct the establishment of new congregations" (Ibid.).

[15] Havlíček, Jakub, and Dušan Lužný, "Religion and Politics in the Czech Republic: The Roman Catholic Church and the State," *International Journal of Social Science Studies* 1, no. 2 (October 2013), 199.

[16] Nešpor, Zdeněk R. "Religious Processes in Contemporary Czech Society," *Sociologický časopis/Czech Sociological Review* 40, no. 3 (2004), 283.

was established, followed by the introduction of Marxist and atheistic ideology. The Czech nation over the last two hundred years made a gradual transition to a secular state and was further pushed along in its anti-religious tendencies by communist rule in the last century. Today the Czech Republic is known as one of the most atheistic countries in the world. Despite census statistics that identify people as not having religious belief, common "street" consensus is that Czechs are more agnostic and opposed to organized religion than actually atheistic in their belief.[17] Having been force-fed religious beliefs like those imposed on them for centuries by the Roman Catholic Church, along with the persecution and martyrdom of Protestants, has created an anti-authoritarian spirit and passion for independent thought. Czechs are distrustful of the church. As a result, if someone were looking for any semblance of belief in Christ, the church is not the place where one would turn for an authoritative answer.

Modern Caricatures of Christ in Society

Communism successfully demonized religion by heralding the abuses of the past. The government used every possible means to advance Marxism, evolutionary theory, and atheism; as well as to caricature Christianity negatively. Examples can be seen in films produced during this time such as the 1956 communist era classic film, *Dobrý voják Švejk* (*Good Soldier Shveyk*). The film was a satire intended to point out the absurdities of the falling Austria-Hungarian empire at the beginning of WWI when Ferdinand d'Este was murdered in Sarajevo. A famous scene in the film portrays a priest who is drunk, smoking, and yelling at a group of soldiers from his pulpit.

A more recent film, *Anděl Páně* (2005), approved by the Roman Catholic Church, depicts Jesus as a rowdy little boy, and angels behaving as drunk and stupid. It was so popular that a sequel premiered December 2016. The education system was also effective in falsely defining the church and indoctrinating students with

---

[17]   John L. Allen Jr., "Czechs Object to Authority, Not Religion, Sociologist Says," *National Catholic Reporter*, September 26, 2009, https://www.ncronline.org/blogs/ncr-today/czechs-object-authority-not-religion-sociologist-says. Allen's statements align with what this author has experienced in speaking with many professing atheists. Several articles can be referenced giving testimony to the fact that for many Czechs, there is "something out there" — light, energy, or some higher power, but not the God of the Bible.

communist, atheist ideology. The remnants of its propagandizing are still prevalent. Teachers who grew up under such teaching continue to promulgate such a worldview as they endeavor to persuade students to reject theistic beliefs.[18] Jesus is often regarded as a mythical figure or a fairy tale.

Movies like *The Da Vinci Code* (2006), ancient documents like the *Gospel of Thomas,* and other works critical of the biblical view of Christ, have effectively made their way into the cultural mainstream. Such distortions further separate the average Czech from any understanding of the biblical Jesus. The thought of having a personal relationship with Christ is viewed as cultic and foreign.

The name "Jesus" is mainly known as a curse word. His name is used together with Mary's as a form of taking God's name in vain. Even small children can be heard saying "Ježíš–Marie" (Jesus–Mary) as a curse. Further conflating the holy and the profane, Czechs teach their children that "Ježíšek" (the baby Jesus) will bring them their gifts at Christmas time. One shopping mall has a children's train during the Christmas season called the "Ježíškův express" (The Little Jesus Express).

Atheists have no problem singing Christian Christmas carols of Christ, all the while denying Him. Concerning Easter, Christ is completely eliminated from all thought except in Christian circles. For many, it is not Sunday but rather Monday that is celebrated, because the Monday following Easter is a state holiday. On this day, men can be seen chasing after and whipping girls, and some pour water on the boys. It is rooted in paganism. Jesus or the resurrection is never thought of, nor is He considered on any other day of the year in the secularized society.

Current Debasement of Christ in His Church

A final contributing factor to the Christological confusion in the Czech Republic, sadly, is the professing church. The bane of Hudson Taylor's soul as a missionary was the mass import of opium to China and the horrible cruelty that arose from its usage. In the Czech Republic, we experience a similar sorrow in witnessing the

---

[18] A mother in the church in which the author serves recently testified of the assistant principal of the school encouraging children to reject theistic views of God, prayer, and religion as a whole. Such attempts at instilling atheistic belief in children are not uncommon.

constant influx, translation, pastoral recommendation, and congregational consumption of books such as *Your Best Life Now* (Joel Osteen), *The Shack* (William Young), and *Jesus Calling* (Sarah Young). Unfortunately, the promulgation and eager acceptance of the false Christology promoted in such books reflects the direction that the leaders of the Czech denominations themselves are going. One of the largest Czech evangelical denominations, the "Církev Bratrska" ("Church of the Brethren"), has been a frontrunner in leading the Bride of Christ away from her Husband to an adulterous deceiver (2 Cor 11:2–3). In 2009, the denominational president at that time, Pavel Černý, also presided as president of the Ecumenical Council of Churches in the Czech Republic.[19] During Pope Benedict XVI's visit to Prague that year, Černy, standing before the enthroned pontiff, addressed him as "Your Holiness—Dear Brother in Christ."[20] His greeting was followed by these words, "For all of us it is a great privilege and joy to meet you on this occasion of your visit to the Czech Republic. As representatives of the churches of the Ecumenical fellowship of the Czech Republic, we very much appreciate this common meeting, welcoming you also on behalf of the believers of our churches."[21] The entire speech is worth reading, and weeping over, as one considers the damage such so-called "unity" is doing. Consider this paragraph from his address:

> In regards to our ecumenical cooperation, we still have areas where we can grow and mature. We recognize the validity of triune baptism executed in other Christian churches, but we miss celebrating Eucharist together. We are all aware of the obstacles, but in

---

[19] As of November 2016, the list of member churches involved included: the Apostolic Church, Unity of the Brethren Baptists, the Brethren Church, the Czechoslovak Hussite Church, the Evangelical Church of Czech Brethren, the Evangelical Church of Augsburg Confession, the United Methodist Church, the Moravian Church, the Orthodox Church in the Czech Lands, the Silesian Evangelical Church of the Augsburg Confession, the Old Catholic Church, the Roman Catholic Church, the Church of Seventh-Day Adventists, the Salvation Army, and the Federation of Jewish Communities in the Czech Republic. http://www.ekumenickarada.cz/in/678/member_churches#.V-TytCN940o

[20] A photo of the visit can be found here: http://www.ekumenickarada.cz/wpimages/foto/Pavel_Cerny_a_Benedikt_XVI_velky.jpg.

[21] The entirety of the brief address can be downloaded from http://www.ekumenickarada.cz/in/1492/promluva_pavla_cerneho_k_papezi_benediktu_xvi#.v-OhJyN940p

spite of that, we long to join together around the
Lord's Table sharing the mystery of His sacrifice.[22]

Any evangelical who knows what the Vatican teaches regarding
the Eucharist and its stance on justification by faith alone should
faint at the thought of evangelicals openly joining Catholics in re-cru-
cifying Jesus Christ.[23] Yet this is exactly what is taking place all
over the country. Ecumenical gatherings and worship services are
too numerous to mention. In the name of unity, important truths are
laid aside, such as justification by faith alone, a regenerated church,
baptism of believers, the sovereignty of God, and the atoning death
of Christ.

Entire evangelical denominations are openly professing unity with
unbiblical denominations and traditions by collaborating on a least
common denominator of Scripture, dismissing real and important disagreements. They are unified by what they overlook. They are united
in intentional obtuseness. Having rubbed off all the sharp doctrinal
edges of Scripture, they are left with nothing more than a two-edged
butter knife unable to pierce paper, let alone soul and spirit.[24]

So how do we proclaim Christ in a culture nearly devoid of any
biblical conception of the true Christ and among churches drenched
in unbiblical Christology?

Proclaiming the Biblical Christ in an Atheistic and Ecumenical Culture

A Presuppositional Approach

As its name suggests, presuppositional apologetics begins with
presuppositions from which the Christian defends his beliefs.[25]

Defensively, the presuppositional approach shows that the
Christian worldview alone has the truthful, logical, and defensible

---

[22] Ibid., 2, emphasis added.

[23] See the *Catechism of the Catholic Church*, esp. §1367: http://www.vatican.va/archive/ccc_css/archive/catechism/p2s2c1a3.htm.

[24] See Heb 4:12 and Jer 23:29 for a definition of what Scripture really is.

[25] Greg Bahnsen, *Always Ready,* (Nacogdoches, Texas: Covenant Media Press, 1996), 19

worldview. This is because the Christian worldview is based upon two foundations:

1. Clear and undeniable general revelation beheld by all men (Psa 19:1–6; Rom 1:18–20).

2. Sovereignly given divine revelation revealing the truth of who God is (2 Tim 3:16), the reason for war between God and man (Rom 1:18–32), and the actions God alone has taken to reconcile His enemies to Himself (Col 1:19–22).[26]

Offensively, presuppositional apologetics' *modus operandi* is to show the unbeliever that his rejection of God is both illogical and immoral. He does this by showing the unbeliever's reasoning to be fallacious. Jay Wetger explains:

> We must remember that the unbeliever has not chosen these strongholds of error as a result of doing careful research. The very opposite is the case. The unbeliever loves his imagined independence from God; he sets aside rationality and welcomes irrationality. In order to evade his accountability to God he chooses to erect arguments against the knowledge of God. [27]

Thus, presuppositional apologetics attacks not only *what* the unbeliever says; it penetrates to the heart of *why* he says what he says. His attacks upon God, Christ, the Scriptures, and the Gospel are not established on neutral ground. The unbeliever's presuppositions are what they are precisely because he is at enmity with God (Col 1:21; Eph 2:1–3).

This approach leads the conversation directly to the question of how the unbeliever can make any claim whatsoever regarding Christ. On what basis does he know anything at all about Christ?

---

[26]   In reality, every single person is a presuppositional apologist. That is, he has preconceived thoughts upon which he builds his case. In the end, though, only those arguments built upon God's divine revelation through His word can stand, defend, and attack.

[27]   Gary Gilley with Jay Wetger, *This Little Church Had None* (Darlington, UK: Evangelical Press, 2009), 176.

The Apostle John had no degree, no titles by his name, no PhD, no DD, and no position at the greatest universities. But in those opening words of his first epistle, John tells us why he is qualified to speak about Christ and upon what ground and facts he makes his claims.

> What was from the beginning, what we have heard, what we have seen with our eyes, what we have looked at and touched with our hands, concerning the Word of Life—and the life was manifested, and we have seen and testify and proclaim to you the eternal life, which was with the Father and was manifested to us—what we have seen and heard we proclaim to you also, so that you too may have fellowship with us; and indeed our fellowship is with the Father, and with His Son Jesus Christ. (1 John 1:1–3).

John says, "I was with Him. I was with Jesus. I saw Him with my own eyes. I was with him day and night for three years. We fished together, ate together, and slept under the stars together." To the Czech atheist he inquires, "Did you see Jesus get down on His hands and knees and wash my feet? Did he wash yours? Were you there when all the disciples ran away as Jesus was being arrested? Did you watch them lay him down on the cross and hammer in the nails—did you feel as I did the hellish weight of guilt knowing that I abandoned my best friend in order to save my own life? When Jesus was dying on the cross, he talked to me, he told me to take care of his mother. And then when he rose again—he took my hands, and he put them into his wounds. I felt the holes the nails had made—deep, dark wounds."

Since the writing of John's letter, thousands of new views about the gospel have arisen. Hundreds of other ideas have emerged: that the Bible is a book of myths, that Jesus married and had children, that Judas was actually the friend of Jesus, that the risen Christ was simply a ghost-like apparition, and so on. Since the time of the writings of the apostles to this very day, thousands have undertaken the attempt to come up with their own explanation and teachings, and today hundreds of thousands of Czechs have imbibed them.

But John asks one simple question that shuts the mouth of the unbeliever: Were you there? Can you say any one thing about Christ or against Christ that you did not get from me and the other apostles? Don't believe in the resurrection—how do you even know about it? Don't believe Christ was God—how would you even know *about* such a claim? Don't believe Jesus was sinless, faced the wrath of God, and was the propitiation for the sin of all those who would believe in Him? How would you even know to refute such claims if such doctrines were not contained in the Scriptures? All the atheist's arguments are built on the very foundation he seeks to destroy. He cuts off the branch he sits upon. He has no argument. For apart from Scripture he has no knowledge of what he argues against! And how can you refute such things, when again John asks, "Were you there?" But more than apologetics is needed. There must be a faithful, bold, and clear preaching of Christ.

A Confrontational Approach

The Apostle Paul was and remains the greatest missionary-evangelist. His life and preaching demand to be imitated and provide the framework for preaching amidst any people with faulty views of Christ (1 Cor 11:1; 2 Tim 2:2; 4:2). When preaching to Jews in the synagogue in Thessalonica he presented Jesus as the true Messiah by saying, "This Jesus whom I am proclaiming to you is the Christ" (Acts 17:3). When speaking to the philosophers in Athens, he preached Jesus and the resurrection of the dead, as well as Jesus as the coming judge (Acts 17:18, 31). Ethnicity and religious background were irrelevant to Paul's thrust: "We preach Christ crucified, to Jews a stumbling block and to Gentiles foolishness" (1 Cor 1:23). When writing to the Galatians, Paul unveils their foolishness and lack of discernment for swallowing the bait by accepting a false depiction of the work of Jesus Christ (Gal 3:1).

Paul had no interest in hiding the motives of his mission. To the Ephesians, he pulled back the curtain to allow them to see the purpose driving his ministry, "to preach to the Gentiles the unfathomable riches of Christ" (Eph 3:8). And in his second letter to the Corinthians, he boldly proclaims, "We do not preach ourselves but Christ Jesus as Lord" (2 Cor 4:5). The sum of his ministry can be described as a proclamation of Christ (Col 1:28). Every true and lasting result was dependent upon this one message.

Conclusion

The Czech Republic needs a large dose of gospel preaching. If Christ is not central in the work of missions, the result is merely humanitarian aid, whether through entrepreneurial enterprise, medical advancement, educational opportunities, or attempts to bring social justice. Christian missions is greater than that. The heart of missions is the person and work of Jesus Christ, the Lord of Glory.

Missionaries serving in the Czech Republic find themselves in a unique set of circumstances as they endeavor to proclaim Christ. The atheistic society, though rooted in Christian tradition, presents various caricatures of Christ that have infiltrated the Christian community. A robust proclamation of Christ is needed to correct the faulty depictions of Christ that prevail, to present a clear understanding of the only way to God, and to see Christ restored to His preeminent position among the churches (Rev 1:12–13). This is the ultimate goal of the missionary.

Will Christ and His gospel heal broken families? Can reclaiming a biblical Christology lead to healthy churches? Can the gospel heal an entire country destroyed by atheism? Yes. But for the missionary, the ultimate goal of preaching Christ in all of His biblically revealed glory must not be to strengthen marriages, increase giving, or send home new reports of fresh baptisms. His ambition must be to see husbands and wives kneeling at the feet of Jesus Christ, and to see fathers and sons bowing in humble adoration to the Lamb who was sacrificed in their stead (Rev 5:11–14). The missionary's goal is that sinners who are willing to exalt anything and everything other than Jesus, (Acts 17:23; Rom 1:23), come to bow in holy reverence to Christ. Our salvation is for His exaltation (John 12:32). It is the desire to see this happen that motivates and sustains the missionary evangelist.

For every believer who has gone out into the harvest, it is Christ and Christ alone who will sustain us in our calling. God has called us to die to ourselves in this ministry. We will never be the heroes, the superstars, the honored guests, or even the keynote speakers. We're lucky even to have an audience to preach to. We are most likely laying a foundation upon which other men will build and whose earthly glory will be greater than ours. In truth, even while we're still alive on this earth, we'll be long forgotten. When we finally retire and move back home, there will be little glory. Few will seek the wisdom we've gained from our experiences. Few will think anything of us, since we spent the majority of our youth laboring in obscurity and building little capital among the churches of our homeland. No one will write biographies about us, name seminaries after us, or give out scholarships in our names. Our tombstones will say "Ichabod."[28]

But the crown of righteousness is stored up in the future for Christ's servants because it is the glory of Christ that is their desire. There will be no regrets on the last day; and even if there could be, the regrets wouldn't be over how few people accepted us, but about how little we labored for our Lord and Savior Jesus Christ. May His cross motivate us, His glory captivate us, and His mercy sustain us.

---

[28] See 1 Sam 4:21; "Ichabod" means "no glory" in Hebrew.

THE EMPIRE STRIKES BACK: THE CATHOLIC COUNTER-REFORMATION IN SPAIN AND THE WORLD

Ruben Videira-Soengas

Berea Seminary, Spain

[Editor's Note: The Protestant Reformation that was sparked 500 years ago has shaped the course of this world, but the Roman Catholic Church did not sit idly by. A Counter-Reformation developed to combat Protestantism and promote the doctrine and practices of the Roman Catholic Church. The undisputed leader of this movement was Spain, whose efforts to counter the Reformation left its own imprint on the world. This essay highlights the development of the Spanish Counter-Reformation and its global impact. It offers much more than mere history; it offers insight that is vital to understanding the spiritual state of the Spanish-speaking world today.]

Introduction

To state that the Roman Catholic Church (RCC) holds a wrong view of Christ is not only an obvious statement from a Protestant perspective, but also a careless generalization with which a Catholic would wholeheartedly disagree. In fact, the RCC Decree Touching the Symbol of Faith, penned during the Council of Trent to shield the Roman Church against the "heresies" of the Reformation, falls within the realm of Evangelical orthodoxy. It states:

I believe in … Jesus Christ, the only-begotten Son of God, and born of the Father before all ages; God of God, light of light, true God of true God; begotten, not made, consubstantial with the Father, by whom all things were made; who for us men, and for our salvation, came down from the heavens, and was incarnate by the Holy Ghost of the Virgin Mary, and was made man; crucified also for us under Pontius Pilate, he suffered and was buried; and he rose again on the third day, according to the Scriptures; and he ascended into heaven, sitteth at the right hand of the Father; and again he will come with glory to judge the living and the dead; of whose kingdom there shall be no end. [1]

This is almost a word-by-word reduplication of the Nicene Creed, written to repudiate Arian heresy[2] that had crept into the Christian Church during the early 4th century. On paper, it would seem that both Catholicism and Protestantism affirm the same Christology. Such a conclusion, however, is misleading, for other dogmas ratified at the Council of Trent corrupted the Catholic orthodox view of Christ's nature and work.[3] Consequently, the Counter-Reformation posed a real and direct threat to the testimony of Scripture regarding Jesus

---

[1]   Council of Trent, Session 3, February 4, 1546. (*The Creeds of Christendom, with a History and Critical Notes,* Philip Schaff, ed., [New York: Harper & Brothers, 1890], 2: 78–79.)

[2]   "This heresy is named after Arius of Alexandria, a fourth-century presbyter in the church at Alexandria. He is best known for his denial of the deity of Christ. His teaching was rejected at the Council of Nicea (325). Arius taught that God created a rational spirit creature called the 'Son-Logos.' At the incarnation the created Son-Logos assumed bodily form. Thus, Arius denied not only Christ's deity (the subject of the Nicene controversy) but also Christ's humanity." (William Greenough Thayer Shedd, *Dogmatic Theology,* Alan W. Gomes, ed., 3rd ed., [Phillipsburg, New Jersey: P & R Pub., 2003], 952. For a more detailed discussion on the Arian heresy, see pages 241–53, 257–67.)

[3]   The RCC differentiates between ecumenical and private councils. The latter do not require the presence of all the Catholic bishops; the former do. It is said that ecumenical councils are infallible. For this reason, since the Council of Trent was ecumenical, it is, according to the RCC, infallible in nature. Hence, every dogma established and reaffirmed during the council becomes absolute truth for the church (see Miguel Valbuena, *La Iglesia Católica ante La Biblia y La Historia,* [Chicago, Illinois: Editorial Moody, n.d.], 51–53). Therefore, even though the Christology of the Decree Touching the Symbol of Faith is orthodox, the Eucharist affirmed during the Council altered Christ's nature and work, as will be shown in this essay.

Christ, which unfortunately, did not stay within the European borders but also reached the American continent. Hence, the present essay addresses the role that Spain played to spread this threat worldwide, and how it silenced the principle that set the world on fire, *sola scriptura*, revealing the most profound need for a Reformation in this country and the countries formerly under its rule.[4]

All That Glitters Is Not Gold

During the 14th and 15th centuries, the RCC was embroiled in a profound crisis that paved the way for the Reformation.[5] The papacy lost its credibility in 1305 when, in order to extend its political influence, it adopted an unprecedented course by moving the Holy See

---

[4] This does not mean that there were no attempts to reform Spain. The fire of the Reformation reached the country, but the Catholic Counter-Reformation extinguished it. There are several Spaniards who labored toward a Reformation in Spain: Juan De Valdes, a true linguist and expert in the biblical languages who fled the country, systematized the Lutheran catechism. Jaime and Francisco de Enzinas were two brothers who published a Protestant catechism. Jaime died a martyr in Rome in 1564. Francisco was the first Spaniard to translate the New Testament from Greek into Spanish. He himself gave a copy of this translation to the Emperor Charles V. Juan Perez de Pineda held a doctorate in theology. He fled the country as well and sought refuge in Geneva. During his time in the Reformers' city, he translated the works of Juan de Valdes on the Pauline epistles into Spanish. He also translated portions of the Old Testament into Castilian, but it is not clear whether he did it from the Hebrew language. Casiodoro de Reina also fled Spain, but during his "exile," he translated the entire Bible into Spanish. After twelve years of hard work, 2,600 copies were finally published in 1567. Cipriano de Valera revised the de Reina translation, resulting in the most famous Bible in the Spanish-speaking world to this day: La Biblia Reina-Valera. He also translated the Institutes of the Christian Religion by John Calvin into Spanish (see Manuel Gutierrez Marin, *Historia de La Reforma en España. Introducción y Selección Antológica*, [Barcelona: Producciones Editoriales del Nordeste, 1973], 37–47). Even though the influence of these men spread over the entire Peninsula, the Reformation that they tried to bring to Spain never took roots deeply enough to transform the church, due to the twofold fact that they had to flee Spain and that some of their works were published in Latin, a language not accessible to the lay Spaniard. For a more detailed explanation on the Spanish Reformation, see Cesar Vidal, *Mitos y Falacias de la Historia de España* (Madrid: Ediciones B, 2010), 27–47; and Thomas M. Lindsay, *Historia de la Reforma: La Reforma en Suiza, Francia, los Países Bajos, Escocia e Inglaterra. Los Movimientos Anabapatista y Sociniano. La Contrarreforma*, trans. Lurá Villanueva, (Buenos Aires, Argentina: Editorial La Aurora, 1959), 383-91.

[5] To speak of the Reformation within the RCC requires the differentiation between the Counter-Reformation and the Catholic Reformation. The latter refers to the transformation that takes place within the RCC, as a result of self-examination. The former is also a transformation but in opposition to the Protestant Reformation's claims.

from Rome to Avignon in France.[6] The unspiritual resolve fueling the RCC set the political tension already present between England and France on fire, having a major ripple effect on the Western world's perspective of the RCC.[7] The European people realized that the papacy sought to become another player in the political arena, hence the saying: "The pope became French and Jesus, English."[8] The Catholic ambition shattered its organizational unity, resulting in the Western Schism, which lasted until 1417. During these years, there were often two different popes and—at one point—even four at once, each of them claiming to be the only legitimate one and anathematizing the rest.[9] By the end of the 15th century, it was clear, even to the Catholic clergy, that the RCC was in a deplorable moral state, rightly described by Sara T. Nalle:

The sanctity of the diocese's churches and shrines (ermitas) was commonly violated; ermitas were the apparent scene of so many sins… . With the excuse of attending all-night vigils on certain holy days, many people would spend the night at ermitas, where the vigils disintegrated into feasting, dancing, singing of secular songs, adultery, and fornication. Corrupt priests would encourage these all-night vigils by agreeing to hold illegal predawn masses, for which they would be paid. The ermitas, although built with pious intentions, rarely were properly endowed, with the result that many soon collapsed in disrepair. Then the decrepit shrines, while still consecrated ground, became the scene for robbery, murder, and adultery. Similar sacrileges took place in parish churches. [10]

The ungodliness of the RCC was even more notorious during the following century. In 1510, when the German monk Martin Luther

---

[6] This period in Roman Catholic history is known as the Babylonian Captivity, and even though the papacy eventually returned to Rome, the integrity and trustworthiness of the RCC was shattered (see Cesar Vidal, *Pontífices: De las Persecuciones al Papa Francisco* [Barcelona: Ediciones Península, 2014], 132).

[7] Cesar Vidal, *La Historia Secreta de la Iglesia Católica en España* (Barcelona: Ediciones B, 2014), 165.

[8] Author's own translation. See Joseph Calmette, *L'Élaboration du Monde Moderne*, (Paris: Presses Universitaires de France, 1942), 41.

[9] For a chronological list of popes and antipopes, see Norman L. Geisler, and Joshua M. Betancourt, *Is Rome The True Church? A Consideration of the Roman Catholic Claim* (Wheaton, Illinois: Crossway Books, 2008), 204.

[10] Sarah T. Nalle, *God in La Mancha. Religious Reform and the People of Cuenca 1500–1650* (Baltimore, Maryland: The Johns Hopkins University Press, 1992), 28–29.

visited Rome, he "found anything but a holy city,"[11] ruled by a worldly, ambitious, warlike pope, Julius II, who sold indulgences to support the building of Saint Peter's Basilica.[12] This practice continued into 1517, the year Luther nailed the Ninety-five Theses to the church door in Wittenberg. By then, Leo X, who was famous for his ostentatious lifestyle, had become the pope. He was determined to finish the Basilica started by Julius II. This project, however, was too expensive, so Leo X also resorted to selling indulgences. However, the money collected from the populace did not always find its way to Rome. Many clerics, who desired a luxurious life as well, kept the proceeds for their own benefit, reducing the collected amount for Rome and leaving the papacy with "no other choice" than to sell more indulgences.[13]

The religious landscape revealed that if the RCC was ever going to escape this deadly whirlwind, it had to start with the papacy. Such transformation, however, was condemned to fail for three reasons. First, the Catholic teaching was diametrically opposed to the doctrine of the New Testament.[14] Second, the abuse of authority, the accrual of wealth, poor doctrinal knowledge, and nepotism shaped the mindset of the Catholic clergy.[15] Third, the popes had eschewed all semblance of piety and rather immersed themselves in political contests and schemes of ambition.[16]

---

[11] Sheldon, *History of the Christian Church*, vol. 3, 52.

[12] Vidal, *La Historia Secreta de la Iglesia Católica en España*, 215.

[13] Moa, *Nueva Historia de España*, 398.

[14] For a more detailed discussion on the Catholic "gospel," see: Geisler, and Betancourt, *Is Rome The True Church?* 165–85; James G. McCarthy, *The Gospel According to Rome: Comparing the Tradition and the Word of God* (Eugene, Oregon: Harvest House Publishers, 1995), 21–121; William Webster, *La Salvación, La Biblia y el Catolicismo Romano* (Edimburgo: El Estandarte de la Verdad, 2015), 82–92; *Saving Faith. How Does Rome Define It?* (Battle Ground, Washington: Christian Resources, 1997); and *The Church of Rome at The Bar of History*, (Carlisle, Pennsylvania: The Banner of Truth Trust, 2003), 133–52.

[15] Erika Tánacs, "El Concilio de Trento y Las Iglesias de La América Española," 123.

[16] This was the reason why Luther wrote a volume against the papacy, namely, "to testify before the entire world, what he thought about the Pope and his evil empire (author's own translation)." Ulrich Köpf, Helmar Junghans, and Karl Stackmann, *D. Martin Luthers Werke. Weimarer Ausgabe (Sonderedition): Abteilung 4, Teil 5: Frühe Vorlesungen Und Späte Schriften, Band 54 (Luthers Werk–Sonderedition/gesamtwerk), special ed.*, (Weimer: Verlag Hermann Böhlaus Nachfolger, 2007), 353.

Between Two Worlds

In Spain, the situation was not any better. The Spanish clergy, more than religious servants, were men of war. They owned fortresses and small armies and spent most of their time fighting medieval lords.[17] They were powerful and wealthy men. Only the treasure of Spain's king surpassed the wealth of Toledo's bishop, who was not interested in the religious affairs of the Spaniards.[18]

During the 15th century, the Catholic monarchs, Ferdinand II of Aragon and Isabella I of Castile, realized that the RCC needed a radical transformation.[19] As Catholic devotees, their motivation was religious, but as monarchs it was political. They understood that the crown's well-being rested on the shoulders of the RCC.[20] Once again, the interests of Catholicism and the Spanish rulers intersected at the same crossroads—political ambition—that has been the trademark of the country's history.

From the very beginning, religion was the nation's unifying element. In 572, the Visigoth king Liuvigild struggled to bring political harmony to the Iberian Peninsula.[21] It was not until his son Reccared I converted to Catholicism in 587[22] that national unity was achieved. His conversion to Catholicism is similar to the Roman emperor Constantine's rejection of Arianism and conversion to Christianity in the 4th century—both were intelligent strategies seeking to unify their respective domains. Two years later, in 589, the Third Council

---

[17] Werner Thomas, *La Represión del Protestantismo en España 1517-1648,* (Leuven: Leuven University Press, 2001), 10.

[18] This was the reason why no Catholic council was held in Toledo from 1379 to 1473, which was a strange situation, since Toledo was the religious center for the Peninsula. This archdiocese included the cities of Toledo, Madrid, Ciudad Real, Guadalajara, Albacete, Badajoz, Cáceres, Cazorla, Jaén, Palencia, Osma, Sigüenza, Segovia, Cuenca and Córdoba (see José Sánchez Herrero, *Concilios Provinciales y Sínodos Toledanos de Los Siglos XIV y XV. La Religiosidad del Clero y Pueblo,* [La Laguna: Universidad de la Laguna, 1976], 58).

[19] Thomas, *La Represión del Protestantismo en España 1517-1648,* 11.

[20] See Moa, *Nueva Historia de España,* 327–30;

[21] Áurea Matilde Fernández Muñiz, *Breve Historia de España,* (La Habana: Editorial de Ciencias Sociales, 2005), 16–17.

[22] Marcelo González Martín, "El III Concilio de Toledo. Identidad Católica de Los Pueblos de España y Raíces Cristianas de Europa," in *Anales de la Real Academia de Ciencias Morales y Políticas* 66 (1989): 70.

of Toledo declared Catholicism the official religion of the Visigoth Empire, securing Spain's political unity.[23] This, according to the historian García Villoslada, signals the official birth of Spain as a nation. Until then the Peninsula was "a mix of races and religions."[24] Only Catholicism was able to unite the country, and from that moment on, Spain became "fully aware of its unity, its sovereignty and independence."[25]

Since Catholicism played a crucial role in the formation of Spain as a nation, a non-Catholic Spain was inconceivable. Hence, when the Catholic monarchs saw the religious debacle of the RCC centuries later, they feared for the political safety of the country.[26] In 1478, the monarchs summoned a national council in Seville, which sought to renew the lost purity of the RCC.[27] During this council, Ferdinand and Isabella objected to the pope's exclusive right to appoint bishops and cardinals in the Church,[28] for if the pope were corrupt, his chosen clerics would be, as well. After six years of tug-of-war between the Spanish crown and the papacy, the pope granted the crown the *Patronato Real of Granada* in 1486.[29] This *Patronato* included two papal bulls, one permitting the crown to ordain their own clergy, and the other endowing the monarchs with the tithes given to the RCC.[30]

---

[23] González Martín, "El III Concilio de Toledo," 72.

[24] R. García Villoslada, *Introducción a La Historia de La Iglesia en España,* quoted in Peter Linehan, *History and the Historians of Medieval Spain* (Oxford, England: Clarendon Press, 1993), 5.

[25] Ibid.

[26] Also the idea that Catholic hegemony was the sole cause of political unity, logically led the conquistadors to enforce Catholicism upon the natives in the Americas. In their mind, the new transcontinental Spanish Empire would only be unified under the same religious umbrella.

[27] Tarsicio de Azcona, *La Elección y Reforma del Episcopado Español en Tiempo de los Reyes Católicos,* (Madrid: Consejo Superior de Investigaciones Científicas, 1960), 201–28.

[28] Felipe Pérez Valencia, "Catolicismo y Conquista del Nuevo Mundo. Función, Apogeo y Decadencia," in *Teología y Cultura* 11 no. 16 (Diciembre 2014): 21.

[29] Because the influence of Huss and Wycliffe began to shatter the political control of the RCC in Europe, the RCC made this concession out of fear of losing their stronghold in Spain (see Jesús Gaite Pastor, "La Cámara de Castilla en Los Siglos XVI y XVII. La Instrucción de Felipe II en 1588," in *IV Jornadas Científicas sobre Documentación de Castilla e Indias en El Siglo XVI,* Juan Carlos Galende Díaz, ed., [Madrid: Universidad Complutense de Madrid, 2005], 143).

[30] See Enrique Dussel, *Historia de La Iglesia en América Latina: Medio Milenio de Coloniaje y Liberación (1492-1992),* 6th edition, (Madrid: Mundo Negro, 1992), 82.

The implications of this *Patronato* were monumental. If the Catholic monarchs were allowed to appoint the leaders of the RCC in Spain, and if they could receive the tithes given to the RCC in Spain, then they controlled the RCC in Spain. For the first time in the history of the nation, the RCC was placed under the rule of the king, setting in motion the concept of church-state in the country. Immediately after this, the Catholic monarchs enacted laws that limited the power of the clergy and dealt with their moral life but to no avail.[31] So, a few years later in 1495, sheltered by the *Patronato Real of Granada,* the Catholic monarchs appointed Francisco Jiménez de Cisneros—a true Catholic—archbishop of Toledo, and, in 1507, grand inquisitor. The sole purpose of his office was to transform and protect against *new doctrines* in the RCC in Spain. In return, he embodied the spirit of the monarchs' reformation,[32] devoting his life to the religious tyranny of the Inquisition.[33] Cisneros became, according to the historian Adolfo de Castro, a worse barbarian than Attila.[34]

In the midst of this turmoil, Christopher Columbus discovered the New World on October 12, 1492, and changed the Old World forever. A year later, in 1493, the shrewd Catholic monarch Ferdinand convinced the papacy to legitimatize the possession and colonization of the Americas.[35] This was a political stratagem that indirectly cleared the way for Catholicism to enter the new continent. The RCC believed it had a God-given right to rule all known lands,[36] and yet it needed

---

31 Herrero, *Concilios Provinciales y Sínodos Toledanos de Los Siglos XIV y XV,* 68.

32 Adolfo De Castro, *Examen Filosófico sobre Las Principales Causas de La Decadencia de España,* (Cádiz: Imprenta de D. Francisco Pantoja, 1852), 20.

33 Under Cisneros' rule, the RCC in Spain imposed its domain forcibly. People converted to Catholicism because the Grand Inquisitor made sure to threaten their life otherwise (Ibid., 32, 35).

34 Adolfo De Castro, *Historia de Los Protestantes Españoles y de Su Persecución por Felipe II,* (Cádiz: Revista Médica, 1851), 246.

35 Cesar Vidal, *El Legado del Cristianismo en la Cultura Occidental: Los Desafíos del Siglo XXI,* (Pozuelo de Alarcón: Espasa, 2000), 212.

36 The Roman Empire saw itself as the climax of universalism, conquering all lands and ruling all seas (Emilio Mitre Fernandez, "Los Límites entre Estados: La Idea de Frontera en El Medievo y El Caso de Los Reinos Hispano-Cristianos," in *El Mundo de Los Conquistadores,* Martín Ríos Saloma, ed., [Madrid: Sílex Ediciones, 2015], 109). No other civilization prior to Rome exerted such a global domain, as the Greek Polybius illustrates: "almost the whole inhabited world was conquered and brought under the dominion of the single city of Rome" (Polybius, *Histories* 1.1); "[To] speak the plain truth, [the Persian Empire] never even knew of the most warlike tribes of the West. The Roman conquest, on the other hand, was not

Spain to conquer the New World. To this end, the pope legitimized the colonization of these newly discovered territories. These Alexandrine Bulls were a political scheme. Both Spain and the RCC needed one another. Spain needed the papacy's influence to assure its domain over the Americas, and the RCC—an unarmed empire—needed an army to rule the New World.[37] This symbiotic union strengthened and extended their influence from the East to the West.

Ironically, this assumed mutual dependence did not always go both ways. Pope Julius II said that Spain was a disgusting country full of Moorish swine.[38] Paul IV also mocked the Spaniards by calling them barbarians.[39] The papacy's attitude toward the Spanish monarchy was, to say the least, startling. Spain was not only fighting to restore the purity of the RCC within its borders, but also to extend it beyond them, and yet the RCC despised Spaniards. This aversion reached its climax when Pope Clement VII attempted to undermine the election of the Spaniard Charles V as emperor of the Holy Roman Empire.[40] After a series of deaths and calamities for the Spanish royal family and a few bribes,[41] Charles V, at sixteen years of age, became Emperor in 1518 against the will of the RCC. Eventually, this ani-

---

partial. Nearly the whole inhabited world was reduced by them to obedience" (Polybius, *Histories* 1.2); "that [the Romans] entered upon those undertakings, which did in fact lead to their becoming masters of land and sea everywhere in our part of the world" (Polybius, *Histories* 1.3). The RCC embraced the universalist mindset of Rome and presented itself as the New Empire, especially during the Middle Ages, hence their claim that the right to dominate the lands conquered by the Romans was theirs (Gustave Schnürer, *La Iglesia y La Civilización Occidental en La Edad Media*, José Miguel de Azaola, trans. and ed., [Madrid: Fax, 1955], 28).

[37]   See Pérez Valencia, "Catolicismo y Conquista del Nuevo Mundo," 22.

[38]   Antonio Sánchez Jiménez, "Fanfarronería Española en 'La Contienda de García de Paredes y El Capitan Juan de Urbina:' Lope de Vega ante La Leyenda Negra," in *Europa (Historia y Mito) en La Comedia Española. XXXIII Jornadas de Teatro Clásico. Almagro, 6, 7, y 8 de Julio de 2010*, Felipe B. Pedraza Jiménez, Rafael González Cañal, and Elena E. Marcello, eds., (Cuenca: Universidad de Castilla La Mancha, 2012), 86.

[39]   Miguel Zorita Bayón, *Breve Historia del Siglo de Oro* (Madrid: Nowtilus, 2010), 182. Melchor Cano says, talking about the discrepancies between Charles V and Paul IV, that Paul IV was a stubborn Holy Father, a man of his own opinions ruled by his passions (see Melchor Cano, *Parecer del M. Fr. Melchor Cano del Orden de Predicadores, Doctor Teólogo de Las Universidades de Alcalá y Salamanca, Obispo de Canarias [Cuyo Obispado Renunció] sobre Las Diferencias entre Paulo IV Pont. Max. y El Emperador Carlos V Primero de Las Españas y de las Indias*, [Madrid: 1736], 15).

[40]   Vidal, *La Historia Secreta de La Iglesia Católica en España*, 209.

[41]   See Vidal, *La Historia Secreta de La Iglesia Católica en España*, 216–17.

mosity caused a chain reaction that ended with the Spanish army conquering and plundering Rome in 1527.[42] From this moment on, the papacy's policy toward Spain changed radically from opposing the emperor to seeing him as a strong ally.

Charles V was by birth the heir both to Spain's kingdom and the Habsburg Empire. His domain, "where the sun never set,"[43] extended beyond European borders and reached into Africa, Asia, and the Americas. It was larger even than the Holy Roman Empire,[44] and by 1529, the RCC saw a golden opportunity to extend its influence worldwide.[45] Almost three decades later, Pope Julius III turned this opportunity into his personal ambition and labored even harder than his predecessors to establish Catholicism in the Americas.[46] Furthermore, during this time some of the political consequences of the Reformation began to appear. Both Europe and the RCC split into two factions: those faithful to the papacy and against the Reformation, and those who questioned the integrity of the RCC and were in favor of, or at least sympathized with, the Reformers.[47] Eventually this division led to the Thirty Years' War, one of the deadliest European conflicts. This war of "apocalyptic proportions" reshaped the political landscape, and severely undermined Spain's hegemony in 1648.[48] But before this took place, the RCC, not being able to foresee the fall of Charles's empire, sided with him, abandoning its hatred toward Spain in hopes of eradicating the Reformation in Europe.[49] Once again, the papacy's political ambition could not be masked, and neither could that of Charles. The emperor was determined to unify

---

[42]   David J. Álvarez, *The Pope's Soldiers. A Military History of The Modern Vatican*, Modern War Studies (Lawrence, Kansas: University Press of Kansas, 2011), 266.

[43]   Jean Bérenger, *A History of The Habsburg Empire 1273–1700*, C. A. Simpson, trans., (New York: Routledge, 1994), 139.

[44]   Trigo Chacón, *La España Imperial*, 109.

[45]   Vidal, *La Historia Secreta de La Iglesia Católica en España*, 218.

[46]   Vidal, *Pontífices*, 162.

[47]   Ibid., 159. Desiderius Erasmus would be one of these sympathizers. He exerted great influence in Spain and is considered by some a spiritual leader that attempted to reform the RCC. Nonetheless, he was more of a humanist and intellectual than a Reformer (see Pierre Chaunu, *La España de Carlos V*, Biblioteca Historia de España, E. Riambau Saurí, trans., [Barcelona: RBA Coleccionables, 2005], 366-68).

[48]   Moa, *Nueva Historia de España*, 578.

[49]   Vidal, *La Historia Secreta de La Iglesia Católica en España*, 218.

Christendom because he shared the medieval dream of creating a universal monarchy[50] rooted in political and religious unity.[51] For Charles, nationalism and Catholicism were not distinct. Therefore, the logical conclusion was the globalization of Catholicism under his reign. If the Spanish Empire was to conquer new groups of people, then their religious ideology also needed to be conquered by Catholicism. Otherwise, it would be understood as a rebellious assault against the crown, which in turn would become an offense against God. Spanish monarchs, including Charles, saw themselves as "vicars of Christ."[52] At first, this meant that the king represented Christ in his administration of justice according to the divine standard.[53] But later this concept evolved to become the imposition of Catholicism on all of the lands.[54] Charles was especially intoxicated with this universal utopia.[55] He longed to exert domain over every national and spiritual affair of his always-sunny Empire. His and the RCC's ambition became the two-edged sword that pierced through the American continent, leaving a trail of physical and spiritual death.[56] The arrival of Catholicism in the New World through the Spaniards was not for the better but for the worse; it darkened the spiritual landscape and exported Spain's imperial nationalism, which became responsible for innumerable deaths.

---

[50] Bérenger, *A History of The Habsburg Empire 1273–1700*, 139.

[51] De Courcelles, "La Historiografía y La Literatura de la Conquista de América en Los Tiempos de Carlos V y Felipe II," 68.

[52] Juan Ricardo Jiménez Gómez, "La Colonización del Pueblo de Tlachco-Querétaro en La Frontera de Chichimecas, 1531-1599," in *El Mundo de Los Conquistadores*, Martín Ríos Saloma, ed., (Madrid: Sílex Ediciones, 2015), 233.

[53] E. F. Jacob, "El Pensamiento Político," in *El Legado de la Edad Media*, C. G. Crump and E. F. Jacob, eds., (Madrid: Ediciones Pegaso, 1944), 671.

[54] Vidal, *La Historia Secreta de La Iglesia Católica en España*, 218.

[55] Ibid.

[56] Sebastian Lorente speaking of the conquistadors' arrival to Peru says: "the Conquistadors like furious bulls struck at the group of women and children, ... the chivalry spread terror and death... ." [author's own translation], Sebastian Lorente, *Historia de la Conquista del Perú* (Lima: Masias, 1861), 152.

A Feeble Excuse

The colonization of the New World was an extension of the Spanish *Reconquista*.[57] Therefore, it needs to be taken into consideration in order to fully understand the Catholicization of the Americas. The *Reconquista* shaped Spain's national identity for centuries, as the cleric Francisco López de Gómara illustrates, writing to Emperor Charles V: "[After] eight hundred years of armed conflict and once the Moors were vanquished, the Spaniards began conquering the Indians so that they will always be at war with infidels and enemies of holy faith of Jesus Christ."[58] The irony is that as the conquistadors advanced their cause in the Americas, they were guilty of committing the same crimes as the Moors against whom they fought for centuries.

In one sense, the *Reconquista* began in 710,[59] when the Moors invaded the Iberian Peninsula. The Islamic conquest forced many Hispanic-Goths, among whom were Vascones, Astures, and Cantabrians, to retreat to northern Spain.[60] This resulted in a diverse community that found its common ground in the same faith—Catholicism—which eventually turned the war against the Moors into a holy war, just like the Crusades three centuries later.[61] This meant that even though the *Reconquista* in itself was a sanctioned war because the Moors illegitimately invaded Spain, its justification became religious.

It was during this time that the Moors derogatorily named the Spanish soldiers "Christians." Interestingly, this is the title that the

---

[57] This term refers to the war between Spaniards and Moors during the Middle Ages that Spain launched in order to reconquer the Iberian Peninsula (Francisco García Fitz, "La Reconquista: Un Estado de La Cuestión," *Clio y Crimen* 6 [2009]: 142).

[58] Author's own translation. Francisco López de Gómara, *Historia General de Las Indias. Prólogo de Jorge Gurría Lacroix*, (Barcelona: Red Ediciones, 2016), 32.

[59] Peter Crawford, *The War of The Three Gods. Romans, Persians and The Rise of Islam* (South Yorkshire: Pen & Sword Military, 2013), 210.

[60] Fernández Muñiz, *Breve Historia de España*, 24.

[61] The Crusaders saw Jerusalem as their possession. It was their Holy City, therefore, it needed to be taken from the Moorish barbarians (at this time in history the term barbarian switched from referring to one whose citizenship was not Roman, to somebody who was not Catholic, and eventually it was used in reference to Muslims [see Federico Mario Beltrán Torreira, "El Concepto de Barbarie en La España Visigoda," *Antiguedad y Cristianismo* 3 (1986): 53–60]), see Jean Flori, *La Guerra Santa. La Formación de La Idea de Cruzada en el Occidente Cristiano*, Rafael Gerardo Peinado Santaella, trans., (Madrid: Trotta, 2003), 402.

conquistadors pinned on themselves during the colonization centuries later.[62] It is evident that the same ideology behind the Crusades and the *Reconquista* was empowering the conquest of the New World.[63] So, logically, as Jerusalem and Spain needed to be delivered from their unlawful master, likewise, the Americas had to be rescued of their illegitimate indwellers. For the conquistadors, the colonization of the New World was an act sanctioned by God Himself.

The intruders, however, were the Spaniards. Therefore, in order to justify their invasion, the natives had to be guilty of a crime that would divest them of their lands. Hence, both Spain and the RCC accused the natives of idolatry and cannibalism.[64] Such accusations were not random. The papacy compared these crimes with those of the Canaanites. So, if God gave Canaan to Israel because of the sins of the peoples in the land, then He also gave the New World to the RCC and the conquistadors because the American natives sinned in a similar manner. The land was defiled and needed to rest and be purified by Catholicism. Thus, the Spanish conquistadors forced the natives to embrace the Catholic faith as they swore loyalty to Spain's crown. The document *Requerimiento* was read to the natives, and then they were asked to embrace its assertions. If they did not fully submit to all of its requirements, it was legitimate to kill them. This document declared that God was the Creator and the pope His sovereign. It also explained the pope's permission for the Spanish king to possess the New World. The army, therefore, as servants of the king, had the right to kill and conquer because the pope, who was God's own sovereign, had given the word.[65]

---

[62] De Courcelles, "La Historiografía y La Literatura de la Conquista de América en Los Tiempos de Carlos V y Felipe II," 66.

[63] Even the title "conquistador" demonstrates this. This term was first used during the *Reconquista* in 1238 when King James I of Aragon delivered Valencia from under Islamic rule and vanquished the Moors (Bernard Grunberg, "Hernán Cortés y la Guerra de los Conquistadores," in *El Mundo de Los Conquistadores*, Martín Ríos Saloma, ed., [Madrid: Sílex Ediciones, 2015], 557).

[64] See Alejandro Morín, "La Frontera de España es de Natura Caliente. El Derecho de Conquista en Las Partidas de Alfonso X El Sabio," in *El Mundo de Los Conquistadores*, Martín Ríos Saloma, ed., (Madrid: Sílex Ediciones, 2015), 398.

[65] Grunberg, "Hernán Cortés y la Guerra de los Conquistadores," 564; and Morales Padrón, *Teorías y Leyes de La Conquista*, 331–477). The Conquistadors often quoted the phrase "to the service of God and to the service of the King," illustrating how in their mind they could not separate loyalty to Spain from Catholicism. For a few examples, see: Bernal Díaz del

The Spanish monarchs, as vicars of Christ, believed that it was their responsibility to conquer these heathens[66] who rejected God, and the conquistadors saw themselves as the instruments of Christ's vicars. Hernán Cortés, for instance, considered it his duty to God "to eradicate the natives' idols, to bring to an end their sacrifices and human killings, and to cause to cease any other moronic evil that they usually commit."[67] This religious approach to the colonization, which was the remnant of the *Reconquista,* gave the Counter-Reformation wings with a span that reached the New World, and it restrained the influence of the Reformation in the Americas because of the intolerance[68] that Spain exported to the countries that it colonized.

The stability that the RCC achieved in the Americas by closing the doors to Protestantism is the direct result of the conquistadors, who saw it as their duty to convert American natives to Catholicism. For centuries since the *Reconquista,* the concept of the holy war had reshaped Spain's nationalism to the degree that for the Spaniard, Catholicism became the cohesive element to attain national unity. In other words, to be a Spaniard meant to be Catholic.[69] This implies that "the conversion of the natives accomplished an ideological

---

Castillo, *Historia Verdadera de la Conquista de la Nueva España,* Carmelo Sáenz de Santa María, ed., (Madrid: Centro Superior de Investigaciones Científicas, 1982), xxii, xxx and xlii; Hernán Cortés, *Cartas de Relación* (México: Porrúa, 1976), 119, 226-27.

[66] Spaniards thought of American natives as second-class humans as the result of the *Reconquista's* inheritance (see Juan Hernández Franco, *Sangre Limpia, Sangre Española. El Debate de los Estatutos de Limpieza (Siglos XV-XVII),* [Madrid: Cátedra, 2011], 79-123). For them, human value was dependent on religion, government, and social status (see Jiménez Gómez, "La Colonización del Pueblo de Tlachco-Querétaro en La Frontera de Chichimecas, 1531-1599," 232). For this reason, the Catholicization of the native and his modernization went hand in hand (Pedro Borges, *Misión y Civilización en América,* [Madrid: Editorial Alhambra, 1987], 5; Francisco Niño, *La Iglesia en La Ciudad: El Fenómeno de Las Grandes Ciudades en América Latina, Como Problema Teológico y Como Desafío Personal,* Tesi Gregoriana Series 13, [Roma: Editrice Pontificia Universita Gregoriana, 1996], 139).

[67] Author's own translation. Díaz del Castillo, *Historia Verdadera de la Conquista de la Nueva España,* lxxvii.

[68] The nation did not tolerate any religion other than Catholicism. Not being Catholic was a sin in itself, but at this point in Spain's history, it also became a social sin. It brought shame upon the country (see J. P. Dedieu, "¿Pecado Original o Pecado Social? Reflexiones en Torno a La Constitución y a La Definición del Grupo Judeo-Converso en Castilla," in *Manuscrits: Revista d'Historia Moderna* 10 (January, 1992): 63–64).

[69] See Dussel, *Historia de La Iglesia en América Latina,* 88.

security,"[70] which offered the means by which Spain and the RCC accomplished their goal of worldwide political influence. This ambition, coupled with Spain's solidified Catholic nationalism after the *Reconquista,* and the global influence of the empire where the sun never set, turned the Spanish monarchy into the ideal candidate to launch a full-on attack against the Protestant Reformation.

Meanwhile in Europe

On the other side of the Atlantic, in the year 1517, not only did Luther spark a fire that rapidly consumed Europe, but Charles V also sat on Spain's throne.[71] In 1555, almost four decades later, the Augsburg Settlement was signed, legalizing Protestantism in the empire.[72] A year after the settlement, the emperor, who was suffering from gout, stepped down.[73] Undoubtedly, religious controversy permeated his reign.[74] The ripple effects of the Reformation weakened the empire,[75] but Charles's administration, wasting its resources to fight wars for the RCC—like reconquering Protestant Europe and the Catholicization of the Americas—brought it to an end.[76] Meanwhile, Turkey gained control over the eastern Mediterranean; France seized imperial cities, such as Metz, Toul, and Verdun; and western Christendom split in two.[77] This chaotic situation agitated the entire

---

[70] Author's own translation. Francisco Tomás Valiente, *Manual de Historia del Derecho Español* (Madrid: Tecnos, 1992), 325.

[71] A year later, in 1518, he was elected emperor of the Holy Roman Empire (Moa, *Nueva Historia de España*, 392–93).

[72] This settlement ended the war in Europe between Catholicism and Protestantism. It established that future religious disputes could be settled only according to law and not by religious councils. The basic principle behind this settlement was that every ruler had the right to determine the faith of his nation. Therefore, the Augsburg Settlement gave Protestantism legal recognition in the Empire (see Michael Hughes, *Early Modern Germany, 1477–1806,* [Philadelphia: University of Pennsylvania Press, 1992], 59–60).

[73] All the battles that the emperor fought, including his personal vendetta against Protestantism, overextended him. His health paid the price. So, in 1556 he abdicated and gave the Holy Roman Empire to his brother Ferdinand the Castilian, and Spain's monarchy to his son Philip II (Moa, *Nueva Historia de España*, 477).

[74] Trigo Chacón, *La España Imperial*, 112.

[75] Vidal, *Pontífices*, 159.

[76] See Chaunu, *La España de Carlos V*, 374–75.

[77] Moa, *Nueva Historia de España*, 477.

empire. Charles V, seeking to maintain the fragile union of his frac-
tured kingdom, convened the Diet of Worms on January 6, 1521.[78]
Two important subjects would be laid before the assembly of princes
and lords of the empire: the Reformation and the nomination of a
regency council.[79] The former, however, became the talk of the town,
and not without reason, since the almost tyrannical ambition of the
RCC hovered over the city of Worms. Before the diet began, a letter
from Rome disclosing the intentions of the papacy was read. It said:

> If I am not mistaken, the only business in your
> Diet will be this affair of Luther, which gives us
> much more trouble than the Turk himself. We shall
> endeavor to gain over the young Emperor [Charles
> V] by threats, by prayers, and feigned caresses. We
> shall strive to win the Germans by extolling the piety
> of their ancestors, and by making them rich presents,
> and by lavish promises. If these methods do not suc-
> ceed, we shall depose the Emperor, and absolve the
> people from their obedience; elect another (and he
> will be one that suits us) in his place; stir up civil war
> among the Germans, as we have just done in Spain;
> and summon to our aid the armies of the Kings of
> France, England, and all the nations of the earth.
> Probity, honor, religion, Christ — we shall make light
> of all, provided our tyranny be saved.[80]

The Swiss historian J. H. Merle d'Aubigné says that these
words accurately described the policy of the RCC, which in the end,
was no other than to exert global domination of the "Great Roman
Empire of Old."[81] Luther, despite this ominous threat, did not recant
from his Ninety-five Theses or his belief on justification by faith
alone. He would only abandon his view if the Bible itself would

---

[78]   Charles summoned the assembly on the 6th but opened the diet on January 28, 1521. See
       ibid., 569–70.

[79]   Ibid.

[80]   John Rae, *Martin Luther: Student, Monk, Reformer* (London: Hodder and Stoughton, 1894),
       252.

[81]   See D'Aubigné, *History of the Reformation of the Sixteenth Century*, 570.

prove him wrong.[82] After the diet, the schism that was ripping the empire apart was even greater.[83] It seemed that the Reformation was about to change the European political landscape. The new religious allegiance of Germany, Hungary, Poland, and the Netherlands to Lutheranism[84] would set them apart from the rest of Catholic Europe.[85] This political instability was the final catalyst to launching the Counter-Reformation, and it was defined by three key elements: the Inquisition, the Society of Jesus, and the Council of Trent.[86]

The Inquisition,[87] which the historian Cesar Vidal compares to the Third Reich,[88] terrified Spain and the Americas. In Mexico, for example, every year during Lent the clerics ordered every Catholic under penalty of excommunication to report anything that they had heard or seen against the RCC, especially if it was related to Islam or Protestantism.[89] In Spain, this reign of terror developed in three phases.[90] The first one, from 1519 to 1539, was characterized by the quest for Protestant literature that had been forbidden.[91] During the

---

[82] Vidal, *Cambiaron la Historia*, 126.

[83] Charles and the papacy could not accomplish the political and religious reunification that they were after.

[84] In this essay, this term is used as a synonym of Protestantism. It does not refer to the Lutheran denomination.

[85] Vidal, *La Historia Secreta de La Iglesia Católica en España*, 228.

[86] Vidal, *Pontífices*, 159–60.

[87] José A. Llorente was a first-hand witness of the Inquisition since the Bishop of Jaen appointed him grand inquisitor in 1789, but as a humanist, he tried to dissolve it (Valentina Fernández Vargas, *La Inquisición y Los Españoles*, Miguel Castellote, ed., [Madrid: Colección Básica, 1973], 10). He wrote several books on this topic. One that describes and explains the different procedures and laws behind the Great Tribunal of the Inquisition is José A. Llorente, *La Inquisición y Los Españoles*, Miguel Castellote, ed., (Madrid: Colección Básica, 1973). Another one explaining its history is José A. Llorente, *The History of the Inquisition of Spain,* (London: Geo B. Whittaker, 1826). For an excellent explanation of the social, cultural, and religious consequences of the Inquisition, see Diana Bianchu, "Inquisición e Ilustración. Un Expediente Reservado de José del Campillo," in *Investigaciones Históricas. Época Moderna y Contemporánea* 22 (2002): 63–82.

[88] Vidal, *La Historia Secreta de la Iglesia Católica en España*, 193–94.

[89] Caraillac, "Lo Morisco Peninsular y Su Proyección en la Conquista de América," 448.

[90] Cesar Vidal writes a brief but insightful section tracing some of the effects of the Inquisition in Spain's culture and society to this day. It is a highly recommended read. See Vidal, *La Historia Secreta de la Iglesia Católica en España*, 350–52.

[91] The creation of the *Index Librorum Prohibitorum* marks the culmination of this first period in the Spanish Inquisition; it is a list of forbidden books first published by the RCC in 1557 (Vidal, *Pontífices*, 160).

second phase, from 1540 to 1557, the Inquisition focused on the eradication of humanism.[92] Finally, from 1558 to 1648—the third phase— the Inquisitorial Tribunal sought to annihilate two of the largest Protestant congregations in Spain located in Seville and Valladolid.[93] This "system of terror"[94] gained control over the religious state of the country by 1573, shutting the doors to Protestantism.[95]

The Society of Jesus (the Jesuits) was established by Ignacio de Loyola, approved by Pope Paul III in 1540, and founded with a twofold purpose in mind: first, to challenge the nonstop spreading of the Reformation, and second, to Catholicize the nations,[96] especially the natives in the new continent.[97] By 1603, there were already 603 Jesuits in Mexico alone[98] who created many schools and universities to convert the upper class to Catholicism.[99] The Society became so influential in the New World and Europe that even their presence threatened the power of the empire and the RCC.[100] Therefore, they were banished from Portugal, Spain, France,[101] and the Americas[102] but not without first extending the fear of the Inquisition and Catholicism on both sides of the Atlantic.

But perhaps even more significant was the Council of Trent, arguably the most important ecumenical council of the RCC. It

---

92   Thomas, *La Represión del Protestantismo en España 1517-1648*, 119.

93   De Mora, *La Iglesia de Jesu-Cristo en España*, 137.

94   Fernández Álvarez, *Sombras y Luces en La España Imperial*, 126. The inquisitors did not seek to be loved but feared (ibid., 135–37).

95   See De Mora, *La Iglesia de Jesu-Cristo en España*, 147–49. The Inquisitorial Tribunal had a reputation for falsely accusing people in order to obtain their wealth and riches. This means that their motivation was not always to preserve the supposed purity of Catholic doctrine (see Juan Ignacio Gutierrez Nieto, "Los Conversos y el Movimiento Comunero," *Hispania: Revista Española de Historia* 94 [1964]: 254–55).

96   Vidal, *Pontífices*, 159.

97   Dussel, *Historia de La Iglesia en América Latina*, 89.

98   Ibid., 113.

99   In Mexico City, they established the Colegio Máximo de San Pedro y San Pablo, together with other schools in Puebla and Guadalajara (see Mónica Ruiz Bañuls, "El Discurso Indígena en El Proyecto Evangelizador Novohispano del Siglo XVI," in *Revista Iberoamericana de Teología* 2, no. 11 [July-December 2010]: 19).

100 Vidal, *Pontífices*, 159.

101 Ibid.

102 See Dussel, *Historia de La Iglesia en América Latina*, 114, 170–73.

represented the definitive Catholic response to the Reformation and the attempt of Charles V to reunify Europe.[103] Trent hosted this Council in three periods that spanned for almost nineteen years. The first period stretched from 1545 to 1547, the second from 1551 to 1552, and the third from 1562 to 1563. The Council was marked by the upheavals of its time.[104] During the first year in 1545, the war between Spain and Germany moved the sessions to Bologna. In 1555, the Augsburg Settlement confirmed the unsurpassable breach between Protestantism and Catholicism.[105] In 1556, Charles V abdicated the throne. From 1555 to 1559, the RCC changed popes three times. Marcellus II was elected pope on April 1555 and died twenty-two days later; his successor, Paul IV, known for his intolerance toward Protestantism and anti-imperial policy, died in August 1559. Pius IV became the next pope in December 1559. It was his determination that was key to restoring the diplomatic network that Paul IV destroyed.[106] He was the pope who convened the last period of the Council of Trent and brought it to a closure, facilitating the installment of its decrees and dogmas.

It was amidst this political and religious turmoil that popes and emperors had to deal with the fragmentation of their respective empires, religious and national. Their common denominator was the Council of Trent. It was at this Council that the RCC became ready to march behind the imperial army against Protestantism in Europe and the Americas. As history developed, the Reformation's enemy grew stronger and stronger. The first serious contestant was Spain, then the RCC, and finally, they both joined forces with the full imperial and political structure of the Holy Roman Empire in order to crush the Reformation under the weight of their might. A greater threat, however, was yet to come.

---

[103] Gonzaga, *Concilios*, 2: 557.

[104] For a more detailed history about the struggles of the Council of Trent, see Hubert Jedin, *A History of the Council of Trent. Volume 1. The Struggle for the Council*, Dom Ernest Graf, trans., (New York: Thomas Nelson and Sons, 1963).

[105] Hughes, *Early Modern Germany, 1477–1806*, 59–60.

[106] Miles Pattenden, *Pius IV and the Fall of the Carafa. Nepotism and Papal Authority in Counter-Reformation Rome*, (Oxford: Oxford University Press, 2013), 44.

The Trojan Horse

The Council of Trent formulated the decrees that reshaped the RCC into what it has become today.[107] Furthermore, if the purpose of the Council was to condemn the teachings of the Reformation, then by definition, Catholicism and Protestantism are antagonistic.[108] In other words, their respective beliefs cannot be reconciled.[109] Therefore, the fight switched from political influence and power to a battle for the truth.[110] The stakes were much higher than ever before, simply because the worst threat is when the truth of God is tampered with.

During the Third Session of the Council of Trent, the Nicene Creed was reaffirmed.[111] Hence, it would seem that Catholicism and Protestantism would share a similar Christology. The RCC, however, often denies in practice what it affirms in theory. Sixteen years after the Third Session, during the Twenty-second Session, the Council denied that the Lord's Supper was a memorial of the death of Christ, stating the now well-known phrase: "And forasmuch as, in this divine sacrifice which is celebrated in the mass, that same Christ is

---

[107] Moa, *Nueva Historia de España*, 496. These decrees have been confirmed at later Councils. Mary Ann Collins writes: "The declarations and anathemas of the Council of Trent have never been revoked. On the contrary, the decrees of the Council of Trent are confirmed by both the Second Vatican Council (1962–1965) and the official *Catechism of the Catholic Church* (1992)" (Mary Ann Collins, *Another Side of Catholicism: Insights from a Former Catholic Nun* [New York: iUniverse, 2004], 41).

[108] The basic beliefs that distinguish Protestantism from Catholicism are summarized in the Five Solas: *sola scriptura* (Scripture alone is the highest authority), *sola fide* (salvation is through faith alone), *sola gratia* (salvation is by grace alone), *solus Christus* (Christ alone is Lord, King, Savior, and Mediator between God and mankind), and *soli Deo gloria* (everything is for the glory of God alone). Justin Holcomb, *Know the Creeds and Councils*, (Grand Rapids, Michigan: Zondervan, 2014), 113. The first four solas, which are essential for the purity of the gospel, were condemned as heresy at the Council of Trent.

[109] The RCC "teaches major false doctrines ... that range from idolatry ... to making works a condition for receiving eternal life.... [It has become] a false church with significant truth" (Geisler, and Betancourt, *Is Rome The True Church?* 180). See also Normal Geisler and Ralph E. MacKenzie, *Roman Catholics and Evangelicals: Agreements and Differences,* [Grand Rapids, Michigan: Baker Books, 2001], 157–358).

[110] For a defense of the reality of absolute truth in a postmodern world, and an explanation of how the RCC altered it, see Ruben Videira, "Catholicism, Postmodernism, and Inerrancy in Southern Europe," in *The Implications of Inerrancy for the Global Church. The Truth of God's Word Defended, Explained and Extolled by Authors from 17 Countries across The Globe,* Mark Tatlock, ed., (Los Angeles: The Master's Academy International, 2015), 217–34.

[111] Compare Council of Trent, Session 3, February 4, 1546, in *The Creeds of Christendom*, 2: 79, with Drobner, *The Fathers of The Church*, 242.

contained and immolated in an unbloody manner who once offered himself in a bloody manner on the altar of the cross."[112] This claim is not only illogical,[113] but it also contradicts Scripture.[114] In addition, it restrains the final efficacy of Jesus' atoning death,[115] and consequently undermines His glory. If Jesus' sacrifice is not sufficient, then, to the extent that the Eucharist is necessary, He was either sinful[116] or not divine.[117] Furthermore, if the Eucharist is an actual

---

[112] Council of Trent, Session 22, September 17th, 1562, "Doctrine on the Sacrifice of the Mass," in *The Creeds of Christendom*, 2:180.

[113] By definition a propitiatory sacrifice requires death, but if in the Mass there is not the shedding of blood, then the sacrifice is not propitiatory (see William Webster, *Roman Catholic Tradition. Claims and Contradictions*, [Battle Ground, Washington: Christian Resources, 1999], 56). Moreover, Scripture itself affirms that without the shedding of blood, there is no forgiveness (Heb 9:22).

[114] The New Testament clearly teaches that there are no more sacrifices for sin (emphasis added): "knowing that Christ, having been raised from the dead, *is never to die again*; death no longer is master over Him. For the death that He died, *He died to sin once for all*; but the life that He lives, He lives to God" (Rom 6:9–10). "For it was fitting for us to have such a high priest, holy, innocent, undefiled, separated from sinners and exalted above the heavens; *who does not need daily*, like those high priests, *to offer up sacrifices*, first for His own sins and then for the sins of the people, *because this He did once for all when He offered up Himself*" (Heb 7:26–27). "By this will, we have been sanctified through the offering of the body of Jesus Christ *once for all*. Every priest stands daily ministering and offering time after time the same sacrifices, which can never take away sins; *but He, having offered one sacrifice for sins for all time,* sat down at the right hand of God, waiting from that time onward until His enemies be made a footstool for His feet. *For by one offering He has perfected for all time those who are sanctified.* And the Holy Spirit also testifies to us; for after saying, 'This is the covenant that I will make with them after those days, says the Lord: I will put My laws upon their heart, and on their mind I will write them.' He then says, 'And their sins and their lawless deeds I will remember no more.' Now where there is forgiveness of these things, there is *no longer any offering for sin*" (Heb 10:10–18).

[115] The sacrifice of Christ happened two thousand years ago completely apart from the participation of its beneficiaries. Moreover, it is a completed work that will never be repeated again (John 19:39), achieved by the only Mediator that there is between God and men (John 14:6; Acts 4:12; 1 Tim 1:15; 2:4). Therefore, only Christ Himself could expiate sin, and since He is risen from the dead and exalted at the right hand of the Father (Rom 1:3; Phil 2:9–11), He will not come back to earth to die for the sins of men again. Thus, His sacrifice on the cross must be sufficient for all the sins—past, present and future—of everyone who has believed, believes, and will believe in Him (John 3:18; Acts 10:43; Eph 1:7; Col 1:14) (see Robert L. Reymond, *A New Systematic Theology of The Christian Faith*, 2nd ed., [Nashville, Tennessee: Thomas Nelson, 1998], 667–69).

[116] Only a sinless Christ could be an acceptable sacrifice to God (1 Pet 1:19). But if the Mass sacrifice is necessary for the propitiation of sins, then, when Jesus claimed the finality of the atonement on the cross (John 19:30), he was not telling the truth (John 14:6, 16:7), making himself a liar. Furthermore, God the Father also becomes a liar since He testified of Jesus' sinlessness by raising Him from the dead (Rom 1:4, 4:25).

[117] Andrew Fuller explains the following: "In short, the Deity and atonement of Christ have always, among thinking people, stood or fallen together; and with them almost every other

unbloody sacrifice, the bread and the wine had to become Christ's literal flesh and blood, although the sensory characteristics of the elements such as taste, smell, and so forth remain the same. This in Catholic theology is called transubstantiation, a doctrine that goes back to the Fourth Lateran Council in 1215,[118] and was reaffirmed at the Council of Trent during the Thirteenth Session:

> And because that Christ, our Redeemer, declared that which he offered under the species of bread to be truly his own body, therefore has it ever been a firm belief in the Church of God, and this holy Synod doth now declare it anew, that, by the consecration of the bread and of the wine, a conversion is made of the whole substance of the bread into the substance of the body of Christ our Lord, and of the whole substance of the wine into the substance of his blood; which conversion is, by the holy Catholic Church, suitably and properly called

---

important doctrine of the gospel. The person of Christ is the foundation-stone on which the church is built. An error, therefore, on this subject affects the whole of our preaching, and the whole of our religion. In the esteem of the apostle Paul, that which nullified the death of Christ was accounted to be another gospel; and he expressed his wish that those who propagated it, and so troubled the churches, were cut off. The principle maintained by the Galatians, it is true, did not consist in a denial of the Deity of Christ; but the consequence is the same. They taught that justification was by the works of the law, from whence the apostle justly inferred that "Christ is dead in vain."' And he who teaches that Christ is a mere creature holds a doctrine which renders his sufferings of none effect. If the Deity of Christ be a Divine truth, it cannot reasonably be denied that it is of equal importance with the doctrine of justification by his righteousness. If therefore a rejection of the latter was deemed a perversion of the gospel, nothing less can be ascribed to the rejection of the former" (Andrew Gunton Fuller, *The Complete Works of the Rev. Andrew Fuller with a Memoir of His Life*, [Boston, Massachusetts: Lincoln, Edmands & Co., 1833], 2: 808–809). For all the biblical data directly or indirectly supporting this, see Reymond, *A New Systematic Theology of The Christian Faith*, 625–28.

[118] Webster, *The Church of Rome at The Bar of History*, 117. A basic form of this Catholic doctrine was already present during the 4th century. Cyril of Jerusalem wrote: "That our Lord Jesus Christ the same night in which He was betrayed, took bread, and when He had given thanks He broke it, and said, 'Take, eat, this is My Body,' and having taken the cup and given thanks, He said, 'Take, drink, this is my Blood.' Since then He Himself has declared and said of the Bread, 'This is My Body,' who shall dare to doubt any longer? And since He has affirmed and said, 'This is My Blood,' who shall ever hesitate, saying, that it is not His blood?" (E. B. Pusey, *The Doctrine of the Real Presence: As Contained in the Fathers from the Death of S. John the Evangelist to the Fourth General Council, Vindicated, in Notes on a Sermon, "The Presence of Christ in the Holy Eucharist," Preached A.D. 1853, before the University of Oxford*, [London: John Henry Parker, 1855], 387–388).

> Transubstantiation... . In [this] sacrament are con-
> tained truly, really, and substantially, the body and
> blood together with the soul and divinity of our Lord
> Jesus Christ, and consequently the whole Christ.[119]

This implies that the Eucharistic wafer dipped in wine becomes Jesus Christ. Such a claim goes both ways. If the wafer and the wine become divine, then the Second Person of the Trinity adds the essence of these elements to His divinity. The essence or nature of a thing, whether inanimate or animate, spiritual or material, created or self-existent "denotes the sum-total of all the essential qualities of that thing."[120] Therefore, at the transubstantiation, if the elements turn into the body and blood of Jesus, then they adopt all of the qualities of His humanity. Moreover, Jesus' humanity cannot be separated from His divinity because if the incarnate Son of God ceases to be divine, He ceases to be Jesus. This means that, since the divine nature cannot be altered or transformed, God Himself needs to take the form of the bread and the wine upon His divine essence, in order for these elements to become the body and blood of Christ. Therefore, the logical implication of the transubstantiation is that Jesus Christ has three natures—divine, human, and wafer.

The teachings of the RCC regarding the Eucharist—reaffirmed at the Council of Trent—have opened the door to a fatal distortion. Even though Catholicism claims to uphold to an orthodox Christology, the practice of the sacrifice of the Mass functions as the Trojan horse that creeps into Catholicism and destroys its seemingly orthodox view of Christ's propitiation and nature. So, the RCC has become "a false church with significant truth,"[121] which has not only distorted the gospel of Jesus Christ as taught in Europe but also exported its errors across the entirety of the New World.

---

[119] Council of Trent, Session 13, October 11, 1551, "Decree Concerning The Most High Sacrament of the Eucharist," in *The Creeds of Christendom*, 2: 130; and 136 (emphasis mine).

[120] Louis Berkhof, *Systematic Theology,* (Grand Rapids, Michigan: Wm. B. Eerdmans Publishing Co., 1938), 321.

[121] Geisler and Betancourt, *Is Rome the True Church?* 180.

The Meeting Point

Most Catholics in Spain and the Americas during these periods were illiterate.[122] They could not read the decrees of the Council of Trent, and yet by 1614, the Eucharist's corruption of Christ's propitiatory work was widespread in both territories.[123] The dissemination of this false Christology came through two intersecting paths: religious and political ambition.

The religious path was built by the Jesuits, who fully adhered to the Council of Trent.[124] They enjoyed a diplomatic network that facilitated their missional work, carrying out the papacy's commitment to ensure that the conciliar decrees were put into practice throughout all the Catholic territories.[125] This was mainly accomplished by means of the Tridentine Confession of Faith and the 1570 Roman Missal.[126] The former was a confession of faith, based on the Tridentine decrees, that was imposed upon all Catholic clerics by Pope Pius IV.[127] It sought to standardize belief and practice in the RCC around the teachings reaffirmed at the Council. For this reason, it succinctly condensed the eight chapters of the *Decree of The Most Holy Sacrament of The Eucharist,*[128] and the nine of the *Doctrine on The Sacrifice of The Mass*[129] into one paragraph:

---

122 For more on the illiteracy of Spaniards, see Vidal, *La Historia Secreta de La Iglesia Católica en España*, 308-309; and for the Americas see Jiménez Gómez, "La Colonización del Pueblo de Tlachco-Querétaro en La Frontera de Chichimecas, 1531-1599," 233-34.

123 Benjamin J. Kaplan, *Divided by Faith. Religious Conflict and the Practice of Toleration in Early Modern Europe,* (Cambridge, Massachusetts: The Belknap Press of Harvard University Press, 2007), 43.

124 Ibid., 47.

125 See Giuseppe Alberigo, "From the Council of Trent to 'Tridentinism,'" Emily Michelson, trans., in *From Trent to Vatican II: Historical and Theological Investigations,* Raymond F. Bulman and Frederick J. Parrella, eds., (New York: Oxford University Press, 2006), 22.

126 Kaplan, *Divided by Faith,* 43–44.

127 This was done through the papal bull *Injunctum nobis* of November 13, 1564, (see Matthew Bunson, *OSV's Encyclopedia of Catholic History,* [Hungtinton, Indiana: Our Sunday Visitor, 2004], 717).

128 See Council of Trent, Session 13, October 11, 1551in *The Creeds of Christendom,* 2: 127–39.

129 See Council of Trent, Session 22, September 17, 1562, in *The Creeds of Christendom,* 2: 176–86.

> I profess likewise that true God is offered in the Mass, a proper and propitiatory sacrifice for the living and the dead, and that in the most Holy Eucharist there are truly, really and substantially the body and blood, together with the soul and divinity of Our Lord Jesus Christ, and that a conversion is made of the whole substance of bread into his body and of the whole substance of wine into his blood, which conversion the Catholic Church calls Transubstantiation. I also confess that the whole and entire Christ and the true sacrament is taken under the one species alone.[130]

This also became the normative text professed by all "converts to Roman Catholicism,"[131] bringing confessional uniformity within Catholicism[132] and changing the definition of Catholic religion itself.[133] Now the doors of Catholicism were opened only to those who adhered to the Tridentine decrees. This meant that the RCC taught their converts that, in order to be saved, they had to internalize a corrupted view of Christ.

The second means that the Jesuits used to implement the Tridentine decrees was through the 1570 Roman Missal[134]—an attempt to bring uniformity into Catholic liturgical practices that included instructions about how to celebrate the Catholic Mass.[135] When Pope Pius V, successor of Pius IV, proclaimed his *Qui Primum* of July 14, 1570, to promulgate the Roman Missal, he sat on the Apostolic Throne. This meant that his words came with infallible authority.[136] Consequently, when he commanded all Catholic churches to follow the Roman Missal, he

---

[130] Henry Bettenson and Chris Maunder, *Documents of The Christian Church*, 4th edition, (New York: Oxford University Press, 2011), 270.

[131] Ibid.

[132] See Kaplan, *Divided by Faith*. 47.

[133] Ibid.

[134] For an English translation of this Missal, see: *The Roman Missal. Translated into the English Language for The Use of The Laity. Published with The Approbation of The Right Rev. The Bishop of Philadelphia*, (Philadelphia: Eugene Cummiskey, 1861).

[135] Dennis C. Smolarsky, *The General Instruction of The Roman Missal, 1962–2002. A Commentary* (Collegeville, Michigan: The Liturgical Press, 2003), 5–6.

[136] James Hitchcock, *History of the Catholic Church. From the Apostolic Age to the Third Millennium* (San Francisco, California: Ignatius Press, 2012), 366–67.

set in stone for all time the nature of the Eucharist as declared by the Council of Trent—the perpetual and repetitious sacrifice of Christ.[137]

Christ's blessed work on the cross was further denigrated by politically motivated factors, beginning with the bull *Benedictus Deus*, when Pope Pius IV solemnly confirmed the decrees of the Council of Trent.[138] This bull gave the Holy See the final authority over any problem of interpretation regarding the decrees. The goal was to avoid a proliferation of interpretations that would delay the implementation of the Council. He desired that this new dogma be enforced by political rulers throughout the territories and, indeed, only a few months later, the king of Spain, Philip II, proclaimed the acceptance of this bull, thereby fully embracing the decrees of Trent.[139] But his motives were not merely religious. Europe's landscape was rapidly changing, making it almost impossible to anticipate the final reconfiguration of the old continent. Hence, Philip still hoped to recover some of the regions lost to Protestantism.[140] He, as a product of Spain's history, could not conceive national unity without religious uniformity. Hence, the monarch thought that through the application of the Council teachings in his lands,[141] he would achieve a much-needed structure for political unity, setting in place the logistics for spreading the Council's decrees in every region of Spain[142] and the New World.[143] So, even

---

[137] See Council of Trent, Session 22, September 17, 1562, in *The Creeds of Christendom*, 2: 177–78.

[138] For the text of the bull in Latin, see Joannis Soteally and Horatii Lucii, *Sacrosancti et Oecumenici Concilii Tridentini sub Paulo III, Julio III, Paulo IV Pontificibus Maximis Celebrati Canones et Decreta: Juxta Exemplar Romae Editum ann. MDLXIV*, (Matriti: Ex Typographia Emmanuelis Martin, 1778), 433–41. See also Alberigo, "From the Council of Trent to 'Tridentinism,'" 21.

[139] Tineo, "La Recepción de Trento en España," 242.

[140] See Vidal, *La Historia Secreta de la Iglesia Católica en España*, 227–38.

[141] See Juan Tejada y Ramiro, *Colección de Cánones y de Todos los Concilios de La Iglesia Española*, (Madrid: Imprenta de Pedro Montero, 1859), 4: 1.

[142] For a detailed explanation of the Tridentine movement in Spain, see: Sara T. Nalle, "Inquisitors, Priests and the People during the Catholic Reformation in Spain," in *The Sixteenth Century Journal* 18 no. 4 (Winter, 1987): 557–87; and Nalle, *God in La Mancha. Religious Reform and the People of Cuenca 1500–1650*, 32–69. Vidal writes an excellent discussion on Philip II, presenting him as the sword that eagerly and violently defended the Catholic Counter-Reformation (see Vidal, *La Historia Secreta de La Iglesia Católica en España*, 227–69).

[143] For some examples on how the Spanish conquistadors were accompanied by Catholic clerics in order to catholicize the New World, and in some cases already apply the Tridentine

though most Catholics on both sides of the Atlantic never read the decrees and canons of the Council of Trent, they learned and came to embrace the insufficient propitiation of Christ and the limitation of His nature as portrayed in the Eucharist. Thus, the Counter-Reformation power play at the Council of Trent cemented a false view of Christ and the gospel into the fabric of the Catholic Church, which was straightaway exported across the world, promoted and applied by kings and popes seeking to gain more power.

The Legacy

The corruption of the papacy infected almost the entirety of the RCC in Spain. Its ambition, coupled with the Spanish monarchs' political thirst for more power after the discovery of the Americas, paved the way for Catholicism to spread its teachings worldwide. Meanwhile, the RCC was also facing a new enemy—the Reformation—causing a violent reaction of far-reaching political–religious significance known as the Counter-Reformation. The papacy was determined to defuse the spark of Protestantism on both sides of the Atlantic. To that end they took advantage of the Spanish conquistadors' mindset, influenced by the *Reconquista,* by turning their quest into a religious event, thereby shrewdly infesting the New World with the doctrines of the Council of Trent. This set the foundations for the RCC as it is known today, and in the end, it shaped the religious landscape of both Europe and the New World. The Catholic Eucharist, reaffirmed at this Council, was forcibly implemented throughout Catholicism, thanks to the Tridentine liturgy of the Holy Mass. Now Catholics believe in an insufficient sacrifice of a Christ whose nature has also been limited to a standard that makes Him less of a Savior.

---

theology, see: Jiménez Gómez, "La Colonización del Pueblo de Tlachco-Querétaro en La Frontera de Chichimecas, 1531-1599,"233-36; Grunberg, "Hernán Cortés y la guerra de los Conquistadores,"557-76; Leften S. Stavarianos, Lorretta Kreider Andrews, John R. McLane, Frank Safford, and James E. Sheridan, *A Global History of Man* (Boston, Massachusetts: Allyn and Bacon, 1974), 310-19; León Cázares, "Entre el Breviario y la Espada," 599-618; López de Gómara, *Historia General de Las Indias,* 289; Vidal, *Cambiaron la Historia,* 167–79; and Vidal, *El Legado del Cristianismo en la Cultura Occidental,* 206–208.

The legacy of the Counter-Reformation and its extension through Spain's political influence is devastating.[144] It has redefined the work of Christ, and taught the Catholic converts to embrace a non-saving Savior. The Counter-Reformation's influence has plunged the Iberian Peninsula and the Spanish-influenced New World into a spiritual darkness that still hovers over these territories. Therefore, Spain and all the countries under its former rule are still under the same urgent need that was found in 16th-century northern Europe—a reformation based on *sola scriptura* that proclaims the true Christ.

---

[144] For an explanation on other cultural, political and social consequences of Catholicism in Spain, see Vidal, *La Historia Secreta de La Iglesia Católica en España*, 289–352.

THE RISEN AND EXALTED CHRIST: A BIBLICAL PERSPECTIVE NEEDED IN MEXICO

Jim Dowdy

Word of Grace Biblical Seminary, Mexico

[Editor's Note: In Mexico, there is a long history of engagement between the indigenous peoples and Catholic foreign powers. These interactions have heavily influenced the Christological beliefs held by many in Mexico today. A survey of this history and its effect on contemporary thinking shows that a new perspective is needed in Mexico, one that reflects the true nature of Jesus' life, death, and resurrection.]

Introduction

On Good Friday, "Jesus" is kicked, beaten, whipped, and covered with cinematic blood. He stumbles and falls. The sounds of nails being hammered into hardwood come across the loudspeakers, and the crowds fall silent. "Jesus" is hoisted aloft and held bound by ropes to the cross and remains there for about twenty minutes as He looks out over the gathered crowd. It is not unusual to see people crying. As "Jesus" hangs on the cross, Judas first gloats and then hangs himself nearby. The play is over. There is no resurrection, no victory, and no triumph over sin, death, and hell—just a defeated and humiliated Christ who is to be pitied. Jesus is not depicted as the conquering Savior of mankind who gave His life as a ransom for many to accomplish His Father's will; instead, He is a man whose unjust sufferings resonate deeply with the Mexican people as a reflection of their own tragic history.

The Passion play described above is the most well-known and elaborate one in all of Mexico. It takes place annually during Holy Week in Iztapalapa, the largest and poorest of Mexico City's sixteen boroughs.[1] It has been reenacted annually since 1843 and includes hundreds of actors. The performance of the Passion play is a revered tradition in Mexico and draws crowds of over 2 million visitors annually, but there is no comparable activity on Easter Sunday, and virtually no teaching concerning the significance of Jesus' atoning death and resurrection to life.[2] In general, it is not the didactic message of the gospel but rather the emotional appeal of tragedy and injustice that strikes a chord with the Mexican people.[3] The purpose of this essay, then, is to explore where this emphasis on *suffering* rather than *saving* comes from, and what must be done to reach the Mexican people with the gospel of Jesus Christ.

Impact of the Spanish Conquest on Mexican Passion Festivals

The roots of the ubiquitous Mexican Passion festivals, which are celebrated even in the smallest of pueblos throughout Mexico, go back to the Spanish Catholic colonization period (1519–1821). The Spanish conquest of the great Aztec Empire in Mesoamerica had its beginnings in the early part of the 16th century, almost 500 years ago. The Aztec Empire of 1519 was one of the most powerful

---

[1]   William Booth, "In Mexico City, Passion Comes Amid Suffering," https://banderasnews. com/0904/nr-centerstage.htm

[2]   There was an attempt in the 1960s to add something about the resurrection, but such a "naïve" attempt failed. According to one historian, "The absolute peak of such naiveté [to try to lead these people to celebrate Jesus" resurrection] ... was the notion that clergy could convert Easter Sunday into a significant feast at Iztapalapa. That day had never figured prominently in the pueblo's festive calendar.... . To this day Easter is still not important in the town's festive calendar." Nor is it important in the rest of Mexico. See Richard C. Trexler, *Reliving Golgotha: The Passion Play of Iztapalapa*, (Cambridge, Massachusetts: Harvard University Press, 2003), 127.

[3]   Mexican Catholics remain fixated on the passion of Christ and not His resurrection. This is why in almost every Catholic cathedral and shrine, one will see wax and plastic figures of the crucified Christ with crown of thorns, nails in hands, and wound in side.

Mesoamerican kingdoms of all time. Against insurmountable odds, Hernán Cortés and his small band of Spanish soldiers triumphed over the empire's 15 million inhabitants. The military triumph came mostly as a result of Cortés' ability to weave together an army consisting of tens of thousands of indigenous (mostly Tlaxcalan) resistance soldiers, who were willing to fight against their hated Aztec overlords.[4] This conquest of the Aztec Empire marked the beginning of Cortés's efforts to bring Catholicism to the indigenous peoples of Mexico.

Cortés received a letter from the governor of Cuba reminding the eager conquistador to "bear in mind from the beginning that the first aim of your expedition is to serve God and to spread the Christian faith."[5] The Spanish Catholic conquistadors wanted to eliminate the pagan elements in indigenous society—most notably the pagan temples, priests, and acts of human sacrifice.[6] At the same time, the Aztec religion included some practices that were similar to those of Spanish Catholicism, such as marriage, penance, baptism, fasting, and offerings. However, in no case were the similarities so exact as to permit a simple and unqualified transfer from one religion to the other.

Though Jesus was presented to the pagan peoples of Mesoamerica, it was not in the biblical and historical way that the Reformers correctly highlighted from the Holy Scriptures *alone*. The earliest Spanish Catholic missionaries, the "apostolic twelve," were Franciscan Mendicants who came to Mexico in 1524.[7] They were the agents of a flourishing conversion program among the native peoples, especially during the first fifty years of the conquest, but "conversion" did not focus on spiritual regeneration so much as on external compliance with the new order. Though Catholicism was communicated in part by teaching and preaching, it was also often forced on the population.[8]

---

[4]   John P. Schmal, "The Indigenous People of Central Mexico, 2," in *The Spanish Conquest of Mexico*, online, houstonculture.org.

[5]   Judith Friedlander. "Mexican Religion and the Virgin of Guadalupe." http://macaulay.cuny.edu/eportfolios/friedlander10/theme/religion/mexican/there/.

[6]   Charles Gibson, *The Aztecs Under Spanish Rule: A History of the Indians of the Valley of Mexico, 1519–1810*, (Stanford, California: Stanford University Press, 1964), 100.

[7]   Ibid.

[8]   Ibid.

The dilemma of Catholicism in early Spanish rule of Mexico was twofold. First, it failed to indoctrinate the masses with a full understanding of its sacraments and doctrines. But second, the indigenous people's "acceptances" of Catholicism were strongly colored by residual and antithetical values.[9] They did not abandon their polytheistic view of worshiping many gods, despite the Catholic insistence upon monotheism. Generally, the Catholics failed to make understandable the basic Christian beliefs of holiness and sin. The Catholic saints were received by the pagan cultures not as intermediaries between God and man (as the Catholics believed), but as a pantheon of anthropomorphic deities. The symbol of Christ's crucifixion was accepted but "with an exaggerated concern for the details of an act of sacrifice."[10] The Christian God was allowed but not as an exclusive or omnipotent deity. Heaven and hell were recognized by the Aztecs but were defined by their own communities, with prominently Aztec attributes. People accepted the concept of the soul but extended it pantheistically to animals and inanimate objects. Indigenous idolatry and pagan superstition persisted despite the Mendicants' best efforts.

Moreover, as historian Charles Gibson notes, "punishment and force played a larger role in conversion than is customarily recognized."[11] Those who refused to convert were sometimes executed, condemned to a lifetime of imprisonment, or tortured with water or strangulation; others were routinely beaten, sentenced to forced labor, or exiled.[12] Influential indigenous leaders would be deputized to force attendance at Mass. The parish priest of Huehuetoca recommended that the excessively brutish natives "be compelled with all necessary force to adopt Christianity."[13] Faced with torture, death, and imprisonment, the Mesoamerican peoples were forced to renounce their local gods and pagan traditions and accept Christian baptism as a sign that they had converted to Christ. The sincerity of these conversions is doubtful, to say the least.

---

[9] Ibid.

[10] Ibid.

[11] Ibid., 117.

[12] Ibid.

[13] Ibid., 116.

Additional confusion was introduced as the Franciscan Mendicants began looking for parallels between the pagan religion of the indigenous peoples and Catholicism. For example, the Aztec god Quetzalcoatl, a primordial god of creation, giver of life and intelligence, was believed to have been born of a "virgin." When the Spanish Catholic missionaries learned this, some began portraying Quetzalcoatl as an actual apostle of Jesus.[14] Also, Huitzilopochtli, the Aztec sun god, was said by the Spanish Catholic priests to be like Jesus since he was also mythically the subject of a miraculous "virgin" birth. Spanish Catholic missionaries believed that it was easy for the Aztecs to understand the Catholic doctrine of transubstantiation because they ate sacrificial victims as part of their pagan rituals to worship their former gods.[15]

The above factors all contributed to great confusion among the Mesoamerican peoples. The Spanish conquistadors, and the Catholic priests who accompanied them, opted for a fusion of Roman Catholic doctrine and pagan beliefs. The indigenous populations were forced to comply externally with the Roman Catholic ordinances without ever being truly regenerated.[16] What this meant was that certain major tenets of Catholicism were impressed upon the Mexican people without them actually understanding their significance or believing in them with saving faith. Jesus was presented to them, but the gospel of the forgiveness of sins by God's grace through faith in Jesus alone was not made clear. Thus, five hundred years later, Mexican Catholicism is perhaps the most syncretistic form of Roman Catholicism in the world, and it strongly influences the way contemporary Mexicans think and feel about the person of Christ and salvation.

---

[14] Friedlander, "The Timeline of the Rise of Mexican Christianity."

[15] Ibid.

[16] Hernan Cortés could not bear the idea of ruling over pagans, and carried out his orders to suppress all pagan activities by means of force. It was not uncommon for the Spanish to simply erect crosses and images of the Virgin Mary over pagan temples in order to "put the devil to flight" and establish their superiority. See Robert Ricard, *The Spiritual Conquest of Mexico*, trans. Lesley B. Simpson, (Los Angeles, California: University of California Press, 1966), 15–19.

The Negative Impact of the Spanish Spiritual Conquistadors

Confusion about Christ and the Gospel

There are several factors that contribute to the confusion that many Mexicans have about Christ and the gospel. First, Catholic conversion was not presented to them primarily in terms of forgiveness and faith; salvation was instead presented in terms of receiving the Catholic sacraments through the medium of the local priest. Baptism was believed to result in regeneration (conversion); for example, the indigenous women who were given to the Spaniards as spoils of war were simply baptized and considered to be Catholics.[17] The priest would offer Christ to the people through the Eucharist. He would impart the Holy Spirit through the sacrament of confirmation, absolve sin through the sacrament of confession, and even offer Mass on behalf of those who were thought to be suffering in purgatory. Thus, salvation was dispensed through a sacramental system, which was parceled out piecemeal by the priest through the installment method, a little at a time.[18]

Second, their distinct view of Christ was set in motion as a result of the way that the indigenous peoples of Mexico suffered at the hand of the Spanish sword. Because conversion was primarily presented in terms of external compliance via the sacraments rather than in genuine repentance and faith in Christ alone, many who were forced to comply with the external rites were never genuinely born again by God's Spirit. For these, all that remained was the emotional appeal of a Christ who suffered unjustly at the hands of the governmental powers of His day, which provided sufficient parallels for the indigenous peoples under Spanish rule to identify with.

These factors inevitably left a tragic gap in the people's understanding about Christ's person and work. Yes, Christ was God, and yes, Christ was without sin, and yes, Christ died on the cross, but He was defeated and humiliated, deserving of our compassion and pity, and calling for self-suffering after His example to atone for our own sins, both through the sacramental system and through more extreme

---

[17]   Ricard, *The Spiritual Conquest of Mexico*, 18.

[18]   Mike Gendron, "Religion Cannot Save Anyone," http://myemail.constantcontact.com/Religion-Cannot-Save-Anyone.html?soid=1103609831924&aid=PPrRLEKvcCs.

measures.[19] This is seen perhaps most distinctly in their ubiquitous local celebrations of the *Via Crucis* (fourteen representations of the passion of Christ). In Pope Francis's sermon to Mexican bishops in February 2016, in one of his few references to Christ, he says that God was brought close to humanity "in the person of his Son Jesus Christ ... who is recognized as such by so many men and women when they behold his bloody and humiliated face."[20]

Further Confusion by the "Appearance" of the Mexican Mary

Early in the Spanish colonization of Mexico the enemy of the true Christ and His gospel manufactured yet another lie to deceive the indigenous populations of the New World. On December 9, 1531, Juan Diego, a recently converted Aztec peasant, was the subject of a series of supposed miraculous apparitions by the Virgin Mary.[21] In the first apparition Mary revealed herself to Diego as the "ever-virgin Mother of God" and spoke to him in the indigenous Náhuatl language to request that the local Catholic bishop build a chapel in that area (Tepeyac) in her honor. The skeptical bishop, however, required a sign of proof.

Diego returned to the Virgin, and she chided him for unbelief, asking him, "Am I not here, I who am your Mother?" She instructed him to pick some nearby roses and carry them in his *tilma* (cloak) and take them back to the bishop. On seeing the bishop, Diego opens his cloak, the flowers fall to the floor, and the bishop sees that they have miraculously left an imprint of the Virgin's image on Diego's mantle, which he then venerates. Interestingly, the image left on Diego's cloak was that of a dark-skinned Virgin Mary. In a subsequent apparition, Mary reveals to Diego that she wants to be known as "Guadalupe."

---

[19] Self-flagellation is the act of flogging or beating oneself to atone for sins or to draw nearer to God. It has been practiced historically in varying degrees by some Roman Catholics, including popes, and remains common in Spain, Mexico, Colombia, and the Philippines. According to Trexler, it had become an accepted and even necessary part of the Spanish celebration of Holy Week by the end of the 15th century. It certainly contributed to the extreme preoccupation on the physical suffering of Christ in Mexico. See Trexler, *Reliving Golgotha*, 23.

[20] Rome Reports, *Full Text of Pope's Speech to Mexican Bishops*, February 13, 2016, http://www.romereports.com/2016/02/13/full-text-of-the-pope-francis-speech-at-mexican-bishops.

[21] Ibid.

The most distinctive feature of the "Virgin of Guadalupe" is her tanned skin, which gives her the likeness of the Mexican indigenous peoples.[22] According to Mexican Catholic tradition, it was because of this likeness and because of her apparition to an Aztec Indian in Mexico that the indigenous peoples were overwhelmed with a desire to convert to Catholicism.

Today, almost five hundred years following the Virgin of Guadalupe's apparition to Juan Diego, Mexico has the world's second-largest Catholic population.[23] Indeed, 81 percent of Mexican adults today claim to be Catholic, and 90 percent say that they were raised Catholic.[24] Though even Catholic scholars have questioned the historicity of the Virgin of Guadalupe, the legend has become so fixed in the minds of Mexican Catholics[25] that they venerate her more than any other single religious figure in Mexico, including Jesus Christ. A former president of Mexico, Felipe Calderón (2006–2012), summed up the sentiments of most Mexicans when he said, "Regardless of what we each believe, we are all followers of the Virgin of Guadalupe."[26] The Basilica of Guadalupe located on the hill Tepeyac, the site of Mary's apparitions to Diego, claims to possess Juan Diego's *tilma* on which the image of the Virgin is said to have been miraculously impressed. With approximately 12 million visitors per year, the Basilica is Catholicism's most popular Marian shrine.[27]

Millions make pilgrimages to the basilica each year on December 12, which is the Virgin of Guadalupe's feast day. Devotees go on foot, knees, bicycles, and motor vehicles from all around the world. Pope Francis visited the basilica on February 13, 2016, telling reporters, "If

---

22   Ibid.

23   Pew Research Center, "A Snapshot of Catholics in Mexico, Pope Francis' next stop," www. pewresearch.org/fact-tank/2016/02/10/a-snapshot-of-catholics-in-mexico-pope-francis-next-stop/accessed.

24   Ibid.

25   Brian Dunning, "The Virgin of Guadalupe," *Skeptoid*, April 13, 2010, https://skeptoid.com/episodes/4201.

26   Claudia Herrera and Bertha Teresa Ramírez, "Sin importar creencias, todos somos guadalupanos," *LaJornada*, October 13, 2011, www.jornada.unam.mx/2011/10/13/politica/005n1pol.

27   Ibid.

it weren't for Our Lady of Guadalupe, I wouldn't go [to Mexico]."[28] In his speech to Mexican Catholic bishops, the pope exclaimed, "How could I not come! Could the Successor of Peter ... deprive himself of seeing *la Virgen Morenita*[29]?"[30] He referred to apparitions of the Virgin of Guadalupe to Juan Diego five centuries ago as the "founding event" of Mexico and the impetus for the "evangelization of the continent."[31] He continued, "I know that no other voice can speak so powerfully to me of the Mexican heart as the Blessed Mother can."[32] He added, "With the thread of mestizo characteristics, God has woven and revealed in *la Morenita* the face of the Mexican people."[33]

When Mexicans think about Christianity, the first image that comes to their minds is not the Christ of the Bible. Rather, it is the Virgin of Guadalupe. She is viewed as the privileged mediator between God and humanity and is faithfully worshipped. She is believed to have been perfectly sinless and transcends the role of Jesus in Mexican Catholicism. The Passion play of Iztapalapa, mentioned above, might commemorate the death of Jesus, but it is the life of the Virgin that is celebrated at her many shrines. Trexler explains, "To the Son ... their feelings seem composed of respectful *pity*, of humble but more distant adoration, while to the Virgin they appear to give all their confidence ... as to a kind and bountiful Queen."[34] Mary shares in the afflictions of the lowly, feels deeply for their unjust treatment, and grants to them "all-powerful intercession."[35] She is worshiped as the living mediator to whom prayers and praises are offered. It is interesting to note that in all of the supposed apparitions of Christ in Mexico during the past few centuries, He has "appeared'

---

[28] David Agren, "Pope's focus on violence and poor likely to make for 'uncomfortable' Mexico visit," The Guardian, December 11, 2015, https://www.theguardian.com/world/2015/dec/11/pope-francis-mexico-visit-february-michoacan-juarez.

[29] Meaning "the dark-skinned Virgin," a reference to the Virgin of Guadalupe.

[30] Rome Reports, *Full Text of Pope's Speech to Mexican Bishops.*

[31] Ibid.

[32] Ibid.

[33] Ibid.

[34] Trexler, *Reliving Golgotha,* 58.

[35] Ibid.

as dead, crucified, and not risen; but in the "apparitions" of the Virgin of Guadalupe, she is alive.[36]

Summary

The sections above have attempted to detail that the prevailing confusion about Christ in Mexico has been exported from Spain via the Roman Catholic "spiritual" conquistadors, and that the single greatest threat to a biblical understanding of Christ in Mexico has, in actuality, been Roman Catholicism. Deeply ingrained in the Mexican consciousness is the suffering the indigenous peoples experienced at the hands of the Spanish Catholics. This works its way out in the countless Passion plays that are repeated every year, which have great emotional appeal to injustice and suffering but little-to-no clear teaching about Jesus' atoning work on the cross, His triumphant resurrection from the dead, and the victory He won for us who simply believe. Also problematic were the syncretistic tendencies of the Franciscan Mendicants, who sought parallels between the pagan religions of the indigenous peoples and Roman Catholicism in order to bring them into the fold.

Furthermore, because conversion was primarily conveyed in terms of compliance (at times by force), and because the gospel of faith was largely overshadowed by the communication of salvation by sacraments, the Mexican people inherited a flawed view of Christ. And though the Mexican Catholic Church for the most part professes an orthodox creedal understanding of Christ, this "orthodox" understanding washes away when one understands that the popular image that most Mexican people have is a defeated, humiliated, and crucified Christ, who depends on the intercession of His mother, Guadalupe (Mary), to bring them to Jesus and perform miracles on behalf of the Mexican people.

Ultimately, the Mexican people—and all people in every place— need clarity about Jesus Christ. They need to know who He truly

---

[36] This cultural way of viewing Christ can also be observed throughout Mexico by noting that "Jesus" is a very popular name given to boys. While most Protestant Christians would probably view naming their child "Jesus" as being sacrilegious, Mexicans view it as an honor. They do not have any greater fear or reverence for Christ than they do for their local saints, and certainly no greater fear and reverence than for the Virgin of Guadalupe.

is and why He truly came to this world. In the following section, we will note a few important focuses for proclaiming Christ in a Mexican context. First, in light of the prevailing confusion it must be explained *why* and *for whom* Christ suffered. Second, it must be explained that He is the only way to God and the only name we should venerate. Finally, it must be explained that the religion of Jesus Christ allows no room for syncretistic compromise, and a complete break from former paganism and Roman Catholic syncretism is necessary.

Proclaiming the Risen, Exalted, and Triumphant Christ

Christ's Suffering

Throughout Mexico's post-conquest history, the passion of Jesus' suffering has been reenacted more than any other religious act. The indigenous peoples throughout Mexico, as had their European conquerors, mourn their own poor lives by identifying with and constantly reenacting the passions of Christ. By repeatedly, and often brutally, depicting the punishment and humiliation of Jesus, they appropriate His experience as if it were identical to their own humiliations and dashed dreams. Through public self-flagellation, bearing crosses on shoulders, falling to the ground and rising again, and being mocked by local citizens, they seek to satisfy Christ in regard to their own sinfulness, equating their own suffering to that of Jesus.

With such widespread confusion regarding Christ's suffering, it is paramount for Christians to bring clarity on this issue. Why *did* Christ suffer? The apostle Peter answers this question in his first epistle, teaching that Christ's death was an efficacious atonement for the sin of repentant believers: "[Christ] Himself bore our sins in His body on the cross ... for by His wounds you were healed" (1 Pet 2:24). Christ suffered on the cross as the believer's substitute for sin. He bore the sins (the punishment and penalty of them) for the believer, thereby completely satisfying, once for all, the just wrath of a holy God. Peter says in the following chapter, "For Christ also died for sins once for all, the just for the unjust, so that He might bring us to God" (3:18). Though Christ had never sinned and had no sin nature, He died in the place of sinners. In doing so, Christ satisfied

God's just penalty for sin required by the law, and opened the way to God for all who would ever believe (John 14:6; Acts 4:12).

Moreover, though Christ suffered unjustly at the hands of the Romans (and Jews), His suffering was also a part of God's good plan. As Acts teaches, God appointed "both Herod and Pontius Pilate, along with the Gentiles and the peoples of Israel, to do whatever [His] hand and [His] plan had predestined to take place" (4:27, 28). It must be proclaimed that Christ suffered *willingly* and *according to God's good plan*. In this respect, it was by no means a defeat but rather Jesus' greatest triumph. Indeed, the heavens rejoiced and hell trembled when He cried out on the cross, "It is finished!" Christ's resurrection from the dead three days later confirms that God was pleased, and that the decisive victory over sin, death, and hell had been won.

Christ Alone

The uniqueness of Christ and His gospel must also be proclaimed. In the sixth "I am" statement in the Gospel of John, Jesus states emphatically "I am the way, and the truth, and the life; no one comes to the Father but through Me" (John 14:6). He teaches that there is only one way to God. Jesus is the only way to the Father because He is the truth of God and the life of God. There are not many gods, but one true and living God. There are not many ways to God, but one. Jesus goes on to say in verse 7 that to know God is to know Christ. That Jesus is God in flesh is stated repeatedly throughout John's gospel (e.g., 1:14; 5:10–23; 10:30; 20:28). Knowing God can only come by knowing Jesus Christ through faith.

The apostle Peter asserts the same truth when he states, "There is salvation in no one else; for there is no other name [than Jesus Christ] under heaven that has been given among men by which we must be saved" (Acts 4:12). All other "names" (i.e., gods and religions) must be forsaken. Peter reaffirms the exclusivity of salvation from sin through faith in the Lord Jesus Christ.

In the closing section of the Sermon on the Mount, Jesus says that there are two possible religious paths. First, the wide gate that insists that there is no single way to God. Although Jesus said there are "many who enter through it," it leads to hell, not heaven (Matt 7:13). On the other hand, entrance through the small gate is very exclusive and precise. Entrance through this gate is by God's grace alone through faith alone in the Lord Jesus Christ alone. It represents God's way of salvation that leads to salvation and eternal life (v. 14). Jesus said that the way is narrow "and there are few who find it" (v. 14). Salvation requires knowledge of the true gospel of Jesus Christ (Rom 10:13–16). This gospel contains the knowledge of the person and work of Jesus Christ for sinners (1 Cor 15:1–4). It demands the forsaking of all worship of false gods and an obedient following and worship of the one true God (Luke 24:46–48).

No Compromise

The apostle Paul and his missionary team repeatedly faced the idolatrous pagan worship of Gentile peoples throughout their missionary journeys (Acts 13–26). Neither Mesoamerica of the early 16th century nor Mexico of the 21st century could be any more similar to the indigenous peoples that Paul was called by God to evangelize. Immediately following his conversion on the Damascus road, Jesus said to him, "Go, for [you] are a chosen instrument of Mine, to bear My name before the Gentiles and kings and the sons of Israel" (Acts 9:15). When Paul later recounted his conversion, he said that Jesus was sending him to the Gentiles in order "to open their eyes so that they may turn from darkness to light and from the dominion of Satan to God, that they may receive forgiveness of sins" (Acts 26:18).

Satan blinds spiritually unregenerate people to spiritual truth (2 Cor 4:4). False religions are the usual vehicle of Satan's deception. Because unbelievers are spiritually blind and dead, they prefer the counterfeit over the genuine and are easily deceived into worshiping the false. This false worship is actually satanic worship (Rev 13:11–15). Evangelical Protestant Christian missionaries working in Mexico need to understand that both the Catholic syncretistic religion in Mexico as well as various pagan religions have no connection to true Christianity. There is only one biblical solution to this: faithfully proclaim the biblical Christ and His gospel without any syncretistic compromise.

Following Paul and Barnabas's proclamation of the gospel at Lystra, the local peoples raised their voices saying, "The gods have become like men and have come down to us." And they began calling Barnabas, Zeus, and Paul, Hermes" (Acts 14:11–12). This strange reaction by the people of Lystra to the healing of the lame man had its roots in local mythological beliefs and traditions. According to local tradition, the Greek gods Zeus and Hermes visited Lystra in disguise asking for food and lodging. Everyone turned them away with the exception of a local peasant and his wife. Zeus and Hermes then took vengeance by drowning everyone in a flood. The survivors converted the lowly peasant couple's house into a temple in honor of the Greek gods. This local religious myth led these people to believe that Barnabas was Zeus and Paul was Hermes.[37]

Here we have a clear example of the initial proclamation of the gospel of Jesus Christ to an idolatrous pagan people. The people in Lystra confused both the Christian message and miracle with their local pagan gods and traditions and began to worship the Christian messengers as Zeus and Hermes. If Paul and Barnabas had responded as did the early Spanish Catholic missionaries to the Mesoamerican Indians, they might have said, "Well, look, these people don't know the Christ of God, nor His power to save. But since it is apparent that they identify us and our message with their local gods and pagan traditions, let's fuse our message and our Christ with their gods and traditions. This will help them accept us, our God, our Christ, and our message; a syncretistic message will be more popular and easily accepted." This they refused to do.

As faithful messengers of the true Christ and His gospel, Barnabas and Paul understood what was going on, and so "rushed out into the crowd … saying, 'Men, why are you doing these things? We are also men of the same nature as you, and preach the gospel to you that you should turn from these vain things to a living God, who made the heaven and the earth and the sea and all that is in them" (Acts 14:14–15). In horror and revulsion, they exposed the local gods (Zeus and Hermes) as "vain things" (v. 15) and charged (not forced) the local people to "turn from" them. The gospel of the living God that they were proclaiming to them required nothing less than turning from idols and turning in faith to the one and only living God and His only Son. There is no confusion of message, no attempted fusion of antithetical religious systems, no syncretism—one God, one gospel, one Creator, one Son, one Savior. Everything else is vain. Turn. Repent.

---

37   John MacArthur, *The MacArthur Study Bible*, (Nashville, Tennessee: Nelson Bibles, 2006), 1625.

Believe. Faithful evangelism must call upon all people everywhere to repent of their sins and idolatry and follow the Lord Jesus Christ in obedience. It must avoid at all costs the fusing, or confusing, of local religious myths, gods, saints, virgins, and relics with the true Christ and His gospel.

Conclusion

Christ must not primarily be known as *sufferer* but as *Savior.* The precious salvation He offers is neither piecemeal nor is it mediated by priests and a sacramental system; it is free, instantaneous, unconditional, and eternal. The atonement of sins need not be accomplished by self-inflicted wounds, for it was Christ who was wounded for our transgressions (Isa 53:5 KJV). The tears of sorrow must be mixed with a triumphant joy in Christ's finished work. He is not a defeated man but the victorious Savior of mankind. He will never again suffer or taste death, and neither will those who belong to Him. It is not the Virgin of Guadalupe but Christ who has purchased for us our redemption. The saints and idols of religious systems accomplish nothing, but God gives eternal life to all who embrace Christ with empty hands of faith (Rom 3:21–25).

When God graciously opened Paul's eyes to the gospel of grace, he realized that religiosity could not save him. Even though he had more religious activities to boast about than anyone (Phil 3:4–6), by God's grace he counted his accomplishments and credentials as loss in exchange for the value of knowing the Lord Jesus Christ (v. 7). He denied his proud, self-righteous, external morality and religious rituals and ceremonies, and clung to the righteousness of God that comes through Christ by faith (v. 9). Paul exchanged his futile religiosity for a personal relationship with the Lord Jesus Christ. He exchanged his futile attempts to become righteous for the gift of Christ's righteousness that comes by faith alone (v.9). He exchanged everything he was *doing* for what Christ had already *done* in His death, burial, and resurrection (Rom 5:6–11). May the truth of God's Word instruct the church to rightly proclaim not only the suffering of Christ but also His saving work on behalf of sinful man. And may the people of Mexico come to worship with great zeal the risen and exalted God and Savior, Jesus Christ.

Suffering for Christ: Biblical Lessons from Chinese Saints

Roger Ng, John Zheng, and Andrew Cho

Grace Bible Seminary, Singapore/China

[Editor's Note: Though the subject is largely ignored in many systematic theologies, the reality of suffering has been a central theme in Christian teaching since the day our Lord Jesus Christ went up on the mountain and began to teach (cf. Matt 5:10–12). He warned that persecution would come as one of the necessary consequences of gospel life (Matt 10:16–25; Luke 21:12–19). Few are better equipped to speak on this subject than our dear brothers from China, who work on the front lines to proclaim Christ in that region and train Chinese pastors to do the same.]

Introduction

The passing of pastor Lee Tian En on May 3, 2016, marks the end of an era in Chinese Christianity. Pastor Lee was the last surviving member of a group of six influential church leaders, each of whom were imprisoned for at least ten years for the cause of Christ in China.[1] One of the authors of this essay met Pastor Lee in the summer of 2004, preaching together to a group of young college students in southern China. For a week, we spent night and day

---

[1]   The other five members were Wang Ming Dao, Watchman Nee, Yuan Xiang Cheng, Lin Xian Gao, and Xie Mo Shan.

preaching, resting, and fellowshipping together. There was not the slightest hint of bitterness in him. He recounted his imprisonment with joy and encouraged his listeners to share in the sufferings of Christ. His love for Christ and his desire to know Him was so evident that he seemed to embody Paul's own heart cry in Philippians—"For his sake I have suffered the loss of all things and count them as rubbish ... that I may know him and the power of his resurrection, and may share his sufferings, becoming like him in his death that by any means possible I may attain the resurrection from the dead" (3:8–11). It was astonishing to witness. How can a man who has suffered so greatly be so full of joy? Moreover, how can we experience this same victory over suffering? Though we cannot provide a comprehensive treatment here on the subject, it is the purpose of this essay to remind readers of the reality of suffering and to provide encouragement, by testimony and teaching, to rightly embrace it for Christ.

Pastor Lee was jailed four times totaling eighteen years[2] and escaped firing squad executions three times. He was first arrested on September 17, 1960, and sentenced to jail for ten years. It was during his second imprisonment that government official Fang Tian Cai pronounced his sentence of capital punishment by firing squad in June 1973. Pastor Lee was spared, however, because there was a widespread flooding, and all the officials were sent to help. The second pronouncement of execution by firing squad was in spring 1976, but there was a riot in the prison and he was spared again. The third sentence of execution came in the fall of 1976, but this time Chairman Mao Zedong passed away. Once again, Lee was spared. He summarized his experiences this way, "I was rescued [by the Lord] from the lion's mouth" (2 Tim 4:17). After the end of the Cultural Revolution,[3] he was released, and he went back to preach

---

[2]   Like most of the Chinese Christians who were imprisoned, Pastor Lee could have chosen to leave at any time. All he had to was recant his faith and renounce Jesus Christ. He then could have walked out a free man. Though that was an easy way out, he was determined never to betray his Lord. Many think that these suffering saints had no choice and were incarcerated against their wills, but they could have walked out of prison and avoided the persecution had they so desired, merely by saying the right words. Faithfulness to Christ, however, was paramount to them—and the price for Pastor Lee was eighteen years of his life.

[3]   This was Chairman Mao Zedong's efforts to preserve his own form of communism and stamp out any competing influences, such as Christianity. The movement was officially known as the Great Proletarian Cultural Revolution.

the Word boldly and fervently. Although Pastor Lee was imprisoned twice more, he continued fearlessly to teach, preach, and strengthen the church of Christ in China. The Lord took Pastor Lee home after a half-century of service, when Lee was eighty-eight years old. During Lee's memorial service, he was eulogized as a faithful witness of Jesus Christ and an example for all Christians.

Persecution in This Age

The church of Christ has been persecuted since its inception at Pentecost. The early church immediately experienced persecution from the Jewish authorities and later from the Romans.[4] Indeed, Christ himself has warned us that "If they persecuted me, they will also persecute you." (John 15:20). Paul also warns us that all who desire to live a godly life in Christ Jesus will be persecuted (2 Tim 3:12).[5] In fact, all Christians should expect persecution in this age and be prepared for it.[6] Paul urges Timothy to not be ashamed of the testimony about our Lord, but to share in suffering for the gospel by the power of God (2 Tim 1:8).

Persecution in China

Like the early church, the Chinese church has known persecution from its inception. When the first Protestant missionary to China, Robert Morrison, arrived in 1807, the Chinese government prevented any Chinese people from teaching their language to him (or other foreigners) under penalty of death.[7] When the Communists took control of China in 1949, the Chinese church faced its greatest per-

---

4   To see the purposes of suffering and persecution, see John MacArthur, *The Power of Suffering* (Colorado Springs, Colorado: David C. Cook, 2011), 121–136, and John Piper, "Why God Appoints Suffering for His Servants," in *Suffering and the Sovereignty of God*, eds. John Piper and Justin Taylor (Wheaton, Illinois: Crossway, 2006), 91–109.

5   To understand more about the mystery of God's sovereignty and suffering and evil see D. A. Carson, *How Long, O Lord?: Reflections on Suffering and Evil* (Grand Rapids, Michigan: Baker, 2006).

6   MacArthur states the importance of proper discipleship to prepare believers for hardship in *The Power of Suffering*, 111–22.

7   Martha Stockment, "Robert Morrison," Biographical Dictionary of Chinese Christianity, http://www.bdcconline.net/en/stories/m/morrison-robert.php.

secution in history. At that time, there were less than one million believers in China.[8] The Communists wanted to make China into what they saw as a utopia. This ambition necessitated the complete transformation of every aspect of the Chinese society, making it conform to Marxist thought. Any institution that contradicted Marxist philosophy and values was seen as a threat and was ruthlessly dismantled. This put the church directly in the government's crosshairs; the Communists began brutally and systematically persecuting the church to make it another political tool. During this time of extreme persecution, however, God protected the Chinese believers' faith and enabled them to endure the persecution. Like the early church, the Chinese church not only survived but thrived under persecution, growing both numerically and spiritually. Today, it is estimated that there are about 100 million Christians in China. According to one analyst, China will become the nation with the most Christians in the world by 2030.[9]

We see in the history of the early church, as well as in the history of the Chinese church, that suffering is a reality—and even a consequence of believing in Christ Jesus. It is precisely because we are united to Christ that we are persecuted and share in His sufferings. Christians must count the cost and expect that the same world that hated Jesus will also hate them. But Scripture does not tell believers to be resigned to suffering weakness and defeat; rather, Jesus Christ conquered the world and commands that His followers take heart. Jesus is able to guard His own to the end, and His words in Scripture give us many reasons for hope in the midst of the suffering. He has endowed His body, the church, with every resource to live godly lives, even in time of extreme persecution. A particularly powerful passage comes from 2 Timothy 1:8–14, wherein the Holy Spirit, through Paul, exhorts Timothy to embrace and endure extreme suffering for the sake of Christ; the same principle exhorts and enables all Christians to join Christ in overcoming the world.

---

[8] David Aikman, *Jesus in Beijing* (Washington DC: Regnery Publishing, 2003), 45.

[9] Brandon Showalter. http://www.christianpost.com/news/china-largest-christian-population-world-200-million-believers-despite-crackdown-166718/ (accessed September 22, 2016). The regenerating work of the Holy Spirit, of course, cannot be predicted by man, but it is worth pointing out that the world has taken notice of the explosive growth of Christianity in China in the midst of great persecution.

Reasons to Suffer for Christ

Paul wrote his second epistle to Timothy around AD 66.[10] Nero blamed a fire in Rome in AD 64 (which he likely started himself) on Christians. As a result, Christians in Rome faced brutal persecution, from torture to execution. Paul was caught up in this wave of persecution during his second Roman imprisonment.[11] He had successfully made his first defense, even though no one supported him (4:16–17). However, Paul expected to be martyred after his second defense (4:6, 18). The two purposes of the letter are to exhort Timothy to suffer with him for the sake of the gospel (1:8) and transmit the gospel to others (1:14, 2:2).[12] Paul encourages Timothy not to be ashamed of suffering, but to embrace it willingly—not that he was ashamed, but he needed this encouragement to stay strong.[13] In 1:9–14, Paul gives three reasons why Timothy should suffer with him for Christ so that Timothy will stay faithful to proclaim the gospel. These three reasons given to Timothy are also given to all Christians in times of suffering.

We Were Saved by Christ's Grace

The first reason to suffer for Christ is that He is our wonderful Savior. We were saved by Jesus Christ Himself, who gave us life, rescued us from hell, and paved the way for us to be adopted into the family of God. Second Timothy 1:9–11 teaches us that we are the beneficiaries and recipients of this great salvation only because of Jesus Christ our Lord. The clear implication is that we should be grateful for such a matchless blessing and great privilege. In verse 9, Paul reminds Timothy of God's love, which saves Timothy not by

---

[10] Most certainly, it occurred after the burning of Rome in AD 64 and before the death of Nero in AD 68 because Paul was martyred during the time of Nero. See Thomas D. Lea and Hayne P. Griffin, *1, 2 Timothy, Titus*, New American Commentary 34 (Nashville, Tennessee: Broadman & Holman, 1992), 41.

[11] His first imprisonment was very different. He was able to have people visit him without fear (Acts 28:30–31) and expected to be released (Philippians 2:24). See George W. Knight, *The Pastoral Epistles*, New International Greek Testament Commentary (Grand Rapids, Michigan: Eerdmans, 1992), 9.

[12] Knight, *Pastoral Epistles*, 11.

[13] The aorist tense suggests Timothy was not ashamed, but the possibility is there in the future, so Paul's exhortation is an attempt to preempt such shame. See Ralph Earle, "2 Timothy," in *Expositor's Bible Commentary*, vol. 11, ed. Frank E. Gaebelein (Grand Rapids, Michigan: Zondervan, 1981), 395.

his own actions, but through God's loving and free grace through His Son Jesus. God called us[14] and saved us not so that we would live however we want, but so that we would live for Christ. Thus, Paul reminds Timothy of this holy calling—to be faithful to God for the sake of His Son.[15] And Timothy was instructed to be faithful to God by being focused on the ultimate task that given to every Christian, which is to fulfill Christ's great commission in Matthew 28:18–20. Timothy was admonished to fulfill the great commission by fulfilling his calling to train faithful men and pass down the gospel to the next generation (2:2).

Paul was aware of God's calling to proclaim Christ as an apostle in order to fulfill the Great Commission. He identifies this in verse 11 as the reason he is suffering, saying he is willing to accept his duty and takes it seriously because he knows and loves his great and glorious salvation. For Paul, Jesus Christ is worth suffering and even dying for. With such love for his Master, Paul reflects great joy and thanksgiving in 1:3, even during this time of extreme suffering. He wrote to remind Timothy of this great Savior so that Timothy will also have the joy and determination to suffer for His sake.

In verse 10, Paul speaks of the greatness of the gospel in detail: it is great because in it, Jesus has abolished death and brought life and immortality to light through His death and resurrection. *Death* here refers to both physical and spiritual death since they are connected. Here Paul is referring to partly to spiritual death since he is contrasting death with spiritual life and immortality. Yet our physical death is the result and symptom of our spiritual death. [16] Jesus did abolish spiritual death on the cross, but He did not abolish physical death for believers, since all believers will still die until Jesus destroys physical death during His second coming (Rev 20:14). However, He did overcome His own physical death through His resurrection; therefore, His resurrection is the guarantee of believers' future resurrection. In

---

[14] This calling is effectual calling (Rom 8:30), not a general gospel calling. See Knight, *Pastoral Epistles*, 374.

[15] The dative case of κλήσει ἁγίᾳ (holy calling) can be dative of means or instrument (by a holy calling), meaning God saved Timothy by His holy calling because God is holy; or it can be dative of interest (for a holy calling), meaning God saved Timothy to a holy calling, which is to spread the gospel. Most likely both ideas are included because both are inseparable. See Knight, *Pastoral Epistles*, 374.

[16] See Knight, *Pastoral Epistles*, 376.

this sense, Jesus has abolished, or made ineffective,[17] physical death because believers are no longer enslaved in fear of physical death (Heb 2:14–15). Jesus didn't just abolish death through the gospel but gives believers life and immortality. The life that Jesus gives is spiritual life. Immortality refers to the continuation of spiritual life after physical death—another way of referring to eternal life.[18] The gospel is great to Timothy, and all Christians, because he has experienced that great spiritual life with God. This great eternal life is worth living and dying for because the life it gives will never die but is immortal. So Paul urges Timothy to be willing to suffer for Christ.

We Know Whom We Believe

Timothy can also suffer willingly and thankfully by knowing whom he has believed (2 Tim 1:12). Timothy believes in the great creator of the universe.[19] Many people die for foolish reasons, but the one whom Timothy believes is no less than the true, living God of this universe. In order to suffer willingly for the gospel, Timothy must be reminded of who God is and His attributes.

God sits on His throne in complete control of the world. Even though believers may suffer, God is no less sovereign. This is demonstrated by the fact that the gospel of Jesus was planned before time began, as Paul explains in 1:9.[20] The grace of salvation in Jesus Christ was not brought about spontaneously, as if God were shooting from His hip. God is not reacting to things He had not foreseen; He planned everything from the beginning. This concept is difficult to understand, but accepting it can grant us peace and assurance in times of extreme suffering. Paul was calm in the midst of the storm and even referred to himself principally as God's prisoner, not Rome's (1:8). Timothy and all Christians can endure suffering for Christ

---

[17] The Greek verb καταργήσαντος is best translated as making ineffective or nullify death, see John R. W. Stott, *Guard the Gospel the Message of 2 Timothy*, The Bible Speaks Today (Downers Grove, Illinois: InterVarsity Press, 1973), 37.

[18] See Knight, *Pastoral Epistles*, 376.

[19] The relative pronoun ᾧ in dative case is the object of the verb *believe*. The object is not specified but based on context it is most likely referring to God. Since emphasis has been laid on God and his power (cf. vv. 6, 7, 8), it is probable that the Father is in view here as well. See Knight, *Pastoral Epistles*, 378.

[20] Scholars agree that πρὸ χρόνων αἰωνίων is best translated as "before time eternal," meaning before time began. See Knight, *Pastoral Epistles*, 375.

because God is eternally sovereign and can be trusted. Trusting in the sovereign God is exactly what Paul urges Timothy to do, namely, by the pattern of his own faith.

In 2:13, Paul urges Timothy to follow his example of suffering by virtue of faith. Timothy must carry out his duties with love and faith that is found in Jesus alone.[21] Timothy (with all Christians) ought to be faithful and loving toward God even in suffering, believing that He is who He claims to be. God is a loyal, trustworthy, and intimate God. We are His children, and He is forever faithful to us. Paul knows God is faithful, and that encourages him to be faithful to God. That is one reason why Paul is willing to suffer for God. If he is not faithful to God, then his conscience will plague him. But he *is* faithful; there-fore, he can say in 1:3 that he serves God with a clear conscience. A clear conscience is so important to Paul that he would rather have a clear conscience and suffer than to have the reverse. Timothy and all Christians should willingly embrace suffering for Christ because of their desire to stay faithful and have a clear conscience before God. They know the God whom they believe. He is sovereign and faithful; therefore, we also ought to be faithful, especially in the midst of suffering.

One man who modeled such faithfulness is Moses Xie (or Xie Mo Shan).[22] Pastor Xie was born in 1918 and was converted when he was fourteen years old.[23] When the Communists took over China, he was the director of the Chinese Christian Mission in Shanghai. The government tried to force him to join the Three Self Patriotic Movement, but he refused and was jailed three times for a total of over twenty-three years. Once he was handcuffed for 133 days straight.[24] The handcuffs cut through his skin into the bone. His hair

---

[21] ἐν Χριστῷ Ἰησοῦ refers to the sphere and the manner by which Timothy must suffer. He must suffer for the gospel with love and faith. These two characteristics are found in Jesus. See Knight, *Pastoral Epistles*, 381.

[22] He is another of the faithful six mentioned in the introduction together with Pastor Lee. One of the authors of this essay visited Pastor Xie in his tiny Beijing apartment in 2006. I was there to seek his advice on how I could serve the churches in China, and he humbly recounted his personal experiences for me and what he thought to be the most desperate need of the churches in China at that time.

[23] Aikman, *Jesus in Beijing*, 65.

[24] Ibid., 66.

was ripped out, and he was beaten. Every day, the guards tried to force him to reject Jesus, but he stayed faithful without compromise. During his first imprisonment, he was so brutally tortured that Xie tried but failed to kill himself by electrocution. It was at that time that he recalled what God said in 2 Corinthians 12:9—"My grace is sufficient for you." His faith in God's sovereignty and sufficiency strengthened him to overcome persecution. From then onward he learned to rely on God and was able to endure the pain until his release in 1975. Xie's suffering mirrored that of the Apostle Paul who said he despaired of life itself so that he would learn to trust God who raises the dead (2 Cor 1:8–9). After Xie was released, he was filled not with hatred or regret, but the love of Jesus. His love testifies to his great character and his zeal to be like Christ. His favorite verse was Philippians 1:21—"For to me, to live is Christ, and to die is gain." He continued to serve the Lord after he was released from prison, until his death in 2011 at the age of ninety-three.

We Know God's Power

A third reason that Timothy, and all Christians, should be willing to suffer for Christ is that we know that God is powerful and able to guard the gospel He entrusted to us (2 Tim 1:12).[25] Paul's encouragement to Timothy is that the God who has preserved the gospel during his own ministry will continue to do so in Timothy's ministry as well.[26] Therefore, Timothy should not fear suffering for the gospel's

---

[25] The meaning of the genitive παραθήκην μου is difficult to determine. There are two views. The first is that this is an objective genitive, which would mean God is able to guard the deposit that he has entrusted to Paul. This deposit would be the gospel. The second view is that it is subjective genitive, which means God is able to guard the deposit that Paul has entrusted to God. This deposit would be Paul's life. The first view can be supported because the word παραθήκην occurs only twice elsewhere in the NT, in 1 Timothy 6:20 and 2 Timothy 2:14. Both places refer to the gospel. Also, the genitive pronoun generally indicates the original owner of the deposit (see Knight, *The Pastoral Epistles,* 379; and Philip H. Towner, *The Letters to Timothy and Titus*, The New International Commentary on the New Testament [Grand Rapids, Michigan: Eerdmans, 2006], 476). The word signifies something deposited with a person to be kept undamaged and unused and returned to the owner, usually while he is absent on a journey. The thought is that whatever happens to Paul personally, God will continue to guard the gospel that he hands over to Timothy. In view of the way in which it is called "the good deposit" in v. 14, the reference must be to the gospel. See I. Howard Marshall and Philip H. Towner, *A Critical and Exegetical Commentary on the Pastoral Epistles*, International Critical Commentary (London: T&T Clark, 2004), 711.

[26] This interpretation fits in better with the thought in the immediate context (1:14; 2:2; cf. 1 Tim 6:20), and a shift in the use of the metaphor is unlikely. See Marshall and Towner,

sake, knowing that the victory is assured. This explains Paul's subsequent commands for Timothy to hold fast to the truth in 1:13–14.[27] In the face of suffering, there is always the temptation for believers to be cowardly and avoid suffering; therefore, it is necessary for Paul to remind Timothy of God's protective power.

Paul also reminds Christians in Romans 8:35 of God's power, when he asks rhetorically who could possibly separate us from God's love: could tribulation, distress, persecution, famine, nakedness, danger, or sword? The obvious answer is that none of these things or any other form of suffering can separate us from the love of God. Likewise, in 2 Timothy 2:14, Paul exhorts Timothy to guard the deposit of the gospel by the power of the Holy Spirit. The Holy Spirit is able to give us new spiritual life and protect it unto eternity. Success in suffering is not ultimate deliverance from suffering and death; instead it is being faithful to God, even until death, by God's power.

The main theme of 2 Timothy 1:8–14 is exhortation for Timothy, and by extension all Christians, to willingly suffer *for* Christ because we were saved *by* Christ, and because we know God and His sovereign power to guard us and the gospel in us. With such truths, Paul expects Timothy and all Christians to live lives of love and faith even in the midst of suffering (1:13–14) so that they will be effective in proclaiming the gospel of Jesus Christ.

Although He Died, His Faith Still Speaks

Years before Lee Tian En and Moses Xie, another Chinese Christian leader, Wang Ming Dao, exemplified these truths. *Christian History Magazine* called Pastor Wang the most influential and respected Chinese Christian leader of the twentieth century.[28] He was born in 1900 in Beijing during the Boxer Rebellion.[29] His mother named him "Tie-zi," which means "Iron," which was very fitting

---

Pastoral Epistles, 711.

[27] The command takes up the theme of the "deposit" that Paul is passing on to him and which was foreshadowed in 2 Tim 1:12. See Marshall and Towner, *Pastoral Epistles,* 712.

[28] https://www.christianhistoryinstitute.org/magazine/article/no-compromise/

[29] Lian Xi, *Redeemed by Fire: The Rise of Popular Christianity in Modern China* (New Haven, Connecticut: Yale University Press, 2010), 111.

because of his strong personality and courageous life. He became a Christian at the age of fourteen and, after serious spiritual struggles, gave himself to be a minister of the gospel at the age of eighteen.[30] In 1920, he changed his name to Ming Dao, which means "understanding the Word," and read the Bible six times in sixty-two days.[31] At the outset of his Christian life and ministry, Wang had a passion to live a godly life according to the pattern of Christ. At that time, such a pursuit of righteousness was not popular, and he often encountered opposition and derision from society and the church. He believed that man was justified by faith but that the integrity of the believer is the fruit of a sanctified life. Wang boldly taught that all kinds of sinful practices in society had their exact counterparts in the church. He preached powerfully and attacked the worldliness of Christians and the apostasy of the churches.

He was also a strong opponent of theological liberalism, which gained popularity in China after the 1920s. These theologians were preaching an earthly kingdom of God that would be established through human effort, but Wang was adamant that society would only be changed through the proclamation of the gospel and the Holy Spirit bringing people to life. The central doctrine of his theology was regeneration in Christ, upon which Christianity stands or falls.

When the Communists came to power in 1949, all foreign missionaries were forced out of China because the government wanted to eradicate "imperialism." The churches were placed under the authority of Three Self Patriotic Movement (TSPM), which was supported by the Communist Party. However, Wang took a firm stance against any form of political involvement, believing that church and state should be separated and that Christians should not be "yoked together with unbelievers."[32] Wang stood for the purity of the gospel.

Around midnight of August 7th, 1955, Wang, his wife, and eighteen young Christians were arrested at gunpoint, tied up with

---

[30] Biographical Dictionary of Chinese Christianity. http://www.bdcconline.net/en/stories/w/wang-mingdao.php.

[31] Wang's personal name was "Yong-shung" until 1920, when he submitted his life to God and formally changed his name to "Ming Dao." *Wang Ming Dao, A Stone Made Smooth* (Littleton, Colorado: OMF Books, 1982), 49.

[32] Wang, *Stone Made Smooth*, 216.

ropes, and taken to prison for refusing to join the TSPM.[33] To the Communists, Wang Ming Dao's refusal to join the TSPM was a counterrevolutionary act, the worst of crimes. The TSPM-controlled magazine *Tianfeng* branded Pastor Wang "a criminal among the Chinese people, a criminal in the church, and a criminal in history." He was sentenced to fifteen years in prison for what was called "resistance to the government."

After being confined to prison for some time, he broke down and signed a confession making a humiliating plea for mercy and promising to participate in the TSPM.[34] Though Wang was allowed to leave prison, his conscience would not let him go. He likened himself to the Apostle Peter who had denied Christ three times. When he could take it no longer, he and his wife went to the government voluntarily in 1963 to rescind their previous confessions. They were immediately sentenced to life imprisonment.[35]

After the United States reestablished diplomatic relations with China in 1972, human rights organizations began to pressure China to release its political prisoners. However, when the Chinese government attempted to release Pastor Wang in 1979, he, like Paul (see Acts 16) refused to leave until his name had been cleared by the government. In Wang's words, "I was not released but ... forced out of the prison by deception."[36]

By the time Wang came out of prison, he was toothless and nearly blind and deaf. In spite of his health, he continued to serve the Lord for another twenty years until he died on July 28, 1991. Wang Ming Dao's example of faithfulness and absolute loyalty to Christ is another great example for all Christians who would ever suffer for the cause of Christ. And, as the author of the book of Hebrews says, "Though he died, his faith still speaks" (see Heb 11:4).

---

[33] Xi, *Redeemed by Fire*, 200–01

[34] Thomas A. Harvey, *Acquainted With Grief* (Grand Rapids, Michigan: Brazos, 2002), 122. Among other things, Wang was forced to confess that he had made personal attacks on Wu Yiaozong, the founder of the Three-Self movement under the direction of the Communist government, by calling Wu a modernist, an unbeliever, and a false prophet.

[35] Harvey, *Acquainted With Grief*, 98–99.

[36] Stephen Wang, *The Long Road to Freedom: The Story of Wang Mingdao* (Lancaster, UK: Sovereign World, 2002), 205–210.

Conclusion

May 3, 2016, marked the end of an era of Chinese Christianity with the passing of Lee Tian En, but his example and that of the other saints who suffered for Christ in China will live on. The way Christians live in this world should testify to the infinite value of our Lord Jesus Christ. Is He worthy to follow? Moreover, is He worthy of suffering on account of His name? Scripture abundantly testifies that He is worth suffering for, and it provides all the encouragement necessary to endure suffering for Christ's sake. He is our wonderful Savior, our blessed Lord, and our gracious King. Scripture also reminds us that God is sovereign. If He ordains that the church be persecuted for righteousness sake, we can trust that He always does what is right for His own glory and the good of those He loves. Both the saints of our modern era and the saints of old testify to the blessedness of suffering for the sake of Christ. As the Scriptures say:

> Since we are surrounded by so great a cloud of witnesses, let us also lay aside every weight, and sin which clings so closely, and let us run with endurance the race that is set before us, looking to Jesus, the founder and perfecter of our faith, who for the joy that was set before him endured the cross, despising the shame, and is seated at the right hand of the throne of God" (Heb 12:1–2).

May He be honored in all that we do, even in the midst of suffering, and even when persecution comes as a result of the gospel impact in our own lives.

Is Justification a Pronouncement or a Process? A Critique of Eastern Orthodox Soteriology

Alexey Kolomiytsev

Word of Grace Bible Institute, USA (Russian Language)

[Editor's Note: Many of the pastors and church leaders that TMAI trains come from regions of the world where Eastern Orthodoxy predominates. Unfortunately, there is relatively little interaction with Eastern Orthodoxy from a Protestant perspective. This essay not only provides a necessary critique of Eastern Orthodoxy's understanding of salvation but it also aims to challenge every reader to believe in the extraordinary grace that is found in Christ Jesus alone.]

Introduction

The great treasure of the church is not her architecture, history, or heritage, but the gospel of Jesus Christ, carried about in jars of clay. This gospel—good tidings of great joy for all people—is the announcement that God has done for us in Christ Jesus that which we could never do for ourselves. It is the good news of the great exchange offered to all by faith: our sin for Christ's righteousness. The apostle Paul put it simply: "He [God] made Him who knew no sin [Christ] to be sin on our behalf, so that we might become the righteousness of God in Him" (2 Cor 5:21). Protestants have always believed that our salvation depends on what Christ has accomplished for us; but this precious truth, this great treasure of the church, is constantly under attack. It comes under attack in many ways, some overt and others subtle. The bottom line is this: anything man hopes to contribute to what Christ has already secured is a major departure from the good news of great joy and a deadly usurpation of Christ's exclusive glory as our God and Savior.

One imminent threat to the gospel that receives far too little attention in the West is Eastern Orthodoxy. Of all the Christian[1] traditions, it is perhaps the most ignored by evangelicals today. Because of this general unawareness, opportunities for evangelism are missed, and certain Orthodox[2] tendencies go unchecked even as they encroach into our churches. The goal of this essay, then, is to shed some light on the soteriological[3] beliefs of Eastern Orthodoxy, focusing specifically on their view of justification. Hopefully, it will help believers recognize that Protestantism and Orthodoxy maintain very different beliefs about salvation. For missionaries who serve in Orthodox contexts, and for anyone whose families or friends come from such a background, it is critical to understand some of the unsound and even dangerous doctrines held by many of this tradition's adherents. In this way, the truth of Jesus Christ and His gospel might be administered where it is needed most. Moreover, there is an increasing trend in the West to borrow concepts from the East, and a variety of Orthodox tendencies are starting to proliferate even within evangelical churches. For this reason, too, it is all the more important to inoculate ourselves and our churches against them. Much more is at stake than some are willing to admit;[4] and the time has come to heed Jesus' warning that many who profess to know Christ will, on the last day, be turned away by Him. As Paul soberly warns, "If anyone is preaching to you a gospel contrary to the one you received,

---

[1]   The word "Christian" is used here in its broadest, historical sense.

[2]   When capitalized, "Orthodox" refers to the Eastern Orthodox Church, not to *orthodoxy* (right belief).

[3]   Soteriology is the doctrine or study of salvation. It comes from the Greek root *soter*, meaning salvation.

[4]   For a variety of views, see *Three Views on Eastern Orthodoxy and Evangelicalism*, Stanley N. Gundry and James J. Stamoolis, eds., (Grand Rapids, Michigan: Zondervan, 2004).

let him be accursed" (Gal 1:9). Implicit in his admonition is the fact that there is only one gospel unto salvation. The question, then, is whether or not Eastern Orthodoxy teaches it.

What Does Eastern Orthodoxy Teach?

Many works have been written by Orthodox theologians on the issue of salvation; however, because of the general lack of systematization and the mystical nature of Eastern Orthodoxy, most of these works are written without a clear delineation of dogma and in nonlinear fashion.[5] This makes it difficult to get a comprehensive picture of *any* aspect of Orthodox theology, let alone one as highly nuanced as soteriology. For this reason, the following discussion focuses primarily on Sergius Stragorodsky's magisterial work, *Orthodox Teaching about Salvation,*[6] which is one of the best extant presentations of an Eastern Orthodox perspective on salvation.

Defined Negatively: What Orthodoxy Does Not Believe

Stragorodsky understands that a church's dogma may be positively and negatively defined. For example, the early church described the union of the two natures of Christ largely by what it *does not* mean, that is, the two natures cannot be confused, changed, divided, or separated. Likewise, central to Stragorodsky's presentation of Orthodox teaching about salvation is a lengthy discussion explaining what Orthodoxy does not believe, providing rationale for why the legal/judicial approach to soteriology (as seen in Roman

---

[5]   Representing this position, Vladimir Lossky writes, "We must live the dogma expressing a revealed truth, which appears to us as an unfathomable mystery, in such a fashion that instead of assimilating the mystery to our mode of understanding, we should, on the contrary, look for a profound change, an inner transformation of spirit, enabling us to experience it mystically... . theology is an expression, for the profit of all, of that which can be experienced by everyone." Lossky, *Mystical Theology of the Eastern Church* (London: James Clarke & Co., 1957), 8–9.

[6]   Sergius Stragorodsky, *Православное учение о спасении* [*Orthodox Teaching about Salvation*], (Sergiyev Posad, 1895). Stragorodsky was the 12th Patriarch of Moscow and the de facto head of the Russian Orthodox Church. Stragorodsky had initially written this work as a thesis for his master of theology degree, which was later adapted into book format. It is in Russian; all quotes used in this essay have been translated into English by the essay author.

Catholicism and Protestantism) is misguided.[7] In his mind, this is clearly a major dividing line between the East and the West. In order to propound exactly what Orthodoxy teaches, then, he must contrast it with the Western error, which comprehends justification as a legal declaration on the merit of Christ rather than a process of moral improvement. Reflecting beliefs common to many Eastern Orthodox thinkers, he argues that: (1) there are insurmountable historical and theological problems involved with this judicial approach to salvation, and (2) such an approach contradicts the testimony of conscience and religious experience. It will help us understand where Stragorodsky (and other Orthodox theologians) come from by briefly sketching his own arguments, to which we may respond later.

Apparent Historical and Theological Problems

Stragorodsky contends that the Western churches adopted a forensic model of salvation because the well-developed legal system in Roman society governed their way of thinking. This system, he argues, had become so deeply rooted in the Western way of life that it exercised an inevitable influence amongst the Christian churches there. He writes:

> Christianity from the very first steps of its existence had to deal with Rome taking into account the spirit and mentality of Roman society. Old Rome is justly considered as carrier of the law. Law ... was the foundation of their personal life. It determined all their relations within the family, society and state. Religion was not an exception—it was one of the spheres where the system of law was applied. Becoming a Christian, a citizen of Rome attempted to understand Christianity from this side, seeking to find its judicial meaning.[8]

---

[7] The judicial nature of justification relates to a forensic declaration of righteousness, which effects a change in one's legal status before God, rather than a process whereby a person actually becomes righteous.

[8] *Православное учение*, 15.

His logic is simple: Christianity was spreading throughout the Roman world, where the well-developed legal system played an important role in the life of all people. This attitude toward civil justice in society was transferred to religious life, which formulated their theological view of salvation. This forensic view of justification, he argues, is not just a minor mistake of the West, but a key element that ruined all the theological thinking of the Roman Catholic and later Protestant churches.

Stragorodsky insists that the forensic view of justification is not just an incorrect one, but that it is also very dangerous. From his point of view, Western soteriology deals only with the *legal status* of man and not with his real, *moral* condition. If one were to assume that man is justified by an outside source in a judicial sense, then any moral change within him, it is argued, becomes absolutely unnecessary. Western concentration on the status of being *declared* righteous before God, instead of on a real-life, *inherent* righteousness, makes, for Stragorodsky, the whole Christian experience fraudulent. If people consider themselves justified before God, when in reality their inner being has not been transformed and when they are not exercising godliness that can be expressed in good works, then they are just cheating themselves, thinking that they are saved while in reality they are not.[9] He views the moral and judicial aspects of salvation as mutually exclusive, writing, "Moral union demands moral conformity, which penetrates the holiest area of a man's conscience with its rules and demands. In contrast, legal order does not penetrate the inner man... ."[10] The concern is that the Western views of justification breed, and cannot be divorced from, antinomianism (*lit.* "against law").

---

[9]   This reflects a subtle misunderstanding of Western soteriology. Protestants would not necessarily disagree with his critique at this point, although terminology would be understood differently. For Eastern Orthodoxy, a man's righteousness before God is *his own* inherent righteousness, expressed by good works; for the Protestant believer, however, a man's righteousness before God is *Christ's* perfect righteousness. Protestants agree with Stragorodsky that there cannot be true justification apart from a real, inner transformation. We *disagree* that such transformation occurs from within; rather, we define it is an act of God's sovereign pleasure in granting new life, defined as *regeneration*, which is inevitably expressed throughout life in a believer's progressive sanctification. Protestants affirm justification, sanctification, and glorification as distinct-yet-inseparable elements of union with Christ.

[10]   *Православное учение*, 17.

Stragorodsky understands both Roman Catholicism and Protestantism to be wrong due to their conception of salvation as a legal transaction rather than a moral transformation of the soul. Eastern Orthodox theologians often point out that all other views of salvation deal with external matters, whether it be declaring man righteous based on the merits of Christ alone (Protestantism), or declaring him righteous based on the merits of Christ and the external works of man (Roman Catholicism). Any attempt to connect imputed righteousness with the internal process of moral transformation of the soul is considered a useless addition, since it is not the person himself whose righteousness is in view. Thus, both Roman Catholics and Protestants are viewed to be in grave error, for they consider justification in one degree or another to be an external recognition of righteousness apart from any inner transformation.

Apparent Contradictions with Conscience and Experience

According to Stragorodsky, the voice of conscience and religious experience is another argument in favor of Orthodoxy. He believes that man's soul in its best part always seeks true life and salvation, and therefore, it can never be satisfied with forensic justification, which he views as merely an external proclamation of righteousness unrelated to inner godliness or goodness.[11] This, he asserts, finds confirmation in the religious experience of all believers. He writes, "Spiritual experience and tradition in one voice are saying that good works are necessary not just as a result, but as a condition of salvation."[12] The Protestant doctrine that good works are the necessary result of imputed righteousness, he contends, contradicts the very nature of justification apart from works.[13] He believes that it is a commonsense truth that a saint or a holy person should really *be*

---

[11] *Православное учение*, 20.

[12] Ibid, 38.

[13] There are some Evangelical voices that have recently agreed with Stragorodsky's contention here, underlining the need for clarity on this point. Evangelical leader Zane Hodges also argues that it contradicts the Protestant doctrine of justification by faith alone to posit that good works necessarily result from saving faith. See Zane Hodges, *Absolutely Free!* (Dallas, Texas: Redencion Viva, 1989), 167. We reject this position, as well as its counterpart in Eastern Orthodoxy. There is nothing inherently contradictory in holding that a person is justified by faith alone, apart from works, while also holding that every person who is justified bears fruit.

holy, not just be *declared* holy. If good works of the heart[14] are not a prerequisite of salvation, he argues, then salvation becomes a mere external declaration of righteousness that does not reflect the reality of the condition of a man's heart.

Orthodox Position: The Moral Approach

According to Eastern Orthodoxy, true salvation must be rooted in the inner moral change of man, which is wrought through a process of achieving God-likeness.[15] Instead of seeking external justification, man must work hard on the transformation of his inner being, starting from the seminal "good" that resides in everyone, and trusting that the grace of Christ would provide all the necessary help in the process. The Spirit's work in the heart of man and His indwelling presence is not the *starting point* but rather the *end* of salvation, according to Orthodox theologians. Vladimir Lossky adds his voice to Stragorodsky, writing, "the end of the Christian life is the acquiring of the Holy Spirit. As for fasts, vigils, prayers, alms, and other good works done in the name of Christ—*these are the means whereby we acquire the Holy Spirit*" (emphasis added).[16] Since the Spirit of God is the end and not the beginning of Christian (i.e., spiritual) life, just how then do Orthodox theologians understand it to begin? Lossky answers, "The beginning of the spiritual life is conversion (Greek: *epistrophe*), … an attitude of the will turning toward God and renouncing the world."[17] He continues, "The heart is the centre of the human being … and *the point from which the whole of the spiritual life proceeds*" (emphasis added). On this point he follows the ascetic tradition of the Christian East, particularly St. Macarius of Egypt, who taught that the heart is the realm of man in which "God, the angels, life and the Kingdom, light and the apostles, and the treasures of grace are to be found."[18]

---

[14]   When speaking about good works, Stragorodsky always has in mind not just external acts, but sincere works of the heart, which are motivated by a desire to be God-like.

[15]   The idea of becoming God-like, or *theosis*, plays a major role in Eastern Orthodox theology. It is well presented by Christoforus Stavropoulos, "Partakers of Divine Nature," in *Eastern Orthodox Theology, A Contemporary Reader,* Daniel B. Clendenin, ed., (Grand Rapids, Michigan: Baker Books, 1995), 183–192.

[16]   Lossky, *The Mystical Theology of the Eastern Church*, 196–97.

[17]   Ibid., 199.

[18]   Ibid., 201. Cited from Hom. Spirit, XV, 32, *Patrologia Graeca*, vol. 34, 597 B.

Spiritual life proceeds from the heart of man and culminates in the acquisition of the Holy Spirit. This is achieved, it is argued, by the means of moral transformation and good works done in the name of Christ. Both justification and regeneration, for Orthodox theologians, are processes. As Stragorodsky writes, "Eternal life, therefore, is not something that happens but rather gradually grows in the man."[19] This is why, he explains, the Holy Scriptures and the works of the church fathers reflect a "constant desire to convince man to work out his salvation, because without self-efforts no one can be saved."[20]

The Eastern tradition has always promoted an indivisible bond in the synergy of divine grace and human freedom. Since the process of salvation concentrates on making man righteous, and not just proclaiming him such, it must involve his full, self-determining cooperation. If this were to be done against or apart from his own self-determination, it is argued, then he could not truly be righteous. Therefore, the only way for man to be saved lies in his conscientious self-efforts, which, with help from God, will eventually make him holy. This reasoning leads Orthodox theologians to reject the possibility of the substitutional nature of salvation. Since true holiness must be built on the innate moral goodness of the person, it requires his autonomous rejection of evil and embrace of good. This alone, it is argued, can make man God-like and thus holy and righteous. The merit of Christ is not needed for this. Stragorodsky writes:

> Holiness, if it were just an involuntary gift, would lose its moral character and be turned into an indifferent condition of the heart. It is not possible 'to be good by necessity.' Therefore, it is not right to understand salvation as an act that is being imputed to him from the outside, or as a supernatural change that happens in a man without the participation of his freedom.[21]

---

[19] *Православное учение*, 114.

[20] Ibid., 159–160. In arguing that it is impossible to "be good by necessity," he apparently overlooks the fact that God Himself is good by necessity and *cannot* sin.

[21] Ibid., 160.

He goes on:

> Every good work, which is being done in man, every
> bit of his moral growth, every turn that happens in
> his soul, is being done not outside of his conscience
> and freedom. It is not somebody else, but he who
> is changing himself, transforming the old into the
> new. Salvation cannot merely be an external-judicial
> event. It should be a moral act, and this supposes as
> an inevitable condition that man himself is accom-
> plishing this act, although with the help of grace.[22]

The point at which Stragorodsky is most emphatic is that man
changes *himself.* He is adamant that it must be man, not someone else
(i.e., God), who decisively effects the change, though he always con-
cedes that God's grace may in some way help. Because moral transformation is understood as a prerequisite to stand rightly before God,
Orthodox theologians reject the notion of Christ's imputed righteousness and substitutionary atonement, thus making personal human
efforts virtually the sole basis for salvation. This is why we recognize
that much is at stake; and it is why we turn now to a biblical critique
of Orthodox soteriology.

Evaluation of Eastern Orthodox Soteriology

Both Lossky and Stragorodsky agree that it is possible for man in
his natural state to begin the process of salvation by his own self-determining volition—indeed, that spiritual life originates and proceeds
from man's own heart!—though both concede the process requires
the help of grace along the way. Stragorodsky writes:

> The essence of baptism and the sacrament of repen-
> tance is in the radical change that is being completed
> in a man's soul.... . Man used to be a slave of sin,
> was carrying out the desires of the devil, and was an
> enemy of God, but now he decides to stop sinning

---

[22] Ibid., 161–62.

and get into fellowship with the Holy Lord. This decision, of course, is an act of man's freedom, but it is being completed in man's soul only in cooperation with and help from grace, which is being transferred to him through the sacraments.[23]

This quote presents a good overview of Eastern Orthodox soteriology. According to Stragorodsky, man is an enemy of God, who at some point decides to be God's friend. With this new desire for fellowship, he turns to the Eastern Orthodox Church, which provides him access to God's grace (through their sacraments) to help him along the way toward salvation. This highlights the first major problem with Orthodox soteriology: it is entirely man-centered, misunderstanding the nature of man, his sinful depravity, and his helpless condition.

Salvation Rooted in God, Not Man

Orthodox theologians speak of a "seminal good" in every man; they believe that spiritual life begins within man's heart, and they assert that man decides to do good and changes *himself*. These notions must be adamantly rejected on biblical authority. The Bible describes man as dead in his trespasses and sins (Eph 2:1–2). God warned Adam that this would happen if he sinned, and the warning was clear, expressed with the strong statement: "You will surely die" (Gen 2:17). It is the first mention of death in the Bible, but it is not the last. The apostle Paul, in Romans 6:23, recalls this tragic event, writing that "the wages of sin is death." Ephesians 2:1–8 is one of the clearest passages in Scripture, teaching that without God's grace, sinful man is incapable of generating any good. The very essence of Adam's sin was an attempt to gain independence from God and put himself at the center. Man's selfishness became the primary element of his fallen nature. This selfish nature does not seek God; indeed, no one does (Rom 3:10–12)! The self-centeredness of fallen man is simply incompatible with any inherent desire to acknowledge God as Master and Lord. It is not within his nature for a fallen man to desire God and to seek His fellowship. Even as fallen man is shown by the

---

[23] *Православное учение*, 169.

sheer power of general revelation that God exists, he does everything possible to suppress this truth in unrighteousness (Rom 1:18). This is why Jesus taught about the absolute necessity that man must be born again (John 3:5). This birth, it should be noted, is "not of blood nor of the will of the flesh nor of the will of man, but of God" (John 1:13). Salvation is not, cannot, and could not ever be of man.

It is necessary, according to the Scriptures, that a force outside of man break in and revive his soul, resurrect him from the dead, and enable him to respond to God. This truth is further demonstrated in the Old Testament history of God's relationship with Israel. Jeremiah 31:31–33 explains it this way:

> "Behold, days are coming," declares the LORD, "when I will make a new covenant with the house of Israel and with the house of Judah, not like the covenant which I made with their fathers in the day I took them by the hand to bring them out of the land of Egypt, My covenant which they broke, although I was a husband to them," declares the LORD. "But this is the covenant which I will make with the house of Israel after those days," declares the LORD, "I will put My law within them and on their heart I will write it; and I will be their God, and they shall be My people."

The history of God's first covenant with Israel shows that when it depended upon people, they failed, breaking it. In this passage, though, God announces the coming of a new covenant, which will differ from the old one in that *God* will make a change within man's heart. The text indicates that He will take the initiative and change man's inner being, making him capable of having fellowship with Him. This proclamation is repeated in several other passages of the Old Testament (e.g., Jer 32:40; Ezek 11:19), and was clearly presented in the New Testament in fulfillment of those prophetic words (cf. Heb 10:16). As mentioned above, Jesus presented salvation in terms of a second birth (John 3:5), which is initiated by the Father (John 6:44). Paul likewise, in a number of passages declares that salvation is God's work in man's heart (e.g., Rom 2:4; 2 Tim 2:25).

The overwhelming testimony of Scripture is that salvation cannot be generated by fallen man but must come from God.

Justification Rightly Understood in Legal Terms

Contrary to the claims of Eastern Orthodox theologians, the judicial aspects of salvation do not originate from the political systems of the West but from the very pages of Scripture itself. It is true, as Stragorodsky proposes, that salvation supposes man's moral transformation in righteousness. In biblical terminology, "righteousness" certainly has an ethical domain, which relates to man's imperfect pursuit of God's righteous standard, but it is also true that many biblical texts speak of righteousness in terms of a legal transaction. As R. Harris notes, "The forensic aspect of *tsedek* [righteousness] applies to the equality of all, rich and poor, before the law. The righteous one, the *tsadik*, is not to be put to death (Exod 23:7) for the law does not condemn him."[24] In fact, the legal understanding of a person being declared right permeates the Old Testament, and provides the foundation for our understanding of salvation in terms of the New.

Judges in the Old Testament are not said to *make* people guilty or innocent; rather, they *declare* them guilty or innocent. Deuteronomy 25:1 reads, "When people have a dispute, they are to take it to court and the judges will decide the case, acquitting the innocent and condemning the guilty." A good judge decides a case by identifying whether the accused is guilty or innocent, and then legally declaring him so. He does not make a person innocent or guilty of a crime; he merely makes a legal decision with legal ramifications. The same is true even for bad judges. Bad judges in the Old Testament are described as those "who acquit the guilty for a bribe, and deprive the innocent of his right" (Isa 5:23). Though the innocent man may be unjustly *declared* to be guilty by an evil judge, he is not *made* inwardly guilty of any crime.[25]

---

[24] R. L. Harris, "Tsedek" in *Theological Wordbook of the Old Testament*, R. L. Harris, G.L. Archer, and B.K. Waltke, eds., (Chicago, Illinois: Moody Press, 1999, c1980), 753.

[25] There are many other OT texts that establish a foundation for the legal aspects of salvation, especially in Job (9:2, 15, 20; 10:15; 11:2; 13:18; 25:4; 40:8) and the prophets (Isa 41:26; 43:26; Jer 12:1). For a fuller discussion on this, see Thomas Schreiner, *Faith Alone*, (Grand Rapids, Michigan: Zondervan, 2015), 158–169.

This is apparent throughout the New Testament in relation to our salvation. Paul argues, for example, that "Abraham believed God, and it was counted to him as righteousness" (Rom 4:3). The Greek word for "count" speaks of a determination or a reckoning. It is the same word used in 1 Corinthians 13:5, wherein love is said to "keep no record of wrongs" (NIV), or which "does not take into account a wrong suffered" (NASB). It is not that wrongs do not exist in actuality, but that love does not *count* them against a person.[26] This idea of love, of course, stems from the love of God, "who justifies the ungodly" by faith (Rom 4:5). Paul continues his argument by quoting David, from Psalm 32:1–2: "Blessed is the one whose transgression is forgiven, whose sin is covered. Blessed is the man against whom the Lord *counts* no iniquity, and in whose spirit there is no deceit" (emphasis added). The idea here is not primarily ethical but forensic. As Schreiner says, "if righteousness is reckoned to sinners, to those who have failed to do what God commands, then it seems that the term designates a status before God instead of describing the transformation of the human being."[27] Sinners are "counted," "credited," or "declared" as righteous, not because of what they have done, but because of what Jesus Christ has accomplished on their behalf.

Righteousness Credited through Faith in Christ

As documented above, Stragorodsky, Lossky, and other Orthodox theologians unambiguously teach that the righteousness of God is achieved by man through works rather than being imputed by God through faith. This is the treacherous lie upon which every form of religious moralism exists today. It was precisely this lie that had infected the medieval Roman Catholic Church of Luther's day, and it was precisely this article (justification) upon which Luther said the church would stand or fall. It is this point at which the strongest disagreement with Eastern Orthodoxy remains, for it cannot be

---

[26] The same concept is found in 2 Samuel 19:20, where Shimei, who confesses his sin, nevertheless asks David not to "hold him guilty"; or again in Psalm 106:31, in which God's reckoning Phinehas as righteous is a declarative act, not an equivalent compensation or reward for his actual status of righteousness. See Douglas Moo, *Romans 1–8*, Kenneth Barker, ed., (Chicago, Illinois: Moody Press, 1991), 264–5.

[27] Schreiner, *Faith Alone*, 165.

sustained on the basis of Scripture that man achieves (or contributes to the attainment of) the righteousness of God.

Romans 3:21 teaches: "But now the righteousness of God has been manifested apart from the Law, although the Law and the Prophets bear witness to it." First, righteousness is apart from the Law. That is, it does not depend on the Mosaic Law or any other moral system that exists among men. Second, it is a righteousness that has been manifested. If it has been manifested to us, it has not been generated by us. It is a righteousness that has been delivered from heaven. It originates from above not within. Third, it is a biblical righteousness, being witnessed by the Law and the Prophets. It was not invented by Paul or the Roman juridical systems of the day. It was according to the eternal plan of God as testified by the eternal Word of God.[28] A fourth point to be made comes from the next verse, wherein we see the means by which this righteousness becomes accessible to us. Romans 3:22 teaches that this righteousness is "the righteousness of God through faith in Jesus Christ for all who believe." So, the righteousness of God is apart from the law, manifested to us from above, according to God's eternal plan, testified to by the Scriptures, and made accessible through faith. This is the linchpin of true Christianity and the litmus test that must be applied to every competitor.

Finally, the righteousness of God is accessible to us through faith in Jesus Christ alone. Whereas Eastern Orthodox theologians want to ascribe it to man, as if man might accomplish it or achieve it, the Bible teaches that it was Jesus Christ who fulfilled all righteousness on our behalf. Faith, then, is trusting in and relying upon Christ to save us. As theologian J. I. Packer notes, "Faith [is] the instrumental means whereby Christ and his righteousness are appropriated."[29] In other words, faith isn't the grounds of our justification—Christ is! It is Christ's righteousness that counts for the believer, not his own. Faith is just the means by which it is ours. This is the heart of Christianity and one of the commonest refrains in Scripture. Paul writes to the faithful in Christ Jesus (Eph 1:1). He explains that God

---

28 Moo writes, "Although God's justifying activity in the new era takes part outside the confines of the Old Covenant, the OT as a whole anticipates and predicts this new work of God." *Romans 1–8*, 223.

29 James I. Packer, "God's Justification of Sinners," *Christianity Today*, March 16, 1959.

has blessed us with every spiritual blessing in Christ (Eph 1:3); moreover, God chose us in Christ before the creation of the world (Eph 1:4), and He has freely given us grace in Christ (Eph 1:6). Paul adds that our redemption is in Him, God's will is revealed in Him, we are chosen in Him, and our hope can only be *found in Him* (Eph 1:7, 9, 11, 12). As the English preacher Charles Spurgeon put it, "Thus, dear believer, rejoice in this: You are 'accepted *in the beloved.*' Don't look at yourself, for you will have to say, 'I see nothing acceptable here!' Instead, look at Christ and see that everything is acceptable there."[30]

Conclusion

Many people who attend evangelical churches rarely consider the real basis of their own salvation. Tragically, they think just as the Eastern Orthodox do. They speak of Christ's righteousness but believe that it is only a supporting grace given to those who prove themselves to be deserving of it, who are sufficiently righteous of their own accord and who have displayed at least a minimal level of righteousness. Only then, they think, might they receive the righteousness of Jesus Christ and be saved. As we have seen, nothing can be further from the truth; this kind of thinking undermines the very heart of the gospel, which proclaims that salvation is by faith, through Christ alone.

The call of this essay is not simply to understand and refute the Orthodox understanding of justification, but also to evaluate our own understanding of the gospel. What is the good news that sounds from our pulpits? Is it that God helps those who help themselves or that God helps the helpless? We must watch that the message of hope we proclaim does not center on man, but on God. The human ego will always fight for a place in the process of salvation, to take credit for any aspect of becoming right with God. This has many manifestations and manners of seeping into our churches. Without a clear understanding of what the gospel is and what it produces time and again, we will fall prey to various perversions of the good news that Jesus Christ saves sinners through faith alone.

---

[30] Charles H. Spurgeon, *Look unto Me: The Devotions of Charles Spurgeon*, Jim Reimann, ed., (Grand Rapids, Michigan: Zondervan, 2008), day 267.

This is not a peripheral issue. This is not something that can be overlooked without tragic consequences. To go astray at the point of justification is to chart a way that prevents sinners from salvation and strips God of his glory in salvation. In 1 Timothy 4:16, Paul admonishes Timothy with words fitting to the conclusion of this chapter, "Keep a close watch on yourself and on the teaching. Persist in this, for by so doing you will save both yourself and your hearers."

Is Christ Clarified or Clouded? A Case Study in Bible Translation from Albania

Brad Lay

Southeastern Europe Theological Seminary, Albania

[Editor's Note: If you are reading this (and are a Christian), your eternal life, your relationship with God, and the salvation of your own soul has depended on translation. You did not hear the gospel in (ancient) Greek, Hebrew, or Aramaic. Somebody gave you this treasure in a language you understood. This treasure reached the Albanian people in the 1800s and continues to bear fruit today. Nevertheless, issues with current Bible translations have the potential to lead to misconceptions about the person and work of Jesus Christ. In the following pages, it is argued that while much progress has been made with regard to Albanian Bible translation, there is still much work to be done to faithfully present Christ in all His glory.]

A Brief History of the Albanian Protestant Church and Bible Translation Efforts

B elievers around the world will soon be celebrating the 500th anniversary of the Protestant Reformation. The nailing of the Ninety-five Theses by an obscure Augustinian monk began, among other things, a domino effect of Bible translations into the national vernacular across many countries of Europe. Sadly, the effects of the Reformation, and Bible translation in particular, didn't extend to Albania, the very area that Paul mentions in Romans 15:19.[1] The reason for this was that the Ottoman Empire conquered Albania and attempted total Islamization from 1389–1912.[2] Without the Scriptures in Albanian, the marvelous person and work of Christ remained hidden from millions of Albanians for another three centuries after their rediscovery in 1517.

The 19th Century

Translation of the New Testament into Albanian was first suggested in 1816[3] and accomplished in 1827.[4] But it wasn't until 1876, more than eighty years after the "Father of Modern Missions" William Carey landed in India, that Albania had its first known Protestant convert. This eventually led to another first: the first Albanian Protestant church in the early 1880s, in modern-day Macedonia. During this time, an updated version of the New Testament, along with the Old Testament books of Genesis, Exodus, Deuteronomy, Psalms, Proverbs, and Isaiah, were translated into Albanian.

The 20th Century

Just prior to World War I, American missionaries came to the southeastern Albanian city of Korça (Core-chah). It was there in Korça, during the years between the World Wars, that the first

---

[1] " ... as far as Illyricum I have fully preached the gospel of Christ." Illyricum is thought to have included at least part of modern-day Albania. "Illyria," in *Encyclopaedia Britannica*, https://www.britannica.com/place/Illyria#ref87154.

[2] This began with the Battle of Kosova on June 15 of 1389 and ended with Albania's declaration of independence on November 28, 1912. Edwin E. Jacques, *The Albanians, An Ethnic History from the Prehistoric Times to the Present* (Jefferson, North Carolina: McFarland, 1995), 195, 357.

[3] Reverend R. Pinkerton wrote the British and Foreign Bible Society in 1816, 200 years ago, urging the society to pursue translating the New Testament into Albanian. Some historians argue that this was one factor in the formation of the Albanian language and thus the declaration of independence from the Ottoman Empire in 1912. James Clark, *1912 dhe Ungjilli (1912 and the Gospel)*. (Gjirokastër, Albania: AEM-Misioni Ungjillor, 2012), 11.

[4] Albanian is an ancient language, but political and religious authorities had prevented Albanian from being produced in a unified, written form. Thus this version had very limited circulation.

Protestant church in modern day Albania[5] was established. Up through the beginning of World War II, more updated versions of the New Testament and portions of the Old Testament were published, particularly as the Albanian language was formalized and oppression under the Ottoman Empire and subsequent political movements waned. The last missionaries departed Albania in 1940, leaving around 100 Albanian Protestant believers.[6]

Under communism (1945–1991), state sponsored persecution gradually erased nearly all the work done by foreign missionaries and national believers. Iron-fisted dictator Enver Hoxha declared Albania the first officially atheistic state,[7] making it the most isolated totalitarian country in the world. In 1967, "every mosque, church, monastery and religious institution in the country was closed down, 2169 of them, and every religious practice outlawed."[8] Children were taught in school to spy on and report their own parents to authorities for crimes against the state, such as possession of the Scriptures or religious expression of any kind. For these reasons, there was no underground church in Albania, and only six believers are known to have survived the communist period.[9] The regime also sought to destroy any and all portions of the Bible, outlawing and burning whatever existing copies they could find.[10]

With the fall of the Iron Curtain in the East, the Albanian communist regime crumbled as well, opening the door to Protestant missions fifty years after that door had closed. Evangelical missionaries soon flooded into Albania, with new churches being planted around the country.[11] During this new democratic era, Bible translation work exploded. By God's grace, Albanians now have abundant access to

---

[5]   Prior to the 20th century, Albania's borders extended into current surrounding countries.

[6]   David Young, *The Protestant Movement Among Albanians 1908–1991* (Prishtina, Kosova: Shtëpia Botuese TENDA, 2011), 147. Original title: *Lëvizja Protestante Midis Shqiptarëve 1908-1991*.

[7]   Ibid., 155.

[8]   Jacques, *The Albanians*, 560.

[9]   David Young, *The Protestant Movement*, 161.

[10] Ibid., 157.

[11] Grace Community Church missionaries came in 1993 to start a church in the capital, Tirana. In 2000, Grace Church of Tirana was officially incorporated, and in 2005, Southeastern Europe Theological Seminary (SETS) was begun in order to train the first generation of Albanian pastors and missionaries in country.

various hard-copy translations, a free digital version of the entire Bible in app form, and two downloadable audio versions of the New Testament. God has certainly blessed His work in Albania through these historic translations. All those who have labored to provide the Albanian people with God's Word in their own language are worthy of commendation. Nonetheless, the work is not finished. In this essay we hope to demonstrate that current Albanian Bible versions still fall short in effectively and accurately conveying Christ and His Work.

Post-Communism Bible Translations (1991–2016)

The first missionaries to Albania in 1991 were starting from square one in church planting and also Bible translation. Thousands, if not tens of thousands, of copies of portions of the Bible in Albanian were in circulation at the advent of the communist era in 1944. However, by the end in 1991, very few copies had survived the systematic destruction of religious literature that occurred under strictly enforced atheism. While these would be recovered in time, the communist regime had been fairly thorough in robbing the church of this precious gift. Thus with the fall of communism in 1991, Bible translation work began not by building on previous translation work, but instead in an unexpected way.

Primary Versions

The Most Popular and Widespread Version
The most popular and widespread version of the Bible in Albania today is also its very first complete Bible.[12] But before we explore how this version came about, it's necessary to understand a bit more about life under communism in Albania. Albania is located directly above Greece and to the immediate east of Southern Italy. Under communism, contact with the outside was strictly forbidden and severely punished. Most Albanians lived in very plain, communist style, four- to five-story apartment buildings with their radio and TV antennas filling the flat roofs of these apartment buildings. All antennas had to be directed toward the state-run station. However,

---

[12] Only portions of the Bible had been published in the Albanian language up to this point.

many Albanians rigged their antennas to swivel, and thus could rotate them from the balcony of their apartments. At nighttime, under cover of darkness, they would frequently rotate these antennas to face Italy, hoping to pick up some Italian station. Then, before they went to bed, they were very careful to rotate their antennas back toward the Albanian station—otherwise the consequences could be swift and harsh. But their intense hunger for knowledge of the outside world, and in particular the West, drove them to take this risk frequently. In this way, the majority of Albanians learned Italian.

Since knowledge of Italian was so widespread, the first Albanian Bible was translated directly from the 1991 Italian Bible, *Nuova Diodati Revisione*.[13] This Italian Bible is based on the Textus Receptus,[14] and therefore those translating this new Albanian version also compared their translation with the New King James Version (NKJV) for accuracy.[15] Additionally, they also checked their translation of the New Testament section against the original Greek New Testament text.[16] The Old Testament was finished in 1993 and then the New Testament in 1994, thus resulting in the first complete translation of the Bible into Albanian. It's astonishing to think that it took 477 years for the Reformation to spread to Albania in the form of the entire Bible translated into Albanian!

In the twenty-two years that have passed, this original Albanian version has undergone some minor changes and one major revision. But this 1994 version has had the most impact for several reasons. One reason is that the first generation of new Albanian believers and soon-to-be church leaders cut their teeth on this translation. They read, memorized, taught, preached, and evangelized using this version. In this way, the next generation of believers after them became familiar with the wording and phrases of the Albanian 1994 text as well. A second reason is that after copies of this first translation were spread throughout churches and homes in Albania and later Kosova, newer, updated and improved versions weren't as likely to replace the original 1994 edition. It's a matter of simple economics. While

---

13   *Bibla* (Tirana: Albanian Bible Society, 1995), vi.

14   It is beyond the scope of this essay to discuss the various Greek text versions.

15   *Bibla* (Tirana: Albanian Bible Society, 1995), v-vi.

16   Ibid., vi.

copies of the first edition were often given to Albanians (who were extremely poor, especially in the 1990s), the subsequent edition was not given away as a gift en masse. They had to be purchased, often times at lower prices than publishing costs, but still very expensive by Albanian wage standards. For some, buying a newer Bible translation meant paying around a day's wage for a simple paperback copy.[17]

There's a third reason this first version continues to be the most widespread. It is readily available in digital form. This factor might now be the main reason why this original, 1994 Albanian Bible text will continue to be the most widely used on a day-to-day basis. With the proliferation of smartphones and tablets in Albania, more and more Albanians are using them to read, study, memorize, preach, teach, and evangelize. Currently, only the 1994 translation is downloadable for free. Unless another, updated digital version is downloadable for free, the 1994 one will continue to enjoy the most widespread use among Albanian speakers.

The Second Most Popular and Widespread Version[18]

The Albanian Bible Society recognized the need for an updated version of the 1994 edition. Thus, in 2002, after receiving much input from Bible readers, and Albanian language experts, together with checking the translation more carefully against the Greek text (Textus Receptus), a new version was released.[19] In terms of accuracy, there were vast improvements. However, it is still not an original language-based version.

Original Language-Based New Testaments

The first original language-based New Testament, by Vladimir Dervishi, was completed in 2000.[20] The second translation project

---

[17] Average wages when the 2002 version was published were about $150/month, or about $7/day, close to the cost of a new paperback Bible. See "Trading Economics: Albania Average Monthly Wages 1996–2016." http://www.tradingeconomics.com/albania/wages.

[18] There's no solid evidence for this but taken more from discussion with, and observation of, Albanian pastors and believers, as well as based upon the reasons already given for the popularity of the 1994 version.

[19] *Bibla e Studimit* (Tirana: Shoqëria Biblike Shqiptare, 2009), viii.

[20] Dr. Dervishi was also translating the Old Testament from Hebrew, but sadly passed away before completing the work. Nevertheless, his New Testament version is a helpful tool for

currently underway is being done by a team of translators from the Interconfessional Bible Society of Albania (IBSA).[21] In 2007, the IBSA published a New Testament Edition.[22]

Problematic Passages

The purpose for this history lesson is to identify and discuss some passages that are insufficiently or erroneously translated and thus fall short in effectively and accurately conveying Christ and His work. We will examine several passages related to the person of Christ and then one related to His work.

Related to Christ's Person

English versus Greek versus Albanian

In English, word order determines the role of each word. The first word is usually the subject of the sentence. New Testament Greek, however, doesn't always follow a certain word order like English. A word can be placed toward the beginning of the sentence in order to emphasize that word.[23] In written English, we would show this by underlining or italicizing the word. But typically Bible translators don't underline words, and italics are generally reserved for words that are implied, but not actually represented by a corresponding Greek word.

If we translated the last phrase of John 1:1 according to the Greek word order, it would be: "And God was the Word."[24] This sounds strange in (normal) English. But this would be a way to convey what John is emphasizing, the deity of "the Word" (identified in the rest

---

comparing with other translations, and is available in audio and online versions.

[21] This team is made up of translators from Orthodox, Catholic, and Protestant churches. Therefore its aim is to produce a text that will be approved by each of these communities among Albanians.

[22] This is based upon the UBS 4th Revised Edition Greek Text. They are currently working on the Old Testament.

[23] William D. Mounce, *Basics of Biblical Greek Grammar* (Grand Rapids, Michigan: Zondervan, 2003), 27.

[24] καὶ θεὸς ἦν ὁ λόγος. (*kai theos ēn ho logos*). Kurt Aland, et al., eds., *The Greek New Testament*, 4th ed. (Stuttgart: Deutsche Bibelgesellschaft, 2000), 312.

of chapter 1 as Jesus Christ). John chose the word order specifically to bring Christ's divinity to the forefront.[25] The Albanian language is similar to biblical Greek in that word order can be changed in order to stress a particular word and thus make a clear point. So, while it sounds strange in English, translating the last phrase of John 1:1 as "And God was the Word," would not sound strange in Albanian. Rather, it would effectively and accurately convey the very emphasis that John intended in an Albanian sounding way. Interestingly enough, all four Albanian versions translate it with the "English"[26] word order: "The Word was God."[27]

Naturally, it is not our position that this word order would cause anyone to question the deity of Christ. But we can point out two issues. First, the translators miss an opportunity to have the Albanian text effectively and accurately convey the author's intent on a very crucial matter—the deity of Christ—in a grammar more closely approximating the original Greek.[28] And it's strangely missed by all of these translations. This leads to the second issue. The fact that the translation was identical[29] among all four versions seems to indicate that the translators involved in all of these translations were *more* influenced by another translation—Italian, English, or the 1994 version—than they were by the original language text. This is concerning to those of us who believe that the inspired and inerrant Word of God should be handled with extreme care and accuracy to produce the best possible translation. At the very least a careful

---

[25] The lack of the definite article on "God" and its placement at the beginning identifies it as a predicate adjective attributing the quality of deity to "the Word."

[26] To be clear, either word order works in Albanian. The "English" word order sounds fine to the Albanian ear, as does the word order as it appears in the Greek text.

[27] "Fjala ishte Perëndi." *Bibla: Dhjata e Vjetër dhe Dhjata e Re* [*The Bible: The Old Testament and the New Testament*] (Tirana: Shoqëria Biblike Shqiptare, 1995), 181. *Bibla: Dhjata e Vjetër dhe Dhjata e Re* [*The Bible: The Old Testament and the New Testament*] (Tirana: Shoqëria Biblike Shqiptare, 2002), 100. *Libri i Jetës: Testamenti i Ri.* [*The Book of Life: The New Testament*] (China: MediaServe, 2014), 130. *Dhjata e Re* [*The New Testament*] (Tirana: Shoqëria Biblike Ndërkonfesionale e Shqipërisë, 2014), 178.

[28] We could add that it's a missed apologetical opportunity as well. Jehovah's Witnesses, for example, are very active in Albania, and also have translated their New World Translation into Albanian. Like in their English translation (purportedly based upon the original language texts), John 1:1c reads, "the Word was a god" ("Fjala ishte një perëndi"). *Dëshmitarët e Jehovait: Bibla Online*, https://www.jw.org/sq/botime/bibla/bi12/libra/gjoni/1/.

[29] The IBSA version omits "And" at the beginning of the phrase. Otherwise they are all identical.

reader of these translations should wonder how often this is true of other passages in these translations.

One or Two Persons?

The next two passages we will examine related to Christ's person are very similar theologically and grammatically. Like the John 1:1 passage, both deal with the deity of Christ. They are Titus 2:13 and 2 Peter 1:1. In Titus 2:13, Paul speaks about "the appearing of the glory of our great God and Savior, Christ Jesus."[30] The New American Standard Bible (NASB) accurately conveys the Greek grammatical construction[31] of one person, not two. In other words, it is clear that the dual title "our great God and Savior" means that Christ is both God and Savior. If it were translated, "the great God and our Savior Jesus Christ" this would convey a much different idea, that of two persons appearing, God and also Christ. And yet this is exactly how all four Albanian versions translate this phrase.[32]

Likewise, Peter chose the same grammatical construction that Paul did in order to unmistakably convey the deity of Christ when he uses the phrase, "the righteousness of our God and Savior, Jesus Christ," in 2 Peter 1:1. Peter is saying that Jesus Christ is both God and Savior. If this phrase were changed slightly and translated, "the righteousness of our God and of the Savior Jesus Christ," "the righteousness of our God and of our Savior Jesus Christ," or, "the righteousness of our God and the Savior Jesus Christ," the meaning

---

[30] All English Scripture quotations in this essay are taken from the New American Standard Bible (NASB) unless otherwise noted.

[31] This grammatical construction in both passages is a clear example of what is known as the Grandville–Sharp Rule. Briefly, this rule of New Testament Greek grammar applies to two nouns connected by the conjunction "καρ" (*kai*) and preceded by an article. The nouns must be singular, personal, not proper, with only one article, and all of the same case. When all of these conditions are met, both nouns refer to the same person. Daniel B Wallace, *Greek Grammar Beyond the Basics* (Grand Rapids, Michigan: Zondervan, 1996), 270–1.

[32] There are some slight variations between the versions, but the translation above into English accurately conveys all of them. Both the 1994 and 2002 primary versions are the same: "të madhit Perëndi dhe të Shpëtimtarit tonë Jezu Krisht." The Dervishi version has: "të madhit Perëndi dhe të Shpëtimtarit tonë Jezu Krisht." The IBSA version has: "të Perëndisë madhështor dhe të Shpëtimtarit tonë Jezu Krisht." The main differences with this one is that the adjective, "madhështor," is behind the noun, "Perëndisë," instead of in front. Also, "madhështor" can be translated "majestic." *Bibla: Dhjata e Vjetër dhe Dhjata e Re*, 423. *Bibla: Dhjata e Vjetër dhe Dhjata e Re*, 233. *Libri i Jetës: Testamenti i Ri*, 311. *Dhjata e Re*, 416.

would change, signifying two persons in all three cases. Yet again, the four Albanian versions translate this phrase in these ways.[33] These two passages are very important in demonstrating the clear New Testament teaching of the deity of Christ.[34] Whereas the John 1:1 passage constituted a missed opportunity on the clarity of the deity of Christ, in the case of these two passages, all four Albanian versions misconstrue Paul and Peter's theological intent, and the value of these verses is lost for the reader.[35] Again, this should cause the careful reader to question how closely the original texts were followed and understood by the translators of all four versions.

Related to Christ's Work

Another problematic passage is Philippians 2:12, where Paul commands the Philippian believers to "work out your own salvation with fear and trembling." This marvelous passage delineates the beautiful, biblical balance in sanctification. We as believers are called to work out our salvation on the basis of God's working in us (as described in verse 13). By using the word *salvation* in verse 12, Paul is clearly not talking about justification, or initial salvation. He has already reminded the believers that God had "begun a good work" in them (1:6). Therefore, the word *salvation* clearly refers to ongoing salvation, that is, sanctification, or becoming more like Christ.

It would be helpful to get a little technical here and mention the exact words as they appear in the Greek text: "with fear and trembling your own salvation be working out." These are all the words

---

[33] The 1994 and IBSA versions both convey this: "the righteousness of our God and of the Savior Jesus Christ." The 1994 version has: "drejtësisë së Perëndisë tonë dhe të Shpëtimtarit Jezu Krisht." The IBSA version reads: "drejtësia e Perëndisë tonë dhe e Shpëtimtarit Jezu Krisht." The Dervishi version translated is: "the righteousness of our God and the Savior Jesus Christ," ("drejtësisë së Perëndisë sonë dhe Shpëtimtarit Jezu Krisht.") The 2002 version conveys this: "the righteousness of our God and of our Savior Jesus Christ," ("drejtësisë së Perëndisë tonë dhe të Shpëtimtarit tonë Jezu Krisht.") *Bibla: Dhjata e Vjetër dhe Dhjata e Re*, 462. *Dhjata e Re*, 462. *Libri i Jetës: Testamenti i Ri*, 342. *Bibla: Dhjata e Vjetër dhe Dhjata e Re*, 254.

[34] Of course, we are not saying that without these two passages, the doctrine of the deity of Christ is undermined. Nevertheless, the clarity of this doctrine is affected.

[35] Not only do these inaccurate translations significantly alter the meaning of these verses, they also rob the church of key apologetical texts in discussions with Muslims and Jehovah Witnesses.

and in the order they appear in this verse.[36] How does this compare with the four Albanian versions? The 1994 edition translates it this way, "work for your salvation with fear and trembling."[37] Word order aside, the translators added the preposition "for." The 2002, updated edition, makes a slight but unsubstantial change, which in English would also read, "work for your salvation with fear and trembling."[38]

One would expect that some inaccuracies might creep into the translation when the original is only consulted and is not the source for translation. How about the two translations that are based directly on the original language texts? The Dervishi version reads this way: "continue to work for your salvation with fear and trembling."[39] This translation is also slightly different, with the translation accurately bringing out the continuous aspect of the present tense command—"continue." Other than this, it is basically the same as the 1994 and 2002 versions. Finally, the Interconfessional translation reads this way, "work for your salvation with fear and trembling."[40] This is identical with the 1994 version.

So each of these translations follows the same pattern—adding the preposition *for* after the verb *work*. Is there any preposition in the Greek text? No; there is no *for* or any other word that could be translated as such. Incidentally, this phrase from Philippians 2:12 in the Textus Receptus is identical with Nestle-Aland 27th edition, so this difference is not due to textual issues.[41]

This raises two issues. First, how did the word "for" get added to each of the Albanian translations, when it is neither in the Greek text nor in the KJV?[42] It's disconcerting that all the translations would have this addition, once again causing careful students of

---

36 μετὰετόετυ καὶ καό κα τκα τκαττκασωτηρίωτηρατεργάτεργε (*meta phobou kai tromou tēn heautōn sōtērian katergazesthe*). *UBS Greek New Testament*, 676.

37 "punoni për shpëtimin tuaj me frikë e me dridhje." *Bibla*, 230.

38 "veproni për shpëtimin tuaj me frikë e me dridhje." The word *veproni* is a synonym with the word *punoni*. *Bibla e Studimit*, 1363.

39 "vazhdoni të punoni për shpëtimin tuaj me frikë dhe të dridhura." *Libri i Jetës: Testamenti i Ri*, 285.

40 "punoni për shpëtimin tuaj me frikë e me dridhje." *Dhjata e Re*, 376.

41 μετα φοβου και τρομου την εαυτων σωτηριαν κατεργαζεσθε (*meta phobou kai tromou tēn heautōn sōtērian katergazesthe*) Textus Receptus Bible, http://www.textusreceptusbibles. com/Strongs/50002012/G1722.

42 The KJV reads: "work out your own salvation with fear and trembling."

God's Word to wonder how carefully the original languages or the immediate and remote contexts for each text were consulted by the translators of each of the four translations.

The second issue is equally serious. Adding the word *for* has huge soteriological implications. The phrase as it occurs in the original—"work out your salvation" (or "work your salvation")—indicates that the believers are to develop the salvation that they already possess. Believers must reflect through their outer behavior that which actually resides within them as a result of their salvation from the penalty of sin. As new creations in Christ (2 Cor 5:17), they must live out their new life (Gal 2:20; Eph 4:21–24). The addition of the preposition *for* paints a picture that believers haven't obtained salvation yet, and so they must do good works in order to gain their salvation. Such a perspective clearly undermines the sufficient, finished work of Christ on the cross, and the matter of sanctification remains obscured and silenced. We must be clear here that we are not implying that the translators intended to cause this confusion. The fact that all four translations have this addition leads one to surmise that the original 1994 translation added the word for whatever reason and thus unwittingly influenced the other three, particularly since the language would be familiar to translators. Again, our purpose is not to guess at motives. Whatever they were, it is clear that the translations do not effectively and accurately convey the work of Christ in their rendering of Philippians 2:12. Rather, these translations open the door for the reader to move toward co-salvation with Christ, thus undermining His perfect work and the doctrine of justification by faith alone.

Conclusion

The Verdict on the Current Versions

As is often the case in communication, it is equally important to state what one is not saying, and not just what is being said. As we've laid out the case of shortcomings in the four current Albanian translations, we are not saying that they are not of immense value to the Albanian church. By and large, whoever reads them, believes them, and obeys them will be saved and grow in Christ. We are also not saying that it was a mistake for early translators to rely more on existing translations than on the original language texts. In the early 1990s, Albanians needed a copy of the Scriptures in their own language. To wait until a translation could be adequately produced from the original languages would have caused the Albanian Church to languish for years without God's Word in its mother tongue.

What is being said? The verdict on the current versions is that while they have served their purposes, they don't demonstrate sufficient reliance on the original biblical language texts. The four sample verses we examined show how the four translations fall short in effectively and accurately conveying the person and work of Christ and thus cause one to wonder about their accuracy in other passages.

The Need for an Official, Modern Version Based on Biblical Languages

It is very easy to be critical and to convey an air of superiority over others who have labored before us. We are indebted to these translators. But we do believe that it is time for a new, official, modern version based on the original biblical languages. By "official" we mean in line with the Albanian Bible Society's 1994 and 2002 versions. These are the ones that are used by the Albanian Protestant church. These versions are historical and also woven into the fabric of the church. Therefore, building on and from within this tradition would be the best path forward.

By "modern," we simply mean taking into account technological trends. The 1994 version is most widely used simply because it is free in app form. Therefore a "modern" version would also need to be free in digital form, perhaps with hypertext options for study.[43] By "based on the original biblical languages," we mean that a team should be composed of expert translators who will translate directly from Hebrew, Aramaic, and Greek, seeking to remain faithful to the original and yet producing a translation expressed in Albanian as it is currently spoken.[44]

---

[43] The current digital version is just plain text.

[44] To most English speakers familiar with the biblical languages, this might seem next to impossible. However, Albanian and biblical Greek have many more grammatical similarities than English and Greek. Therefore, such a translation is achievable.

Apart from Himself (through the Son and the Spirit), God's most precious gift to us is His Word. For centuries, this treasure was kept from people in desperate need of it. The Reformation returned this treasure to people so that they might know Christ and what He accomplished for them. And in God's sovereign timing, His Word was finally brought to the Albanian people. Because it contains clear, definitive truth about Christ and His work, it must be translated with utmost accuracy. As we have demonstrated, Albanians are still in need of a translation of the Scriptures that reflects this clarity. If the Lord allows, such a translation would lay a solid foundation within the Albanian Church for generations to come.

THE BANKRUPTCY OF ISLAM AND THE RICHES OF CHRIST

Henry Anderson (with testimony from "Ramiz")

Southeastern Europe Theological Seminary, Albania

[Editor's Note: Islam is the fastest growing religion in the world, with over one billion adherents. Due to the increasingly globalized world in which we live, an interaction between Christianity and Islam is inevitable. This essay cuts to the heart of this false system and highlights the need that Muslims have for Jesus Christ. Included is the testimony of Ramiz, a former Muslim and the current academic dean at the TMAI training center in Tirana, Albania. His testimony provides a timely reminder that God is actively rescuing Muslims through the gospel of Jesus Christ, which alone provides true forgiveness and eternal life.]

Introduction

What is the most frightening thought that one can contemplate? This author solemnly contends that it is the thought of standing guilty and unforgiven before a holy God. For many, this frightening thought will one day be realized, as Christ Himself warns, "I will declare to them, 'I never knew you; depart from me, you who practice lawlessness'" (Matt 7:23). Anyone who dies in their sins will be cast into the outer darkness of hell forever. Thus, it is of primary importance that a person understand exactly how to be forgiven before it is too late.

With every day that goes by, Judgment Day looms nearer and nearer. In light of this, saints throughout the centuries have cried out with the apostle Paul to lost men, "We beg you on behalf of Christ, be reconciled to God" (2 Cor 5:20b). There is only one way by which man might be restored to God, and that is through the finished work of the Sovereign Lord, Jesus Christ. This essay aims to expose the bankruptcy of Islam while pleading with Muslims to come to Christ.[1] Muslims profess that Allah is holy and that all people are sinners, but because of their tragic rejection of the sinless Savior's sacrifice, there is no basis for the salvation of sinners and no hope for eternal life.

Central Islamic Tenets

Muslims Profess That Allah Is Holy

The Qur'an claims that Allah is holy and is set apart from humanity. It says, "He is ... the Holy One" (59:23). As the "Holy One," there should be no error or sin within his nature. The hadith teach that Allah is pure and undiluted in nature (*Sahih Muslim* 5:2214). Accordingly, not only is there no compromise in him, but Allah cannot compromise. Because he is deemed holy and pure, Allah cannot accept sin.

Muslims Profess That Man Is Sinful

Muslims also recognize man is sinful and in need of restitution. Allah tells Muhammad to ask for forgiveness for his own sins and for the sins of other Muslims (Qur'an 47:19). The Qur'an teaches that good Muslims confess sins and seek forgiveness. They are taught to say, "Forgive us our sins, and spare us the agony of the hellfire" (3:16). Even Muhammad, the greatest prophet of Islam, was in dire need of forgiveness and recognized his own wickedness. Muhammad is recorded to say, "By Allah! I ask for forgiveness from Allah and turn to Him in repentance more than seventy times a day" (*Sahih al-Bukhari* 75:319). So Muslims confess that Allah is perfectly holy and that all mankind is utterly sinful, including Muhammad, who sought forgiveness more than seventy times a day.

---

[1]   Islam, as a system, enslaves over a billion souls and is the fastest growing religion in the world. See Michael Lipka. <http://www.pewresearch.org/fact-tank/2016/07/22/muslims-and-islam-key-findings-in-the-u-s-and-around-the-world/>.

The Unfortunate and Untenable Conclusion

There is no clear answer in Islam as to how Allah could be holy and pure while simply forgiving and forgetting about the repeated abuses he suffers at the hands of sinful, rebellious men. Muslims, like many people, believe that good works somehow atone for bad ones (Qur'an 101:6–11)[2], but there is no objective basis for such forgiveness. In fact, there is no concept of total forgiveness of sin for the Muslim. The Qur'an states, for example, that giving to the poor will atone for *some* of one's bad deeds (2:271)—but what about the rest? Throughout Islamic teaching, there is only promised partial restitution for Muslims, and even this is on arbitrary terms nowhere explained.

The true God of our Lord Jesus Christ repudiates the idea that fallen man achieves righteousness by "good works." Quite the contrary, man's works condemn him, as it is written, "Cursed is he who does not confirm the words of this law by doing them" (Deut 27:26a). The standard for man is that he keep all things written in the Book of the Law. This does not require more good deeds than bad but rather demands perfect obedience to God. No Muslim has ever done that. No Christian has ever done that. "For whoever keeps the whole law and yet stumbles in one point, he has become guilty of all" (Jas 2:10). Stumbling at one point in the law is all it takes to be separated from God for eternity. The apostle John tells us, "if we say that we have no sin, we are deceiving ourselves and the truth is not in us" (1 John 1:8), and Romans 6:23 begins by saying, "For the wages of sin is death." All people are separated from God and are unable to work toward Him (Isa 59:2; Eph 2:1).

On the contrary, Islam teaches that if enough "good" deeds are done, then one can go to paradise. The Qur'an states, "the one whose good deeds are heavy on the scales will have a pleasing life, but the one whose good deeds are light will have the Bottomless Pit for his home ... a blazing fire" (101:6–9, 11). But even a pious Muslim does not know what sins are forgiven, how many sins are forgiven, how many sins he has, or how many good deeds that he must complete

---

[2]   Muslims vigorously perform works to appease Allah, "(The superstructure of) al-Islam is raised on five (pillars), testifying (the fact) that there is no god but Allah, that Muhammad is His bondsman and messenger, and the establishment of prayer, payment of Zakat, Pilgrimage to the House (Ka'ba), and the fast of Ramadan" (*Sahih Muslim* 1:18).

to be right before Allah. This is a dangerous reality for any Muslim. Allah forgives subjectively, "He will forgive whoever He will and punish whoever He will ..." (Qur'an 2:284).

Christian apologist James White points out the logical implication, "This brings us to the all-important question of how Allah can be holy and just and yet act arbitrarily, forgiving some sins and retaining others without reference to sacrifice or the fulfillment of his own law. In Islamic belief, Allah can forgive sins while providing no basis in justice or equity."[3] If there is not a full payment for sin, the holiness of Allah must be compromised. Allah must simply absorb, absolve, or acquit the guilty, which is a big problem, implicating Allah with objectively evil actions. On the one hand, Allah promises to punish wrongdoers and uphold his universal justice, but at the same time chooses to forgive some. What kind of judge refuses to uphold the law when a crime has been committed? As the Bible says, "He who justifies the wicked and he who condemns the righteous, both of them alike are an abomination to the LORD" (Prov 17:15). Since there is no complete forgiveness in Islam, because there is no payment for sin, this practice of Allah is actually an abomination to the Lord.[4]

There Is Only Forgiveness in Christ

It has been shown in brief that Muslims see Allah as holy and themselves as sinners, but within Islam, there is no objective basis for forgiveness. In this section, we will explain in more detail why this is the case. There is no objective basis for salvation in Islam because they reject two vital truths: the righteousness of Christ and His atoning work on the cross.

No Objective Basis for Salvation Apart from Christ's Righteousness
Christ alone has abided by all things written in the Book of the Law. In order to be righteous before God, Muslims must call upon and believe in the Son of God (Acts 4:12). Faith in Him alone provides salvation because Christ alone is "without sin" (Heb 4:15).

---

3   James R. White, *What Every Christian Needs to Know About the Qur'an*, (Bloomington, Minnesota: Bethany House Publishers, 2013), 139–40.

4   White, *The God Who Justifies*, (Bloomington, Minnesota: Bethany House Publishers, 2001), 73–92.

Christ's righteousness alone is sufficient to stand in the presence of a truly holy God. He came as the Son of Man to obey the Father in all things and fulfill the very law that we have broken. In this way, He, as the perfect man, fulfilled all righteousness on behalf of mankind. And His perfect righteousness is the only righteousness that can satisfy God's perfect standard. Everyone else falls short, but Christ actively and perfectly obeyed the law while on the earth in our stead.[5] Thus, believers in Christ are not simply in a neutral state because of forgiveness, but they are actually given a positive status before God as they now have Christ's righteousness as well.[6] Christians live through Christ's life. A Christian's story is Christ's obedience in life and death.

According to Matthew 3:15, Christ came to do what no human could, to "fulfill all righteousness." In this verse, the word "fulfill" means to make complete or to bring to an end.[7] In this instance, Christ slams the gavel, saying that He *will* "fulfill all righteousness." The requirement will be fully satisfied, and the final verdict will be settled.

When Christ speaks of fulfilling *all* righteousness, He speaks both of the totality of requirements as well as duration.[8] The word itself can mean total, whole, every kind of, or all.[9] Christ walked throughout His life in perfect obedience to all of the law. Each and every precept was followed with absolute precision. Theologian

---

5   "Christ's whole work of reconciliation, from the cradle to the grave, was one act of obedience for sinners. Just as penal substitution focuses on Christ's vicarious curse-bearing, active obedience addresses the positive prescription of God's law, and asserts that Christ was also a substitute for sinners in perfectly obeying God throughout his life on earth." (Micah McCormick, *The Active Obedience of Jesus Christ*, [Ann Arbor, Michigan: UMI Dissertation Publishing, 2010], 1–29.)

6   McCormick observes, "The sacrificial lamb truly had to be a lamb without blemish. However, the doctrine of active obedience says more—it says not just that his obedience qualified him to offer a vicarious sacrifice to God, but that his whole obedience was itself vicarious." (McCormick, *The Active Obedience of Jesus Christ*.)

7   James Swanson, *Dictionary of Biblical Languages with Semantic Domains: Greek (New Testament)*, (Oak Harbor, Washington: Logos Research Systems, 1997).

8   "The use of "all" points to a developing and unfolding process that may involve a number of stages. The culmination of this process remains the purification and judgment John anticipates at the hands of the one he heralded (vv. 11–12), but first a preliminary role for the historical Jesus, quite unanticipated by John, is to be intercalated." John Nolland, *The Gospel of Matthew*, (Grand Rapids, Michigan: W. B. Eerdmans, 2005), 154.

9   Nolland, *The Gospel of Matthew*.

Edward Bigelow writes, "All that was involved in Christ's keeping of the law's positive demands were kept by Christ both internally (attitudes, motivations), and externally (actions, rites, ceremonies)."[10] In all things He is righteous.

"Righteousness" here refers to the will of God, or simply, that which is right. Christ came to fulfill all of the will of God, as He states in John 6:38: "For I have come down from heaven, not to do My own will, but the will of Him who sent Me." And what was the will of the Father? The Father willed that through Jesus' perfect life, death, and resurrection, He would representatively make perfect the righteousness of man.[11] Peter Sammons explains, "God's plan for Jesus goes beyond His position as Messiah King; it also involves His actions as the representative head in fulfilling God's righteous demands on His people."[12] This righteousness Christ fulfilled for the sake of His people. He did it so that the unrighteous might be counted as righteous through faith in Him.

When God looks at a Christian, He sees Christ's righteousness. Theologian Wayne Grudem writes, "When we say that God *imputes* Christ's righteousness to us it means that God *thinks of* Christ's righteousness as belonging to us, or regards it *as belonging to* us. He 'reckons' it to our account. We read, 'Abraham believed God, and *it was reckoned to him as righteousness'"* (Rom 4:3, quoting Gen 15:6).[13] This righteousness is a gift given ultimately at the expense of Christ paying for the sins of all who believe (2 Cor 5:21). Pastor John MacArthur explains:

> Jesus lived a perfectly righteous life from childhood, through adulthood, and in His death, so that His righteous life could be imputed to believers. Salvation

---

[10]   Edward Bigelow, *An Exegetical Approach to the Saving Accomplishments of Christ's Atonement*, (Sun Valley, California: The Master's Seminary, 1997), 113–124.

[11]   "Jesus obeys because He understands the demands of God's law upon His image bearers as a task essential to be fulfilled. The fulfillment element then must be of Christ's substitutionary position to the natural demands of God." (Peter Sammons, *No Hope Without It!: The Doctrine of Active Obedience Defined and Vindicated*, [Sun Valley, California: The Master's Seminary, 2013], 13–68.)

[12]   Sammons, *No Hope Without It!*

[13]   Wayne Grudem, *Systematic Theology: An Introduction to Biblical Doctrine*, (Nottingham, UK: Inter-Varsity Press, 2007), 726.

comes only to those who do not have a "righteousness of [their] own derived from the Law, but that
which is through faith in Christ." (Phil 3:9) [14]

Islam rejects this notion. Muslims deny that Christ was the son of
God, and the Qur'an curses the idea: "Christians call Christ the son
of Allah... . Allah's curse be on them; how they are deluded away
from the Truth" (9:30). In affirming this, they separate themselves
from their only hope of reconciliation, and they mar the Perfect One
who gave His life as a ransom for many. Muslims vehemently deny
that Jesus is the Christ. In stark contrast, the apostle John, who knew
Jesus personally, writes, "Who is the liar but the one who denies that
Jesus is the Christ? This is the antichrist, the one who denies the
Father and the Son" (1 John 2:22). As MacArthur warns:

> Do not be deceived. There's a world of Muslims
> deceived about the person of Jesus Christ. You
> cannot accommodate that by saying, 'Isn't that won-
> derful, they love Jesus.' They don't. Any other Jesus
> than the true Jesus is not Jesus. And if you worship
> any other than the true Jesus, you are cursed.[15]

The Qur'an goes as far as to say that Christ was no more than a
slave (43:59). This is a blasphemous assertion against Jesus' deity,
and a tragic rejection of the marvelous righteousness He earned for
the sake of all who would believe.

No Objective Basis for Salvation Apart from Christ's Sacrifice
Muslim's do not only reject the righteousness of Christ, but also
His sinless sacrifice. This poses a particularly significant problem, for
without bloodshed there can be no forgiveness for sins (Lev 17:11).
Sin has a cost that demands death and damnation (Rom 6:23). This
cost was ultimately paid for in Christ's death. The debt for all past,
present, and future sins of all who believe in Him have been paid for.

---

[14] John MacArthur, *Philippians*, (Chicago, Illinois: Moody Publishers, 2001), 197–8.

[15] John MacArthur, "The Grim Reality of the Last Days." <http://www.gty.org/resources/
sermons/41–66/The-Grim-Reality-of-the-Last-Days>.

As Peter writes, "He Himself bore our sins in His body on the cross" (1 Pet 2:24). Since sin is never truly paid for in Islam, it is not truly forgiven. When Muslims reject Christ's ultimate sacrifice, they deny their only means of true salvation.

The author of Hebrews writes, "All things are cleansed with blood, and without shedding of blood there is no forgiveness" (Heb 9:22). This cleansing bloodshed took place in Christ's death on the cross, where He bore sin in His body. This is called "penal substitutionary atonement."[16] Redemption is not possible outside of Christ's shed blood. This doctrine of substitutionary atonement is not new. Rather, it is consonant with the whole counsel of the Word of God.

In Genesis 22, there is a vivid account of substitutionary atonement. Abraham is asked by God to take his promised son, Isaac, to Moriah and offer him as a burnt offering unto the Lord. Abraham loved Isaac (v.2) but was going to be faithful unto God. Abraham bound Isaac on an altar, and just as he was to slay him, the angel of the LORD called to him, "Abraham, Abraham!" And he said, "Here I am." He said, "Do not stretch out your hand against the lad, and do nothing to him; for now, I know that you fear God, since you have not withheld your son, your only son, from Me." Then Abraham raised his eyes and looked, and behold, behind him was a ram caught in the thicket by his horns; and Abraham went and took the ram and offered him up for a burnt offering in the place of his son (Gen 22:11–13). The ram was substituted for Isaac. The ram's blood was spilled in the place of Isaac's. Theologian Kenneth Mathews comments, "The death of the discovered ram 'instead of [Abraham's] son' (v. 13) epitomizes the idea of substitutionary atonement, which characterized the Levitical system."[17]

Muslims have a festival called Eid al-Adha in which they remember the sacrifice of Genesis 22. Each year during the Hajj

---

[16] "Christ (perfectly and eternally righteous in death) received from God the Father the eternal punishment due to all the unrighteous who would believe in Him for eternal life. He was the believer's substitute; He who deserved no condemnation received eternal condemnation on behalf of condemned sinners who repented in His name…. Without Christ's penal substitution on behalf of sinners, an efficacious atonement rendered by Christ to redeem sinners would not be real." (Richard L Mayhue, "The Scriptural Necessity of Christ's Penal Substitution." <https://www.tms.edu/m/tmsj20f.pdf>.)

[17] K. A. Mathews, *Genesis 11:27–50:26, Vol. 1B* (Nashville, Tennessee: Broadman & Holman Publishers, 2005), 297.

pilgrimage they sacrifice a ram in remembrance of the blood that was shed in Isaac's stead.[18] Some believe that the sacrifice they make is "a sort of atonement for sins."[19] Muslims will perform this action as a good work in accordance with Muhammad's teaching. Samuel Zwemer, an early 20th-century missionary, points out, "It is a notable fact and an enigma that while Mohammed professed to abrogate the Jewish ritual ... yet [he] made the Day of Sacrifice the great central festival of his religion."[20] In promoting this festival, Muhammad affirms the need for the shedding of blood for the forgiveness of sins.[21] Muslims still misunderstand that this event was a beautiful precursor to Jesus Christ, God's only begotten Son, offering Himself as the final sacrifice on behalf of mankind.

The Passover in Exodus 12 is another picture of Christ, this time foreshadowing Him as the Lamb of God who was slain (Rev 5:12) and who takes away the sins of the world (John 1:29). Israel had been enslaved in Egypt, and God revealed that His final plague would involve the death of the firstborn son of each family. He told His people, Israel, to have a meal together of lamb and to put the blood on their doorposts, so that the firstborn would not be killed (Exod 12:1–13).[22] For Israel, the lamb was slain in the place of the firstborn. This is explicitly referenced in the New Testament as Jesus celebrates the Passover, only this time the center of the meal is not the lamb but rather His own body and blood of the covenant (Mark 14:22–24). Jesus' references to his body and blood allude to His death, which He once for all establishes as the ultimate fulfillment of the Passover.

---

[18] Muslims incorrectly claim, on the basis of the Qur'an, that it was actually *Ishmael* and not *Isaac* who was to be sacrificed. The point, however, remains the same. For more on the subject, see "Eid-ul-Adha: Abraham and the Sacrifice," <http://www.answering-islam.org/gilchrist/eid.html>.

[19] Charles R. Marsh, *Share Your Faith with A Muslim*, (Chicago, Illinois: Moody Press, 1975), 27.

[20] Samuel M. Zwemer, *Islam: A Challenge to Faith*, (New York: Layman's Missionary Movement, 1909), 114.

[21] Thomas Patrick Hughes, *A Dictionary of Islam,* (Clifton, New Jersey: Reference Book Publishers, 1965), 25.

[22] "The blood on the doorpost showed a connection between the family inside and the lamb they had offered for their sins. *Eating* the lamb made the connection even closer ... they were making a total identification with the sacrifice that God had provided for their salvation. It was more than a symbol; it was a spiritual reality." (Philip Graham Ryken, *Exodus*, [Wheaton, Illinois: Crossway Books, 2005], 357–67.)

The Passover centered on the body and blood of a lamb, slain as a penal substitutionary sacrifice for the redemption of Israel, but the Lord's Supper centers on the body and blood of Christ, who gave Himself as a penal substitutionary sacrifice for His people.

Isaiah 53 strongly confirms penal substitutionary atonement. This passage depicts the Suffering Servant, the Christ, bearing the sins of those who would believe in Him. It provides some of the clearest language in the Old Testament on this concept:

Surely our griefs He Himself bore ... He was pierced through for our transgressions, He was crushed for our iniquities; The chastening for our well-being fell upon Him, and by His scourging we are healed... . The LORD has caused the iniquity of us all to fall on Him... . Because He poured out Himself to death, and was numbered with the transgressors; yet He Himself bore the sin of many, and interceded for the transgressors" (Isa 53:4–6, 12).

The Hebrew word for *to bear* in verse 4 often carries the connotation of bearing griefs or sins, that is, to receive the penalties which another has deserved.[23] The implication is that, for those who are followers of Christ, He has taken upon Himself all the sins that the believer would ever commit—not just some but the totality of his sins. In this chapter, the word *all* refers to those who believe in Jesus Christ as Lord and Savior.[24] The offer of salvation is available to all Muslims but only by faith in Christ, trusting Him alone for righteousness and the forgiveness of sin.

Turning to the New Testament, the full weight of penal substitutionary atonement is brought to the forefront. Paul writes:

But God demonstrates His own love toward us, in that while we were yet sinners, Christ died for us. Much more then, having now been justified by His blood, we shall be saved from the wrath of God through Him. For if while we were enemies we were reconciled to

---

23 W. Gesenius and S.P. Tregelles, *Gesenius' Hebrew and Chaldee Lexicon to the Old Testament Scriptures* (Bellingham, Washington: Logos Bible Software, 2003), 578.

24 "The 'we' for whom the servant suffers most immediately (Isa 53:1–6) are God's chosen people. However, the benefits of the suffering is [sic] not limited to Israel. The servant also bears the sins of the [*ravim*, "many"]. The occurrences of ["many"] in 53:11–12 encompass both Israel and the nations. Yahweh's provision of reconciliation for the nations by means of His servant begins with the servant's ministry to Israel." (Michael A. Grisanti, *The Relationship of Israel and the Nations in Isaiah*, [Dallas, Texas: Dallas Theological Seminary, 1993], 197–291.)

God through the death of His Son, much more, having been reconciled, we shall be saved by His life (Rom 5:8–10).

In this passage Paul uses the word *reconcile* twice, revealing the importance of the ramifications of the atonement. In verse 10, the word *reconciled* indicates the complete union between God and man.[25] In the book of Romans, because of Christ's sacrifice, God's wrath has been satisfied. Believers in Christ have been justified and reconciled by His blood.[26] Since we have been reconciled, Paul details the effects of reconciliation, writing: "we shall be saved."

No works are required in the true gospel, as Paul says, "For by grace you have been saved through faith; and that not of yourselves, it is the gift of God; not as a result of works, so that no one may boast" (Eph 2:8–9). No amount of works or good deeds can reconcile anyone to God. Man's natural state before God is not weakness or simply moral blemish; we are dead in our trespasses and sins before God (Eph 2:1). Man is a corpse that needs to be born again (John 3:3). Islam's erroneous soteriological understanding is deeply rooted in Islam's misplaced object of faith.

Logical Conclusion

Because there is no objective basis for the forgiveness of sins within Islam, there is no full assurance of salvation. The only hope for a Muslim is built upon the number of good works completed and the subjective whims of Allah. The Bible gives specific objective

---

[25] Kittel writes that it "denotes a transformation or renewal of the state between God and man, and therewith of man's own state. In 2 Corinthians 5:18 it is introduced as the basis of the most comprehensive renewal possible for man, namely, that he has become a new creature, that old things have passed away and that all things have become new." (G. Kittel, G.W. Bromiley, and G. Friedrich, eds. *Theological Dictionary of the New Testament, Vol 1*, [Grand Rapids, Michigan: Eerdmans, 1964], 255.

[26] "We are reconciled by the death of Jesus (Rom 5:10). As He was made sin for us, we were made the righteousness of God in Him (2 Cor 5:21). To this extent reconciliation is parallel to justification (cf. also Rom 5:10 in relation to 5:9). This is why λογίζεσθαι, which is vital to Paul's view of justification (Rom 4:3, 4, 5, 6, 8, 9, 10, 11, 23, 24), occurs again in 2 Cor 5:19: μὴ λογιζόμενος αὐτοῖς τὰ παραπτώματα αὐτῶν. Yet there can be no question that in reconciliation more takes place than a mere removal of the relationship of guilt. God has sent to men His messengers through whom He addresses men and whom He beseech them for Christ's sake: 'Be ye reconciled to God' (2 Cor 5:20). Through the revelation of the superabounding love of God which did not find the sacrifice of the Son too great, and which does not regard it as too humiliating to plead with men, we are renewed in the total state of our life." (Kittel, et al., *Theological Dictionary of the New Testament*.)

assurance of salvation because of Christ's work on behalf of those who believe in Him. The apostle John says, "These things I have written to you who believe in the name of the Son of God so that you may know that you have eternal life" (1 John 5:13). This section will look at the characteristics of faith based on love and walking in the light within both Christianity and Islam.

Christians are called to love one another (John 13:34–35), to serve one another (Gal 5:13), and to go the extra mile (Matt 5:41). In fact, "the one who hates his brother is in the darkness" (1 John 2:11). The reason Christians love their brothers (1 John 2:10) is because of what Christ has done. In the Qur'an, Muslims are told not to kill other Muslims (4:92–93), but they are told to fight against hypocritical Muslims (66:9). If a Muslim is seemingly not honoring Allah, that person should be fought. There is not an objective way to determine the faithful Muslims, and therefore anyone can be accused and fought. In the hadith, there are verses about love for other Muslims (*Sahih al-Bukhari* 2:12). Once again, due to there being no objective standard, love is relative and, in the Muslim's case, self-centered. This is in sharp contrast to Christ's teaching, "If you love those who love you, what credit is that to you? For even sinners love those who love them" (Luke 6:32). Muslims and Allah only love those who love them.[27]

Christ, however, expects Christians to love their enemies (Matt 5:44). All people by nature are sinners and enemies of God (Rom 5:8), but because of His unmerited love, those who have been forgiven of their sins and believe in Christ reflect that same gracious love to all (Rom 5:8). Within Islam, Allah is declared to be "the Loving" (Qur'an 85:14); however, Muslims are told, "wherever you encounter the idolaters, kill them" (Qur'an 9:5). For any who is not worshipping Allah, they are to be not loved, but murdered. If someone is to wage war against Allah, or the religion of Islam, that person should be, "punished by death, crucifixion, the amputation of an alternate hand and foot, or banishment from the land" (Qur'an 5:33). This is in stark contrast to the love Christ's followers are to show: "You have heard that it was said, 'an eye for an eye, and a tooth for a tooth.' But I say to you, do not resist an evil person; but whoever slaps you on your right cheek, turn the other to him also" (Matt 5:38–39). The fruit

---

27   Farid Mahally, <http://www.answering-islam.org/Quran/Themes/love.htm>.

and assurance of one's salvation in Christianity is a love for others, whereas in Islam it is warring against any opposition to Islam.

Christians walk in the light (1 John 1:5–7). Once someone believes in Christ, that person walks in the light of God's holiness and righteousness (1 John 3:10). This person can be assured of salvation because he walks in the light. The love of Christ is what compels a Christian to walk in the light. The Christian has a desire to follow Christ, to love like Christ, and to be like Christ. Muslims walk in the darkness, for they do not have true love for their brothers and because they follow unholy Allah. In light of these truths, out of their doubt, Muslims seek for extra duties in the Qur'an and hadith in hopes that Allah will be gracious to them. "Whoso fights in the Cause of Allah, and is killed or gets victory, We shall bestow on him a great reward" (Qur'an 4:74). Fighting and violence are a means by which Muslims gain favor in Allah's sight. The terrorist leader Osama bin Laden understood this and taught that it was the only way to be assured of standing before Allah, "A martyr's privileges are guaranteed in paradise."[28] This is an effective recruiting measure, but even this bears no weight on Allah's subjective standards. In Islam, there simply is no assurance of salvation, for there is no salvation. Tragically, many Muslims who are left without security seek extreme measures to gain Allah's favor. This has led to much confusion, pain, and destruction around the world both historically and today. But the glorious message of Christ, the true light of man, continues to save Muslims from the darkness of Islam. The following testimony bears mighty witness to God's power to save through Christ.

Ramiz's Testimony

The testimony of Ramiz,[29] a former nominal Muslim and now a follower of Jesus, is an example of God's grace and love for Muslims and people of any background. Ramiz was born a few months after Albania was declared an atheist state by the communists in 1967.

---

[28]   Roxanne L. Euben, ed, "Declaration of War against the Americas," in *Princeton Readings in Islamic Thought*, (Princeton, New Jersey: Princeton University Press, 2009), 436–60.

[29]   Name changed for security purposes.

He grew up in a dark place and a dark time, when churches and other religious places were closed and some of them were destroyed, when religious literature was banned, and possession of religious books was punishable by incarceration.

Even in that dark place, however, God could not be taken away. Many people in Albania believed in God, though they kept their faith private. During the years under atheistic communism, God drew Ramiz to read the Bible out of curiosity to know why this book had been banned from society. It was difficult to find a Bible, not to mention that it was dangerous. The only place where the Bible could be found then was at the National Library, but it could only be borrowed with a special permit by a few people in good standing with the communist regime. The only reason it had even been allowed in the library was to grant a few select people the opportunity to study it in order to undermine the existence of God and attack biblical claims.

In the 1990s when European communism fell to pressure from Western democratic nations, religious literature was once again allowed. Ramiz found a New Testament in Albanian and read it. What he found on the pages of Scripture changed his life forever. The main figure who stood out from the New Testament was Jesus Christ. His teachings on unconditional love, gracious forgiveness, and prohibitions on vengeance against enemies, were completely different from anything Ramiz had ever heard under communism and Islam. Though to some, these teachings may have appeared like weakness, he immediately saw in them great strength and power. He recognized that the teachings of Jesus Christ demanded a response and a change of heart. The more he read, the more he became convinced that it was the very Word of God and the absolute truth. He saw that he was a sinner before a holy God and was led to repent of his sins and believe in Jesus Christ for forgiveness.

Conclusion

God found Ramiz and rescued him out of a harsh life surrounded by false religion, and He can do the same with every Muslim who hears the gospel. It is the Christian duty to bring this message of light to those who are lost in darkness. Islam is antithetical to the gospel of Jesus Christ. Islam says that Muslims can be righteousness on account of their own efforts. The Bible, however, reminds us of the truth that none is righteous, not even one (Rom 3:10). Islam says that good works somehow atone for bad ones. The Bible says that one is saved by grace alone through faith alone (Eph 2:8). Islam says that Jesus Christ is not the way to come to God. The Bible says Jesus Christ alone bridges the gap between God and man (John 14:6).

Out of sheer obedience to Allah, every day, multiple times a day, Muslims bow their knees and incline their hearts toward Mecca. They repeat prayers they have been taught to them since childhood, all the while calloused to the core. Claiming to worship the one true God, they speak vanity into thin air, as Allah is not listening. As empty tombs, dead, face to the ground, they wonder in desperation, "Does he hear? Can a sinner such as me be forgiven? Will I ever find paradise?" They look up for a moment, hoping toward the sky, only to bow back down to the Allah of this world.

In rejecting Christ, Muslims have no hope. Christ, however, has come to seek and save the lost. No matter how far away, no matter how long He has been rejected, no matter how much wrong has been done, the offer of forgiveness stands. He will take every broken heart, every battered soul, and every fallen man or woman who calls out to Him for rescue. Repentant sinners formerly clothed in filthy garments are newly wrapped in the robes of Christ's own perfect righteousness (Isa 61:10; 64:6). Jesus provides full forgiveness and final assurance of salvation. To the Muslims who are friends, family, or even far off, please know that everyone who believes in Jesus will find paradise, "For God so loved the world, that He gave His only begotten Son, that whoever believes in Him shall not perish, but have eternal life" (John 3:16).

THE THREAT OF RELIGIOUS PLURALISM IN POST-COMMUNIST CROATIA

Miško Horvatek
Theological Biblical Academy, Croatia

[Editor's Note: The fall of Communism and the establishment of Croatia as a new sovereign state have led to massive ideological shifts within the span of just one generation. Though the newfound religious freedom is to be celebrated with great joy, it has presented new challenges that the believers in Croatia must face. From a Croatian context, this essay details the danger of religious pluralism and how to overcome it with the exclusive gospel of Jesus Christ.]

The Importance of Christological Clarity for Christ's Church in Croatia

The doctrine of the person and work of Christ should be studied and taught by all Christians with the greatest degree of reverence and precision. The importance of accuracy in understanding and communicating this doctrine should be especially evident in the preacher's sermon or the theologian's text—so evident that he leaves no one in his audience confused about where he stands concerning the God-man, Jesus Christ. Over such a person, there is no room for ambiguity or vacillation. The message must be certain: Jesus Christ is not one among many religious teachers. As Peter rightly confessed, Jesus "is the Christ, the Son of the living God" (Matt 16:16).

This has been the conviction of the church during its brightest moments. The Nicene Creed of AD 325, for example, spells out Christ's exclusivity and authority with some of the best theological eloquence and accuracy:

> We believe ... in one Lord Jesus Christ, the Son of God, begotten of the Father, only-begotten, that is, of the substance of the Father, God of God, Light of Light, true God of true God, begotten not made, of one substance with the Father, through whom all things were made, things in heaven and things on earth; who for us men and for our salvation came down and was made flesh, and became man, suffered, and rose on the third day, and ascended into the heavens; [and] is coming to judge the living and dead.[1]

The 1646 Westminster Assembly produced an equally qualitative article of faith that beautifully yet simply extols the majesty of Christ's humanity and divinity:

> The Son of God, the second Person in the Trinity, being very and eternal God, of one substance, and equal with the Father, died, when the fullness of time was come, took upon him man's nature, with all the essential properties and common infirmities thereof, yet without sin; being conceived by the power of the Holy Ghost, in the womb of the Virgin Mary, of her substance. So that two whole, perfect, and distinct natures, the Godhead and the manhood, were inseparably joined together in one person, without conversion, composition, or confusion. Which person is very God, and very man, yet one Christ, the only Mediator between God and man.[2]

---

[1]   Henry Bettenson, ed., *Documents of the Christian Church*, 2nd ed. (Oxford, UK: Oxford University Press, 1963), 25.

[2]   The Westminster Confession of Faith, VIII.2.

Yet the history of the church has not always been so bright. A surprising number of theologians from within Christianity have labored to wrest away from Jesus His deity and to rob Him of His divine attributes. To them it is more rational to believe in a Jesus who is more like Daniel among the lions. He is a *little* better than the average man—but only a little. In their minds, Jesus is the ultimate humanitarian, who, as Roman Catholic theologian Walter Kasper states, had "absolute trust in God, and unselfish interest in people."[3] According to Kasper, a distinction must be made between the man Jesus and the ideal Christ of the church: "He is the historical Jesus, who is something else from the Christ of the church's faith, and he did not demand for Himself divine authority."[4]

But the testimony of Scripture itself could not be more clear. Take, for example, the apostle Paul's understanding of Jesus based on his encounter with Him on the Damascus road. This glorious Lord who appeared to Paul is "Jesus of Nazareth" (Acts 22:8), and this Jesus is worthy of absolute obedience (22:10). As Seyoon Kim writes, "The gospel that he received on the Damascus road Paul defines, first of all, Christologically: it is Jesus Christ, the Son of God (Gal 1.12, 16), 'the glory of Christ, who is the image of God'" (2 Cor 4.4).[5] There is no distinction for Paul. The historical Jesus who appeared to Paul is the Christ, the sovereign Lord of his life. Recognizing this truth was the essence of his conversion.

In light of Paul's conversion accounts (cf. Acts 9:1–19; 22:1–21; 26:9–23) we see that the person of Jesus Christ is central to conversion—and thus central to evangelism. To speak of the work of evangelism, not to mention Christian edification, can only make sense if at the very outset we understand and believe in Jesus Christ as apostle Paul came to believe on that Damascus road. The hope and prayer of the writer of this study, then, is that the spiritual leaders of the church in Croatia—and wherever else these words go—will reexamine their Christology in the light of God's Word so that their conclusion would

---

[3]   Walter Kasper, *Krist da Crkva ne, in Teološke meditacije*, (Družba katoličkog Apostolata: Zagreb 1980).

[4]   Ibid., 13.

[5]   Seyoon Kim, *The Origin of Paul's Gospel*, (Eugene, Oregon: Wipf & Stock, 2007), 100.

be the same as the apostles: the historical Jesus of Nazareth is the Christ, the Son of the Living God, the Lord, very God and very man.

The Rise of Religious Pluralism in Post-Communist Croatia (1990s to 2016)

The first references to the arrival of the gospel in Croatia are found in Paul's mention of Illyricum in Romans 15:19 ("from Jerusalem and all the way around to Illyricum I have fulfilled the ministry of the gospel of Christ"[6]), and to Dalmatia in 2 Timothy 4:10 ("Titus [has gone] to Dalmatia").[7] In other words, already by Paul's third missionary journey, in the mid-50s AD, gospel seeds had already been sown in Croatian soil. But that was two millennia ago, and much has happened since then. This essay picks up the history of the gospel and its impact as of two decades ago, with the fall of Communism in the early 1990s.

The Fall of Communism and Croatia's Transition to an Independent State
The Socialist Federal Republic of Yugoslavia was established in the aftermath of World War II. It was constituted as a socialist state made up of six republics (Slovenia, Croatia, Bosnia and Herzegovina, Serbia, Montenegro, and Macedonia) and five nationalities (Croats, Serbians, Slovenians, Macedonians, and Bošnjaks-Muslims). Four languages were recognized (Croatian, Slovenian, Serbian, and Macedonian) along with two alphabets (Latin and Cyrillic) and three main religions (Serbian Orthodox, Roman Catholicism, and Islam). It had one political party, the Communist Party. Communist marshal Josip Broz Tito united the peoples in one country for forty-six years (1953–1980). Following his death in 1980, the unity of the six republics continued artificially for another decade. Eventually, the festering political climate ignited a revolt by the pro-Western republics of Slovenia and Croatian, and on October 8, 1991, Croatia became an independent state, dissolving all ties with the Socialist Federal Republic of Yugoslavia. Although Croatia dates its history

---

[6] Illyricum was a large district along the eastern and northeastern coast of the Adriatic Sea. It included the area of what is today known as Croatia, Bosnia, Serbia, Montenegro, Macedonia, and Albania.

[7] Dalmatia today is a province along Croatia's southwestern shore, on the Adriatic Sea.

all the way back to 7th century BC, 1991 marked a new beginning for its history. The worldwide recognitions that followed strengthened Croatia and gave the young European state political, social, and economic stability. It also raised an issue that concerns our study most, that of new religious freedom.

The Role of Religion in Post-Communist Society

All Croatian patriots rejoiced when Croatia became a sovereign state. The dream that many Croats had held for almost half a century now became a reality. Democracy, which was taken away from Croats by communist dictators, slowly began appearing in all spheres of life.

Coinciding with the dawn of new political freedom came the dawn of the freedom of religion. However, the clergy of the Roman Catholic Church (RCC) quickly took advantage of this freedom and turned it into a new form of one-party rule. Soon, to be a "real Croat" meant to be a Roman Catholic. Almost overnight the RCC became politically and socially aggressive, demanding from the new government special privileges. In turn, the RCC was granted significant influence in education and government and began receiving considerable subsidies and grants from the national budget. Today, the RCC is by far the largest religious body in Croatia.

Nevertheless, after the collapse of Communism, a variety of religious groups have grown in Croatia's new era of religious freedom. One recent poll gives the following statistical summary: Roman Catholics constitute 76 percent of the population; Serbian Orthodox, 11 percent; and Protestants, only 0.4 percent.[8] The RCC maintains its supremacy, but other religious groups like Muslims, Jews, and Mormons are accepted as part of the Croatian culture. The traditional religions of Serbian Orthodoxy, Judaism, and Islam are treated with special favor because of their roots in the various ethnicities present in Croatia. Ultimately, these multicolor spiritual dynamics demonstrate that Croats who typically claim to be Roman Catholic by birth are nonetheless open to the messages being preached by others than just the RCC.

---

[8] http://journeymart.com/de/croatia/religion.aspx.

The Roman Catholic Church—a State within a State

As with other countries in Eastern Europe, the rapid development of democracy in Croatia left Communism without influence. In the formerly communist countries of Romania, Bulgaria, and Serbia, the Orthodox Church quickly became the de facto state religion. In the countries of Poland, Hungary, Slovenia, and Croatia, the RCC rose to social and political dominance.

Thus, soon after the Croatian War of Independence (1991–1995), a special concordat between the president of Croatia and a representative of the Vatican was signed on February 13, 1997. Article 2 of this agreement acknowledges the priority of the RCC in the development of the nation and in its role—both historically and in the present—in governmental, civil, cultural, and educational spheres.[9] Soon, RCC leaders were speaking on the same level and with the same social authority as politicians. Whenever a crisis hit or elections came, members of the political parties in Croatia would make their pilgrimages to the church hierarchy to barter for the support of the RCC clergy. It is difficult to deny that the RCC replaced Communism as the Croatian state's ideology, with true freedom of religion existent only on paper.

The Pressure to Embrace Religious Pluralism

The Spirit of the Present Age

The idea of religious pluralism as an ideology is a postmodern worldview. Yet the pluralism of twenty years ago is completely different when compared with the thought of current writers. As McGrath explains, pluralism is nothing new: "Christian proclamation has always taken place in a pluralist world, in competition with rival religious and intellectual convictions."[10]

In Christian contexts, the ideology of pluralism pressures all Christians to be "open minded," brotherly, and tolerant of the beliefs of all the faiths. According to religious pluralists, evangelical Christians must cease to be theologically exclusive and should

---

[9]   http://narodne-novine.nn.hr/clanci/medunarodni/1997_02_3_19.html.

[10]   Alister E. McGrath, *Christian Theology: An Introduction*, 5th ed. (Malden, Massachusetts: Blackwell, 2011), 425.

embrace their so-called spiritual brethren despite differences in their formal denominations. Although their own pluralistic ideology is non-negotiable, others must abandon their convictions and assertions and exercise love and tolerance. All roads, they claim, lead to God. Todd Miles explains:

> The rise of religious pluralism is tied to rise of philosophical pluralism. Often labeled the philosophy of postmodernity, philosophical pluralism is easier to identify by what it denies than by what it affirms. It is characterized by a gnawing epistemological skepticism and a rabid suspicion of any truth claim.... Philosophical pluralism is attended by a commitment to culturally situated nature of truth and a radical perspectivalism. Reality cannot be known as it actually is but only how it appears to the knower. Because of this, objective knowledge is impossible. The result is that, if absolute truth exists at all, it cannot be know with certainty. Therefore, any suggestion that particular ideology of religions truth claim is superior to another is necessarily false.[11]

As this ideology infects the church, the church becomes more and more inconsistent and confused in its teachings. Yes, evangelism of the lost—including pluralists—is necessary. But this evangelism cannot contain truth claims. The central feature of the gospel which the church has proclaimed during her brightest moments, that Jesus Christ is the exclusive mediator between God and man, is now increasingly questioned, if not silenced. Ironically, in the West in general and Croatia in particular, Protestant churches continue talking about the need for evangelization, all the while imbibing the tenets of ideological pluralism. How can this be?

Churches of the Reformation's Heritage

Churches of Reformation's Heritage in Croatia, a book written by Croatian historian Stanko Jambrek, provides a short and objective

---

[11] Todd L. Miles, *A God of Many Understandings* (Nashville, Tennessee: Broadman & Homan Academic, 2010), 139.

history of the Protestant church in Croatia, including its organizational structures and creeds, with a special emphasis on the Baptist and Pentecostal movements.[12] In his assessment of the ecclesiological activities of Christ Pentecostal Church in particular, the author points to the growth of ecumenism in the denomination and consequently in other Reformation-heritage churches in Croatia. It is noteworthy that in his assessment, the spread of ecumenical pluralism in Croatian evangelical churches is due in significant part to the efforts of John Stott, Bill Bright, and Billy Graham.[13] All three evangelists visited Croatia at different times, and all three labored to unite Protestant churches while minimizing differences. However, in terms of the largest, most general influence toward ecumenical pluralism among these churches, the writer points to the efforts of the RCC for its part in inviting evangelical leaders under its umbrella of influence and pursuing influence among evangelical believers in general.

For example, during a week of prayer organized under the banner of Christian unity, the RCC would invite leadership and believers of other Christian groups, including evangelicals, to participate in their celebrations. During the same week, RCC believers—most often led by their bishop responsible for ecumenical relations—would be encouraged to visit Orthodox, Lutheran, Baptist, and Pentecostal churches. Such unity efforts would raise the concern of conservatives within their ranks, but over time their voices were increasingly ignored. Slowly but surely, the majority of the members of those Protestant churches, whose leaders had been invited to fellowship with the leadership of the RCC, and whose members welcomed the presence of RCC members into their midst, were caught up in the ecumenical spirit. Joint worship services, intermarriage between confessions, participation in the Mass, and pilgrimages to holy shrines came to be common among the more progressive, liberal elements within these churches. The spirit of *semper reformanda,* "always reforming," which was supposed to mark the churches in the heritage of the Reformation, soon came to be applied to the doctrines of this ecumenical system.

---

[12] Stanko Jambrek. *Crkve Reformacijske baštine,* [*Churches of Reformation heritage in Croatia*] (Zagreb: Bogoslovni Institut, 203).

[13] Ibid., 131.

Acceleration of Pluralism via Mass Media

With the development of modern communications and the Internet age has come the spread of all kinds of religious information, including disturbing and destructive influences. As a result, mass media has become the new battleground for building religious followings.

In Croatia, the RCC holds a monopoly over religious programming. Though it may convey a spirit of congeniality publicly, it fiercely guards its territory through the steady control of the religious media. The state ensures that the RCC has ample time and unparalleled access to spread its dogmas and practices with the widest audiences of TV viewers and Internet users. Always in the media, RCC leaders convey to the population that it is a power to be reckoned with and is owed homage; to be associated with them is to be on the right side of power. Conservative evangelicals, however, have no such access to the media. To find a niche requires considerable amounts of money, and those who do find access either have their programs censored by the RCC or by those in the secular media who are friendly to the RCC.

Ultimately, mass media instills and protects the mantra that the RCC is the only true church. From this standpoint of power, the RCC hierarchy effectively says to all other churches, "you are either with us or against us." The ecumenism it preaches, like all ecumenism, is all about who holds power. Those who naïvely believe they can influence members of the RCC with the true gospel through closer participation are simply pulled in by the RCC's gravity; they ultimately do the RCC's bidding.

Rediscovering Christological Clarity

At the center of the matter is *Christology*—what is believed and taught about the person of Jesus, the Christ, the Son of the living God. If we are to understand at all what constitutes the true church, we must first understand this person. It is He who said, "I will build my church" (Matt 16:18). The church is His; He is its head. He is the One who holds it together and the One who is preeminent within it (Col 1:18). He is the One who holds it or removes it like a lampstand (Rev 1:20). Therefore, it is vitally important that all who would call themselves followers of Christ seek to understand the truth about Him and communicate it without partiality, fear, or divided allegiance, in order that mankind would give Him the glory which He alone is worthy (Phil 2:10–11).

However, it is the very fact that Christ demands this exclusive loyalty and love that gives rise to the claims of false christs. Since the true Christ demands complete loyalty in thought, affection, and deed, and since some refuse to bow, those same rebellious ones will endeavor to confuse and distract others from that end as well. The teaching of the RCC is one such example.

Roman Catholic Christology Is Sacrilegious

The RCC's dogmas, sacraments, hierarchy, and traditions all show that it is more interested in its own role as head, its own pre-eminence, and its own authority—rather than the headship and rule of Christ. While it is true that a cursory reading of what some of their theologians teach about Christ comes very close to the message of Scripture, it must not be forgotten that all of this is still filtered through the lens of RCC creeds and magisterial teaching. To some it may seem that the RCC has a great tolerance for different views, even evangelical views. But this must always be understood as ultimately submissive to the official teaching of the Church.

The Sacrifice of Christ

Roman Catholic theologian Tomislav Šagi Bunić wrote the following about Christ: "In all mankind He expressed Himself as the best man. However, he was at the same time God, God's Son, the eternal Word of the Father. He was like a man in everything, but exceptionally different from man, because He was God."[14] While this seems to agree with biblical teaching, the truth is that the incarnate Christ in writings of RCC theologians is not the same Christ as the one that they present in the consecration of the Mass, though they themselves would see no difference. He is the perpetual sacrifice at the beck and call of a sinful, human priest who orders Him down to suffer in the Mass. As one Catholic source explains:

---

[14] Tomislav Šagi—Bunić, *But There is no Other Way, Ecumenical Opening*, trans. Ali Drugog puta Nema (Zagreb: Kršćanska Sadašnjost, 1972), 92.

> When the priest pronounces the tremendous words
> of consecration, he reaches up into the heavens,
> brings Christ down from His throne, and places Him
> upon our altar to be offered up again as the Victim
> for the sins of man. It is a power greater than that
> of monarchs and emperors: it is greater than that of
> saints and angels, greater than that of Seraphim and
> Cherubim. Indeed it is greater even than the power
> of the Virgin Mary. While the Blessed Virgin was
> the human agency by which Christ became incarnate
> a single time, the priest brings Christ down from
> heaven, and renders Him present on our altar as the
> eternal Victim for the sins of man—not once but a
> thousand times! The priest speaks and lo! Christ,
> the eternal and omnipotent God, bows His head in
> humble obedience to the priest's command.[15]

This statement is entirely at odds with biblical teaching. The RCC has trivialized the deity of Christ by making Him the slave of men, always suffering on the cross at their beck and call.

The Work of Salvation

Because the RCC employs an allegorical approach to the Bible, it abandons the biblical author as the objective authority over the meaning of his text. Allegorization as a method of interpretation seeks to uncover the multiple hidden meanings in the biblical text.[16] As this system developed in the early church, it resulted in a spiritualization of the Scriptures and a neglect of its literal meaning. Over time, it became the interpretational norm, with a great deal of emphasis placed on the concept of *sensus plenior,* or "fuller sense" — an aspect of meaning in the text which is beyond the grammatical meaning. Using allegorization, a reader can potentially read into

---

15   John A. O'Brien, *The Faith of Millions: The Credentials of the Catholic Church* (Huntington, Indiana: Our Sunday Visitor, 1874), 255–56. For an analysis of the mass from a former Catholic, see James G. McCarthy, *The Gospel According to Rome* (Eugene, Oregon: Harvest House, 1995).

16   Gerhard Maier, *Biblical Hermeneutics*, trans. Robert W. Yarbrough (Wheaton, Illinois: Crossway, 1994), 70.

the text whatever meaning he believes is best—even to the point of heresy.

This allegorization impacts not just minor issues, but the interpretation of the gospel itself. Through allegorization, the way of salvation can be explained as a synergistic effort of works—the works of God and the works of man. For the RCC, salvation is a process (of which baptism is only the beginning), controlled from start to finish by the Church itself.[17] A prominent Croatian RCC theologian, Bonaventura Duda, explained the way of salvation as follows:

> Salvation is self-realization. Without his own contribution, nobody can be saved... . This contribution can be achieved by ministering to others ("I was hungry, and you gave to me something to eat ..."). Salvation is indeed a series of events in which only God can judge it... . Sometimes, even a small bit of love and goodness is a deciding factor—salvation simply should be worked out. Salvation is mystery.[18]

This does not come from a direct, grammatical reading of the biblical text in its historical context.[19] Yet that is what is preached from Rome, and that is what many churches in the heritage of the Reformation are becoming more and more comfortable with, even in Croatia. In fact, as one evangelical has argued, it is best for evangelical Christians to stop contending with Catholics face-to-face over the soteriological issues of the gospel, and instead endeavor to work more with them shoulder-to-shoulder in an ecumenical fashion. If this transition is not made, then evangelical Christianity will lose all of its platform for preaching the gospel.[20] Such an approach only tramples underfoot the person and work of Jesus Christ.

---

[17] McCarthy, *The Gospel According to Rome*, 28–29.

[18] Dragan Kalajdžić 'Bonaventura Duda, *Are We Alone on the Way?* (Zagreb: Kršćanska Sadašnjost, 1980), 60–61.

[19] McCarthy, *The Gospel According to Rome*, 65.

[20] Roko Kerovec, "Kristovo uskrsnuće i eshatološka vizija Božjeg kraljevstva kao platforma evangelizacijske prakse: izazovi i mogućnosti evanđeoskog poslanja" [Christ's Resurrection

Ecumenical Christology as Relativistic

Proponents of ecumenism typically make their case by several arguments. First, ecumenism is advanced as the "real solution to the problem of divided Christian Church."[21] Ecumenical success boosts "the civilization of the world, social involvement, promotion of peace, the fight against racism, economic development in Third World countries, human rights, and the fight against hunger."[22]

Yet participation and success in bringing civility is not the most pressing need of the undeveloped or underdeveloped regions of the world. In principle, ecumenical efforts—rightly understood—should involve the joining together of true believers to bring the message of Jesus Christ to those in spiritual need. But the reality is that ecumenical circles, the spiritual need of man is quickly lost. Why? Most ecumenists are doctrinally naïve and passive, even though they may be active and educated ethically and materially. As they progress, their "social passion ingests salvific passion."[23] As that happens, the true doctrine of the person and work of Christ is obscured.

For evangelicals whose only rule for faith and practice is Scripture, the highly acclaimed ecumenical document, "Evangelicals and Roman Catholics Together" (ECT), signed in 1994 by representatives of both camps, is an ecclesiological and theological scandal that only confuses the person and work of Christ. Its signatories set aside the most important and fundamental doctrines of Christianity in order to advance a lesser cause. Fundamentally, this document and its signatories gave direct instruction that both evangelicals and Catholics are to look on each other uncritically as already "saved" or "evangelized." For example, it states, "In view of the large number of non-Christians in the world and the enormous challenge of our common evangelistic task, it is neither theologically legitimate nor a

---

and the Eschatological Vision of God's Kingdom as a Platform of Evangelistic Practice: Challenges and the Possibilities of Evangelical Mission], *Kairos* 2, no. 2 (2008): 259–260.

[21]   Bert Beverly Beach, *Ecumenism—Boon or Bane* (Washington, DC: Review and Herald, 1985), 9.

[22]   Ibid., 160.

[23]   Ibid., 158.

213

prudent use of resources for one Christian community to proselytize among active adherents of another Christian community."[24]

The signatories went so far in their ecumenical zeal that they even curtailed the simple command of the Lord, that the gospel should be preached to every creature (Mark 16:15), and this certainly does not just apply to those who are non-Christian by tradition or heritage. As MacArthur concludes, ECT leaves the instruction that "people who believe they are 'born again' because they were baptized Catholic 'must be given full freedom and respect' to remain Catholic. That is, they should not be approached by evangelicals and told that no amount of sacraments or good works can make them acceptable to God."[25]

Yet believers are nowhere called to withhold the preaching of the gospel of Christ, even to those in their own churches who are self-deceived by a false profession. Such ecumenism only silences the gospel and prevents people from hearing, all for the sake of formal "peace" between churches. This kind of ecumenism, in the end, tends toward the inhibition of evangelization.

The Rich Heritage of Biblical Christology

Religious pluralism in post-communist Croatia holds a significant control on Croatian society, especially in spiritual realm. The spiritual erosion of society is reflected in every aspect of life. Romanization, pluralization, and secularization produce confusion and apathy across the population.

Sadly, many once-evangelical churches have lost their message for the lost. The only remedy for such confusion is the return to the source of this message. Just as the Reformer Martin Luther preached in the darkness of his time, so the Croatian churches must preach *sola scriptura* [scripture alone]! And it is not simply "scripture alone" for antiquity's sake. It is "scripture alone" because only the Bible contains the truth about the person and work of Christ. It is this message, found only in the Scriptures, which can excite and embolden us in light of the darkness of our own day.

---

[24] "Evangelicals and Catholics Together: The Christian Mission in the Third Millennium" (29 March 1994), 22–23. For a full response to this document, see John F. MacArthur, Jr., "Evangelicals and Catholics Together," *MSJ* 6 no. 1 (Spring 1995): 7–37.

[25] MacArthur, "Evangelicals and Catholics Together," 14.

The return to the Bible and its primary focus, Jesus Christ, requires not a quick glance but careful study—not a snapshot but a timed exposure. The development of a truly biblical Christology requires the right hermeneutics: literal interpretation rather than the allegorical spiritualization of the RCC, and study of the entire biblical witness. Some crucial areas of examination are as follows:

Jesus' Authority. Whereas the prophets in the Old Testament would say, "The word of the Lord came to me," or "thus says the Lord," Jesus Christ simply says, "I say unto you" (e.g. Matt 5:21–48). It is not that what the prophets said was less authoritative, since Christ did not come to abolish the Law or the Prophets (Matt 5:17), and all Scripture is equally inspired by God (2 Tim 3:16). Rather, whereas Moses and the prophets were mere channels of divine revelation, Christ is the source—the climax (Heb 1:1–2). Any truly biblical Christology, therefore, must exalt Christ as the exclusive sovereign One, the Word, the One from whom all revealed knowledge comes.

Jesus' Equality. In John 10:30 Jesus says, "I and the Father are one." The statement is vastly important for understanding the person of Jesus Christ. He is not inferior to the Father but equal. He is not simply a man but is of the same category as God. He is not in need for man to complete Him, serve Him, or finish what He could not accomplish. But He—like the Father—"has life in Himself" (John 5:26).

Jesus' Forgiveness. The narrative of the paralytic's healing in Mark 2:2–12 clearly teaches that Jesus Himself has the prerogative to forgive sins: "My son, your sins are forgiven" (v. 5). The scribes rightly recognized the implications of Jesus' statement: "Who can forgive sins but God alone?" (v. 7). To prove that His words were not just wishful thinking, Jesus then proceeds to heal the man as the demonstration of His ability to forgive: "But that you may know that the Son of Man has authority on earth to forgive sins ... I say to you, rise, pick up your bed, and go home" (v. 10). If Jesus' words were effective in causing the paralytic to be healed, His words were no less effective in forgiving the man's sins.

215

Jesus' Titles. The title "Lord" means much more than the simple "sir." For example, when Paul teaches that "everyone who calls upon the name of the Lord will be saved" (Rom 10:13), he is connecting this promise—which was originally given in the Old Testament—directly to Jesus Christ, the One who must be confessed by one's mouth as "Lord" in order to be saved (10:9). It is noteworthy, however, that this Old Testament promise which Paul cites in Romans 10:13 is taken from Joel 2:32, "And it shall come to pass that everyone who calls on the name of the LORD shall be saved." There the word "LORD" translates the Hebrew "Yahweh." By connecting the name of Jesus (Rom 10:9) with the name of Yahweh (Joel 2:32) in this manner, we see that Jesus is ascribed the highest possible honor. He is recognized as God.

Ultimately, any true return to Scripture and focus upon the person and work of Jesus Christ will not lead to minimizing of the facts that are discovered. Any true understanding of Jesus Christ will not allow His person or work in any way to be subjugated by humanitarian, ecumenical efforts. Rather, it will motivate the greatest evangelistic efforts to preach the gospel to all people, regardless of official, religious identities.

Conclusion

Certainly, there is a small minority of evangelicals in Croatia who, in spite of pressure to identify with either the RCC or Protestant ecumenists, are not distracted by endless dialogues about improving social services and interreligious relations. These faithful believers are active in the true work of evangelism, of preaching the Christ of Scripture to people who are perishing in their sins. Indeed, God is building His church. This church is not the church of the majority, which is visible and corrupted by human wisdom, but the church of those who have been truly changed by God's grace. More help is needed. Missionaries to Croatia are needed: faithful messengers who will uphold biblical Christology, win Croats to the biblical Christ, plant biblical churches of which Christ is truly the head, and help train new national pastors who will obey uncompromisingly everything Christ has commanded. May it all be done for the sake of our only Lord and Savior Jesus Christ.

THE STRAW KINGDOM: A FALSE CHRIST IN THE PHILIPPINES EXPOSED

Vincent Greene

The Expositor's Academy, The Philippines

[Editor's Note: In the Philippines today, there may be fewer followers of the true Christ than there are followers of a false one. Apollo Quiboloy's "Kingdom of Jesus Christ" is one of many cults around the world today wherein impostors masquerade as the true Christ. This essay aims to expose the well-known, self-proclaimed Christ of the Philippines by addressing his claims in light of the unique and exclusive glory of our Lord Jesus Christ, the only begotten from the Father (John 1:14).

Introduction

In the islands of the Philippines, defending the biblical teaching concerning Christ is of primary importance. A recent attack on Christ's person and work has surfaced in the claims of Apollo Carreon Quiboloy, the leader of a large cult called "The Kingdom of Jesus Christ," which boasts over six million followers worldwide.[1] As stated on the ministry's website, Quiboloy has declared himself to be "the appointed Son of God" based upon hearing God person-

---

[1] By some estimates, there are fewer Filipinos following the true Christ than this false one. See Jack Miller, "Religion in the Philippines," http://asiasociety.org/education/religion-philippines.

ally speak to him for many years of his life. He claims that God told him, "Now, You are My Son, you are My residence." This supposed appointment by God has led Quiboloy to assume that he has full control over the Kingdom of God. Thus, he commands:

> Follow me because this is where the Father is! You will be freed from the greatest bondage of all. It is a Luciferic, Satanic bondage of the serpent seed, which means obeying your will until you die and go to hell. You can be freed from that now. Come out, and let us have a feast in the wilderness. Let us have a feast, a thanksgiving worship presentation that is acceptable to the Almighty Father.[1]

He claims to have received this divine appointment to Sonship because Jesus only completed *part* of the plan for mankind. Quiboloy teaches that Jesus' death on the cross merely secured "the Sonship and Kingship" for mankind. It did not, however, provide a path for that "Sonship and Kingship" to be restored to mankind in a practical and personal way. The one who will bring complete restoration is ostensibly none other than Quiboloy himself, "the appointed Son of God."

Some of those who criticize Quiboloy focus their discussion either on the crass extravagance of his ministry and lifestyle or the way in which he has influenced Filipino politics. The greater issue to be examined, however, is how his teachings contradict Scripture regarding the uniqueness of Jesus as the only begotten (*monogenes*)[2] Son of God. An examination must take place that compares the bib-

---

[1] "The Threefold Ministry." http://www.kingdomofjesuschrist.org/the-threefold-ministry.

[2] This essay follows the NASB translation of *monogenes* as "only begotten," but it should be noted that there is considerable debate regarding the term's etymology and semantic domain. The controversy transcends the scope of this essay and does not ultimately affect its conclusions. Whether the word is best translated as "only begotten," "one of a kind," or "only," the point for the sake of this essay is the same: Jesus is unique, the only Son of the Father in a way shared by no one else—a basic notion that is communicated by each of the proposed translations in (primarily Johannine) contexts. Even where *monogenes* is not used, John portrays Jesus and Jesus alone as "the Son" of the Father (John 3:17, 35, 36; 5:19, 20, 21, 22, 23, 25, 26; 6:40; 8:35, etc.). For the seminal work that challenged longstanding assumptions about the word, see Dale Moody, "God's only Son: The Translation of John 3:16 in the Revised Standard Version" *Journal of Biblical Literature* 72, no. 4 (1953): 213–19.

lical teaching regarding the person and work of Jesus to the teachings and assertions of Quiboloy. Are Quiboloy's claims true? Is he the newly appointed Son of God? Or is Jesus unique as the only begotten Son of God? This essay will address these crucial questions. First, a description of the specific Christological claims of Quiboloy will be explained. Second, a theological understanding of Jesus' uniqueness as the only begotten Son of God will be discussed. Finally, the implications of Quiboloy's teachings to the body of Christ will be elucidated.

The Christological Claims of Apollo Quiboloy

Recipient of the Threefold Ministry

When examining the Christological claims made by Apollo Quiboloy, a logical sequence of ideas is apparent within his theological framework in that he has placed considerable thought into his claims and actually believes in them as factual truth. For example, he describes an incident where he was indwelt by three spirits that he received from God the Father. These spirits represented the "Threefold Ministry," meaning "the Mosaic, Solomonic, and the Prophetic ministries."[3] He believes that these three ministries were entrusted to him by God for the purpose of leading the rest of humanity into securing the victory over Satan, who presently holds the keys to the kingdom of this world. He claims this prerogative because God said to him, "You will talk to the one who, by deception, is sitting upon that mountain as the king of the world. You have to go to the summit of that mountain and vanquish the enemy by telling him, 'Let my people go!'"[4]

This threefold ministry, he claims, is the mechanism by which he has been empowered to spread God's full revelation to the world. Since God spoke to him and gave him these three powerful spirits, Quiboloy claims he has exclusive possession of certain truths that must be believed by everyone. The following quote reveals his repeated assertions that no one but he (and anyone who follows him) knows the truth about the gospel, Jesus Christ, and God the Father:

---

[3]   "The Threefold Ministry." http://www.kingdomofjesuschrist.org/the-threefold-ministry.

[4]   Ibid.

But many don't know what happened in Calvary. They think all that happened there was that He [Jesus] was crucified and died for them. As for me, I know—and many Christians don't—that when Adam and Eve sinned, in them was implanted a seed that cannot be solved by human means, because it is a spiritual problem. It is a spiritual seed.

Christians do not know that there are seeds of the spirit implanted in our souls. They only know of physical seeds implanted in the womb of their wives, creating a physical life. After nine months it is born, bearing 36 of their chromosomes—18 from the wife and 18 from the husband. All they know is the physical life; they don't know the spiritual life—that spirits also have seeds. They don't know that Lucifer the devil and the Almighty Father are also spirits and they have seeds.

And these seeds are words that have been planted in them. When you receive them, they become implanted into your soul. And they will create a spiritual life—either of obedience or disobedience. I know that because it was revealed to me and I am the only one preaching about it. You cannot hear it from any other preacher... . What I am revealing to you, as it was revealed to me, was not revealed to others; that's why nobody knows about it. And nobody can preach about it like I do.[5]

Quiboloy uses this "new revelation to teach that the solution to mankind's sin problem lies ultimately in trusting that God has given him the keys to Sonship and Kingship. Jesus could not fully secure our salvation because God still needed someone from the fallen human race to be His new Son. Quiboloy claims that this is what God did to him—God made him His Son. He explains, "The

---

[5] Ibid.

Begotten Son [Jesus] in the Jewish setting paid the price! Now, the problem is: the mission of the Son was not only *to take back* the Sonship and the Kingship, but *to give it back to the rightful heir.*"[6] And, since a rightful heir was not available after Jesus, God the Father began to look for someone who would be found worthy enough to be that heir.[7] In His search, God was able to discover Quiboloy and through the threefold ministries of the Mosaic, Solomonic, and the Prophetic ministries, God gave him the Sonship and Kingship that would finally offer mankind freedom from sin.

The Sonship and Kingship

Quiboloy defines the Sonship as the ability to give eternal life to whomever he wills. But he considers the Kingship as the "greatest entrustment of all" because it grants to him "the power to rule over the Father's Kingdom and to implement the Father's spiritual laws all over the world."[8] He teaches that everyone since Adam and Eve have failed to "be implanted with the Father's spirit [i.e., seed]," thereby losing "not only the Sonship, but the Kingship as well."[9] Although Quiboloy does not include Jesus in his list of failures and states that His death on the cross was "not a defeat, but a victory," he nonetheless denies that Jesus is the true Son (i.e., the rightful heir of the Father) and true King. He teaches that Jesus *regained* the Kingship for mankind, but that it remained for the rightful heir to come and *inherit* it.[10] Central to Quiboloy's teaching is the dogma

---

[6]   Ibid. Italics mine.

[7]   Ibid. Quiboloy teaches that Christians are not the rightful heirs because there exist too many divisions of them. He states, "The Jewish Age was phased out. Another body was called, not from the Jews, but from the gentiles. There came Christianity ... [however,] there are so many factions in Christianity, there are Catholics, there are Protestants, there are Pentecostals, there are Charismatics, there are Mormons, there are the Iglesia [Ni Kristo], there are Jehovah's Witnesses. All of these received a portion of the revelation. But just like the Jewish people, their mistake was that they stopped somewhere. They did not continue. The first faction got so happy with their little revelation; they were content with where they were. So there's no difference between them and the Jewish people... . [Therefore,] the Father had to leave and go to another dimension in the spirit." Quiboloy claims it was in this new dimension of the spirit where God met and spoke to him.

[8]   Ibid.

[9]   Ibid.

[10]   Ibid.

that he alone—not Jesus—is the rightful heir of the Kingdom of God and the ultimate fulfilment of God's plan of salvation.

A Biblical Understanding of the Uniqueness of Jesus Christ

In contrast to the beliefs of Apollo Quiboloy, the Bible teaches that Jesus is the only begotten Son of God, that Jesus is unique in His role as Son, and that there is none like Him (cf. John 1:14, 18; 3:16, 18; 1 John 4:9). Jesus did not merely begin but completed the work of redemption that was planned before the creation of the universe (cf. John 6:37, 40; 17:23–24, 26; 2 Tim 1:9; Titus 1:2–3; Heb 13:20), which awaits its consummation in the future (cf. 1 Cor 15:24–28; Rev 11:15–18). The exclusivity of Jesus Christ as the unique Son of God may be demonstrated in many ways, but here we will highlight just three. Jesus, the true Son of God, is unique in that He shares underived oneness with the Father; uncaused eternality with the Father; and was given a mission from the Father that cannot be repeated.

Jesus' Oneness with God the Father

When Scripture states that Jesus is the only begotten Son of God, the implication is that He shares with God a oneness that no one else possesses. Friedrich Büchsel writes, "As the only begotten Son, Jesus is in the closest intimacy with God. There is no other with whom God can have similar fellowship. He shares everything with this Son.... He knows God, not just from hearsay, but from incomparably close intercourse with Him."[11] The way that the Bible identifies Jesus as the Son of God suggests a remarkable oneness. As John MacArthur notes, "In calling Jesus His Son, the Father declared Him to be of identical nature and essence with Himself."[12] The oneness is so complete that Jesus says, "If you had known Me, you would have known My Father also; from now on you know Him, and have seen Him" (John 14:7). His claim of full and comprehensive deity confirms

---

[11]   See Gerhard Kittel, Geoffrey W. Bromiley, and Gerhard Friedrich, eds., *Theological Dictionary of the New Testament* (Grand Rapids, Michigan: Eerdmans, 1964–), 740.

[12]   John MacArthur, *MacArthur New Testament Commentary: Matthew 16–23* (Chicago, Illinois: Moody, 1988), 68.

oneness with the Father that no one else has,[13] let alone a member of fallen humanity, as Quiboloy likes to suggest. No one can add to or improve upon Jesus' role as God's only Son because Jesus possesses a unique relationship with His Father that is greater and deeper than all other relationships. Jesus possesses all the same attributes as God the Father (Ps 102:25–27; Matt 28:18, 30; Mark 2:5, 7, 10; John 1:1, 4; 2:25; 4:18; 14:6; 16:30; Heb 1:11–12; 13:8). He is God of God, Light of Light, perfectly one with the Father. Indeed, when He became flesh His glory was seen, and it was glory as of the only begotten from the Father, full of grace and truth (John 1:14).

Jesus' Unique Eternality with God the Father

Jesus also uniquely shares eternality with the Father (and the Spirit). Jesus asserted His own eternal existence when He said, "Before Abraham was born, I am" (John 8:58). He also told Nicodemus that He had come down from heaven, implying that He is eternal (John 3:13). This is why Paul writes that Jesus is "before all things" (Col 1:17), and why the author of Hebrews notes that Jesus' throne is "forever and ever" (Heb 1:8), a claim Quiboloy directly contradicts and a prerogative he foolishly seeks for himself.

Additionally, the Gospel of John begins by establishing Jesus' existence at the time of creation. It states, "In the beginning was the Word, and the Word was with God, and the Word was God. He was in the beginning with God" (John 1:1–2). As George Beasley-Murray summarizes, "[Jesus], the Word, and none other, was with God in the beginning ... he was with God before all times and did not come into being at the 'beginning.'"[14] The fact that He was with God in the beginning makes Him uniquely suited to "narrate" the Father to man, for no one has ever seen God, but God the only Son, who is *at the Father's side,* has made Him known (John 1:18). Who can claim to be "the appointed Son of God" but the only one who was with God in the beginning and who is God from the beginning? Anyone else who makes such a claim contradicts biblical teaching and places himself in the realm of severe judgment (2 Pet. 2:1–2; Jude 25).

---

[13] John MacArthur, *MacArthur New Testament Commentary: John 12–21* (Chicago, Illinois: Moody, 2008), 104.

[14] George R. Beasley-Murray, *John*, 2nd ed., Word Biblical Commentary 36 (Dallas, Texas: Word, 2002), 11.

Jesus' Unique Mission with God the Father as Messiah

Not only does Jesus alone share oneness and eternality with God the Father (and the Spirit), but He was also given a unique mission by God the Father that no one else can perform. Jesus was and is the only true Messiah (the Christ). Though some might take it for granted, this is indeed the crux of the matter, since whoever denies that Jesus is uniquely the Christ is, according to the apostle John, a *liar* and the *antichrist* (1 John 2:22). These are serious accusations that warrant explanation. Jesus of Nazareth is uniquely qualified as God's Messiah in several ways, four of which are highlighted here.

First of all, only Jesus of Nazareth — not Quiboloy — was heralded into life by God's appointed forerunner, John the Baptist. In Malachi 3:1, we learn that God would send a messenger to prepare the way for the Messiah. That forerunner comes and bears testimony to Jesus, saying of Him, "Behold, the Lamb of God, who takes away the sin of the world!" (John 1:29). Quiboloy claims to have been given the prerogative of taking away people's sins, but God's messenger testified that it was Jesus, God's beloved Son, who would accomplish such a marvelous thing. This was, of course, publicly confirmed by none other than God the Father and God the Spirit at Jesus' baptism (Matt 3:13–17), something entirely unlike Quiboloy's crass self-promotion and utter lack of any external verification for his presumptuous claims.

Second, Jesus is uniquely in the Messianic lineage that traces back directly both to King David and Abraham (Matt 1:1–17). The Messianic genealogy is not superfluous but rather absolutely critical in establishing Jesus as the rightful son of Abraham and heir of David's kingdom (and thus heir of God's covenantal promises). Though Quiboloy claims that he has inherited the kingship that Jesus made available, the Scriptures from the very beginning tell a very different story about the Messiah figure. Genesis 49:10, for example, teaches explicitly that the kingship will *never depart* from the tribe of Judah. Quiboloy has no claim to Judah's heritage or the promises later given to King David's dynasty; yet both of Jesus' earthly parents, Mary and Joseph, came from the tribe of Judah, and were direct descendants of David himself.

Third, Quiboloy had a normal birth, but Jesus' birth was a sign of His wonderful Messiahship. The prophet Isaiah writes, "The Lord himself will give you a sign. Behold, the virgin shall conceive and bear a son, and shall call his name Immanuel" (Isa 7:14). This was, of course, fulfilled in Jesus' birth. Luke records that the angel Gabriel was sent from God to a virgin named Mary, and told her, "Behold, you will conceive in your womb and bear a son, and you shall call his name Jesus. He will be great and will be called the Son of the Most High. And the Lord God will give to him the throne of his father David, and he will reign over the house of Jacob forever, and of his kingdom there will be no end" (Luke 1:31–33). Such precious truths, such a unique coming into the world, such tidings of great joy, all are threatened by the false claimant Quiboloy, who leads millions astray from the true King and Savior Jesus the Messiah.

Finally, Jesus' miracles were numerous, public, and showed His undeniable love for mankind. His many miracles were signs that manifested His glory as of the *only* Son of the Father (cf. John 1:14; 2:11). Moreover, these unparalleled miracles and demonstrations of divine power and favor were recorded once and for all so that we would believe that Jesus of Nazareth is the Messiah (John 20:31). Who has Quiboloy healed? Who has he raised from the dead? Has he calmed a storm with a word? Does he exercise power of the spiritual realm and exorcise demons by a word? Has he fed the multitudes with a few loaves of bread and fish? He has done none of the above, nor will he ever. Quiboloy is a liar and an imposter who must be unmasked (see 1 John 2:22).

The Dangerous Implications of Quiboloy's Christological Claims

Those who believe in the claims of Quiboloy are truly in danger of following a mere man toward the fire of eternal judgment. Since Quiboloy continually declares that John 14:6 is a reference to him and only him, those who believe in him for salvation are the blind being led by the blind.[15] Sadly, his outreach continues to grow and gain more followers, thereby creating an environment by which many more are turned away from an opportunity to hear the gospel.[16] As

---

[15] "Signs of a Cult and Pastor Apollo Quiboloy." https://carm.org/signs-of-a-cult-pastor-apollo-quiboloy.

[16] "Pastor Apollo Quiboloy's prophecy." http://www.philstar.com/opinion/2016/06/12/1592040/pastor-apollo-quiboloys-prophecy. Writing in the *Philippine Star*, Babe Romualdez recounts,

they follow after him, they empower him even more to control their thinking regarding spiritual matters. They allow him to influence their thoughts to make them believe in, not Jesus as the Son of God, but rather to commit their lives to a fallen man. Tragically, they do not realize the dangerous implications in adhering to Quiboloy's Christological claims. In affirming Quiboloy as their savior, they have forsaken the true Savior and Son of God and have negated three significant truths about Jesus as taught in Scripture.

The Deity of Christ Undermined
The first truth Quiboloy's claims negate is Jesus' deity. In his system, when compared with Quiboloy, Jesus being thought of as God is both unnecessary and ridiculous. Even though Scripture clearly affirms the deity of Jesus, those who follow Quiboloy have now a new God and Lord. Based on his claims, he is the Son of God for today. God only works through him and none other. He alone is the dispenser of truth, righteousness, grace, and mercy. This belief in Quiboloy causes his followers to suspend their rationality and give credence to his claims of deity. The result of this will be a terrible awakening of judgment for all of them because as Paul declares in Galatians 1:8–9, "But even if we, or an angel from heaven, should preach to you a gospel contrary to what we have preached to you, he is to be accursed! As we have said before, so I say again now, if any man is preaching to you a gospel contrary to what you received, he is to be accursed!" The repetition in Paul's statement should convince anyone of the danger of denying the deity of Christ which is central to the gospel.

The Salvation of Christ Undermined
Quiboloy's followers are also led to reject Jesus' power to save. Since they believe that salvation is only through Quiboloy, there is no longer any reason for them to think that Jesus can save them from their sins. In fact, Quiboloy himself takes all the Scripture passages that relate to salvation in Christ and applies these to himself. He

---

"I'm told that KJC has now expanded its reach to about 200 countries covering 2,000 cities, with the pastor's teachings spread through a Davao-based TV network (Sonshine Media Network International), a radio station (Sonshine Radio), several newspapers and a magazine, and a website where he is able to touch base with his overseas followers."

teaches that he is the current Christ. As he claims, Jesus died on the cross to secure our salvation; however, it was not in God's plan for Him to be the one who would give it to others. God would give that responsibility to someone else who would be the heir from fallen humanity (i.e., Quiboloy). As a result, Quiboloy now decides who will be a recipient of salvation.[17] By making salvation through Jesus Christ as no longer relevant, there is no need to hear the antiquated teachings of biblical Christianity. As is clear from God's Word, this misplaced belief in Quiboloy for salvation has dangerous and eternal consequences.

The Resurrection of Christ Undermined

The third truth Quiboloy's followers negate is Jesus' resurrection. The words of 1 Corinthians 15 have no meaning or significance for them. Their focus is not on Jesus, but Quiboloy himself. Only his words carry any weight. Even though he would not deny the resurrection of Jesus, he minimizes its importance because, as he teaches, God has appointed him the Son of God for today, meaning that what Jesus did many years ago does not have the same importance as it once did. Thus, sadly, the truth regarding the resurrection as taught in Scripture is no longer precious and meaningful. Rather, since Quiboloy teaches that he is the appointed Son of God for today, he has twisted the resurrection of Jesus to be something which personally gives him the power to grant salvation to people.

Conclusion

The teachings of Apollo Quiboloy are dangerous. These teachings have blinded many to the truth of Scripture that Jesus alone is the Son of God. Sadly, Quiboloy's followers do not realize the gravity of his wicked claims against the true Christ. Jesus is uniquely the Son of God, He alone died for the sins of mankind, and only He rose again from the dead. He alone provides the salvation that mankind

---

[17]   "The Entrustments." http://www.kingdomofjesuschrist.org/the-entrustments. As his website states, "When the Sonship was entrusted to Pastor Apollo, he was given the power to give eternal life to whomsoever he will… . When the Kingship was given to him, he was entrusted with the power to rule of the Father's Kingdom and to implement the Father's spiritual laws all over the world."

desperately needs. Though Quiboloy claims to be the appointed Son of God of today, the Word of God calls him a liar and a false teacher. The church in the Philippines needs to remain committed to the truth that Jesus alone is the Son of God. We need to share with our friends and families, and proclaim from the pulpits across the nation, that in Jesus Christ alone is eternal life, and that Jesus Christ alone will reign forever and ever as the rightful King of kings. And woe to those who would seek to claim His exclusive glory and worship for themselves, "for their judgment from long ago is not idle, and their destruction is not asleep" (2 Pet 2:3).

SIN AND SAVIOR: THE RIGHT DIAGNOSIS NEEDED IN THE CENTRAL AMERICAN CHURCH

Robert D. Kensinger

Ministerios Evangélicos de las Américas, Honduras

[Editor's Note: In order to rightly understand and love the Savior, people must first understand and hate their sin. As one of the great Puritan divines once wrote, "Until sin be bitter, Christ will not be sweet." This essay brings much-needed clarity to the topic of sin, recognizing that churches in Latin America and beyond will only glorify man's Savior, Jesus Christ, insofar as they rightly diagnose man's problem, sin.]

The Importance of a Biblical Hamartiology

Whatever the issue may be, if you want to understand the solution, you must first understand the problem. This especially holds true in the world of medicine. To simply prescribe medication without an accurate diagnosis can prove disastrous to one's health. Similarly, in the theological realm an errant understanding of man's true problem before God will lead to flawed solutions and disastrous results. According to God's Word, man's greatest problem is sin. Simply put, "all have sinned and fall short of the glory of God" (Rom 3:23).[1] However, to understand correctly the solution to this hamartiological

---

[1] All Scripture quotations are from the New American Standard Bible (NASB), unless otherwise noted.

diagnosis with all of its resultant symptoms, one must first comprehend correctly the details of the condition.

Unfortunately, many churches, especially the most prominent denominations in Central America, do not hold to a proper perspective of the extent and impact of sin (the problem); and thus, they are inclined to diminish the person and work of Christ in redemption (the solution). Therefore, if one desires to address the anthropological, soteriological, and Christological errors within many Central American churches, the place to begin is by addressing the misdiagnosis of the sin problem.

A History of Biblical and Unbiblical Hamartiology

Historically and theologically, the central issues in making an accurate hamartiological diagnosis are: (1) the effect of original sin; (2) the existence of the freewill of man or, more specifically, the capacity of man to choose that which is good and pleasing to God; and (3) the role of predestination and election by an omniscient and sovereign God in relation to the first two issues. In order to consider these matters and the resultant effects of misunderstanding them, a review of the historical and biblical perspectives is necessary.

Augustine and Pelagius

In church history, the debate over the impact of original sin, the existence of freewill in man, and the necessity of the doctrine of predestination and election originated in earnest in the early fifth century with the well-known dispute between Pelagius, a British monk "of clear intellect, mild disposition, learned culture, and spotless character,"[1] and Augustine, the North African bishop of Hippo, who was redeemed from a former life of youthful indiscretion[2] and false teachings.[3] As occurred previously with the Trinitarian and Christological doctrines, the early church wrestled to clearly define and describe a biblical hamartiology.

---

[1] Philip Schaff, and David S. Schaff, *History of the Christian Church*, vol. 3 (New York: Charles Scribner's Sons, 1910), 790.

[2] Ibid., 787.

[3] Justo L. Gonzalez, The Story of Christianity: The Early Church to the Dawn of the Reformation, vol. 1 (New York: HarperCollins, 1984), 209–10.

Prior to his interactions with Augustine, Pelagius had visited Rome and was deeply troubled by the moral corruption that he encountered, and furthermore, he was disturbed upon hearing of Augustine's prayer to God in his book *Confessions:* "Give what you command, and command what you will."[4] To Pelagius, this prayer "encouraged waiting on God for courage, strength, and ability to do his will. But human beings are already designed by God himself to carry out his will ... He believed that whereas God had given human beings the *capacity* to fulfill the commandments, both *volition* and *action* are strictly human faculties."[5] In other words, Pelagius believed that God had graciously provided a moral capacity in human beings which gave them the ability to perfectly obey God's law; otherwise, God would not have commanded such obedience. Therefore, it was not up to God to will and act in man, but rather for man to enact within himself that which was already possible through the ability graciously provided by God.

Pelagius' doctrine of divine capacitation enabling human volition and action reflected his perspective of the effect of original sin and the freewill of man. To him, mankind suffered no ill effects from Adam's sin other than the negativity of a poor example. According to his creationist perspective,[6] he believed that, like Adam, all men have the capacity to choose between good and evil according to their freewill, and "the nature which God created remains, as to its substance, good."[7]

Augustine, on the other hand, had an entirely different perspective on the significance of the fall of Adam. "In Adam human nature fell, and therefore all, who have inherited that nature from him ..."[8]

---

[4]   Cited in Gregg R. Allison, *Historical Theology: An Introduction to Christian Doctrine* (Grand Rapids, Michigan: Zondervan, 2011), 345. In Allison's citation of Augustine's statement he personalizes the prayer, "Give [me] what you command, and command [me to do] what you will."

[5]   Ibid.

[6]   Schaff and Schaff, *History of the Christian Church*, 809. "Pelagius was a creationist, holding that [in human reproduction] the body alone is derived from the parents, and that every soul is created directly by God [at the time of conception], and is therefore sinless."

[7]   Ibid., 810.

[8]   Ibid., 824. In fact, Augustine would take it so far as to say that in some manner, all men sinned directly in Adam so that all men are guilty for the sin "they themselves committed in Adam."

This is known as the doctrine of original sin or hereditary guilt, and it indicates that Adam's sin was more than simply a poor example; rather, the result of Adam's sin was a hereditary, sinful, totally depraved nature that has been passed to every human being except Christ. Every part of man is corrupted by sin, and all people are born guilty of sin. "In other words, people are not sinners because [they] sin; [they] sin because [they] are born sinners."[9]

Semi-Pelagianism, Arminianism, and the Free Will of Man
In church history, two additional theological perspectives that don't coincide with a biblical understanding of sin have been suggested. The first was introduced in Southern France near the end of Augustine's life and is commonly referred to as semi-pelagianism.[10] "Its leading idea is that divine grace and the human will jointly accomplish the work of conversion and sanctification, and that ordinarily man must take the first step."[11] According to semi-pelagianism, a right relationship with God is obtained not by the personal choice of one's own will and action as Pelagius believed; yet it is also not by the predestined choice of a sovereign God giving his grace and faith to those whom he chooses as Augustine believed. Instead, man, in a sickened but not completely spiritually dead state, participates with God's grace to jointly accomplish the work of salvation.[12] Once again, this perspective gives the capacity in some manner back to man to participate in his sanctification, only this time with more interaction by God's grace to assist the will. One of the early proponents of this perspective, John Cassian, explained it this way: "When he sees in us some beginnings of a good will, he immediately enlightens it and strengthens it and urges it on toward salvation. He increases that which he himself planted or which he sees has arisen from our own efforts."[13]

---

[9]   Justin S. Holcomb, *Know the Heretics* (Grand Rapids, Michigan: Zondervan, 2014), 115.

[10]   Schaff and Schaff, *History of the Christian Church*, 858. The title of "semi-pelagianism" was given to these ideas during the scholastic age many centuries later.

[11]   Ibid.

[12]   Ibid.

[13]   John Cassian, *The Third Conference of Abbot Chaeremon*, 8, in NPNF[2], 11:426; quoted in Gregg R. Allison, *Historical Theology*, 349–50.

The second theological viewpoint, commonly known as Arminianism, named after Jacobus Arminius (1560–1609), does not necessarily deny man's totally depraved, sinful nature, but it does insist upon the existence of man's freewill to accept or reject God's provision for salvation. While most Arminians would agree that salvation in and of itself is totally of God's grace, they would suggest that man has the capacity to choose to accept or reject the gift of Christ's substitutionary sacrifice, making God's election conditioned upon his foreknowledge of man's choice of whether to believe in Christ. Soteriologically, this doctrine also results in an unlimited atonement and the uncertainty of the perseverance of the saints because every man has the ability to choose at any time to accept or reject God's gracious offer of atonement.

John Calvin and his followers, as is well known, took an opposing view, generally consistent with Augustine's hamartiology, declaring that man in his totally depraved state does not have the capacity to choose to accept Christ's sacrifice (the "good" in this case), leaving men lost and without hope apart from the predestined, loving election of a sovereign and all-knowing God in salvation.[14]

A Biblical Hamartiology

Throughout Scripture, the total depravity of man as a result of the impact of original sin, his inability to choose that which is pleasing to God, and his dependence upon the predestined election of a sovereign, all-knowing and loving God are evident. The consequence of original sin is clearly seen in Romans 5:12, 18 and Psalm 51:5. Even though the Word of God doesn't explain the details of exactly how the sin of Adam passed to all humanity, it is clear that it did.

As to original sin's impact on man's ability to choose that which is pleasing to God, one need only look to Romans 3:10–12, 18 for an answer. "… there is none righteous, not even one; there is none who understands, there is none who seeks God; all have turned aside, together they have become useless; there is none who does good, there is not even one… . There is no fear of God before their eyes." Man, after the effect of original sin, is within himself completely

---

unable to choose that which is pleasing to God which includes an incapacity to express faith in the substitutionary sacrifice of Jesus Christ. Whereas some would argue that even unbelievers can do good and charitable things, it's worthwhile to take a moment and explain what exactly is meant by total depravity and its consequences.[15] First, it's helpful to state what it does not mean. Total depravity does not indicate that men are as sinful as they might be (Luke 6:33; Rom 2:14), nor does it mean that non-Christians cannot do acts of external good (Matt 7:11). Finally, it does not mean that the unbeliever cannot appreciate things of beauty or good things in this world (Acts 14:17). However, it does mean that every man is completely a sinner, and sin has contaminated every area of his being, from his thoughts, desires, and reasoning to every other area of his material and immaterial being (Jer 17:9; Eph 2:1; Tit 3:2–3; Rom 3:10–18). Finally, men cannot please God in and of themselves (Rom 8:8). Even what appears to be good externally is corrupted by sinful, impure motives that are not for the glory of God (Matt 6; Isa 64:6).

So where does that leave mankind? As a result of original sin, man is a totally depraved sinner deserving of death (Rom 6:23a), and he is completely unable to please God. Beyond that, according to Romans 3:11, he doesn't even seek after God. That's not a good place to be. For this reason, some theologians prefer to use the phrase "total inability" instead of "total depravity" referring to the utter incapacity of man to be pleasing to God and thus his powerlessness to save himself from God's wrath.[16]

When the doctrines of original sin and the total depravity, or total inability, of man are properly understood, then the doctrine of predestination and election expressing the *necessity* of God's choice to save sinners becomes clear. Man cannot please God or save himself from God's wrath. Moreover, man doesn't even seek after God, nor can he choose to accept or reject the sacrifice provided by God; left to himself, totally depraved man cannot choose that which is pleasing to God. So, if man is to become pleasing to God, he must

---

[15]   John MacArthur Jr., "Counseling and the Sinfulness of Humanity," *Introduction to Biblical Counseling: A Basic Guide to the Principles and Practice of Counseling* (Dallas, Texas: Word, 1994), 102.

[16]   John M. Frame, *Systematic Theology: An Introduction to Christian Belief* (Phillipsburg, New Jersey: P&R Publishing, 2013) 863.

depend upon a means outside of himself, both for the merit of the sacrifice itself (1 Pet 2:24) and for the capacity to accept that sacrifice by faith (Eph 2:8–9).

Current Errant Perspectives within the Central American Church

Romanism and Its Semi-Pelagian Perspective on Man's Sinful Nature
According to data derived from the Pew Research Center reported in 2014, a survey of the six Spanish-speaking Central American countries[17] reveals that 55 percent of the average population are Roman Catholic, 34 percent Protestant, and 11 percent unaffiliated or other. Of the percentage who identify as Protestant, the majority identify with Pentecostalism or some other charismatic church.[18] While some would suggest that the doctrine of the Roman Catholic Church is more in line with Arminianism,[19] it would seem that in truth Roman hamartiology is semi-pelagian. Robert Duncan Culver explains Rome's perspective succinctly in his systematic theology:

> In Rome's theology, grace is not as in Paul's doctrine a way God saves sinners apart from their lack of merit. Grace in salvation, for Rome, is something God imparts to sinners through sacraments by means of which, by works of righteousness, they come to merit salvation…. Roman theology for all its sincere concern about sin and sins has not discerned the depths of fallen human nature…. There is no point in theology where Rome and evangelical theology are both so near and so far apart. Rome teaches that salvation is all of grace—as a freely imparted divine enablement to merit salvation.[20]

---

[17]   These countries include Costa Rica, El Salvador, Guatemala, Honduras, Nicaragua, and Panama. (Belize is not included in this data as its official language is English.)

[18]   "Religion in Latin America: Widespread Change in a Historically Catholic Region," Pewforum.org http://www.pewforum.org/2014/11/13/religion-in-latin-america/.

[19]   Tim Challies, "An Introduction to Calvinism & Arminianism," Challies.com, http://www.challies.com/articles/an-introduction-to-calvinism-arminianism.

[20]   Robert Duncan Culver, *Systematic Theology*, 368.

Arriving at such a conclusion demonstrates a misdiagnosis of a biblical hamartiology. It denies original sin and its resultant total depravity that makes it impossible for man to in any way merit salvation, as is clearly stated in Scripture (Eph 2:8–9; Titus 3:5). Another distinction is that while Arminians would hold to the capability of man's freewill to accept or believe in Christ Jesus as Savior and Lord, they would in general agree that man can in no way merit his salvation; whereas Roman Catholics in the main hold to a doctrine of grace enabling human merit (although they would label them "the works of Christ"), which is semi-pelagian.

Arminianism as the Predominant Perspective of the Rapidly Growing Charismatic Church

Of the Pentecostal and charismatic churches in Central America, the vast majority would be considered Arminian, which in and of itself does not deny salvation by grace alone, through faith alone, in Christ alone. However, the hamartiological discrepancy lies in their belief that man has the capacity and ability to accept or reject the free gift of grace that God offers. As noted previously, according to the Pew Research Center report in 2014, the majority of Protestants in Central America, and even throughout all of Latin America, consider themselves to be Pentecostals.[21] In fact, taking an average of the six Spanish-speaking Central American countries, 88 percent of all Protestant churchgoers suggest that they have witnessed speaking in tongues, praying for a miraculous healing, and/or prophesying at church at least occasionally. The point? With the rapidly growing Pentecostal and charismatic church in Central America, at least two-thirds, and probably many more, believe that man has the ability to accept or reject Christ, based upon their own capacity to believe apart from the sovereign, unconditional election of God.

While some would argue for the prevenient grace of God to enable the freewill choice or the foreknowledge of God to choose those whom he knew would first choose him,[22] these arguments also

---

[21] The survey study suggests 65% attend a Pentecostal church or self-identify as Pentecostals. "Religion in Latin America," http://www.pewforum.org/2014/11/13/religion-in-latin-america/.

[22] Millard J. Erickson, *Christian Theology*, 2nd ed. (Grand Rapids, Michigan: Baker, 1998), 933.

do not adequately coincide with a biblical hamartiology. The first is a theological argument in defense of a theological proposal (that man must choose God rather than the other way around in order for God to be fair and just to all men) for which Scriptural evidence is referenced, but which is in no way convincing.[23] Rather, these passages would better coincide with a totally depraved man, who cannot choose God, leaving only God in his grace to choose him. The second is also a theological argument to protect God's honor in the choice of those who would and would not be saved, and the Scriptural evidence is generally based upon the word translated *foreknowledge* in Romans 8:29 and 1 Peter 1:1–2. The problem with this perspective is that while Peter does not specifically clarify the content of this foreknowledge, Paul does; and it is the foreknowledge of specific individuals (chosen by him before the foundation of the world: Eph 1:4–5, 11) rather than the foreknowledge of any decision made by men, especially a theoretical decision made by a totally depraved man without the ability to choose that which is pleasing to God.

The Predilection toward a Man-Centered Gospel

One of the significant problems with both the semi-pelagian, Roman Catholic perspective and the Arminian perspective, which is pervasive in the Protestant Central American church, is the predilection toward a man-centered gospel, or a man-centered soteriology, in place of a God-centered or Christ-centered gospel. What is indicated by a man-centered gospel in this case is the fact that man's salvation in some way depends upon a choice made by him. Whether it's the Roman Catholic's meriting of salvation through divine enablement or the Arminian's freewill choice of man in accepting Christ's sacrifice, both put the onus upon a man who is totally depraved and according to Romans 3:11–12 does not seek God, is useless, and cannot do what is good and pleasing to God.

From discussions with a number of Central American pastors, this form of a gospel leads to preaching without a discussion of the true sin problem. Instead, the Roman priests teach a man-centered gospel of at least partial self-reliance upon the works of penance and the sacraments; while those of an Arminian persuasion frequently

---

[23] Jer 1:5; 31:3; Ezek 34:11, 16; Luke 19:10; John 6:44; 12:32; Rom 2:4; Eph 1:13; Phil 2:12–13; 1 John 4:19

preach a results-oriented gospel which many believe creates problems in the communication of the true, Christ-centered gospel. From the perspective of pastors who have studied at the Seminary for Expository Preaching in Honduras,[24] this response-oriented approach to the gospel has created many false confessions of faith without a true understanding of the root problem—the person's sinfulness and total depravity. This commonly results in an assenting level of understanding of the true gospel, but it does not result in the complete, "*fiduciary*" total reliance upon Christ alone, which is essential for saving faith as described by the reformers.[25] The concern of these pastors then includes many churchgoers who think that they are saved from God's wrath, when in reality they don't even understand the true problem. As one pastor put it, "they don't want to put on a raincoat because they don't think that it's raining." Others are without assurance of their salvation because they believe that at some level, it is theirs to gain or lose, and still others believe that because they followed the instructions of the pastor and prayed the required prayer, they are then free to continue to live in sin because it is now covered by grace based upon their free choice. However, in many ways, the worst effect of these errant perspectives has yet to be explained.

The Impact of an Errant Hamartiology

The Anthropological Problem of an Errant Hamartiology

Anthropologically, the greatest problem of an errant view of sin is that it makes man something that he is not, or it makes him capable of accomplishing something that in reality is outside of his capacity as a fallen creature.

From a study of the Greek word *sarx*, ("flesh") in the New Testament, one finds that it is true to its semantical foundation: the Old Testament Hebrew word *basar*, which "is used to connote

---

[24] The Seminary for Expository Preaching (SEPE) is the primary ministry of Ministerios Evangélicos de las Américas (MEDA) located in Siguatepeque, Honduras, and it is a member school of The Master's Academy International (TMAI).

[25] R. C. Sproul, *Faith Alone: The Evangelical Doctrine of Justification* (Grand Rapids, Michigan: Baker, 1995), 80.

mankind as weak, fragile, transitory, etc."[26] In some biblical contexts such as 1 Peter 1:24 (quoting Isa 40:6–8), the focus is on human limitation and frailty; however, in hamartiological contexts, it is clear that "the finiteness of the human creature is *not* the reason for his falleness, *nor* is his physical 'flesh' the high-handed agent of sin. In such contexts the term's physical connotation is overwhelmed by a whole-man-apart-from-God-and/or-His resources significance"[27] In other words, the Bible does not speak of a Platonic understanding of the flesh (material part of man) as evil and the spirit (immaterial part of man) as good;[28] rather, the biblical distinction lies in man's fragility and debility apart from God as opposed to his strength and fortitude with God. This is as a result of man's totally depraved sinful nature and is contrasted repeatedly in Romans, chapters 7 and 8. Furthermore, Paul makes this contrast abundantly clear in Ephesians 2:1–5:

> And you were dead in your trespasses and sins, in which you formerly walked according to the course of this world, according to the prince of the power of the air, of the spirit that is now working in the sons of disobedience. Among them we too all formerly lived in the lusts of our flesh (*sarx*), indulging the desires of the flesh (*sarx*) and of the mind, and were by nature children of wrath, even as the rest. But God, being rich in mercy, because of His great love with which He loved us, even when we were dead in our transgressions, made us alive together with Christ (by grace you have been saved).

Due to original sin and its resultant effect of total depravity, all men, apart from God's gracious, predestined election (as explained in chapter 1 of Ephesians), are spiritually dead, "by nature children

---

[26] George J. Zemek, *A Biblical Theology of the Doctrines of Sovereign Grace: Exegetical Considerations of Key Anthropological, Hamartiological and Soteriological Terms and Motifs* (Little Rock, Arkansas: n.p., 2002), 25.

[27] Ibid.

[28] This was the philosophy of the Gnostics and Manicheans. See Holcomb, *Know the Heretics*, 35, 67–8.

of wrath." As such, man is not only without the capacity to do that which is pleasing to God, but he is not even interested in doing so. Therefore, apart from the merciful, loving, gracious act of Christ's atoning sacrifice and God's loving choice "according to the kind intention of his will" (Eph 1:5), man is without hope.

The Impact of an Errant Hamartiology on a Biblical Soteriology

Having been created in Adam, who fell into sin, "humans were preconditioned to commit wrong because Adam and Eve had sinned, [and] all humans were guilty of that sin.... [Thus] they are 'not able not to sin.'"[29] The biblical description of this condition of man is "dead in ... trespasses and sins." The problem then of the Arminian perspective of man's capacity through free will is that dead men can't respond. Totally depraved sinners *sin* by nature. That's what they do because that's what they are. They don't understand. They don't seek for God. They do not do what is good. John Calvin puts it this way:

> But faith is the principal work of the Holy Spirit.... Paul shows the Spirit to be the inner teacher by whose effort the promise of salvation penetrates into our minds, a promise that would otherwise only strike the air or beat upon our ears.... faith itself has no other source than the Spirit" (John 1:12–13; Matt 16:17; Eph 1:13).[30]

And again Calvin states, "For, as regards justification, faith is something merely passive, bringing nothing of ours to the recovering of God's favor but receiving from Christ that which we lack."[31]

Roman Catholic doctrine is even further afield to the extent that it is not even the same gospel. Among other errors, Catholicism adds the works of man in the name of penance to the atoning work of Christ in order to attain and maintain a right relationship with God. Catholic theologian Ludwig Ott explains, "The virtue of penance ...

---

[29]   Holcomb, *Know the Heretics*, 115.

[30]   John Calvin, *Institutes of the Christian Religion*, ed. John T. McNeill, trans. Ford Lewis Battles (Philadelphia, Pennsylvania: Westminster Press, 1960), 3:541.

[31]   Ibid., 768.

which at all times was a necessary precondition for the forgiveness of sins, is that moral virtue, which inclines the will to turn away inwardly from sin, and to render atonement to God for it."[32] This not only demonstrates an errant soteriology as the Bible clearly states that Christ atoned for sins "once for all when he offered up Himself" (Heb 7:27); but it once again reveals an errant hamartiology. Due to man's totally depraved sin nature, he in no way can "precondition" or add to the atoning work of Christ. In response to Titus 3:4–7, Calvin explained, "By this confession we deprive man of all righteousness, even to the slightest particle until, by mercy alone, he is reborn into the hope of eternal life, since if the righteousness of works brings anything to justify us, we are falsely said to be justified by grace."[33] Furthermore, only God in his love and the kind intention of his will can make the choice to redeem man on account of man's sinful incompetence and "total inability." "If all men are by nature utterly incompetent to do good, if it is grace that works in us to will and to do good, if faith itself is an undeserved gift of grace: the ultimate ground of salvation can then be found only in the inscrutable counsel of God."[34]

The Resultant Diminishing of the Person and Work of Christ in Redemption

Finally, an errant hamartiology diminishes the person and work of Christ in redemption. Paul makes clear in Romans 11:33–36 that God's wisdom and knowledge is far greater than man could ever fathom, and that man can in no way merit anything from such an infinite God. For all things are from him and through him and to him, and the glory is to be his forever. In addition, every good gift that man has is from God (James 1:17), including the gift of Jesus Christ as the propitiation for sin (1 John 4:10). The sacrifice of the Son of God was perfect and without spot (Heb 9:14), completely atoning (Col 1:13–14; Romans 6:23), and accepted by the Father (Acts 4:12; Heb 9:12). Therefore, to think that sinful man could in some way add to

---

[32] Ludwig Ott, *Fundamentals of Catholic Dogma*, trans. Patrick Lynch (Charlotte, North Carolina: TAN Books, 1974), 150.

[33] Calvin, *Institutes*, 772.

[34] Schaff and Schaff, *History of the Christian Church*, 856.

Christ's atonement diminishes his glory and the work of redemption that only he was able to accomplish. Even to suggest that man could in some way take part in choosing to receive God's gift of redemption runs counter to the very ideas of total depravity and salvation by grace alone from a sovereign God.

Conclusion

Whatever the issue may be, if you want to accurately understand the solution, you must first understand the problem because similar to the medical world, a misdiagnosis of the problem could lead to a damaging and even fatal response. Sadly, many Central American churches have misdiagnosed the problem of sin resulting in errant treatments of the doctrines of man, salvation and Christ. Whether they might be trying to resolve the biblical tension between the responsibility of man and the sovereignty of God by giving man a freewill ability that he does not have, or whether they might be trying to justify their system of religion through a semi-pelagian doctrine of co-effort between God and man, the result is a diminished Christocentric gospel caused by confusion of the doctrines of original sin and the total depravity of man. At best, this misdiagnosis results in a minimizing of the glory of Christ and his saving work on the cross. At worst, it results in belief in a false gospel that leads to eternal damnation. Therefore, to understand and accept the true biblical solution of grace alone through faith alone in Christ alone, the churches of Central America need to make the right diagnosis regarding man's greatest problem—sin.

CHRIST, THE ETERNAL WORD: GOD, MAN, REDEEMER, AND REVEALER

Benedikt Peters

European Bible Training Center, Germany/Switzerland

[Editor's Note: The light of the Protestant Reformation was the light of Jesus Christ. From the Scriptures, the reformers recognized that it was Christ—fully God and fully man—upon whom the church truly stands or falls. Though the church must be made aware of the contemporary threats to the gospel, it is equally critical that she be firmly and positively rooted in the biblical doctrine of Christ. Nowhere in Scripture is this more natural or compelling than from the prologue to the Gospel of John.]

Introduction

The life and work of the Lord Jesus Christ has been recorded in four historical accounts, and yet we say that there is but *one* gospel. All four Gospels have *one* common theme, namely Jesus, the Christ, the Son of God. The gospel is about Him; without Him there is no gospel. Therefore Mark introduces his gospel with the words: "The beginning of the gospel of Jesus Christ, the Son of God" (Mark 1:1). And Paul opens his epistle to the Romans, that glorious treatise on the gospel, with the words: "Paul, a bond-servant of Christ Jesus ... set apart for the gospel of God, which He promised beforehand through His prophets in the holy Scriptures, concerning His Son"

(Rom 1:1–3). Again we see: the gospel of God is concerning His Son; He is the theme and the substance of the word which God sent for our salvation.

Matthew, Mark and Luke emphasize the human side of the One who came into this world as the Son of David, the Servant of the Lord, and the Perfect Man. Some decades later, John wrote his gospel. He starts his account by saying that Jesus was from the beginning, that the man from Nazareth was from eternity with God, and that He Himself is God, the Creator of all things.

The Gospel of John was written between AD 80 and 90, when the gospel of the grace of God had been preached already for more than half a century. Innumerable souls had been saved, and churches had been planted throughout the Roman Empire. But as the word of salvation spread, false teachings sprang up, and false teachers infiltrated the churches. In attacking the truth, the enemy aimed at the very heart of the gospel: the person of Christ. In 1 John 2:18–23, we learn that there were false teachers who denied the divine Sonship and in 1 John 4:1–3 that there were those who denied the true humanity of Christ. In 2 John we hear that "many deceivers have gone out into the world" (v. 7), people who "[do] not abide in the teaching of Christ" (v. 9). So we have reasons to believe that John wrote his gospel to fight these errors in order to establish the believers and the churches in the truth about Christ. John 1 contains non-negotiable and indispensable truths of the gospel: Christ is the eternal God (vv. 1–3), Christ is true man (v. 14), He is sinless (v. 17), and in Him alone God has revealed Himself (v 18). If we give up but one of these truths, we have no gospel to preach.

"In the beginning was the Word, and the Word was with God, and the Word was God" (John 1:1).

This verse states three great facts about the Word:
1. He was in the beginning.
2. He was God.
3. He was with God.
    a. The Word "was" (Gk. *ēn)*; the Word did not become, and He was not made. Contrasting this, verse 3 says that all things "were made" (Gk. *egeneto,* lit. "became," cf. John

1:6, 14; 8:58). As we must say concerning all created things that they "were made," we can say only of One that He never was made, and He is God.

b. The Word was "in the beginning." That means: He had no beginning, He is without beginning, and He is eternal. Besides Him everything *has* a beginning, but He *is* in the beginning; He Himself *is* "the Beginning" (Rev 3:14).

c. The Word was "with God." If the Word Himself is God, we can formulate the sentence: "God was with God." That means that the one God is a plurality.

"All things came into being through Him, and apart from Him nothing came into being that has come into being" (John 1:3).

Since the Word was in the beginning, He is necessarily omnipotent, and that is exactly what John says in this verse. Being in the beginning, He has no originator; He is Himself the Originator of all things that have come into being. John wants to be clear that the word *all* is to be taken in its fullest, in its absolute sense, since the word *all* can be used in a relative sense, like in Matthew 3:5: "Then Jerusalem was going out to him and *all Judea,*" which evidently does not mean that all and sundry went out. So John emphasizes: the Word created all things; nothing is exempt; nothing came into being without Him. The Son of God is the Creator of all things, visible and invisible (Col 1:16; Heb 1:10–12).

Let us sum up what the first three verses teach us about the Son of God:

a. He is eternal.
b. He is God.
c. He is a Person with God.
d. He is the Creator of *all* things.

This first verse contains the first basic truth concerning all works of God: as in creation, so in redemption God is in the beginning. Salvation begins with God, not with man. The third verse contains the second basic truth about salvation: in creation, God alone works all things; in redemption likewise He works all things: from beginning to the end God "works all things after the counsel of His will"

(Eph 1:11). "From Him and through Him and to Him are all things" (Rom 11:36a). So by acknowledging that Christ is God, we acknowledge that salvation is monergistic.[1]

"And the Word became flesh, and dwelt among us, and we saw His glory, glory as of the only begotten from the Father, full of grace and truth" (John 1:14).

When we consider what John has said in verses 1–3 about the Word, reading verse 14 we are speechless. The eternal and omnipotent God becomes man! But how can that be? The Bible says: "God is not a man" (Num 23:19); and: "For I am God and not man, the Holy One in your midst" (Hos 11:9). And the Bible teaches that man is not God (see 2 Kings 5:7). But here we are told that the impossible has come true. When Mary said that she could not possibly conceive and give birth to a son since she was a virgin, the angel answered that, with God nothing is impossible (Luke 1:34–37). As God made it possible for a virgin to conceive, so He made it possible for God to become man. In order to bridge the insuperable gulf between God and man, God first created man in His image (Gen 1:26). By doing that He prepared the incarnation of His eternal Son, who is the Image of the invisible God (Col 1:15; 2 Cor 4:4; Num 12:8). Because man was created in the image of God, the Son of God could become man without changing His nature. He can never be what He is not, nor can he do anything which is against His nature (2 Tim 2:13; Titus 1:2). In other words, He cannot change (Mal 3:6; Heb 13:8). This means: The Son of God could not have been incarnated into anything else; He could only assume humanity without changing His being.

Let us carefully consider what John says in this verse about the eternal Word who became flesh. Every word is purposely chosen, every one counts, and none is amiss.

    a. He *became*—John deliberately contrasts the form "became" to the form "was" in v. 1. He *was* in the beginning; he *was* God, but in time, on a historically established day, the eternal Son who always was, *became* flesh: "When the fullness of the time came," He was "born of a woman" (Gal 4:4). The day

---

[1]   God alone (Gk. *monos*) works (Gk. *ergazomai*) in salvation. Therefore, we say, it is *mon-ergistic*.

had come which Psalm 2:7 calls "today": "I will surely tell of the decree of the LORD: He said to Me, 'You are My Son, Today I have begotten You.'"

b. The Word became man, fully and completely man, wherefore John employs the unexpected term *flesh*. Flesh is used for humanity (Isa 40:5; Heb 2:14), for human frailty (Isa 40:6–8) and for human sinfulness (Rom 8:7). But we must pay very close attention to all John's statements. He who became flesh, was "full of truth," which can only be said of a sinless person (as I shall explain below). And we must heed the complete testimony of the Scriptures concerning the humanity of our Lord. Yes, He became flesh, but He did not have sinful flesh. The term *flesh* is used in the Bible for man before he became sinful (Gen 2:23, 24). That the Word in His incarnation became sinless Man is established beyond doubt in the announcement of His conception and birth: "The Holy Spirit will come upon you, and the power of the Most High will overshadow you; and for that reason the holy Child shall be called the Son of God" (Luke 1:35). Being conceived by a virgin, he is a truly human child; being begotten of God, He is a "holy Child," who is without sin. Therefore, Paul can say that God sent His Son "in the *likeness of* sinful flesh" (Rom 8:3), not "in sinful flesh." As true man, He could be "tempted in all things as we are, *yet without sin*" (Heb 4:15). Christ became fully man, but sinless Man, as the apostles Paul, Peter, and John explicitly affirm: Christ *knew* no sin (2 Cor 5:21); He *committed* no sin (1 Pet 2:22); and in Him there *is* no sin (1 John 3:5).

c. The *Word* became flesh. When Christ became man, He did not only put on a human shape like a cloak in which He would pass through this world, only to shed it at the end of His journey. He did not come as a king, who chooses to dress like a common man and travel incognito through his lands to be close to his subjects for a season. That king would not truly become a common man; he would only appear as one. But Christ did not merely appear as a man; He became man by being conceived and born of a woman. He grew in His mother's womb and was nourished by her blood. So He entered fully and without reserve into real humanity. And what is most glorious: having become man he did not shed His humanity after His resurrection and ascension. We, as the writer of the epistle to the Hebrews says, see Jesus "crowned with glory and honor" (Heb 2:9). The writer deliberately uses only the human name Jesus, without the titles Lord and Christ, to stress his humanity. And Stephen, being full of the Holy Spirit, saw "the Son of Man" in heaven (Acts 7:56). By becoming man, living, suffering, and dying as man, He wrought redemption for sinful man. The truth that Christ "has come in the flesh" (1 John 4:2) is so important, that any spirit denying it is defined as the spirit of antichrist (1 John 4:3).

d. As the Word became flesh, He did not cease to be the eternal Word. That could not be; God cannot cease to be God. John underlines this truth by adding: "We saw His glory." What was this glory like? It was "glory as of the only begotten from the Father." John saw in the man Jesus all the perfections of God (Heb 1:3). The fullness of God's essence and the sum total of all God's attributes dwelt in Him, as Paul affirms: "In Him all the fullness of Deity dwells in bodily form" (Col 2:9). That was only possible because the Word in His incarnation remained God. None but God can contain the whole fullness of Deity.

e. The Word was "full of ... truth." That can only be said of a sinless Person, since no child of Adam has ever been full of truth: "Men of low degree are only vanity and men of rank are a lie" (Psa 62:9a). They are all "of [their] father the devil" and want to do the desires of their father, in whom there is no truth (John 8:44). "False witness" is in their hearts (Matt 15:19). "With their tongues they keep deceiving, the poison of asps is under their lips" (Rom 3:13). But Christ was full of truth; He spoke the truth, and He is the Truth (John 14:6). That proves beyond doubt that He was sinless.

Let us now sum up the three great truths concerning salvation in John 1:14:

1. It was necessary that God, the Savior, should become man.
2. It was necessary that He was man and at the same time was God.

3. It was necessary that He was without sin.

Why was all this necessary?
1. Had He not become man, He could not have died as a substitute in our stead; man must pay the penalty for the sins of man. No animal can do that (Heb 10:4).
2. Had He been only man and not God, He as a substitute could only have paid for one single man.
3. If He had been guilty of only one sin, He could not have died as a substitute for others; His death would have been but the penalty of His own sin.

We have seen that none of the truths taught in John 1 concerning the Son of God is dispensable. Deny any of them, and there can be no salvation. That explains why John fought with such determination against all who denied Christ's divinity and Christ's humanity:

- "Who is the liar but the one who denies that Jesus is the Christ? This is the antichrist, the one who denies the Father and the Son. Whoever denies the Son does not have the Father; the one who confesses the Son has the Father also" (1 John 2:22, 23).
- "By this you know the Spirit of God: every spirit that confesses that Jesus Christ has come in the flesh is from God; and every spirit that does not confess Jesus is not from God; this is the spirit of the antichrist" (1 John 4:2, 3).

And it explains why he insisted that Christ was and is without sin:
- "You know that He appeared in order to take away sins; and in Him there is no sin" (1 John 3:5).

"No one has seen God at any time; the only begotten God who is in the bosom of the Father, He has explained Him" (John 1:18).

This verse makes three important statements concerning the Word:
1. The Word is "the only begotten God."
2. The Word is "in the bosom of the Father."
3. The Word "has explained" the invisible God.

a. If the Word is "the only begotten God" (Psa 2:7), He is Himself God. When Christ called God His own Father, the Jews immediately understood that he was "making himself equal with God" (John 5:18).

b. The Word was not only "with God," but He is "in the bosom of the Father." That term does not signify a locality, as if the Son had to leave the Father when He came into this world. Rather it expresses a relationship: they are distinct, but they are never separate. He is in the Father, and the Father is in Him (John 10:38; 14:11, 20). Being in the bosom expresses the mutual love between the Son and the Father (John 3:35; 14:31; 17:24), and in that love the Father and the Son shared in all their purposes and works. Whatever God knows the Son knows.

c. "No one has seen God"; Abraham did not see him, nor did Moses, nor David nor Isaiah. But did Isaiah not see the Lord sitting on an exalted throne (Isa 6:1)? And did not Moses together with the elders of Israel see the God of Israel (Exod 24:10)? Yes, they did: they saw God, the Son, and in seeing the Son, they saw God. He who has seen the Son has seen the Father (John 14:9). None but God can know all that is in God (1 Cor 2:11), and none but God can make God known. John uses the verb *exegeomai,* which literally means "to lead/ bring out," translated as *explain* here. The Son takes the hidden things of God and brings them out for the believing person to see.

The Son of God has made known the invisible God. He could do that:

1. Because He is Himself God; and
2. Because He is man.

Because Christ is God, He can reveal God in all His fullness, and because He is man, He can reveal God in such a way that man can bear that revelation. In verse 14, we saw that the Word by necessity must be both God and man in order to work redemption. Now we see that He must be God and man in one Person in order to be the Light that enlightens man (John 1:9).

What has John achieved by the prologue to his gospel? He has led us to believe that the man Jesus who was born in Bethlehem, who lived, taught, worked in Israel and was executed in Jerusalem in AD 30, is the eternal Word, the Creator of all things, the Son of God, the Holy One who alone is able to accomplish the great work of redemption and to enlighten man so that he believes unto eternal life.

What else follows from the truths we have learned of John in his prologue to the gospel? We learn to see ourselves as we really are. As we grow in the knowledge of Christ who, as true God, became sinless Man to be our substitute in suffering and dying for our sins (2 Cor 5:21), and in rising for our justification (Rom 4:25) we begin to see that we are utterly powerless. Therefore, God Himself had to intervene to save man. He had to do the complete work of salvation for us, we who were dead in our trespasses and sins. He is the One who had the power to create all things (John 1:3); He alone is the One who has the power to redeem us and create us anew (2 Cor 5:17).

And when we understand that Christ had to become man to reveal God to us, we begin to feel that we are absolutely blind. We sit in darkness and have neither the knowledge nor the power to dispel it; we are absolutely dependent upon the Son of God to enlighten us (John 1:9). So we thank God for His indescribable gift (2 Cor 9:15), and we worship Him who is full of grace and of truth. He alone is worthy to receive thanksgiving and honor and glory. As the apostle John said in another portion of Scripture, "Salvation to our God who sits on the throne, and to the Lamb!" (Rev 7:10).

Unmasking the False Christ of the Prosperity Gospel in Latin America

The Spanish Expositors Institute, USA (Spanish Language)

[Editor's Note: The so-called prosperity gospel has taken Latin America by storm, oftentimes presenting a false Christ and undermining the majesty of the real one. While one must never glory in controversy, when a people's understanding of Jesus Christ is at stake, and when the preservation of the truth of the gospel is threatened, the people of God are left with no other option than to decry falsehood and unmask error. This chapter sets forth a firm response to the false Christ presented in prosperity teaching.]

Introduction

Within the last half-century, no movement within American Christianity has seen such explosive growth as prosperity theology. Born out of the Pentecostalism, the influence of prosperity theology has grown exponentially in the United States since the 1970s. Prosperity theology may be defined as any kind of positive message that promises health, wealth, and temporal prosperity, using the Bible as its source material. Prosperity teachers such as Joel Osteen, Joyce Meyer, T. D. Jakes, Creflo Dollar, and Benny Hinn have exploded in popularity in the United States and have significantly expanded the influence of prosperity theology.

However, prosperity theology has not just gained influence in North America. In the last forty years, this teaching has also taken

Latin America by storm. Initially, prosperity teaching was exported via Western missionaries to countries throughout South and Central America (as well as many other countries in the world). Since that time, future generations of prosperity preachers have been steadily rising up from within the Spanish-speaking world. Today, a myriad of such prosperity teachers have come on the scene with remarkable popularity, and their teaching has swept through the Spanish-speaking world like wildfire. Latin American prosperity gospel preachers, such as Cash Luna (from Guatemala), have become household names in the Spanish-speaking world and have gained massive followings.

In Latin America, as in much of the rest of the world, prosperity teachers are among the highest-profile preachers and church leaders. They dominate Christian television through networks like The God Channel and TBN (or its Spanish Channel, Enlace TV). They are among the loudest religious voices on the Internet and social media, and they have some of the largest churches in the world. For example, César Castellanos pastors a "church" in Colombia with nearly a quarter of a million members. His books include prosperity titles such as *Sueña y Ganarás el Mundo* (Dream and You Will Win the World) and *La Escalera del Éxito* (Ladder of Success).

Statistics on the growth of the Pentecostal church in Latin America help give us insight into the state of prosperity teaching in the region.[1] A recent study shows that of all Protestant believers in Latin America, over half are associated with Pentecostalism either by denomination or by personal identification.[2] In countries, such as the Dominican Republic, Brazil, Nicaragua, Guatemala, and Argentina, the number is above 70 percent.[3] An earlier study revealed that between 1970 and 2005, the percentage of the total population

---

[1] We acknowledge that not all Pentecostal or Charismatic preachers teach a prosperity gospel. In Latin America, however, the connection is so strong that for general statistical purposes, looking at trends related to Pentecostal churches gives the reader a very good idea of the trends related to prosperity teaching.

[2] Pew Research Center Study: Religion in Latin America; Widespread Change in a Historically Catholic Region. <http://www.pewforum.org/files/2014/11/Religion-in-Latin-America-11-12-PM-full-PDF.pdf>, p. 62.

[3] Ibid.

in Latin America that identified as Pentecostal or Charismatic grew from 4.4 percent to 28.1 percent.[4]

With this massive growth of prosperity theology in Latin America, it is critical that we honestly assess and evaluate the impact of this movement. Is this supposed prosperity "gospel" and its widespread popularity good for the Latin American church? Or is there something that believers in Latin America should beware of? In this paper, we will analyze four of the main tenets of the prosperity gospel and show how this teaching critically and dangerously undermines the truth about Jesus Christ. We will see that not only is the teaching of the prosperity gospel flawed, but it substitutes a false (and inferior) Christ in place of the true majestic, glorious Christ who is revealed in Scripture.

The Followers of the Prosperity Gospel

Before considering the errant teachings of the prosperity gospel, it is important to first examine the nature of those whom this false gospel is primarily reaching. One of the great (and tragic) ironies of the prosperity gospel movement is that even though many of the most prominent prosperity teachers live in opulence and wealth, most of their followers live at various levels of poverty. This is clearly seen in the Spanish-speaking world. In Latin America, two-thirds of the population live on less than ten dollars per day.[5] And yet, one Latin-American blogger laments, "Prosperity theology is not just a system of belief, but the culture in which we live."[6] He goes on to say that in Latin America, "the charismatic, Word-of-faith, prosperity form of Christianity is, by and large, the only form of Protestantism people know."[7]

It is a heart-wrenching reality that many peddlers of the prosperity gospel live off the backs of the very people they claim to be

---

[4]   Pew Research Center Study, <http://www.pewforum.org/2006/10/05/overview-pentecostalism-in-latin-america/>.

[5]   http://www.worldbank.org/content/dam/Worldbank/document/LAC/chronic_poverty_overview.pdf.

[6]   Jairo Namnún, "Encountering Prosperity Theology in Latin America," https://www.thegospelcoalition.org/article/the-prosperity-gospel-in-latin-america.

[7]   Ibid.

helping, fleecing the vulnerable masses by exploiting their desperation. Like the scribes of Jesus' day, they "devour widows' houses" (Mark 12:40) and prey on the most destitute in society. Thus, it is very common for the prosperity gospel to gain popularity in particularly poor areas of the world. For many followers of this false gospel, the promises of health, wealth, and happiness offer a strong emotional appeal through positive messages and guarantees of a "better life." People who are weary of oppression long to gain an upper hand in life, and this is exactly what prosperity teachers promise, though usually with a price tag attached in the form of donations to the preacher's ministry.

The Message of the Prosperity Gospel

When trying to precisely define the prosperity gospel, it becomes evident that there is no fixed doctrinal template that outlines a consistent theology among all prosperity preachers. Therefore, attempts to biblically critique the movement are forced to deal with generalities, emphases, and trends within prosperity teaching, rather than with concrete doctrinal statements and creeds. At the same time, given that the brevity of this article makes it impossible to deal with all the errors of prosperity theology, we will focus specifically upon teachings that undermine Christ and the gospel itself.

For the purpose of this paper, we have identified four of the most serious errors in the Christ of the prosperity gospel.[8] These false portrayals of Jesus are hallmarks of the movement and are characteristic of nearly every "mainline" prosperity gospel message. These four Christological deviations are as follows:

1. The Christ of the prosperity gospel is a passive master who awaits activation and enablement through our faith and prayers. He wants to bless, heal, and prosper us, but our lack of faith or righteousness, hinders him from carrying out

---

[8] It should be noted that while the promise of health, wealth, and prosperity are central to the prosperity understanding of the cross, a small minority of teachers do rightly place emphasis on the forgiveness of sin and the promise of eternal life (to varying degrees). This paper will deal with the overwhelming majority of prosperity preachers who do not fit into this category.

those desires. We will refer to this as the error of the "captive Christ."

2. The Christ of the prosperity gospel delegates Christ's sovereignty to people who can supposedly control reality through the words they speak. Christ's power is seen as effective only insofar as we maintain a positive confession. We will address this error as the "commandeered Christ."

3. The Christ of the prosperity gospel treats our sin, and its eternal consequences, as a peripheral issue. His sacrificial death is presented as *primarily* concerned with gaining our access to the divine benefits that are rightfully ours: health, wealth, and victory over all adversity in the here and now. We will refer to this as the error of the "carnal christ."

4. The Christ of the prosperity gospel was not given as a propitiation[9] for sin through his physical death on the cross. He is widely believed to have atoned for our sins through a spiritual death in hell during the three days following his crucifixion. Christ's physical death is downplayed in prosperity theology, which places a far greater emphasis on a supposed ransom he paid to Satan in hell to deliver the captives. This error will be addressed as the "cross-less Christ."

The Error of the Captive Christ

The first deviation may be described as "the captive Christ." The captive Christ of the prosperity gospel earnestly desires for us to receive his bountiful blessings. He wants us to release his miracle-working ability so that he can provide Christians with an easy exit ramp off the road of human hardship. However, he cannot act unless believers initiate his work through their actions. Our prayers, faith, and generosity are the keys to stirring him to action, so that he can bless us with an easy life of perfect health, significant influence, the removal of suffering, and an abundance of material wealth.

---

[9] By *propitiation*, the biblical authors mean that Christ was given to satisfy God's justice by bearing His holy wrath against sin. Sin is a great offense to God, and it provokes Him to righteous anger. Since God does not acquit the guilty nor does He overlook sin, His anger remains with Him until the sin is dealt with. The Bible teaches that it was on the cross that Jesus bore our sins, taking our punishment upon Himself, thus being the *propitiation* for our sins.

A careful examination of internationally known prosperity teachers will reveal constant references to God or Jesus in this "captive" sense. Christ is seen as a force than we manipulate, not as a Divine person who works all things according to the counsel of His will (Eph 1:11). According to Creflo Dollar, "God needs your consent and cooperation to bring forth manifestation in the earth."[10] Another prosperity gospel author writes, "Prayer is man giving God permission, or license, to interfere in earth's affairs."[11]

It is man who is sovereign in each of the above statements. The Christ that is presented is captive to the will and action of man. One must "allow," "give God permission," and give "consent and cooperation." Christ's divine power is "held captive" until man decides. The believer makes the ultimate and decisive determination without which Christ cannot accomplish His purposes. This is not just an acknowledgment that God uses means; it is a rejection of Christ's ultimate lordship. This kind of teaching reduces the Creator and Sustainer of the universe (Heb 1:3–4) to a genie in a bottle whose confined power can be harnessed through the right formulas of faith and finances.

And as we shall now see, this genie requires that we speak words of faith in order to activate and apply his atoning work to your bank balance and medical record.

The Error of the Commandeered Christ

Another deviation from the biblical portrait of our Lord Jesus Christ seen in prosperity teaching may be termed, "the commandeered Christ." For certain prosperity teachers, the idea that Christ's sheep hear His voice and submit to Him (John 10:27) is a foreign concept. As far as they are concerned, it is *our* words that Jesus must obey, so long as they are spoken with enough "faith" or "spiritual power." Through positive thinking and laying hold of the "promises" of Scripture, the spoken word of faith functions as a key to unshackle Christ and employ Him for whatever purposes are desired—health, deliverance from all suffering, limitless success, and untold riches.

---

[10] Creflo Dollar, https://twitter.com/Creflo_Dollar/status/684017696510312448.

[11] Myles Munroe, "Benny Hinn and Myles Munroe Say 'God Needs our Permission,'" https://www.youtube.com/watch?v=c5BDAwnH7SE.

In the introduction of his book *¡Cree, todo es posible! La fe que mueve a Dios* (Believe, Anything Is Possible! The faith That Moves God), Latino prosperity teacher Marco Barrientos writes, "You will be inspired to *determine and decree words that will provoke changes from God* in your life, your marriage, your children, your finances, and your congregation" (emphasis and translation added).[12] If a person is sufficiently optimistic to "declare and decree," they will receive from the commandeered Christ whatever they want. Why? Because their wish is his command.

Speaker and writer Joel Osteen has authored a bestselling book devoted to this very subject. In this book, *The Power of I Am*, which has also had a massive impact in Latin America (*El Poder del "Yo Soy"*), he attempts to Christianize pagan philosophies with his own version of what the New Agers call the "laws of attraction." He believes his readers can alter their personal reality through positive "I am" confessions:

> Here's the principle. Whatever follows the "I am" will always come looking for you. When you say, "I am so clumsy," clumsiness comes looking for you. "I am so old." Wrinkles come looking for you. "I am so over-weight." Calories come looking for you. It's as though you're inviting them. Whatever you follow the "I am" with, you're handing it an open invitation, opening the door, and giving it permission to be in your life.

> The good news is you get to choose what follows the "I am." When you go through the day saying, "I am blessed," blessings come looking for you. "I am talented." Talent comes looking for you ... "I am strong." Strength starts tracking you down. You're inviting those things into your life.[13]

So, Osteen's solution to the problems of life is to declare yourself healthy when you are sick, declare yourself wealthy when you

---

[12] Marco Barrientos, *¡Cree, todo es posible! La fe que mueva a Dios* (Lake Mary, Florida: Casa Creación, 2013).

[13] Joel Osteen, *The Power of I Am: Two Words That Will Change Your Life Today,* (New York: FaithWords, 2015), 2.

cannot pay the bills, and declare yourself successful when you are unemployed. A Latin-American blogger writes, "Active faith activates the power of heaven ... Faith brings the miracle down from heaven ... The miracle is activated by the word" (translation mine).[14]

Pastor John MacArthur explains that prosperity theology redefines the meaning of faith: "Faith [in the prosperity paradigm] ... is not submissive trust in God; faith is a formula by which to manipulate the spiritual laws [prosperity] teachers believe govern the universe."[15] Not only does this teaching imply a manipulation of spiritual laws, but it also implies a manipulation of our spiritual Lord. The King of kings is portrayed as a slave that submits to his master's every carnal desire. But the Bible presents Jesus Christ in a very different light. As God, He alone has the authority and power to bring things about by His spoken word: "For by Him all things were created, both in the heavens and on earth, visible and invisible, whether thrones or dominions or rulers or authorities—all things have been created through Him and for Him" (Col 1:16). Any suggestion that we can determine our reality by the words that we speak is an attempt to deify man and dethrone Christ.

The Error of the Carnal Christ

In the realm of prosperity preaching, not much is made of Christ's bearing God's wrath or atoning for man's sins. Instead, the message of Christ focuses more on the fulfilment of man's "carnal" (physical and temporal) desires. Televangelist Creflo Dollar boldly states, "Jesus bled and died for us so that we can lay claim to the promise of financial prosperity."[16] Aquiles Azar, a pastor in the Dominican Republic, promotes his book, *Prosperados por la Palabra* (*Prospered by the Word*), with a similar, though more expansive, claim:

Divine prosperity is something more than money. Prosperity does not only include material blessings,

---

14 https://radiopalabraviva.wordpress.com/2010/11/09/%C2%A1activar-tu-fe-activa-el-poder-del-reino/.

15 John MacArthur, *Charismatic Chaos*, (Grand Rapids, Michigan: Zondervan, 1993), 280.

16 Creflo Dollar, https://twitter.com/ForeverGraceMin/status/593822451873816577.

it also encompasses healing, wisdom, success, well-being, and the protection and favor of God ... Christ on the cross of Calvary redeemed you from poverty, so that today you can live in God's blessing. If you have Christ, you have it all (translation mine).[17]

The problem with such a statement lies in how Christ's redemption is interpreted. From Azar's point of view, the death of Christ guarantees a person's freedom from poverty, sickness, and unhappiness. The objective of Christ's death was to pour out material blessings on all who believe upon His name. In other words, Christ came to give to people exactly what they want—namely money, power, fame, success, and health—without any transformation of the heart necessary. But in truth, these are all things the biblical Christ teaches His followers to forego. Rather than deny oneself, the carnal Christ teaches to indulge. Barrientos writes:

What God can and will do for you is linked to what matters most to you ... God has not given you more because of a certain evil that has taken over your soul. If up to this moment you have not had the courage to pray and live a life of greater faith, there is something within your heart that has subconsciously persuaded you that you cannot do these things correctly and that you do not deserve them. Those thoughts should not be yours. They are excuses for those who do not wish to succeed.[18]

What is being promoted here has nothing to do with the Jesus of the Bible who overcame the world and its lusts; it has much more to do with the devil's temptation of worldly wealth and power that Jesus resisted (see Matt 4:8–10).

---

[17] In his book, the author makes a connection to 88 verses that "prove" the Bible's promise of prosperity. In the words of the author, "This book is a recompilation of quotes about prosperity that are found throughout the Word of God (the Bible) so that you can know that: God wants to prosper you; what are the principles of abundance that we find in the Word of God; tithes and offerings as a door to your prosperity; and that God is who gives you power to make wealth." He adds "The main purpose of taking and compiling these quotes is so that you can realize that the salvation of God is a package that includes eternal life, healing, liberation, but also prosperity." Aquiles Azar, *Prosperados por la Palabra,* (Santo Domingo, Dominican Republic: Ministerios Aquiles Azar , 2016), PDF format, 3.

[18] Barrientos, 10–11.

You may be wondering, where do prosperity teachers find biblical support for claims that so obviously contradicts Jesus' clear teaching that we should not seek treasure on earth, but rather store up treasures in heaven (Mat 6:19–21)? Most appeal to 2 Corinthians 8:9, which states: "For you know the grace of our Lord Jesus Christ, that though He was rich, yet for your sake He became poor, so that you through His poverty might become rich." Here, they explain, is the justification for a life in hot pursuit of money. Singaporean prosperity preacher Joseph Prince comments on this verse, saying, "On the cross, Jesus bore the curse of poverty ... Don't let anyone tell you that the verse is referring to 'spiritual' riches."[19]

But this assessment is incorrect on two levels. John MacArthur points out that Jesus did not live His life in abject poverty, nor does 2 Corinthians 8:9 have anything to do with a lack of financial means:

> This verse is not a commentary on Jesus' economic status or the material circumstances of His life ... The Lord's true impoverishment did not consist in the lowly circumstances in which He lived but in the reality that "although He existed in the form of God, [He] did not regard equality with God a thing to be grasped, but emptied Himself, taking the form of a bond-servant, and being made in the likeness of men" (Phil 2:6–7).[20]

MacArthur expands on that idea by explaining the extent of the heavenly riches Christ willingly gave up during His incarnation:

> Though as God, Jesus owns everything in heaven and on earth (Exo 19:5; Deut 10:14; Job 41:11; Psa 24:1; 50:12; 1 Cor 10:26), His riches do not consist primarily of what is material. The riches in view

---

[19] Joseph Prince, *Unmerited Favor: Your Supernatural Advantage for a Successful Life*, (Lake Mary, Florida: Charisma House, 2010), 29.

[20] John MacArthur, *The MacArthur New Testament Commentary: 2 Corinthians*, (Chicago, Illinois: Moody Publishers, 2003), 291–92.

here are those of Christ's supernatural glory, His
position as God the Son, and His eternal attributes.[21]

Therefore, Christ offers us riches which far surpass anything
this world can offer. Through and in Christ, the blessings of salvation are granted to the believer. Who can compare the vain things
of this world to the forgiveness of sin and the promise of eternal
life? How inferior is a padded bank account compared to the riches
of joy everlasting, the presence of God's Holy Spirit, the adoption
into the family of God, and eternal fellowship with the Triune God!
Moreover, this spiritual inheritance is imperishable and undefiled and
will never fade away (1 Pet 1:4).

Thus, although the broader context of 2 Corinthians 8 does
speak of financial giving, Paul's point here is that Christ loved us by
giving up what was His so that we might share in it. He wanted the
Corinthian church to understand that they would be reflecting this
same love by giving up with they had in order to share it with those
in greater need. Loving others sacrificially at one's own expense is
precisely the kind of love that Christ showed to mankind. Jesus did
not leave behind a bank account, jet skis, and a mansion so that we
might obtain these things. The Word in His perfect righteousness took
upon Himself human flesh so that human flesh might be redeemed in
perfect righteousness. He impoverished Himself by assuming human
nature so that man might be enriched by partaking in the divine.

The above emphasis on worldly and carnal things is directly
related to a misunderstanding of the cross. This leads to the fourth
and final faulty portrayal of Christ among prosperity teachers: the
crossless Christ.

The Error of the Crossless Christ

Many well-known prosperity preachers teach that Christ's major
transaction did not take place on the cross, but rather *after* His crucifixion, when He descended, they claim, to hell. American prosperity preacher Fred Price writes: "Do you think that the punishment
for sin was to die on a cross? If that were the case, the two thieves

---

[21] Ibid., 289–90.

could have paid your price. No, the punishment was to go into hell itself and serve time in hell separated from God.... . Satan and all the demons of hell thought that they had him bound, and they threw a net over Jesus, and they dragged Him down to the very pit of hell itself to serve our sentence."[22]

Yet the Bible teaches the opposite. Scripture teaches us that Christ "bore our sins in His body *on the cross*" (1 Pet 2:24, emphasis added), not in hell. Our redemption came through the shedding of His blood (Eph 1:7), when Christ canceled the debt of our sin "having nailed it to the cross" (Col 2:14). As MacArthur puts it, instead of serving a sentence in hell, "He served *notice* to hell that the powers of evil were defeated."[23]

The idea that Christ was tortured in hell by demons makes Satan out to be the lord of hell and the one who requires payment for sin. But it is God—not Satan—who requires this. It is God who will by no means acquit the guilty (Exod 34:7) and demands payment in blood (Heb 9:22). It is God's wrath that must be atoned for by a penal substitute (Rom 3:25–26). It was God the Father who crushed His Son (Isa 53:10) under the weight of His holy wrath. And when Jesus said, "It is finished" (John 19:30), it was.

Conclusion

Paul warns us that people "will accumulate for themselves teachers to suit their own passions" (2 Tim 4:3). Since people lust for more wealth, more health, and more prominence, prosperity preachers promise these very things. They preach a Christ who exists to exalt man, in any and every way. Unfortunately, when man is exalted, the Christ of the Scriptures is brought down. This reality can be summarized with the prosperity teaching of Cash Luna, pastor of the largest "church" in Guatemala,[24] who tickles peoples' ears with the lie that they are sons of God like Christ is the Son of God.

---

[22] Frederick K. Price, *The Ever Increasing Faith Messenger* (June 1980), 7, cited in MacArthur, *Charismatic Chaos*, 278.

[23] MacArthur, *Charismatic Chaos*, 280.

[24] https://en.wikipedia.org/wiki/Casa_de_Dios.

"What is your father's name? Jehovah. And what is your name? Junior ... Jehovah junior ... We are not God, but we are gods, we are juniors. Are we not? ... Jesus became flesh, right? So, what's wrong with you, in your flesh, being the son of God as well? This is what Jesus came to do, to make us participants in the divine nature" (translation mine).[25]

The truth that our sonship is through adoption (Rom 8:15) is overlooked in order to elevate man and tell him what he wants to hear—that he is like God (Gen 3:5), thereby bringing the Son of God down to our level.

Thus, the Christ of prosperity theology is humbled and enslaved to our lusts. He is not the pearl of greatest price for which we sell all our earthly pleasures to gain. He is but a means to obtain more temporal treasure. But the Bible never promises that Christ will satisfy man's lust for material and temporal things. Rather, the opposite is true. Christ warned against the riches of this world because they could place our souls in eternal peril (Luke 9:25). He promised persecution (John 15:20), suffering (Matt 10:17–18), and even death for some (Luke 21:16). He is Lord, and as such, expects His followers to forsake the things of this world and follow Him, no matter the cost (Mark 8:34–36).

In Latin America, as in many parts of the world today, the Person and work of Jesus Christ is under siege, and we must stand against every effort to diminish Him. We should exhort mankind to "count all things to be loss in view of the surpassing value of knowing Christ Jesus," even counting the health, wealth, and prosperity of this world to be rubbish so that they may instead gain Christ (cf. Phil 3:7–8). He is the true treasure, "far more excellent, more glorious, and more filled with rays of divine wisdom and goodness, than the whole creation ... can contain or afford."[26]

Christ is Lord. He is the Almighty and Sovereign Savior who reigns over all, and men shall not prosper unless they bow their wills

---

[25]   https://www.youtube.com/watch?v=jc2rEPw7nn4.

[26]   John Owen, *The Glory of Christ: Meditations and Discourses,* (Chicago, Illinois: Moody Press, 1949), 25–26.

and desires to Him, taking up their cross and following Him unto death. Yet this is the great irony of the prosperity gospel and its "best life now" promise. It actually cheapens the eternal prosperity Christ purchased for us when He bore God's wrath on our behalf. Christ promises His redeemed something far greater than temporal treasures. He offers the health of a new resurrected body, the wealth of the New Jerusalem, and the opportunity to reign upon a new earth with Him. There we will have the greatest prosperity imaginable, as we rejoice in the privilege of worshipping His glorious majesty forever.

CHRIST ALONE AND THE FATE OF THE UNREACHED

Alexander Gurtaev

Samara Center for Biblical Training, Russia

[Editor's Note: In a volume that addresses the exclusivity of Christ and the uniqueness of His gospel, the question may arise, "But what of those who have never heard?" This final essay labors to help the reader think about this question from a biblical perspective. It also serves as a fitting conclusion, challenging every believer to take hold of Christ's final command to go and make disciples (Matt 28:18–20).]

Introduction

The name of Christ is unique because it is inextricably connected to the salvation of fallen humanity. Jesus Christ is fully glorified when sinners who formerly opposed their Creator later come to embrace the gospel of salvation that is accomplished by Christ's perfect life, sacrificial death, and glorious resurrection on their behalf. The person of Jesus Christ is the core of the gospel (Rom 3:21–26).

When the gospel reaches people, it leaves no one unaffected. For some, it results in salvation when they trust in Christ alone for their deliverance from eternal condemnation. When this happens, Scripture describes the impact of the gospel as "an aroma from life to life" (2 Cor 2:16). For the rest, the gospel message leaves them in a state of spiritual darkness and condemnation because of their unbelief. Instead of giving life, the gospel is a sentence of death for people who reject it (2 Cor 2:16). When someone consciously rejects the gospel and openly resists the Savior, his fate is not to be envied. Most evangelical Christians can easily call to mind the passage from the gospel of John, which states: "He who believes in the Son has eternal life; but he who does not obey the Son shall not see life, but the wrath of God abides on him" (John 3:36). It is impossible to contemplate eternal damnation without a sense of anguish and grief. Nevertheless, we must come to terms with the clear teaching of the Bible concerning God's righteous judgment against those who reject the Savior (John 3:36; Rom 2:8).

However, what can be said about the fate of those whom the gospel has never reached? What is the destiny of those who have never heard the good news? What does eternity hold for people who are able to reason but have never had the opportunity to consciously consider God's call to salvation proclaimed through the preaching of the gospel?[1] The emotional side of these questions is even more complex, since for many people they evoke innate questions of the fairness of the gospel. Such feelings are intensified by the fact that there are many who have not heard the gospel.

Regardless of the pain that one undoubtedly endures when contemplating the fate of the unevangelized, we must turn to the Scriptures to find a satisfactory answer to this question. It behooves us to take into consideration the biblical teaching concerning the universal sinfulness of man, the role of faith in the gospel presentation of salvation, the mission of gospel preachers, and the eternal destiny of those who have not come to know God. These complex questions demand complex answers, and answering them has become increasingly difficult in our day.

The Winds of Contemporary Thought

Before turning to the Scriptures, we must recognize how the modern outlook on the world seriously complicates the search for an objective answer to this question. Voices outside the revelation of God in Scripture are prepared to destroy the very foundation on

---

[1]   Writers frequently use the term "the unevangelized." These are people who "have lived at some time in history and died without ever hearing the gospel of Jesus Christ." See Todd Miles, *A God of Many Understandings? The Gospel and a Theology of Religions* (Nashville, Tennessee: B&H, 2010), 3. See also David M. Doran, *For the Sake of His Name: Challenging a New Generation for World Missions* (Allen Park, Michigan: Student Global Impact, 2002), 175.

which the question of the fate of the unevangelized rests—namely: is Jesus Christ the only way of salvation?[2] Does faith in Jesus Christ play an exclusive role in the salvation of sinners?

If the Church affirms the exclusive role of Christ in salvation, it immediately becomes vulnerable to the pressure of contemporary culture, which insists on rejecting any claim to exclusivity.[3] First, the dominant concept of religious pluralism[4] casts doubt on the very possibility of one single path to salvation. "All roads lead to God," declare the advocates of this belief system. They insist that it is possible to find salvation in every world religion, and thereby they reject the necessity of Christ's sacrifice. People who reason this way compare the world's religions to pathways ascending different sides of the same mountain, all leading to God at the top. The exclusive claims of Christ and Christianity do not fit into their "open-minded" worldview, so those who hold to exclusive truth claims are branded as intolerant and unyielding.[5]

Second, relativism,[6] which permeates our contemporary society, considers the possibility of finding a single path to salvation highly doubtful, if one path even exists. Advocating diversity for the sake of diversity, relativism rejects the existence of any objective truth as well as the likelihood of having any knowledge of it.[7] As a result, it turns out that every person is right in his own way; everyone possesses his own path to God, which is neither right nor wrong. Moreover, no person's path can possibly be the only way.

---

[2] See John Piper, *Let the Nations be Glad: the Supremacy of God in Missions*, 2nd ed. (Grand Rapids, Michigan: Baker Academic, 2003), 111.

[3] See Robert D. Culver, *Systematic Theology: Biblical and Historical* (Fearn, Ross-shire, UK: Christian Focus, 2005) 781; Douglas Gievett, "Is Jesus the Only Way?" in *Jesus Under Fire: Modern Scholarship Reinvents the Historical Jesus*, eds. Michael Wilkins and J. P. Moreland (Grand Rapids, Michigan: Zondervan, 1995), 178; Miles, *A God of Many Understandings?*, 7.

[4] "Pluralism is the belief that every religion is true, that each provides a genuine encounter with the Ultimate" (Norman Geisler, *Systematic Theology* [Minneapolis: Bethany House, 2002], 1:126).

[5] See Geivett. "Is Jesus the Only Way?" 178.

[6] "Relativism is similar to pluralism, claiming each religion is true to the individual who holds it. Relativists believe that since there is not objective truth in religion, there are no criteria by which one can tell which religion is true or which religions are false" (Geisler, *Systematic Theology,* 1:126).

[7] See Doran, *For the Sake of His Name*, 174.

This means, therefore, that Christ and Christianity do not have the exclusive ability to save. Pressure from society, along with the need to coexist with members of differing religions,[8] adds fuel to the fire in the debate concerning the exclusivity of Christ and the destiny of those who have not been reached with the gospel.

These challenges that Christians face from society are nothing new. Christians in the first century also confronted the same choice to be in step with society and avoid persecution by recognizing Christ as one of many gods, or to defend the exclusivity of Christ as the Savior of the whole world (cf. John 4:42). In doing so, they were defying the culture and religion of the Roman Empire and thereby exposing themselves to the danger of persecution. New Testament scholar Scott Hafemann underscores this conclusion:

> Indeed, the pluralism of the modern world is no more dramatic than that faced by Israel or Paul. In Paul's day every Roman was born into a nexus of personal religious affiliations and family household cults. Add to this milieu the Roman imperial cult, the Greco-Roman pantheon of deities descending down from Jupiter, and the mystery religions venerating gods from Greece, Anatolia, Egypt, Persia, and Syria, and our situation looks tame in comparison... . To assert the One God of Israel and Jesus as his Messiah, the Son of God, was just as startling and exclusive then as it is now (cf. 1 Cor 8:5–6; Phil 2:9–11)."[9]

The history of the Christian Church testifies to the fact that the first Christians were prepared to sacrifice their lives for belief in

---

[8]   Even though people, at all times of history, have had some contact with followers of various world religions, the 20th and 21st centuries have been characterized by the process of globalization. As a result of this, adherents of a variety of religions live side-by-side in the same region, preserving their practices and religious worldviews. See M. Erickson, "The Fate of Those Who Never Hear," *Bibliotheca Sacra* 152, no. 605 (January 1995): 9; Clark Pinnock, "Toward an Evangelical Theology of Religions," *Journal of the Evangelical Theological Society* 33, no. 3 (September 1990): 359.

[9]   Scott Hafemann, "The SBJT Forum: Responses to Inclusivism," *Southern Baptist Journal of Theology* 2, no. 2 (Summer 1998): 56.

the exclusive nature of faith in the Lord Jesus Christ for salvation. The beginning of the second century shows Christian apologists like Aristides, Justin, Tatian, and Athenagoras setting dangerous precedents by seeking compromise with the culture; they explained Christianity in terms of contemporary philosophy and attempted to discover biblical truths within the sphere of pagan thought.[10]

The Question Posed Even in Evangelicalism

It is not surprising that unbelievers would cast doubt on God's justice when considering the fate of those who have never heard the gospel. But it may surprise some to discover just how widespread this kind of thinking is, even within the professing church. Several evangelical scholars support the notion of salvation by means of the teaching of other religions and other factors without faith in Jesus Christ. They do insist on the exclusive role of universal redemption through the blood of Christ and the necessity of some kind of faith in God,[11] but they are not prepared to affirm that a conscious confession of Christ within the span of one's lifetime is essential for salvation. Proponents of compromising solutions to this question can be found in a variety of denominations, including Baptists, Lutherans, Presbyterians, and Methodists, and among adherents of different theological traditions, such as Calvinism and Arminianism.[12]

One example is C. S. Lewis, who, in his books, affirmed the possibility of salvation outside of Christianity. Of course, it would be unfair to think that he was the first or the last evangelical Christian who promulgated similar ideas. However, his books and essays

---

[10] See Culver, *Systematic Theology*, 795.

[11] See Clark Pinnock, "Overcoming Misgivings about Evangelical Inclusivism," *Southern Baptist Journal of Theology* 2, no. 2 (Summer 1998): 32; Pinnock, "Toward an Evangelical Theology of Religions," 360, 362; John Sanders, "Introduction," in Gabriel Fackre, Ronald H. Nash, and John Sanders, *What About Those Who Have Never Heard?: Three Views on the Destiny of the Unevangelized*, ed. John Sanders (Downers Grove, Illinois: InterVarsity Press, 1995), 10. This article will often reference both Pinnock and Sanders. This has nothing to do with the author's love of western theology or these two scholars in particular, but rather the fact that they have expressed their views more completely than others.

[12] Sanders, "Inclusivism," in *What About Those Who Have Never Heard?*, 55. See the analysis of the spread of inclusivism among evangelical Christians in Miles, *A God of Many Understandings?*, 210; Kenneth C. Fleming "No Other Way, No Other Name," *Emmaus Journal* 4, no. 2 (Winter 1995): 126.

are extremely popular in the Christian world. In *Mere Christianity* he writes:

> Is it not frightfully unfair that this new life should be confined to people who have heard of Christ and been able to believe in Him? But the truth is God has not told us what His arrangements about the other people are. We do know that no man can be saved except through Christ; we do not know that only those who know Him can be saved through Him.[13]

In another place he explains, "There are people in other religions who are being led by God's secret influence to concentrate on those parts of their religion which are in agreement with Christianity, and who thus belong to Christ without knowing it."[14]

In his essay, "Man or Rabbit," Lewis adds one more thought about an "honest error or an honest mistake:"

> We all know there have been good men who were not Christians; men like Socrates and Confucius who had never heard of it, or men like J. S. Mill who quite honestly couldn't believe it. Supposing Christianity to be true, these men were in a state of honest ignorance or honest error. If their intentions were as good as I suppose them to have been (for of course I can't read their secret hearts) I hope and believe that the skill and mercy of God will remedy the evils which their ignorance, left to itself, would naturally produce both for them and for those whom they influenced.[15]

Consequently, according to Lewis, a person can be saved without believing the gospel.

---

[13]   C. S. Lewis, *Mere Christianity* (New York: Macmillan, 1970), 65.

[14]   Lewis, *Mere Christianity*, 176.

[15]   C. S. Lewis. *God in the Dock: Essays on Theology and Ethics,* ed. W. Hooper (Grand Rapids, Michigan: Eerdmans, 1970), 110.

Lewis is not the only author who expressed such sentiments. Several evangelical scholars have joined their voices to his. Clark Pinnock claims that "There is no salvation except through Christ, but it is not necessary for everybody to possess a conscious knowledge of Christ in order to benefit from redemption through him."[16] John Sanders echoes the same idea: "The unevangelized may be reconciled to God on the basis of the work of Christ even though they are ignorant of Jesus."[17]

Christians, with relative ease, use terminology that describes salvation outside the gospel. Some examples are "a wider hope," "anonymous Christians," "believers, but not Christians," "the holy heathen," "Christ incognito," and so on. The quantity of literature dedicated to this topic in the past two decades, attests to the debate within evangelical Christianity over the necessity of a conscious faith in Jesus Christ for salvation. This also includes similar issues like universal access to salvation and the possibility of an encounter with the gospel after death.

What Is All the Fuss About?

What has given rise to this revision of the traditional view? What factors have been part of this movement toward inclusivism? In addition to cultural pressure, addressed above, we need to note two presuppositions that explain the rise of inclusivism. These can be described as the theological and the emotional question.

The Theological Question

A major presupposition of advocates of inclusivism involves their perception of God's character. In particular, inclusivists redefine God's love and justice. They insist that their understanding of God's love is what motivates them to seek "a wider hope" for mankind. Clark Pinnock openly confesses, "It is the presupposition [about God's love] which gives rise to wider hope and the inclusivist

---

[16]   Pinnock, *A Wideness in God's Mercy: The Finality of Jesus Christ in a World of Religions* (Grand Rapids, Michigan: Zondervan, 1992), 75.

[17]   Sanders, "Inclusivism," 38.

theory."[18] Adherents of inclusivism characteristically affirm that love is the predominant and determining quality of God.[19] They consider the words of the apostle John, "God is love" (1 John 4:8), as proof of the preeminent place of love in God's character, even though the Scriptures contain similar descriptions of God as light (1 John 1:5) or as a consuming fire (Heb 12:29).

Endeavoring to substantiate their views, inclusivists frequently rely on narrative texts—stories from the Old and New Testaments—that describe God's relationship with people. Their choice of texts is not accidental. For example, Pinnock describes his hermeneutical approach in the following way: "In terms of biblical interpretation, I give particular weight to narrative and to the language of personal relationships in it.... I seek to recover the dynamism of biblical revelation."[20] In other words, the foremost defenders of inclusivism, Pinnock and Sanders, confess that they prefer to base their theological views on narrative passages and not on clear, didactic texts from the Scriptures. This increases the risk of unjustified generalizations and nonliteral interpretations.

Consequently, the concept of God's love, drawn from interpretation of narrative texts, motivates inclusivists to agitate against what they call "ghetto mentality"[21] in the question of salvation, in order to accentuate God's desire to save all people (cf. 1 Tim 2:4), and to insist that God's love, of necessity, is expressed in universal access to salvation and, if necessary, by means of other religions. However, in order to avoid a deep philosophical rendering of God's love and justice,[22] it is important to seriously examine the biblical basis of the inclusivists' optimism, since the Scriptures alone are able to shed

---

[18] Pinnock "Overcoming Misgivings," 34.

[19] Ibid., 33; see also Pinnock, *The Most Moved Mover: A Theology of God's Openness* (Grand Rapids, Michigan: Baker Academic, 2001), 45; Sanders, "Divine Providence and the Openness of God," in Paul Helm, Bruce A. Ware, Roger E. Olson, and John Sanders, *Perspectives on the Doctrine of God: Four Views,* ed. Bruce A. Ware (Nashville, Tennessee: B&H Academic), 197.

[20] Pinnock, *The Most Moved Mover*, 20. It is easy to see that John Sanders employs the same principles, since in defending the inclusivist position he resorts primarily to narratives. See Sanders, "Inclusivism," 26–29.

[21] This is Pinnock's expression. See Pinnock "Overcoming Misgivings," 33.

[22] See the warning in Paul R. House, "Biblical Theology and the Inclusivist Challenge," *Southern Baptist Journal of Theology* 2, no. 2 (Summer 1998): 2.

light on how God's love must be expressed, and in what sense God wishes that all people be saved.

The Question of Emotions

The second factor explaining the rise and spread of inclusivism is the emotional pain Christians experience when they think about the great multitude of people who, having lived at one time on earth, have been condemned to eternal damnation.[23] Indeed, "Inclusivism deals with the emotional and cultural disturbances created by the exclusivist viewpoint, especially the claim that God would be unfair to condemn the unevangelized."[24]

Of course, those who are saved sympathize with others and wish that they too could enjoy the same blessings they receive. Therefore, from an emotional point of view, the question of the destiny of the unevangelized is completely understandable.[25] However, some Christians do not stop there but openly express their revulsion at a portrait of God that depicts Him in somber hues as someone who condemns those who have rejected the gospel or have never encountered Him.[26] Such people look with suspicion on exclusivistic statements or directly accuse exclusivists of several deficiencies, including religious and cultural hubris, fear of competition, and dialogue with other religions, intolerance, a tendency toward defensiveness, and self-exaltation.[27]

Evangelical theologian Bruce Demerest has rightly observed, in dealing with these kinds of topics, that "it is imperative that we be guided by clear evidence and not merely by our emotions."[28] The actual issue is not which party loves perishing sinners more, but which understanding of biblical teaching is more correct from an exegetical standpoint. When thinking about the important issue of those who have never heard the gospel, we need to rely on a firmer foundation than

---

[23] See Ramesh P. Richard, "Soteriological Inclusivism and Dispensationalism" *Bibliotheca Sacra* 151 , no. 601 (January 1994):. 85.

[24] Doran, *For the Sake of His Name*, 185.

[25] See Erickson, "The Fate of Those Who Never Hear," 4.

[26] See Sanders, "Inclusivism," 25–26.

[27] See Pinnock, "Toward an Evangelical Theology of Religions," 361n8.

[28] Bruce Demerest, *The Cross and Salvation: The Doctrine of Salvation* (Wheaton, Illinois: Crossway, 1997), 87.

human emotions. A position relying on one's feelings may turn out to be simply speculation, or, what is worse, theologically unhealthy.[29]

So it is important to remember the apostle Paul's perspective on the relationship between human wisdom and God's truth: "For the word of the cross is to those who are perishing foolishness ... the world through its wisdom did not come to know God ... Because the foolishness of God is wiser than men, and the weakness of God is stronger than men" (1 Cor 1:18, 21, 25). Therefore, in finding an answer concerning the destiny of perishing sinners, we must not rely on the shaky foundation of human feelings and notions, but rather the firm foundation of biblical truth discovered through diligent exegesis of the text.

What Is at Stake?

One can question the value of dedicating whole books, chapters, and hours of private reflection and deliberation with other believers on this issue. Even though unreached people groups may be far removed from us geographically, the problems that are raised by discussing their destiny span a wide spectrum of issues that are fundamental for every Christian.

Theological Considerations

Ideas concerning the fate of those who have never heard the gospel are linked to a broad range of theological issues. The fate of the unevangelized touches upon the doctrine of God[30]—His nature, His power, and the dynamic between His love and justice. It also directly concerns the doctrine of Christ—the historical significance of His incarnation, the necessity and sufficiency of His death for the salvation of mankind, and the importance of the proclamation of His death and resurrection. The doctrine of salvation is also at stake, since it involves questions such as the necessity of faith, the nature of saving faith, the mental capability and moral incapability of man, the role and mission of the Church in spreading salvation, and the

---

[29] See Ronald Nash, "Restrictivism," in *What About Those Who Have Never Heard?* 139; see also House, "Biblical Theology and the Inclusivist Challenge," 3.

[30] See Geivett, "Is Jesus the Only Way?" 179–181.

possibility of gaining salvation after death. Biblical teaching on revelation also comes into play when discussing the destiny of those who have not heard the gospel. It involves teaching on the value and role of general revelation, on the power and sufficiency of special revelation, and on the superiority of recorded revelation over personal experience. Finally, the discussion encompasses various other applied aspects of theology, such as hermeneutics, apologetics, evangelism, and Christian missions.[31]

The Glory of Christ

Another critical element at stake when discussing the fate of those who have not known the gospel is the uniqueness, superiority, and glory of Jesus Christ. God intentionally purposed that His Son would be at the center of His plan to save mankind. The main motivating force in the life and ministry of the apostle Paul was the glory of Jesus Christ through the salvation of the nations. At the beginning of the Epistle to the Romans, he writes about his ministry of proclaiming the gospel of Jesus Christ, "through whom we have received grace and apostleship to bring about the obedience of faith among all the Gentiles, for His name's sake" (Rom 1:5). John Piper has rightly noted: "It is a stunning New Testament truth that since the incarnation of the Son of God, all saving faith must henceforth fix on him … Christ is the focal point of the Church's missionary activity."[32]

The Christian Church is called to continue the work begun by the apostle Paul, who wrote:

> To me, the very least of all saints, this grace was given, to preach to the Gentiles the unfathomable riches of Christ, and to bring to light what is the administration of the mystery which for ages has been hidden in God, who created all things; in order that the manifold wisdom of God might now be made known through the church to the rulers and

---

[31] For more information on the theological topics listed in this paragraph, see John MacArthur and Richard Mayhue, eds., *Biblical Doctrine: A Systematic Summary of Bible Truth* (Wheaton, Illinois: Crossway, forthcoming). For more on the doctrine of Scripture itself, see John MacArthur, ed., *The Inerrant Word* (Wheaton, Illinois: Crossway, 2016).

[32] Piper, *Let the Nations Be Glad!* 111.

the authorities in the heavenly places. This was in accordance with the eternal purpose which He carried out in Christ Jesus our Lord, in whom we have boldness and confident access through faith in Him (Eph 3:8–12).[33]

In proclaiming the gospel, the followers of Christ must operate in accordance with the Holy Spirit, as the Lord has commanded "When the Helper comes, whom I will send to you from the Father, that is the Spirit of truth, who proceeds from the Father, He will bear witness of Me, and you will bear witness also, because you have been with Me from the beginning" (John 15:26–27). And the Spirit acts with the express aim of glorifying the name of Jesus Christ (see John 16:14). As Todd Miles writes, "The Church exists for the glory of Christ and the sake of missions. When the Church ceases to proclaim, she denies the fundamental reality of who she is."[34]

However, what is clear and logical from the point of view of Scripture is incompatible with religious pluralism and various compromising theories. If Christ is not the one and only Savior, then He stands in the same line with other deities, and God's words, "My glory I will not give to another" (Isaiah 48:11), are forgotten. If the gospel of Christ is not the sole means of salvation, then the good news of the death and resurrection of Christ becomes a message about a significant, but not unique event in the history of mankind. If faith in Christ is not the essential condition for salvation, then Christ and His appeal, "believe in God, believe also in Me" (John 14:1) can be totally ignored. If the Holy Spirit leads people to salvation but bypasses the name of Christ, then Jesus Christ, God's Son, is deprived of the glory that he deserves (cf. Rev 5:12).

Nevertheless, despite the changes in contemporary culture, the task of the Church remains the same: to glorify Christ and not deprive Him of His glory. In other words, the fundamental principle of the Reformation, *solus Christus* (Christ alone), must be expressed not

---

[33] Emphasis added.

[34] Miles, *A God of Many Understandings?*, 6; see also Henry, "The SBJT Forum: Responses to Inclusivism," *Southern Baptist Journal of Theology* 2, no. 2 (Summer 1998): 53.

only by way of proclamation but also through practical application in the sphere of missions.

Missionary Motivation

The matter of the destiny of the unevangelized is directly connected to missions. Traditionally, the motivating force behind evangelism and missionary work has been the conviction that it is essential that people hear the good news, since all of humanity is subject to God's wrath due to sin and because humanity is at risk of ending up eternally in hell.[35] However, in pursuit of a theodicy,[36] compromising theories propose that God possesses other means of reaching people apart from the missionary activity of the Church.[37] In connection with this, there is the tremendous danger that the arguments presented in these theories will reach the ears of not only non-believing critics and academics, but also individuals who are interested in missionary service. Todd Miles expresses his dismay concerning this: "When a Christian's theology of religions moves from exclusivism to inclusivism, pluralism, or universalism, the result is a diminished commitment to missions and evangelism."[38] Liberal theologians have honestly admitted that pluralistic trends have had an adverse effect on Christian missions. For example, Paul Tillich writes: "This approach discourages contemporary Christianity from engaging in missions in the traditional and reprehensible sense of the word."[39]

Consequently, exclusivist notions threaten the very nerve center of motivation for missions. If there is another way or other means of acquiring salvation that might possibly be more effective than the

---

[35] See Erickson, "The Fate of Those Who Never Hear," 14.

[36] Theodicy is "a term used to refer to attempts to justify the ways of God to man. A successful theodicy resolves the problem of evil for a theological system and demonstrates that God is all-powerful, all-loving, and just, despite evil's existence." J. S. Feinberg. "Theodicy," in *Evangelical Dictionary of Theology*, ed. Walter A. Elwell (Grand Rapids, Michigan: Baker, 1984), 1083.

[37] See, for example, Sanders, "Introduction," in *What About Those Who Have Never Heard?*, 8; Gabriel Fackre, "Divine Perseverance," in *What About Those Who Have Never Heard?*, 87.

[38] Miles, *A God of Many Understandings?*, 329; see also ibid., 5.

[39] Paul Tillich, *Christianity and the Encounter of World Religions* (Philadelphia: Fortress, 1963).

preaching of the gospel by missionaries, then why should Christians risk their families, their health, their finances, their comfort, and even their lives for the sake of the gospel?[40] Therefore, any attempt to discover sufficient motivation in a simple desire to share the joy of salvation and the blessedness of the Christian life with people of other nations, could scarcely be met with any success.[41] If there are other avenues to salvation for those who have never heard the gospel, then it becomes extremely difficult to explain the missionary zeal of the apostles and early Christians, and to motivate contemporary believers to get involved in missions.

The Need for a Scriptural Understanding

All of this underscores the need for a trusted foundation when solving these issues. It is important to remember, in this endeavor, that Scripture must be the foundation and not philosophical reasoning, even more so, since at times there are sentiments expressed which are contrary to Scripture.[42] For example, inclusivist John Sanders, working on a theodicy while discussing divine providence, states: "A straight-forward appeal to scriptural teaching will not settle the matter. We do not have a universally objective and neutral approach to Scripture, so appeals to scriptural texts, though necessary, will not settle this dispute."[43] An approach like this is unacceptable since Sanders explicitly neglects biblical teaching in favor of philosophical argumentation. Therefore, it is vital that any answer to the question of the destiny of those unreached by the gospel be firmly based on biblical and theological perspectives.

Five Points to Consider

Paul's words in Romans 10:13–17 are of great value in deciding the question of the fate of the unevangelized:

---

40 See Doran, *For the Sake of His Name*, 171.

41 Piper, *Let the Nations Be Glad!*, 115.

42 Doran, *For the Sake of His Name*, 172.

43 Sanders, "Divine Providence and the Openness of God," in *Perspectives on the Doctrine of God*, 214.

For "Whoever will call on the name of the Lord will be saved." How then shall they call upon Him in whom they have not believed? And how shall they believe in Him whom they have not heard? And how shall they hear without a preacher? And how shall they preach unless they are sent? Just as it is written, "How beautiful are the feet of those who bring glad tidings of good!" However, they did not all heed the glad tidings; for Isaiah says, "Lord, who has believed our report?" So faith comes from hearing, and hearing by the word of Christ (Rom 10:13–17).

This text testifies that eternal salvation from the torment of hell is possible only by means of a conscious confession of Jesus Christ as Savior and Lord in response to the proclamation of the Good News by a preacher of the gospel. We can break this down into five points.

First, consulting the Old Testament, the apostle Paul reminds us of *the necessity of salvation:* "Whoever will call on the name of the Lord will be saved" (Rom 10:13). This affirmation, taking for granted the universal need for salvation, is based on the apostle's previous, extended deliberation in chapters 1–3 (esp. 3:9, 19) on the all-encompassing sinfulness of mankind. Here, Paul convincingly demonstrates that God is absolutely justified in condemning all people, including those who have not been reached by the good news, for rebelling against Him and rejecting general revelation (see 1:18–20). The apostle's conviction is extensively backed up by biblical teaching from the Old Testament (cf. Gen 6:5; 8:21; 1 Kgs 8:46; Ps 130:3; 143:2; Prov 20:6, 9; Eccl 7:20; Jer 17:9), as well as the New Testament (see, for example, Eph 2:1–3; 4:17–19; Titus 3:3).[44]

Second, using the first of four short rhetorical questions, the author begins to narrow the circle of saved individuals by setting

---

[44] There are people who may not like the original, universal condemnation of humanity preached by Paul because it does not correspond with their understanding of God's love. Consequently, they may offer universalism (salvation for everyone) and annihilation (final destruction of condemned sinners without eternal torment in hell) as alternatives. However, these alternatives directly contradict the clear testimony of Scripture concerning the two destinies of people, destinies which cannot be altered after death (see Luke 16:26; Heb 9:27); and further, the eternal nature of punishment in hell, and the parallel eternal perpetuation of the joy of the saved in heaven (see Dan 12:2; Matt 25:46).

down *the first condition of salvation:* the necessity of faith and a conscious conversion. He asks, "How then shall they call upon Him in whom they have not believed?" (Rom 10:14a). The text preceding and following these words convincingly argues in favor of the conscious nature of conversion and a conscious faith in the Lord. The New Testament says quite a bit about this, insisting on a conscious confession of the name of Jesus and conscious faith in Him (see John 3:16; 1 John 5:11–12; 1 Tim 2:5). The Lord Jesus Christ Himself was especially clear about this, saying, "I am the way, and the truth, and the life. No one comes to the Father but through me" (John 14:6). It is plain from Peter's testimony before the Jewish leaders in Acts 4, that the apostles understood His words perfectly: "And there is salvation in no one else, for there is no other name under heaven given among men by which we must be saved" (Acts 4:11–12).

Third, the second half of Romans 10:14 indicates *the gospel prerequisite of salvation:* "And how shall they believe in Him whom they have not heard?" The context of this verse leaves no doubt that the text is referring to a particular revelation of the Good News. The New Testament repeatedly affirms that it is the gospel that "is the power of God for salvation to everyone who believes" (Rom 1:16; cf. 1 Cor 1:21–23; Jas 1:18; 1 Pet 1:22–25). In other words, there is a required minimum (cf. 1 Cor 15:1–4), taking into account progressive revelation, which is necessary for salvation. General revelation, despite all of the good intended from it, does not possess that minimum (cf. Rom 1:18–20).[45]

The fourth point concerns Paul's next rhetorical question, which expresses his certainty concerning *preaching as the means of*

---

[45] The proponents of inclusivism are not satisfied with this state of things and state two objections which are close one to another in essence. They point to the salvation of Old Testament believers and formulate a so-called "principle of faith" (cf. Heb 11:6), which posits that the minimum for salvation is not information about God but rather trust in Him. The answer to this objection is that Scripture contains enough indications that Old Testament saints (within Israel and outside of her borders) were unequivocally saved not by means of pagan cults, but with the aid of special revelation. This proves that there is an enormous difference between Old Testament believers and contemporary pagans. If one believes in the uninterrupted uniformity of God's design for salvation throughout all periods of history, then one can discover in the convictions of Old Testament saints—with greater or lesser certainty—practically all of the qualitative elements of the gospel message. On the other hand, if the argument presupposes that God's methods are discontinuous in various periods, then in accounting for the progressive nature of revelation, one will find particular, clearly defined components of faith in every dispensation and will unabashedly insist on the need for faith in the gospel in the present age.

salvation: "And how shall they hear without a preacher?" (10:14b). The apostle's certainty rests on God's plan of salvation: "For since in the wisdom of God the world through its wisdom did not come to know God, God was well-pleased [εὐδόκησεν, *eudokēsen*] through the foolishness of the message preached to save those who believe" (1 Cor 1:21; cf. 1 Thess 2:16). Furthermore, the apostle himself demonstrated from his own life the urgency of spreading the gospel by striving to extend his missionary activity into new territories: "And thus I aspired to preach the gospel, not where Christ was already named, so that I would not build on another man's foundation; but as it is written, "They who had no news of Him shall see, And they who have not heard shall understand" (Rom 15:20–21).[46]

The fifth and final point deals with the last rhetorical question Paul asks in Romans 10. His quote from the Old Testament demonstrates the necessity of a human mediator who will preach the gospel: "And how shall they preach unless they are sent? Just as it is written, 'How beautiful are the feet of those who bring glad tidings of good things!'" (Rom 10:15). There is no small number of advocates, both of inclusivism and exclusivism, who cite direct revelations from God to the unevangelized, but who do not see the need for them. However, the apostle Paul has laid down the general principle of special revelation with certainty. In addition, this principle, reinforced by numerous biblical examples, totally agrees with teaching on the sufficiency of Scripture, expresses God's intentions (cf. Acts 4:12), and provides the required motivation for missionaries, as human mediators, who bring to fruition God's plan in life.

Conclusion

In summing up his series of rhetorical questions, Paul emphasizes that responsibility for unbelief in response to the gospel message lies

---

[46] In contrast to Paul's position, inclusivists cast doubt on the necessity of the gospel message insisting that the message of salvation has been universally accessible to all people, in all places, and at all times. This alteration of special revelation, which is essential for salvation, cannot, in general, be justified from a theological point of view and is rooted in untrustworthy conclusions based on faulty application of texts concerning the universal nature of the atonement (1 John 2:2; 1 Tim 4:10), or on an erroneous understanding of texts supposedly affirming prevenient grace with a Wesleyan twist (John 1:9; Titus 2:11). At fault as well is an inaccurate harmonizing of texts about God's desire to save everyone (John 12:32; 2 Pet 3:9; 1 Tim 2:4–5) with God's specific plan of salvation.

with the hearer: "However, they did not all heed the glad tidings; for Isaiah says, 'Lord, who has believed our report?' So faith comes from hearing, and hearing by the word of Christ" (Rom 10:16–17). In other words, conscious faith, based on a hearing of the Word of God, is necessary for salvation.

In conclusion, the Scriptures teach that after the death and resurrection of Christ, in the Church age, eternal salvation from the torment of hell is possible only by means of a conscious confession of Jesus Christ as Savior and Lord. This confession must be in response to a proclamation of the good news by a preacher of the gospel. Only this kind of understanding of God's plan of salvation motivates God's servants to choose missionary ministry for the sake of the salvation of nations. And, most of all, it brings particular glory to Christ as the only hope for the nations, the only light of men, and the only name given by which we must be saved. Thus, the message (and messengers) of Christ must go to every nation—and this is exactly what Christ has commanded us to do.

Bibliography

Between God and Men: Proclaiming Christ as Mediator in Light of the South African Concept of Mediation

Adeyemo, Tokunboh. *Salvation in African Tradition*. Nairobi: Evangel Publishing House, 1997.

Bruce, F. F. *The Epistle to the Hebrews*. New International Commentary on the New Testament. Grand Rapids, Michigan: Eerdmans, 1990.

Carson, D.A. *The Gospel according to John*. The Pillar New Testament Commentary. Grand Rapids, Michigan: Eerdmans, 1991.

de Visser, A.J. *Kyrios and Morena: The Lordship of Christ and African Township Christianity*. Potchefstroom, South Africa: n.p., 2001.

Ellingsworth, Paul. *The Epistle to the Hebrews*. The New International Greek Testament Commentary. Grand Rapids, Michigan: Eerdmans, 1993.

Gade, Christian B. N. "What is Ubuntu? Different Interpretations among South Africans of African Descent." *South African Journal of Philosophy* 31, no. 3, 2012.

Gehman, Richard J. *African Traditional Religion in Biblical Perspective*. Nairobi: Kesho Publications, 1989.

Gérard, Albert S., ed. *European-Language Writing in Sub-Saharan Africa*. Budapest: Akadémiai Kiadó, 1986.

Lewis, Peter. *The Glory of Christ*. Chicago, Illinois: Moody Press, 1997.

Luther, Martin. *Festival Sermons of Martin Luther: The Church Postils*. Translated by Joel R. Baseley. Dearborn, Michigan: Mark V Publications, 2005.

Mbiti, John S. *Introduction to African Religion*, 2nd ed. London: Heinemann, 1975.

Meiring, P., ed. *A World of Religions: A South African Perspective*. Pretoria: Kagiso, 1996.

O'Donovan, Wilbur. *Biblical Christianity in African Perspective*. Carlisle, UK: Paternoster, 1992.

Olowola, Cornelius. "The Person and Work of Christ" in *Issues in African Theology*. Nairobi: East African Educational Publishers, 1998.

Yri, Norvald. "Luther Speaks to Africa." *Issues in African Theology*. Nairobi: East African Educational Publishers, 1998.

Pali, K. J. "Christ as Once for All Sacrifice: A Cultural Reading of Hebrews." *Acta Theololgica* 34, no. 1, Jan 2014.

Parrinder, Edward Geoffrey. *African Traditional Religion*. London: SPCK, 1954.

Should We Take the Road Back to Rome? An Analysis of Roman Catholic Ecumenical Trends

English Sources
Allison, Gregg R. Roman Catholic Theology and Practice: An Evangelical Assessment. Wheaton, Illinois: Crossway, 2014.

Catechism of the Catholic Church. New York: Doubleday, 1995.

Cyprian of Carthage. The Epistles of Cyprian 72.21. New Advent. http://www.newadvent.org/fathers/050672.htm.

De Chirico, Leonardo. Evangelical Theological Perspectives on Post-Vatican II Roman Catholicism. Religions and Discourse 19. Bern, Switzerland: Peter Lang, 2003.

—— "Evangelicals and Catholics: A New Era?" Vatican Files. May 1, 2016, http://vaticanfiles.org/2016/04/124-evangelicals-and-catholics-a-new-era-4.

——. "Roman Catholic Ecumenism: Let the Italian Evangelicals Speak." Vatican Files. July 23, 2014. http://vaticanfiles.org/2014/07/84-roman-catholic-ecumenism-let-the-italian-evangelicals-speak.

Estrada, David. "The Joint Declaration on the Doctrine of Justification by the Lutheran World Federation and the Catholic Church." *Christianity & Society* 11, no. 1. January 2001.

Holy See, The. Dominus Iesus. August 6, 2000. http://www.vatican.va/roman_curia/congregations/cfaith/documents/rc_con_cfaith_doc_20000806_dominus-iesus_en.html.

——. "From Conflict to Communion: Lutheran-Catholic Common Commemoration of the Reformation in 2017." VI.238. http://www.vatican.va/roman_curia/pontifical_councils/chrstuni/lutheran-fed-docs/rc_pc_chrstuni_doc_2013_dal-conflitto-alla-comunione_en.html.

——. "Joint Declaration on the Doctrine of Justification by the Lutheran World Federation and the Catholic Church." http://www.vatican.va/roman_curia/pontifical_councils/chrstuni/documents/rc_pc_chrstuni_doc_31101999_cath-luth-joint-declaration_en.html.

——. Indulgentiarum Doctrina. January 1, 1967. https://w2.vatican.va/content/paul-vi/en/apost_constitutions/documents/hf_p-vi_apc_01011967_indulgentiarum-doctrina.html.

——. "Lumen Gentium." November 21, 1964. http://www.vatican.va/archive/hist_councils/ii_vatican_council/documents/vat-ii_const_19641121_lumen-gentium_en.html.

——. Misericordiae Vultus. April 11, 2015. https://w2.vatican.va/content/francesco/en/apost_letters/documents/papa-francesco_bolla_20150411_misericordiae-vultus.html.

——. "Mortalium Animos." January 6, 1928. http://w2.vatican.va/content/pius-xi/en/encyclicals/documents/hf_p-xi_enc_19280106_mortalium-animos.html.

——. "Munificentissimus Deus." November 1, 1950. http://w2.vatican.va/content/pius-xii/en/apost_constitutions/documents/hf_p-xii_apc_19501101_munificentissimus-deus.html.

——. Mystici Corporis Christi. June 29, 1943. http://w2.vatican.va/content/pius-xii/en/encyclicals/documents/hf_p-xii_enc_29061943_mystici-corporis-christi.html.

——. "Unitatis redintegratio." November 21, 1964. http://www.vatican.va/archive/hist_councils/ii_vatican_council/documents/vat-ii_decree_19641121_unitatis-redintegratio_en.html.

——. "Ut Unum Sint" May 25, 1995. http://w2.vatican.va/content/john-paul-ii/en/encyclicals/documents/hf_jp-ii_enc_25051995_ut-unum-sint.html.

Schaff, Philip and David S. Schaff. History of the Christian Church 3. New York: Charles Scribner's Sons, 1910.

Schaff, Philip. The Creeds of Christendom, with a History and Critical Notes. New York: Harper & Brothers, 1877.

Webster, William. Roman Catholic Tradition: Claims and Contradictions. Battle Ground, Washington: Christian Resources, 1999.

——. Saving Faith: How Does Rome Define It? Battle Ground, Washington: Christian Resources, 1995.

——. The Church of Rome at the Bar of History. Carlisle, Pennsylvania: Banner of Truth, 1997.

Italian Sources

Chiesi, Tito. Lasciò la Chiesa per seguire Cristo: La vita e l'opera di Luigi Desanctis (1808–1869). Mantova, Italy: Passaggio, 2014.

De Chirico, Leonardo. "Il Vaticano II, banco di prova della teologica evangelica." Studi di Teologi 50. February 2013.

———. "La giustificazione come questione ecumenica irrisolta." Studi di Teologia NS 53. January 2015.

———. Quale unità cristiana? L'ecumenismo in discussione. Italy: Alfa e Omega, 2016.

Santa Sede, La. "Discorso del Santo Padre Giovanni XXIII [Address of Pope John XXIII]." October 11, 1962. https://w2.vatican.va/content/john-xxiii/it/speeches/1962/documents/hf_j-xxiii_spe_19621011_opening-council.html.

The Danger of Karma and the Doctrine of Christ

Boyd, Robin. An Introduction to Indian Christian Theology. Delhi: ISPCK, 2004.

Calvin, John. Commentary on the Gospel according to John 1. Translated by William Pringle. Bellingham, Washington: Logos Bible Software, 2010.

Carson, D. A. The Gospel according to John. *The Pillar New Testament Commentary*. Grand Rapids, Michigan: Eerdmans, 1991.

Mangalwadi, Vishal. *When the New Age Gets Old: Looking for a Greater Spirituality*, 2nd ed. Westmont, Illinois: Inter-Varsity Press, 1992.

———. *The World of Gurus: A Critical Look at the Philosophies of India's Influential Gurus and Mystics*. Chicago, Illinois: Cornerstone Press, 1992.

McClelland, Norman C. *Encyclopedia of Reincarnation and Karma*. Jefferson, North Carolina: McFarland, 2010.

Poisonous Pragmatism: The Harmful Effects of Western Missiological Trends on the Churches in Ukraine

English Sources

Demarest, Bruce. *The Cross and Salvation: The Doctrine of Salvation*. Foundations of Evangelical Theology. Wheaton, Illinois: Crossway, 2006.

Doran, David M., et al. *For the Sake of His Name: Challenging a New Generation for World Missions*. Allen Park, Michigan: Student Global Impact, 2002.

Geisler, Norman L. *Baker Encyclopedia of Christian Apologetics*. Grand Rapids, Michigan: Baker, 1999.

Gilley, Gary E. *This Little Church Had None: A Church in Search of the Truth*. Carlisle, Pennsylvania: EP Books, 2009.

Kruedener, Julia and Anna Lion. *Evangelist John Onyshchenko*. Morris Plains, New Jersey: All-Ukrainian Evangelical Baptist Fellowship, 2002.

Kreeft, Peter and Ronald K. Tacelli. *Pocket Handbook of Christian Apologetics*. Downer Grove, Illinois: Inter-Varsity Press, 2003.

MacArthur, John F., Jr. *Ashamed of the Gospel: When the Church Becomes Like the World*. 3rd ed. Wheaton, Illinois: Crossway, 2010.

———. *Our Sufficiency in Christ*. Electronic ed. Dallas, Texas: Word Publishing, 1997.

McBeth, H. Leon. *The Baptist Heritage: Four Centuries of Baptist Witness*. Nashville, Tennessee: Broadman, 1987.

Murray, Andrew. *Key to the Missionary Problem*, 2nd ed. Fort Washington, Pennsylvania: Christian Literature Crusade, 1993.

Nichols, Gregory L. *The Development of Russian Evangelical Spirituality: A Study of Ivan V. Vargel*. Eugene, Oregon: Wipf & Stock, 2011.

Noll, Mark A. "Pietism." *Evangelical Dictionary of Theology*, 2nd ed. Edited by Walter A. Elwell. Grand Rapids, Michigan: Baker Academic, 2001.

Piper, John. *God is the Gospel: Meditations on God's Love as the Gift of Himself*. Wheaton, Illinois: Crossway, 2005.

Prigodich, Raymond P. "Ukraine." *Evangelical Dictionary of World Missions*. Edited by A. Scott Moreau. Grand Rapids, Michigan: Baker, 2000.

Puzynin, Andrey P. *The Tradition of the Gospel Christians: A Study of Their Identity and Theology during the Russian, Soviet, and Post-Soviet Periods*. Eugene, Oregon: Wipf & Stock, 2011.

Rowe, Michael. *Russian Resurrection: Strength in Suffering—A History of Russia's Evangelical Church*. London: Marshall Pickering, 1994.

Sawatsky, Walter W. "Ukraine." *The Encyclopedia of Christianity*. Edited by Erwin Fahlbusch, Jan Milic Lochman, and John Mbiti. Translated by Geoffrey William Bromiley. Grand Rapids, Michigan: Eerdmans, 2008.

———. "Return of Mission and Evangelization in the CIS (1980s-present): An Assessment." *Mission in the Former Soviet Union*. Edited by Walter W. Sawatsky, Peter F. Penner. Schwarzenfeld, Germany: Neufeld-Verlag, 2005.

Schwarz, Christian A. *Natural Church Development: A Guide to Eight Essential Qualities of Healthy Churches*. Carol Stream, Illinois: Churchsmart Resources, 1996.

Simonian, Craig. "Natural Church Development: A Review." Fall 1999. http://www.ourvineyard.org/files/A_Review_of_Christian_Schwarz1.htm.

Terry, John Mark. *Evangelism: A Concise History*. Nashville, Tennessee: Broadman & Holman, 1994.

Warren, Rick. *The Purpose Driven Church: Every Church is Big in God's Eyes*. Grand Rapids, Michigan: Zondervan, 1995.

Washer, Paul. *The Gospel Call and True Conversion*. Recovering the Gospel. Grand Rapids: Reformation Heritage, 2013.

White, John. "Three Periods of Awakening in Eastern Slavic Lands." *Theological Reflections, Euro-Asian Theological Journal*. Special Edition, 2013.

Yurash, Andrij. "Ukraine." *Worldmark Encyclopedia of Religious Practices*. Edited by Thomas Riggs. New York: Thomson Gale, 2006.

Zabko-Potapovich, L. *The Life of a Church*. Winnipeg, Manitoba: Doroga Prawdy, 1977.

Ukrainian and Russian Sources

Антонюк, Валерій, ред. Євангельські християни-баптисти: історія і сучасність. Київ: ВСО ЄХБ, 2012.

Глик, Дэниел. Что говорят новообращенные христиане Украины. Запорожье, Укр.: Пилигрим, 2008.

Головащенко, С. И., сост. История евангельско-баптистского движения в Украине. Материалы и документы. Одесса: Богомыслие, 1998.

Головин, Сергей. Мировоззрение—утраченное измерение благовестия. Симферополь, Укр.: Диайпи, 2008.

Иванов-Клышников, П. В. «Наше шестидесятилетие 1867–1927». Баптист Украины, №9. Харьков, Укр.: ВСОБ, 1927.

Іваськів, Й. Український народ і християнство. Харків: Глобус, 2005.

Коваленко, Леонид. Облако свидетелей Христовых. Киев: Центр христианского сотрудничества, 1997.

Московка, Сергій, ред. Каталог ідей для вашої церкви. Київ, Укр.: «Дорожче за кубок», 2012.

Поллок, Джон. Жизнь Билли Грема. Киев: Христианский центр «Возрождение» ЕХБ, 2006.

Регіональна конференція служителів. Березень 2016. «Церква, яка впливає на суспільство». Тема 4. Критерії успішності у благовісті (Сергій Мороз). http://ecbua.info/index.php?option=com_content&view=article&id=3992%3Aregonalna-konferenczya-sluzhitelv-berezen-2016-lczerkva-yaka-vpli-

va-na-susplstvor-tema-4-kriter-uspshnost-u-blagovst-sergj-moroz&-catid=13%3As-&Itemid=53&lang=ua (01 September 2016).

Савинский, С. Н. История евангельский христиан-баптистов Украины, России, Белоруссии 1867–1917. Санкт-Петербург: Библия для всех, 1999.

_____ . История евангельский христиан-баптистов Украины, России, Белоруссии 1917–1967. Санкт-Петербург: Библия для всех, 2001.

Уорен, Рик. Целеустремленная церковь. Пер. с англ. Н. Демянов. Киев: Центр Христианского Сотрудничества, 1997.

Яроцький П., ред. Протестантизм в Україні. Історія релігії в Україні. 5 томів. Київ: Світ знань, 2002.

Reclaiming the Forgotten Christ in the Czech Republic

English Sources

Allen, John L., Jr. "Czechs Object to Authority, Not Religion, Sociologist Says." *National Catholic Reporter.* September 26, 2009. https://www.ncronline. org/blogs/ncr-today/czechs-object-authority-not-religion-sociologist-says.

Bahnsen, Greg L. *Always Ready: Directions for Defending the Faith.* Covenant Media Press, November 1996.

Gilley, Gary and Jay Wegter, *This Little Church Had None: A Church in Search of the Truth.* Darlington, UK: Evangelical Press, 2009.

Gregor, Frances. *The Story of Bohemia.* Cincinnati, Ohio: Cranston & Curts, 1895.

Havlíček, Jakub and Dušan Lužný. "Religion and Politics in the Czech Republic: The Roman Catholic Church and the State." *International Journal of Social Science Studies* 1, no. 2. October 2013.

Horák, Záboj. "Religion and the Secular State in the Czech Republic." *National Report: Czech Republic.*

Kaminsky, Howard. *A History of the Hussite Revolution.* Eugene, Oregon: Wipf & Stock, 2004.

Lewis, C. S. *Mere Christianity.* New York: HarperCollins, 2001.

Nešpor, Zdeněk R. "Religious Processes in Contemporary Czech Society." *Sociologický časopis/Czech Sociological Review* 40, no. 3. 2004

Otter, Jiří. *Five Circuits through Prague in the Footsteps of the Czech Reformation.* Translated by Michael Joyce. Prague: Kalich, 2006.

Spinka, Matthew. *John Hus and the Czech Reform*. Princeton, New Jersey: Princeton University Press, 1966.

Workman, Herbert B. *The Letters of John Hus*. London: Hodder and Stoughton, 1904.

Czech Sources

Ekumenická rada církví. "Členské církve." November 23, 2004. http://www.ekumenickarada.cz/in/678/member_churches#.V-TytCN940o

Ekumenická rada církví. "Promluva Pavla Černého k papeži Benediktu XVI." October 2, 2009. http://www.ekumenickarada.cz/in/1492/promluva_pavla_cerneho_k_papezi_benediktu_xvi#.V-OhJyN940p

The Empire Strikes Back: The Catholic Counter-Reformation in Spain and the World

English Sources

Adam, Karl. *The Spirit of Catholicism*. Translated by Justin McCann. Garden City, New York: Doubleday Image Books, 1954.

Alberigo, Giuseppe. "From the Council of Trent to 'Tridentinism.'" Translated by Emily Michelson. *From Trent to Vatican II: Historical and Theological Investigations*. Edited by Raymond F. Bulman and Frederick J. Parrella, 19–38. New York: Oxford University Press, 2006.

Álvarez, David J. *The Pope's Soldiers. A Military History of the Modern Vatican*. Modern War Studies. Lawrence Kansas: University Press of Kansas, 2011.

Bainton, Roland H. *Here I Stand: A Life of Martin Luther*. Nashville, Tennessee: Abingdon Press, 1978.

Barrett, Matthew M. *God's Word Alone. The Authority of Scripture*. The Five Solas. Edited by Matthew Barrett. Grand Rapids, Michigan: Zondervan, 2016.

Bérenger, Jean. *A History of the Habsburg Empire 1273–1700*. Translated by C. A. Simpson. New York: Routledge, 1994.

Berkhof, Louis. *Systematic Theology*. Grand Rapids, Mighigan: Eerdmans, 1938.

Bettenson, Henry and Chris Maunder. *Documents of the Christian Church*, 4th ed. New York: Oxford University Press, 2011.

Boehmer, Heinrich. *Road to Reformation. Martin Luther to the Year 1521*. Translated by John W. Doberstein and Theodore Gerhardt Tappert. Philadelphia, Pennsylvania: Muhlenberg Press, 1946.

Bunson, Matthew. *OSV's Encyclopedia of Catholic History*. Revised edition. Hungtinton, Indiana: Our Sunday Visitor, 2004.

Cairns, Earle E. *Christianity Through The Centuries. A History of the Christian Church.* Grand Rapids, Michigan: Academie Books, 1981.

Collins, Mary Ann. *Another Side of Catholicism. Insights from a Former Catholic Nun.* New York: iUniverse, 2004.

Crawford, Peter. *The War of the Three Gods. Romans, Persians and the Rise of Islam.* South Yorkshire, UK: Pen & Sword Military, 2013.

D'Aubigné, J. H. Merle. *History of the Reformation of the Sixteenth Century,* vol. 1. Translated by H. White. New York: American Tract Society, 1849.

De Noxeto, P. "The Bull Romanus Pontifex (Nicholas V) January 8, 1455." *European Treaties Bearing on the History of the United States and Its Dependencies to 1648.* Edited by Frances Gardiner Davenport. Clark, New Jersey: The Lawbook Exchange, 2004.

Drobner, Hubertus R. *The Fathers of the Church. A Comprehensive Introduction.* Translated by Siegfried S. Schatzmann. Peabody, Massachusetts: Hendrickson Publishers, 2007.

Enns, Paul. *The Moody Handbook of Theology Revised and Expanded.* Chicago, Illinois: Moody Publishers, 2008.

Ferguson, Sinclair. "Scripture and Tradition: The Bible and Tradition in Roman Catholicism." *Sola Scriptura: The Protestant Position on the Bible.* 2nd ed. Edited by Don Kistler. Lake Mary, Florida: Reformation Trust, 2009.

Fisher, George P. *The Reformation.* New York: Charles Scribner's Sons, 1903.

Fuller, Andrew Gunton. *The Complete Works of the Rev. Andrew Fuller with A Memoir of His Life.* Boston, Massachusetts: Lincoln, Edmands & Co., 1833.

Geisler, Norman L. and Joshua M. Betancourt. *Is Rome The True Church? A Consideration of the Roman Catholic Claim.* Wheaton, Illinois: Crossway Books, 2008.

Geisler, Norman L. and Ralph E. MacKenzie. *Roman Catholics and Evangelicals: Agreements and Differences.* Grand Rapids, Michigan: Baker Books, 2001.

Gifford, Edward Hamilton. "The Catechetical Lectures of S. Cyril: Introduction." *A Select Library of the Nicene and Post-Nicene Fathers of the Christian Church, Second Series. Translated into English with Prolegomena and Explanatory Notes,* vol.7. Edited by Philip Schaff and Henry Wace. New York: Christian Literature Company, 1894.

Gombrich, E. H. *A Little History of the World.* Translated by Caroline Mustill. London: Yale University Press, 2008.

Henry, Carl F.H. *God, Revelation, and Authority.* 5 volumes. Wheaton, Illinois: Crossway Books, 1999.

Hitchcock, James. *History of the Catholic Church. From the Apostolic Age to the Third Millennium.* San Francisco, California: Ignatius Press, 2012.

Holcomb, Justin. *Know the Creeds and Councils*. Grand Rapids, Michigan: Zondervan, 2014.

Hughes, Michael. *Early Modern Germany, 1477–1806*. Philadelphia, Pennsylvania: University of Pennsylvania Press, 1992.

Jedin, Hubert. *A History of the Council of Trent*, vol. 1. Translated by Dom Ernest Graf. New York: Thomas Nelson and Sons, 1963.

Jones, Michael Keenan. *Toward a Christology of Christ the High Priest*. Rome: Editrice Pontificia Università Gregoriana, 2006.

Kaplan, Benjamin J. *Divided by Faith. Religious Conflict and the Practice of Toleration in Early Modern Europe*. Cambridge, Massachusetts: The Belknap Press of Harvard University Press, 2007.

Kinder, Arthur Gordon. "Spain." *The Early Reformation in Europe*. Edited by Andrew Pettegree, 215–37. Cambridge, Massachusetts: Cambridge University Press, 1992.

Kolb, Robert. "The Bible in the Reformation and Protestant Orthodoxy." *The Enduring Authority of the Christian Scriptures*. Edited by D. A. Carson. Grand Rapids, Michigan: Eerdmans, 2016.

Levie, Jean. *The Bible, Word of God in Words of Men*. Translated by S. H. Treman. New York: P. J. Kennedy, 1961.

Llorente, José A. *The History of the Inquisition of Spain. From The Time of Its Establishment to the Reign of Ferdinand VII. Composed from The Original Archives of The Supreme Council and from Those of Subordinate Tribunals of The Holy Office*. London: Geo B. Whittaker, 1826.

Linehan, Peter. *History and the Historians of Medieval Spain*. Oxford, UK: Clarendon Press, 1993.

McCarthy, James G. *The Gospel According to Rome: Comparing the Tradition and the Word of God*. Eugene, Oregon: Harvest House Publishers, 1995.

McGrath, Alister E. *Christian Theology: An Introduction*. 6th edition. Malden, Massachusetts: Wiley Blackwell, 2017.

McNally, Robert. "The Council of Trent and the German Protestants." *Theological Studies* 25 no. 1. February, 1964.

Nalle, Sarah T. *God in La Mancha. Religious Reform and the People of Cuenca 1500–1650*. Baltimore, Maryland: The Johns Hopkins University Press, 1992.

———. "Inquisitors, Priests and the People during the Catholic Reformation in Spain." *The Sixteenth Century Journal* 18 no. 4. Winter 1987.

———. "Private Devotion, Personal Space: Religious Images in Domestic Context." *La Imagen Religiosa en La Monarquía Hispánica: Usos y Espacios*. Colección de La Casa de Velázquez. Edited by María Cruz de

Carlos, P. Civil, F. Pereda, and C. Vincent-Cassy, 255–72. Madrid: Casa de Velázquez, 2008.

———. "Self-Correction and Social Change in the Spanish Counter Reformation." *Religion and the Early Modern State: Views from China, Russia, and the West.* Edited by James D. Tracy and Marguerite Ragnow. Cambridge, Massachusetts: Cambridge University Press, 2004.

———. "The Millennial Moment: Revolution and Radical Religion in Sixteenth-Century Spain." *Toward the Millennium: Messianic Expectations from the Bible to Waco.* Edited by Mark Cohen and Peter Schäfer. Studies in the History of Religions 77. Edited by H. G. Kippenberg and E. T. Lawson, 153–73. Leiden, Netherlands: Brill Press, 1998.

Nichols, Stephen J. *The Reformation. How a Monk and a Mallet Changed The World.* Wheaton, Illinois: Crossway Books, 2007.

Noble, Thomas F. X., Barry Strauss, Duane J. Osheim, Kristen B. Neuschel, Elinor A. Accampo, David D. Roberts, and William B. Cohen. *Western Civilization: Beyond Boundaries.* 6th edition. Boston, Massachusetts: Wadsworth Cengage Learning, 2011.

O'Collins, Gerald. *Christology. A Biblical, Historical, and Systematic Study of Jesus.* 2nd edition. New York: Oxford University Press, 2009.

Ortiz-Griffin, Julia and William D. Griffin. *Spain and Portugal: A Reference Guide from the Renaissance to the Present.* Edited by Frank J. Coppa. New York: Facts on File, 2007.

Owen, John. *The Death of Death in the Death of Christ.* Carlisle, Pennsylvania: The Banner of Truth Trust, 2007.

———. *The Doctrine of Justification by Faith through The Imputation of The Righteousness of Christ Explained, Confirmed, and Vindicated.* Grand Rapids, Michigan: Reformation Heritage Books, 2006.

Pastor, Ludwig. *The History of the Popes from the Close of The Middle Ages. Drawn from the Secret Archives of the Vatican and Other Original* Sources, vol. 11. Edited by Ralph Francis Kerr. London: Kegan Paul, Trench, Trübner & Co., 1912.

Pattenden, Miles. *Pius IV and the Fall of the Carafa. Nepotism and Papal Authority in Counter-Reformation Rome.* Oxford: Oxford University Press, 2013.

Pérez, Joseph. *The Spanish Inquisition: A History.* Translated by Janet Lloyd. New Haven, Connecticut: Yale University Press, 2005.

Plummer, Marjorie Elizabeth. *From Priest's Whore to Pastor's Wife: Clerical Marriage and the Process of Reform in the Early German Reformation.* St. Andrews Studies in Reformation History. New York: Routledge, 2016.

Polybius. *Histories.* Medford, Massachusetts: Macmillan, 1889.

Pusey, E. B. *The Doctrine of the Real Presence: As Contained in the Fathers from the Death of Saint John the Evangelist to the Fourth General Council, Vindicated, in Notes on a Sermon, "The Presence of Christ in the Holy Eucharist," Preached A.D. 1853, before the University of Oxford.* London: John Henry Parker, 1855.

Rae, John. *Martin Luther: Student, Monk, Reformer.* London: Hodder and Stoughton, 1894.

Reymond, Robert L. *A New Systematic Theology of the Christian Faith.* 2nd ed. Nashville, Tennessee: Thomas Nelson, 1998.

Roman Missal, The. Translated into the English Language for The Use of The Laity. Published with The Approbation of The Right Rev. The Bishop of Philadelphia. Philadelphia, Pennsylvania: Eugene Cummiskey, 1861.

Schaff, Philip. *The Creeds of Christendom, with a History and Critical Notes,* vol. 2. New York: Harper & Brothers, 1890.

Schreiner, Thomas. *Faith Alone. The Doctrine of Justification.* The Five Solas. Edited by Matthew Barrett. Grand Rapids, Michigan: Zondervan, 2015.

Shedd, William Greenough Thayer. *Dogmatic Theology.* Edited by Alan W. Gomes. 3rd ed. Phillipsburg, New Jersey: P & R Publishers, 2003.

Sheldon, Henry C. *History of the Christian Church: The Modern Church Part Two.* Peabody, Massachusetts: Hendrickson Publishers, 1998.

Smolarsky, Dennis C. *The General Instruction of the Roman Missal, 1962–2002. A Commentary.* Collegeville, Michigan: The Liturgical Press, 2003.

Stavarianos, Leften S., Lorretta Kreider Andrews, John R. McLane, Frank Safford, and James E. Sheridan. *A Global History of Man.* Boston, Massachusetts: Allyn and Bacon, 1974.

Trueman, Carl R. *Grace Alone. Salvation as a Gift of God.* The Five Solas. Edited by Matthew Barrett. Grand Rapids, Michigan: Zondervan, forthcoming.

———. *Luther on the Christian Life, Cross and Freedom.* Theologians on the Christian Life. Edited by Stephen J. Nichols and Justin Taylor. Wheaton, Illinois: Crossway, 2015.

VanDrunen, David. *God's Glory Alone. The Majestic Heart of Christian Faith and Life.* The Five Solas. Edited by Matthew Barrett. Grand Rapids, Michigan: Zondervan, 2015.

Videira, Ruben. "Catholicism, Postmodernism, and Inerrancy in Southern Europe." *The Implications of Inerrancy for the Global Church. The Truth of God's Word Defended, Explained and Extolled by Authors from 17 Countries across the Globe.* Edited by Mark Tatlock. Los Angeles, California: The Master's Academy International, 2015.

Watanabe, Morimichi. *Nicholas of Cusa: A Companion to His Life and His Times.* Edited by Gerald Christianson and Thomas M. Izbicki. Burlington, Vermont: Ashgate, 2011.

Webster, William. *Roman Catholic Tradition. Claims and Contradictions.* Battle Ground, Washington: Christian Resources, 1999.

———. *Saving Faith. How Does Rome Define It?* Battle Ground, Washington: Christian Resources, 1997.

———. *The Church of Rome at the Bar of History.* Carlisle, Pennsylvania: The Banner of Truth Trust, 2003.

Wellum, Stephen J. *Christ Alone. The Uniqueness of Jesus as Saviour.* The Five Solas. Edited by Matthew Barrett. Grand Rapids, Michigan: Zondervan, forthcoming.

Spanish Sources

Alcalá, Angel, ed. Inquisición Española y Mentalidad Inquisitorial: Ponencias Del Simposio Internacional Sobre Inquisición, Nueva York, Abril de 1983. Ariel Historia. Sección Historia Moderna y Contemporánea. Barcelona: Ariel, 1984.

Alexander IV, Pope. Primera Bula Inter Caetera. May 3, 1493.

———. Segunda Bula Inter Caetera, May 4, 1493.

Archivo General de Indias. Escribanía de Cámara. Legislatura 159B. Rollo II. Petición: Estancia de Guanajuato de Rodrigo Basquez. Provincia de Michoacán, January 13th, 1547.

Atkinson, James. Lutero y El Nacimiento Del Protestantismo. Grandes Obras de Historia 66. Barcelona: Altaya, 1997.

Baschet, Jérôme. La Civilisation Féodale: De l'an Mil à La Colonisation de l'Amérique. 3rd ed. Champs Histoire. Paris: Flammarion, 2006.

Bataillon, Marcel. Erasmo y España. Estudios sobre La Historia Espiritual. Translated by Antonio Alatorre. Méjico-Madrid-Buenos Aires: Fondo de Cultura Económica, 1991.

Beltrán Torreira, Federico Mario. "El Concepto de Barbarie en La España Visigoda." Antiguedad y Cristianismo 3, 1986.

Bianchu, Diana. "Inquisición e Ilustración. Un Expediente Reservado de José del Campillo." Investigaciones Históricas. Época Moderna y Contempóranea 22, 2002.

Borges, Pedro. Misión y Civilización en América. Madrid: Editorial Alhambra, 1987.

Cano, Melchor. Parecer del M. Fr. Melchor Cano del Orden de Predicadores, Doctor Teólogo de Las Universidades de Alcalá y Salamanca, Obispo de Canarias (Cuyo Obispado Renunció) sobre Las Diferencias entre Paulo

IV Pont. Max. y El Emperador Carlos V Primero de Las Españas y de las Indias. Madrid: n.p., 1736.

Caraillac, Louis. "Lo Morisco Peninsular y Su Proyección en la Conquista de América." In El Mundo de Los Conquistadores. Edited by Martín Ríos Saloma. Madrid: Sílex Ediciones, 2015.

Castañeda Delgado, Paulino. La Teocracia Pontifical en Las Controversias sobre El Nuevo Mundo. Instituto de Investigaciones Jurídicas. Serie C: Estudios Históricos 59. México: Universidad Nacional Autónoma de México, 1996.

Chaunu, Pierre. La España de Carlos V. Biblioteca Historia de España. Translated by E. Riambau Saurí. Barcelona: RBA Coleccionables, 2005.

Cortés, Hernán Cartas de Relación. México: Porrúa, 1976.

De Cadenas y Vicent, Vicente. El Concilio de Trento en La Época del Emperador Carlos V. Instituto "Salazar y Castro." Madrid: Hidalguia, 1990.

De Castro, Adolfo. Exámen Filosófico sobre Las Principales Causas de La Decadencia de España. Cádiz: Imprenta de D. Francisco Pantoja, 1852.

———. Historia de Los Protestantes Españoles y de Su Persecución por Felipe II. Cádiz: Revista Médica, 1851.

De Courcelles, Dominique. "La Historiografía y La Literatura de la Conquista de América en Los Tiempos de Carlos V y Felipe II: El Ejemplo de Un Conquistador, Escritor e Historiador, Bernal Díaz del Castillo." El Mundo de Los Conquistadores. Edited by Martín Ríos Saloma. Madrid: Sílex Ediciones, 2015.

De Encinas, Diego. Cedulario Indiano, Reproducción facsímil de la edición única de 1596. Madrid: Cultura Hispánica, 1945–1946.

De Mora, A. H. La Iglesia de Jesu-Cristo en España. Nueva York: Sociedad Americana de Tratados, n.d.

Dedieu, J. P. "¿Pecado Original o Pecado Social? Reflexiones en Torno a La Constitución y a La Definición del Grupo Judeo-Converso en Castilla." Manuscrits: Revista d'Historia Moderna 10. January 1992.

Delumeau, Jean. El Catolicismo de Lutero a Voltaire. Barcelona: Editorial Labor, 1973.

———. La Reforma. Nuevo Clio: La Historia y Sus Problemas. Barcelona: Editorial Labor, 1977.

Díaz del Castillo, Bernal. Historia Verdadera de la Conquista de la Nueva España. Edited by Carmelo Sáenz de Santa María. Madrid: Centro Superior de Investigaciones Científicas, 1982.

Diestre Gil. Antolín. El Sentido de La Historia y La Palabra Profética. Un Análisis de Las Claves Históricas para Comprender El Pasado, Presente y El Futuro Político-Religioso de La Humaniación desde La Civiliación Babilónica hasta El Nuevo Orden Mundial. Terrassa: Editorial CLIE, 1995.

Dussel, Enrique. "Concilios, Clero y Religiosos." In Historia General de La Iglesia en América Latina: Introducción General a La Historia de la Iglesia en América Latina, 472–560. Salamanca: Ediciones Sígueme, 1983.

———. Historia de la Iglesia en América Latina: Medio Milenio de Coloniaje y Liberación (1492–1992). 6th ed. Madrid: Mundo Negro, 1992.

Erlanger, Philippe. Carlos V. Translated by Manuel Morera. Madrid: Ediciones Palabra, 2000.

Escault, Rene-H. "La Reforma en Su Perspectiva Histórica: La Historiografía Más Reciente y Significativa." Actualidad y Catolicidad de La Reforma. Colección Pensamiento Evangélico. Edited and translated by José Grau, 39–57. Barcelona: Ediciones Evangélicas Europeas, 1967.

Esteve Barva, Francisco. La Historiografía Indiana. 2nd ed. Madrid: Gredos, 1992.

Fernandez Álvarez, Manuel. Carlos V. El César y El Hombre. Espasa Forum. Madrid: Grupo Planeta, 2014.

———. Sombras y Luces en La España Imperial. Madrid: Espasa, 2004.

Fernández Muñiz, Áurea Matilde. Breve Historia de España. La Habana: Editorial de Ciencias Sociales, 2005.

Fernández Terricabras, Ignasi. Felipe II y El Clero Secular. La aplicación del Concilio de Trento. Madrid: Sociedad Estatal para la Conmemoración de los Centenarios de Felipe II y Carlos V, 2000.

Fernández Vargas, Valentina. "Prologo." In La Inquisición y Los Españoles. Edited by Miguel Castellote. Madrid: Colección Básica, 1973.

Florescano, Enrique. El Ocaso de La Nueva España. México: Clío, 1996.

Flori, Jean. La Guerra Santa. La Formación de La Idea de Cruzada en el Occidente Cristiano. Translated by Rafael Gerardo Peinado Santaella. Colección Estructuras y Procesos. Madrid: Trotta, 2003.

Gaite Pastor, Jesús. "La Cámara de Castilla en Los Siglos XVI y XVII. La Instrucción de Felipe II en 1588." In IV Jornadas Científicas sobre Documentación de Castilla e Indias en El Siglo XVI. Edited by Juan Carlos Galende Díaz, 144–61. Madrid: Universidad Complutense de Madrid, 2005.

García Fitz, Francisco. "La Reconquista: Un Estado de La Cuestión." Clio y Crimen 6 (2009): 142–215.

García Villoslada, R. Introducción a La Historia de La Iglesia en España. Madrid: BAC, 1979.

Gonzaga, Javier. Concilios. 2 volumes. Grand Rapids, Michigan: International Publications, 1965–66.

González Cremona, Juan Manuel. *Carlos V. El Señor de Dos Mundos*. Colección Memoria de La Historia 28. Madrid: Planeta, 1989.

González Martín, Marcelo. "El III Concilio de Toledo." Identidad Católica de Los Pueblos de España y Raíces Cristianas de Europa." *Anales de la Real Academia de Ciencias Morales y Políticas* 66. 1989.

Grau, José. "La Reforma, 1517 y 1967." *Actualidad y Catolicismo de La Reforma*. Colección Pensamiento Evangélico. Edited and translated by José Grau. Barcelona: Ediciones Evangélicas Europeas, 1967.

Grunberg, Bernard. "Hernán Cortés y la guerra de los Conquistadores." *El Mundo de Los Conquistadores*. Edited by Martín Ríos Saloma. Madrid: Sílex Ediciones, 2015.

Guerra Orozco, María Cecilia. "Alcance del Concilio de Trento en América: Justo Donosto y Su 'Guía del Buen Párroco.'" Miradas desde La Historia Social y La Historia Intelectual. *América Latina en Sus Culturas: De Los Procesos Independentistas a La Globalización*. Edición Literaria. Edited by Hugo Cancino, Rogelio de la Mora V, Lená Medeiros de Menezes, and Silvano G.A. Benito Moya. Córdoba: Centro de Estudios Históricos Profesor Carlos S.A. Segreti, Facultad de Filosofía de Humanidades Universidad Católica de Córdoba, Universidad Vercruzana México, Instituto de Investigaciones Histórico-Sociales, 2012.

Gutierrez Marin, Manuel. *Historia de La Reforma en España. Introducción y Selección Antológica*. Barcelona: Producciones Editoriales del Nordeste, 1973.

Gutierrez Nieto, Juan Ignacio. "Los Conversos y el Movimiento Comunero." *Hispania: Revista Española de Historia* 94. 1964.

Hernández Franco, Juan. *Cultura y Limpieza de Sangre en la España Moderna. Puritate Sanguinis*. Murcia: Universidad de Murcia, 1996.

——. *Sangre Limpia, Sangre Española. El Debate de los Estatutos de Limpieza (Siglos XV-XVII)*. Madrid: Cátedra, 2011.

Howard, Jorge P. *La Otra Conquista de América*. Buenos Aires: La Aurora, 1951.

Jacob, E. F. "El Pensamiento Político." *El Legado de la Edad Media*. Edited by C. G. Crump and E. F. Jacob. Translated by J. M. F. Madrid: Ediciones Pegaso, 1944.

Jiménez Gómez, Juan Ricardo. "La Colonización del Pueblo de Tlachco-Querétaro en La Frontera de Chichimecas, 1531–1599." *El Mundo de Los Conquistadores*. Edited by Martín Ríos Saloma. Madrid: Sílex Ediciones, 2015.

Kamen, Henry. *La Inquisición Española. Una Revisión Histórica*. Biblioteca Historia de España. Translated by María Morrás. Barcelona: RBA Coleccionables, 2005.

Konetzke, Richard. Colección de Documentos para la Historia de la Formación de Hispanoaméricana 1493–1810. Madrid: Centro Superior de Investigaciones Científicas, 1953.

Kovaliov, Sergei Ivanovich. Historia de Roma. Básica de Bolsillo 142. Edited by Domingo Plácido. Translated by Marcelo Ravoni. Madrid: Akal, 2007.

León Cázares, María del Carmen. "Entre el Breviario y la Espada. Los Mercedarios como Capellanes en Las Huestes Conquistadoras." El Mundo de Los Conquistadores. Edited by Martín Ríos Saloma. Madrid: Sílex Ediciones, 2015.

Lindsay, Thomas M. Historia de la Reforma: La Reforma en Suiza, Francia, los Países Bajos, Escocia e Inglaterra. Los Movimientos Anabpatista y Sociniano. La Contrarreforma. Translated by Lurá Villanueva. Biblioteca de Cultura Evangélica IX. Buenos Aires: Editorial La Aurora, 1959.

Llorente, José A. Colección Diplomática de Varios Papeles Antiguos y Modernos sobre Dispensas Matrimoniales y Otros Puntos de Disciplina Eclesiástica. Madrid: Imprenta de Ibarra, 1809.

———. La Inquisición y Los Españoles. Edited by Miguel Castellote. Madrid: Colección Básica, 1973.

López de Gómara, Francisco. Historia General de Las Indias. Prólogo de Jorge Gurría Lacroix. Barcelona: Red Ediciones, 2016.

López Lamerain, María Constanza. "El Concilio de Trento y Sudamérica: Aplicaciones y Adaptaciones en el III Concilio Limense." Anuario de Historia de la Iglesia en Chile 29. 2011.

López y Andrés, Jesús María. "Real Patronato Eclesiástico: La Iglesia de Almería, como Iglesia de Estado, en Época de los Reyes Católicos." Boletín del Instituto de Estudios Almerienses 1. 1981.

Lorente, Sebastian. Historia de la Conquista del Perú. Lima: Masias, 1861.

Lortz, Joseph. Historia de la Reforma. 2 volumes. Translated by Lucio Garcia Ortega. Madrid: Tuarus Ediciones, 1963.

Lutz, Heinrich. Reforma y Contrarreforma. Europa entre 1520 y 1648. Madrid: Alianza Editorial, 1992.

MacKay, Juan A. El Otro Cristo Español. Un Estudio de La Historia Espiritual de España e Hispanoamérica. Colecciones Renovación IV. Buenos Aires: La Aurora, 1952.

Martínez, José María. La España Evangélica Ayer y Hoy. Esbozo de Una Historia para Una Reflexión. Barcelona: Editorial CLIE, 1994.

Menéndez Pelayo, Marcelino. Historia de Los Heterodoxos Españoles II: Protestantismo y Sectas Místicas. Regalismo y Enciclopedia. Heterodoxía en El Siglo XIX. Biblioteca de Autores Cristianos 151. Madrid: La Editorial Católica, 1987.

Mitre Fernández, Emilio. "Los Límites entre Estados: La Idea de Frontera en El Medievo y El Caso de Los Reinos Hispano-Cristianos." El Mundo de Los Conquistadores. Edited by Martín Ríos Saloma. Madrid: Sílex Ediciones, 2015.

Moa, Pío. Nueva Historia de España. De la II Guerra Púnica al Siglo XXI. Madrid: La Esfera de Los Libros, 2010.

Morales Padrón, Francisco. Los Conquistadores de América. Madrid: Espasa-Calpe, 1974.

———. Teorías y Leyes de La Conquista. Madrid: Ediciones de Cultura Hispánica, 1979.

Morín, Alejandro. "La Frontera de España Es de Natura Caliente. El Derecho de Conquista en Las Partidas de Alfonso X El Sabio." El Mundo de Los Conquistadores. Edited by Martín Ríos Saloma. Madrid: Sílex Ediciones, 2015.

Niño, Francisco. La Iglesia en La Ciudad: El Fenómeno de Las Grandes Ciudades en América Latina, Como Problema Teológico y Como Desafío Personal. Tesi Gregoriana Series 13. Roma: Editrice Pontificia Universita Gregoriana, 1996.

O'Malley, John W. Trento, ¿Qué Pasó en El Concilio? Panorama 18. Translated by Isidro Arias Pérez. Maliaño, Cantabria: Editorial Sal Terrae, 2015.

Palazzo, Eric. "La Iglesia, La Formación del Imaginario Medieval y Su Recepción en América Después de La Conquista." El Mundo de Los Conquistadores. Edited by Martín Ríos Saloma. Madrid: Sílex Ediciones, 2015.

Palomo, Federico. "Apuntes Historiográficos en Torno a La Disciplina y El Disciplinamiento Social Como Categorías de La Historia Religiosa de La Alta Edad Moderna." Cuadernos de Historia Moderna 19. 1997.

Passuth, Laszlo. Poker de Papas. Translated by Elisabeth Szel. Barcelona: Luis de Caralt, 1981.

Pérez Valencia, Felipe. "Catolicismo y Conquista del Nuevo Mundo. Función, Apogeo y Decadencia." Teología y Cultura 11 no. 16. Diciembre 2014.

Paolo Prodi. El Soberano Pontífice. Un Cuerpo y Dos Almas: La Monarquía Papal en La Primera Edad Moderna. Madrid: Akal, 2010.

Prosperi, Adriano. El Concilio de Trento. Una Introducción Histórica. Valladolid: Junta de Castilla y León, 2008.

Recopilación de Las Leyes de Los Reinos de Las Indias. Madrid: Gráficas Ultra, 1943.

Rodríguez García, Pedro. A Tumba Abierta (Entrevistas en el Diario «Arriba»). PPC: Madrid, 1971.

Rubial García, Antonio. "Los Santos Reyes Magos en el Imaginario Medieval y Novohispano." El Mundo de Los Conquistadores. Edited by Martín Ríos Saloma. Madrid: Sílex Ediciones, 2015.

Ruiz Bañuls, Mónica. "El Discurso Indígena en El Proyecto Evangelizador Novohispano del Siglo XVI." Revista Iberoamericana de Teología 2, no 11. July-December 2010.

Salom Franco, Nicolás. Dos Colosos Frente al Mar. Colección Estudio de Derecho Internacional 6. Bogotá: Pontificia Universidad Javeriana, 2003.

Sánchez Herrero, José. Concilios Provinciales y Sínodos Toledanos de Los Siglos XIV y XV. La Religiosidad del Clero y Pueblo. La Laguna: Universidad de la Laguna, 1976.

Sánchez Jiménez, Antonio. "Fanfarronería Española en 'La Contienda de García de Paredes y El Capitan Juan de Urbina:' Lope de Vega ante La Leyenda Negra." Europa (Historia y Mito) en La Comedia Española. XXXIII Jornadas de Teatro Clásico. Almagro, 6, 7, y 8 de Julio de 2010. Edited by Felipe B. Pedraza Jiménez, Rafael González Cañal, and Elena E. Marcello. Colección Corral de Comedias 29. Cuenca: Universidad de Castilla La Mancha, 2012.

Schatz, Klaus. Los Concilios Ecuménicos. Encrucijadas en La Historia de La Iglesia. Valladolid: Trotta, 1999.

Schnürer, Gustave. La Iglesia y La Civilización Occidental en La Edad Media. Edited and translated by José Miguel de Azaola. Madrid: Fax, 1955.

Tánacs, Erika. "El Concilio de Trento y Las Iglesias de La América Española: La Problemática de Su Falta de Representación." Fronteras de la Historia 7. 2002.

Tejada y Ramiro, Juan. Colección de Cánones y de Todos los Concilios de La Iglesia Española. 5 volumes. Madrid: Imprenta de Pedro Montero, 1859.

Thomas, Werner. La Represión del Protestantismo en España 1517–1648. Leuven, Belgium: Leuven University Press, 2001.

Tineo, Primitivo. "La Recepción de Trento en España (1565). Disposiciones sobre La Actividad Episcopal." Anuario de Historia de la Iglesia 5. 1996.

Trigo Chacón, Manuel. La España Imperial. Testamentos de los Reyes de La Dinastía Austríaca Española. Madrid: Editorial Liber Factory, 2009.

Tubau, Xabier. "Las Alianzas a La Luz del Derecho Canónico: El Tractatus Dialogicus de Confoederatione Principum et Potentatum (c. 1495) de Juan López de Segovia." Anuario de Estudios Medievales 40 no 2. July-December 2010.

Valbuena, Miguel. La Iglesia Católica ante La Biblia y La Historia. Chicago, Illinois: Editorial Moody, n.d.

Valiente, Francisco Tomás. Manual de Historia del Derecho Español. Madrid: Tecnos, 1992.

Vidal, Cesar. Cambiaron la Historia. Barcelona: Planeta, 2010.

———. Diccionario de Los Papas. Barcelona: Ediciones Península, 1997.

———. El Caso Lutero. Madrid: EDAF, 2008.

———. El Legado del Cristianismo en la Cultura Occidental: Los Desafíos del Siglo XXI. Pozuelo de Alarcón: Espasa, 2000.

———. La Historia Secreta de la Iglesia Católica en España. Barcelona: Ediciones B, 2014.

———. Mitos y Falacias de la Historia de España. Madrid: Ediciones B, 2010.

———. Momentos Cumbre de la Historia que Cambiaron Su Curso. Madrid: EDAF, 2009.

———. Pontífices: De las Persecuciones al Papa Francisco. Barcelona: Ediciones Península, 2014.

Vizuete Mendoza, Juan Carlos. La Iglesia en la Edad Moderna. Madrid: Síntesis, 2000.

Webster, William. La Salvación, La Biblia y el Catolicismo Romano. Edimburgo: El Estandarte de la Verdad, 2015.

Zorita Bayón, Miguel. Breve Historia del Siglo de Oro. Madrid: Nowtilus, 2010.

French Sources

Calmette, Joseph. *L'Élaboration du Monde Moderne,* CLIO Introduction Aux Études Historiques 5. Paris: Presses Universitaires de France, 1942.

Guéranger, Prosper. *Institutions Liturgiques,* vol. 1. Paris: Chez Débécourt Libraire, 1840.

Latin Sources

Index auctorum et librorum, qui tanquam haeretici, aut suspecti, aut perniciosi, ab officio S. Ro. Inquisitionis reprobantur, et in universa Christiana republica interdicuntur. Rome: Antonio Blado, 1557.

Soteally, Joannis and Horatii Lucii. Sacrosancti et Oecumenici Concilii Tridentini sub Paulo III, Julio III, Paulo IV Pontificibus Maximis Celebrati Canones et Decreta: Juxta Exemplar Romae Editum annum MDLXIV. Matriti: Ex Typographia Emmanuelis Martin, 1778.

German Sources

Geiler von Kaysersberg, Johann. Ein heilsam kostliche Predig Doctor Johans Geiler von Keisersperg Predicanten and Loblicße Flat Straßburg die er zu Bischoff Albrechten von Straßburg und andern erwirdigen Prelaten und seiner gantzen ersamen Priesterschafft vor Zeiten gethon hat. Strasbourg, France: n.p., 1513.

Köpf, Ulrich, Helmar Junghans, and Karl Stackmann. D. Martin Luthers Werke. Weimarer Ausgabe (Sonderedition): Abteilung 4, Teil 5: Frühe Vorlesungen und Späte Schriften, Band 54 (Luthers Werk — Sonderedition/ gesamtwerk). Special edition. Weimar, Germany: Verlag Hermann Böhlaus Nachfolger, 2007.

The Risen and Exalted Christ: A New Perspective Needed in Mexico

English Sources

Agren, David. "Pope's focus on violence and poor likely to make for 'uncomfortable' Mexico visit." *The Guardian*. December 11, 2015. https://www.theguardian.com/world/2015/dec/11/ pope-francis-mexico-visit-february-michoacan-juarez.

Booth, William. "In Mexico City, Passion Comes Amid Suffering." April 2009. http://banderasnews.com/0904/nr-centerstage.htm.

Dunning, Brian. "The Virgin of Guadalupe." *Skeptoid Podcast*. April 13, 2010. https://skeptoid.com/episodes/4201.

Friedlander, Judith. "Mexican Religion and the Virgin of Guadalupe." http://macaulay.cuny.edu/eportfolios/friedlander10/theme/religion/ mexican/there/.

Gendron, Mike. "Religion Cannot Save Anyone." October 2016. http:// myemail.constantcontact.com/Religion-Cannot-Save-Anyone. html?soid=1103609831924&aid=PPrRLEKvcCs.

Gibson, Charles. *The Aztecs under Spanish Rule: A History of the Indians of the Valley of Mexico, 1519–1810*. Stanford, California: Stanford University Press, 1964.

Pew Research Center. "A Snapshot of Catholics in Mexico, Pope Francis' next stop." February 10, 2016. www.pewresearch.org/fact-tank/2016/02/10/a-snapshot-of-catholics-in-mexico-pope-francis-next-stop.

Ricard, Robert. *The Spiritual Conquest of Mexico: An Essay on the Apostolate and the Evangelizing Methods of the Mendicant Orders in New Spain, 1523–1572*. Translated by Lesley Byrd Simpson. Berkeley: University of California Press, 1966.

Rome Reports. *Full Text of Pope's Speech to Mexican Bishops*. February 13, 2016. http://www.romereports.com/2016/02/13/ full-text-of-the-pope-francis-speech-at-mexican-bishops.

Schmal, John P. "The Indigenous People of Central Mexico, 2." 2003. http:// houstonculture.org/mexico/mexico2.html.

Trexler, Richard C. *Reliving Golgotha: The Passion Play of Iztapalapa.* Cambridge, Massachusetts: Harvard University Press, 2003.

Spanish Source

Herrera, Claudia and Bertha Teresa Ramírez."Sin importar creencias, todos somos guadalupanos: Calderón." La Jornada. October 13, 2011. http:// www.jornada.unam.mx/2011/10/13/opinion/005n1pol.

Suffering for Christ: Biblical Lessons from Chinese Saints

Aikman, David. Jesus in Beijing: How Christianity is Transforming China and Changing the Global Balance of Power. Washington DC: Regnery Publishing, 2003.

Biographical Dictionary of Chinese Christianity. "Wang Mingdao." http://www. bdcconline.net/en/stories/w/wang-mingdao.php.

Carson, D.A. How Long, O Lord?: Reflections on Suffering and Evil. Grand Rapids, Michigan: Baker Academic, 2006.

Earle, Ralph H. "2 Timothy." Ephesians through Philemon. The Expositor's Bible Commentary. Edited by Frank E. Gaebelein. Grand Rapids, Michigan: Zondervan Publishing House, 1978.

Harvey, Thomas Alan. Acquainted With Grief. Grand Rapids, Michigan: Brazos Press, 2002.

Knight, George William, III. The Pastoral Epistles. New International Greek Testament Commentary. Grand Rapids, Michigan: Eerdmans, 1992.

Lea, Thomas D. and Hayne P. Griffin. 1, 2 Timothy, Titus: An Exegetical and Theological Exposition of Holy Scripture. The New American Commentary 34. Nashville: Broadman & Holman Publishers, 1992.

Lian Xi. Redeemed by Fire: The Rise of Popular Christianity in Modern China. New Haven: Yale University Press, 2010.

Li Yading. "No Compromise." Christian History Institute. 2008. https://www. christianhistoryinstitute.org/magazine/article/no-compromise/.

MacArthur, John F., Jr. The Power of Suffering: Strengthening Your Faith in the Refiner's Fire, 2nd ed. Colorado Springs, Colorado: David C Cook, 2011.

Marshall, I. Howard. A Critical and Exegetical Commentary on the Pastoral Epistles. London: T&T Clark International, 2004.

Piper, John. "Why God Appoints Suffering for His Servants." *Suffering and the Sovereignty of God.* Edited by John Piper and Justin Taylor. Wheaton, Illinois: Crossway, 2006.

Showalter, Brandon. "China on Track to Have World's Largest Christian Population by 2030." *The Christian Post.* July 21, 2016. http://www.christianpost.com/news/china-largest-christian-population-world-200-million-believers-despite-crackdown-166718/.

Stockment, Martha. "Robert Morrison." Biographical Dictionary of Chinese Christianity. http://www.bdcconline.net/en/stories/m/morrison-robert.php.

Stott, John Robert Walmsley. *Guard the Gospel: The Message of 2 Timothy.* The Bible Speaks Today. Downers Grove, Illinois: Inter-Varsity Press, 1973.

Towner, Philip H. *The Letters to Timothy and Titus.* New International Commentary on the New Testament. Grand Rapids, Michigan: Eerdmans, 2006.

Wang, Stephen. *The Long Road to Freedom: The Story of Wang Mingdao.* Translated by Ma Min. Tonbridge, United Kingdom: Sovereign World, 2002.

Wong Ming Dao. *A Stone Made Smooth.* Littleton, Colorado: OMF Books, 1982.

Is Justification a Pronouncement or a Process? A Critique of Eastern Orthodox Soteriology

English Sources

Stamoolis, James, ed. *Three Views on Eastern Orthodoxy and Evangelicalism.* Grand Rapids, Michigan: Zondervan, 2004.

Lossky, Vladimir. *The Mystical Theology of the Eastern Church.* Cambridge: James Clarke & Co., 1957.

Hodges, Zane. *Absolutely Free: A Biblical Reply to Lordship Salvation.* Dallas: Redencion Viva, 1989.

Stavropoulos, Christoforus. "Partakers of Divine Nature." *Eastern Orthodox Theology: A Contemporary Reader.* Edited by Daniel B. Clendenin. Grand Rapids, Michigan: Baker, 1995.

Harris, R. Laird. "Tsedek." *Theological Wordbook of the Old Testament.* Edited by R. Laird Harris, Gleason L. Archer, Jr., and Bruce K. Waltke. Electronic ed. Chicago, Illinois: Moody Press, 1999.

Schreiner, Thomas. *Faith Alone: The Doctrine of Justification.* The Five Solas. Grand Rapids, Michigan: Zondervan, 2015.

Moo, Douglas. *Romans 1–8.* Wycliffe Exegetical Commentary. Edited by Kenneth Barker. Chicago, Illinois: Moody, 1991.

Packer, James I. Packer. "God's Justification of Sinners." *Christianity Today.* March 16, 1959.

Spurgeon, Charles Haddon. *Look Unto Me: The Devotions of Charles Spurgeon.* Edited by Jim Reimann. Grand Rapids, Michigan: Zondervan, 2008.

Russian Source

Stragorodsky, Sergius. Православное учение о спасении [Orthodox Teaching about Salvation]. n.p.: Sergiyev Posad, 1895.

Is Christ Clarified or Clouded? A Case Study in Bible Translation from Albania

English Sources

Abbott-Smith, G. *A Manual Greek Lexicon of the New Testament.* New York: T&T Clark, 2001.

Aland, Kurt, Matthew Black, Carlo M. Martini, Bruce M. Metzger, and Allen Wikgren, eds. *The Greek NewTestament,* 4th ed. Stuttgart, Germany: Deutsche Bibelgesellschaft, 2000.

Dana, H. E., and Julius R. Mantey. *A Manual Grammar of the Greek New Testament.* New York: Macmillan, 1955.

Encyclopædia Britannica. "Illyria." Last updated October 3, 2015. https://www. britannica.com/place/Illyria#ref87154.

Han, Nathan E. *A Parsing Guide to the Greek New Testament.* Scottdale, Pennsylvania: Herald Press, 1971.

Hendriksen, William. *Philippians, Colossians and Philemon.* New Testament Commentary. Grand Rapids, Michigan: Baker, 1994.

Jacques, Edwin E. *The Albanians: An Ethnic History from Prehistoric Times to the Present.* Jefferson, North Carolina: McFarland, 1995.

Kubo, Sakae. *A Reader's Greek-English Lexicon of the New Testament.* Grand Rapids, Michigan: Zondervan, 1975.

MacArthur, John F., Jr. *Philippians.* Chicago, Illinois: Moody, 2001.

Morris, Leon. *The Gospel According to John.* Grand Rapids, Michigan: Eerdmans, 1971.

Mounce, William D., *Basics of Biblical Greek Grammar,* 2nd ed. Grand Rapids, Michigan: Zondervan, 2003.

Rogers, Cleon L., Jr. and Cleon L. Rodgers III. *New Linguistic and Exegetical Key to the Greek New Testament.* Grand Rapids, Michigan: Zondervan, 1998.

Summers, Ray. *Essentials of New Testament Greek*. Edited by Thomas Sawyer. Nashville, Tennessee: Broadman & Holman, 1995.

Tasker, R. V. G. *The Gospel According to John: An Introduction and Commentary*. Grand Rapids, Michigan: Eerdmans, 1975.

Trading Economics. "Albania Average Monthly Wages 1996–2016." http:// www.tradingeconomics.com/albania/wages.

Wallace, Daniel B., *Greek Grammar Beyond the Basics: An Exegetical Syntax of the New Testament with Scripture, Subject, and Greek Word Indexes*. Grand Rapids, Michigan: Zondervan, 1997.

Zerwick, Maximilian, and Mary Grosvenor. *A Grammatical Analysis of the Greek New Testament*, 5th ed. Rome: Pontifical Biblical Institute, 1996.

Albanian Sources

Bibla: Dhjata e Vjetër dhe Dhjata e Re [The Bible: The Old Testament and the New Testament]. Tirana: Shoqëria Biblike Shqiptare, 1995.

Bibla: Dhjata e Vjetër dhe Dhjata e Re [The Bible: The Old Testament and the New Testament]. Tirana: Shoqëria Biblike Shqiptare, 2000.

Bibla: Dhjata e Vjetër dhe Dhjata e Re [The Bible: The Old Testament and the New Testament]. Tirana: Shoqëria Biblike Shqiptare, 2002.

Bibla e Studimit [The Study Bible]. Tirana: Shoqëria Biblike Shqiptare, 2009.

Buda, Aleks, Giusi Zanichelli, Kaliopi Naska, Kosta Naço,Kristo Frashëri, Liljana Bërxholi, Luan Rama, Nevila Nika, Roderic L. Mullen, Shaban Sinani, Theofan Popa, Violeta Rakipi. Kodikët e Shqipërisë. [Codices of Albania]. Edited by Shaban Sinani, Arian Leka, and Lila Plasari. Tirana: Drejtoria e Përgjithshme e Arkivave, 2003.

Clark, James. 1912 dhe Ungjilli [1912 and the Gospel]. Gjirokastër, Albania: AEM-Misioni Ungjillor, 2012.

Dhjata e Re [The New Testament]. Tirana: Albanian Bible Society, 2002.

Dhjata e Re [The New Testament]. Tirana: Shoqëria Biblike Ndërkonfesionale e Shqipërisë, 2014.

Dhjata e Re e Zotit edhe Shpëtimtarit t'ënë Jisu Krisht, Kthyerë prej Elinishtesë Shqip, Ndë të folë Toskërisht [The New Testament of our Lord and Savior, Jesus Christ, Translated from Greek into Albanian, in the Tosk Dialect]. Tirana: Shoqëria Biblike Ndërkonfesionale e Shqipërisë, 1998.

Dhjata e Re në Krahasim [The New Testament in Comparison]. Tirana: Shoqëria Biblike Shqiptare, 2005.

Dhjata e Re, Psalmet, Fjalët e Urta [The New Testament, Psalms, Proverbs]. Tirana: Shoqëria Biblike Shqiptare, 2013.

Libri i Jetës: Testamenti i Ri. [The Book of Life: The New Testament]. China: MediaServe, 2014.

Thomson, Alexander. Rruga Biblike Në Shqipërinë e Vjetër. [Bible Ways in Old Albania]. Gjirokastër, Albania: Misioni Ungjillor, 2002.

Young, David. Lëvizja Protestante Midis Shqiptarëve 1908–1991 [The Protestant Movement Among Albanians 1908–1991]. Prishtina, Kosovo: Shtëpia Botuese TENDA, 2011.

The Bankruptcy of Islam and the Riches of Christ

Bigelow, Edward G. An Exegetical Approach to the Saving Accomplishments of Christ's Atonement. Sun Valley, California: The Master's Seminary, 1997.

Euben, Roxanne L., ed. "Declaration of War against the Americas." Princeton Readings in Islamist Thought. Princeton, New Jersey: Princeton University Press, 2009.

Gesenius, W. and S.P. Tregelles. Gesenius' Hebrew and Chaldee Lexicon to the Old Testament Scriptures. Bellingham, Washington: Logos Bible Software, 2003.

Gilchrist, John. "Eid-ul-Adha: Abraham and the Sacrifice." http://www.answering-islam.org/Gilchrist/eid.html.

Grisanti, Michael A. The Relationship of Israel and the Nations in Isaiah 40–55. Dallas, Texas: Dallas Theological Seminary, 1993.

Grudem, Wayne. Systematic Theology: An Introduction to Biblical Doctrine. Nottingham, United Kingdom: Inter-Varsity Press, 2007.

Hughes, Thomas Patrick. A Dictionary of Islam. Clifton, New Jersey: Reference Book Publishers, 1965.

Kittel, Gerhard and Gerhard Friedrich, eds. Translated by Geoffrey William Bromiley. Theological Dictionary of the New Testament, Vol 1. Grand Rapids, Michigan: Eerdmans, 1964.

MacArthur, John F., Jr. Philippians. Chicago, Illinois: Moody Publishers, 2001.

———. "The Grim Reality of the Last Days." March 20, 2011. http://www.gty.org/resources/sermons/41–66/The-Grim-Reality-of-the-Last-Days.

Mahally, Farid. "A study of the word 'love' in the Qur'an." http://www.answering-islam.org/Quran/Themes/love.htm.

Marsh, Charles R. Share Your Faith with a Muslim. Chicago, Illinois: Moody Press, 1975.

Mathews, K.A. The New American Commentary, Vol 1B, Genesis 11:27–50:26. Nashville: Broadman & Holman Publishers, 2005.

McCormick, Micah John. The Active Obedience of Jesus Christ. Ann Arbor, Michigan: UMI Dissertation Publishing, 2010.

Nolland, John. The Gospel of Matthew. Grand Rapids, Michigan: Eerdmans, 2005.

Pew Research Center. "Muslims and Islam: Key findings in the U.S. and around the world." July 22, 2016. http://www.pewresearch.org/fact-tank/2016/07/22/muslims-and-islam-key-findings-in-the-u-s-and-around-the-world.

Ryken, Philip Graham. Exodus: Saved for God's Glory. Wheaton, Illinois: Crossway Books, 2005.

Sammons, Peter. No Hope Without It!: The Doctrine of Active Obedience Defined and Vindicated. Sun Valley, California: The Master's Seminary, 2013.

Swanson, James. A Dictionary of Biblical Languages with Semantic Domains: Greek (New Testament). Oak Harbor, Washington: Logos Research Systems, 1997.

White, James R. What Every Christian Needs to Know About the Qur'an. Bloomington, Minnesota: Bethany House Publishers, 2013.

———. The God Who Justifies. Bloomington, Minnesota: Bethany House Publishers, 2001.

Zwemer, Samuel Marinus. Islam: A Challenge to Faith. New York: Layman's Missionary Movement, 1909.

The Threat of Religious Pluralism in Post-Communist Croatia

English Sources
Beach, Bert Beverly. *Ecumenism: Boon or Bane?* Washington, DC: Review and Herald, 1985.

Bettenson, Henry, ed. *Documents of the Christian Church,* 2nd ed. Oxford: Oxford University Press, 1963.

First Things. "Evangelicals and Catholics Together: The Christian Mission in the Third Millennium." May 1994. https://www.firstthings.com/article/1994/05/evangelicals—catholics-together-the-christian-mission-in-the-third-millennium-2.

Journey Mart. "Religion in Croatia." http://journeymart.com/de/croatia/religion.aspx.

Kim, Seyoon. *The Origin of Paul's Gospel.* Eugene, Oregon: Wipf & Stock, 2007.

MacArthur, John F., Jr. "Evangelicals and Catholics Together." *The Master's Seminary Journal* 6 no. 1. Spring 1995.

Maier, Gerhard. *Biblical Hermeneutics.* Translated by Robert W. Yarbrough. Wheaton, Illinois: Crossway, 1994.

McCarthy, James G. *The Gospel According to Rome: Comparing Catholic Tradition and the Word of God*. Eugene, Oregon: Harvest House, 1995.

McGrath, Alister E. *Christian Theology: An Introduction*, 5th ed. Malden, Massachusetts: Wiley-Blackwell, 2011.

Miles, Todd L. *A God of Many Understandings?: The Gospel and Theology of Religions*. Nashville, Tennessee: B&H Publishing Group, 2010.

O'Brien, John Anthony. *The Faith of Millions*. Huntington, Indiana: Our Sunday Visitor, 1974.

Croatian Sources

Duda, Bonaventura and Dragan Kalajdžić. *Jesmo li sami na putu [Are We Alone on the Way?]*. Zagreb: Kršćanska Sadašnjost, 1980.

Hrvatski sabor. "O proglašenju zakona o potvrđivanju ugovora između Svete Stolice i Republike Hrvatske o pravnim pitanjima." February 13, 1997. http://narodne-novine.nn.hr/clanci/medunarodni/1997_02_3_19.html.

Jambrek, Stanko. *Crkve Reformacijske baštine, [Churches of Reformation heritage in Croatia]*. Zagreb: Bogoslovni Institut, 2003.

Kasper, Walter. *Krist da Crkva ne, in Teološke meditacije*. Družba katoličkog Apostolata: Zagreb 1980.

Kerovec, Roko. "Kristovo uskrsnuće i eshatološka vizija Božjeg kraljevstva kao platforma evangelizacijske prakse: izazovi i mogućnosti evanđeoskog poslanja" [Christ's Resurrection and the Eschatological Vision of God's Kingdom as a Platform of Evangelistic Practice: Challenges and the Possibilities of Evangelical Mission]. *Kairos: Evangelical Journal of Theology* 2, no. 2, 2008.

Šagi-Bunić, Tomislav. *Ali Drugog puta Nema [But There is no Other Way]*. Zagreb: Kršćanska Sadašnjost, 1972.

The Straw Kingdom: A False Christ in the Philippines Exposed

Beasley-Murray, George R. Beasley-Murray. *John*, 2nd ed. Word Biblical Commentary 36. Nashville, Tennessee: Thomas Nelson, 1999.

Kingdom of Jesus Christ, The. "The Entrustments." http://www.kingdomofjesuschrist.org/the-entrustments.

Kingdom of Jesus Christ, The. "The Threefold Ministry." http://www.kingdomofjesuschrist.org/the-threefold-ministry.

Kittel, Gerhard, Gerhard Friedrich, and Geoffrey W. Bromiley, eds. *Theological Dictionary of the New Testament*. Grand Rapids, Michigan: Eerdmans, 1985.

MacArthur, John F., Jr. *Matthew 16–23*. The MacArthur New Testament Commentary. Chicago, Illinois: Moody, 1988.

———. *John 12–21*. The MacArthur New Testament Commentary. Chicago, Illinois: Moody, 2008.

Miller, Jack. "Religion in the Philippines." Center for Global Education. http://asiasociety.org/education/religion-philippines.

Moody, Dale. "God's only Son: The Translation of John 3:16 in the Revised Standard Version." *Journal of Biblical Literature* 72, no. 4. December 1953.

Rodger, Daniel and Ryan Turner. "Signs of a Cult and Pastor Apollo Quiboloy." Christian Apologetics and Research Ministry. https://carm.org/signs-of-a-cult-pastor-apollo-quiboloy.

Romualdez, Babe. "Pastor Apollo Quiboloy's prophecy." *The Philippine Star.* June 12, 2016. http://www.philstar.com/opinion/2016/06/12/1592040/pastor-apollo-quiboloys-prophecy.

Sin and Savior: The Right Diagnosis Needed in the Central American Church

Allison, Gregg R. *Historical Theology: An Introduction to Christian Doctrine*. Grand Rapids, Michigan: Zondervan, 2011.

Calvin, John. *Institutes of the Christian Religion* 3. Edited by John T. McNeill, translated by Ford Lewis Battles. Philadelphia: Westminster John Knox Press, 1960.

Challies, Tim. "An Introduction to Calvinism & Arminianism." November 24, 2003. http://www.challies.com/articles/an-introduction-to-calvinism-arminianism.

Culver, Robert Duncan. *Systematic Theology: Biblical and Historical*. Fearn, Tain, UK: Christian Focus, 2005.

Erickson, Millard J. *Christian Theology,* 2nd ed. Grand Rapids, Michigan: Baker, 1998.

Frame, John M. *Systematic Theology: An Introduction to Christian Belief*. Phillipsburg, New Jersey: P&R Publishing, 2013.

Gonzalez, Justo L. *The Story of Christianity: The Early Church to the Dawn of the Reformation*. New York: HarperCollins, 1984.

Holcomb, Justin S. *Know the Heretics*. Grand Rapids, Michigan: Zondervan, 2014.

MacArthur, John F., Jr. "Counseling and the Sinfulness of Humanity." *Introduction to Biblical Counseling: A Basic Guide to the Principles and Practice of Counseling*. Dallas, Texas: Word, 1994.

Ott, Ludwig. *Fundamentals of Catholic Dogma*. Translated by Patrick Lynch. Charlotte, North Carolina: TAN Books, 1974.

Pew Research Center. "Religion in Latin America: Widespread Change in a Historically Catholic Region." November 23, 2014. http://www.pewforum. org/2014/11/13/religion-in-latin-america/.

Schaff, Philip and David S. Schaff. *History of the Christian Church 3*. New York: Charles Scribner's Sons, 1910.

Sproul, R. C. *Faith Alone: The Evangelical Doctrine of Justification*. Grand Rapids, Michigan: Baker, 1995.

Zemek, George J. *A Biblical Theology of the Doctrines of Sovereign Grace: Exegetical Considerations of Key Anthropological, Hamartiological and Soteriological Terms and Motifs*. Little Rock, Arkansas: n.p., 2002.

Unmasking the False Christ of the Prosperity Gospel in Latin America

English Sources

Armstrong, John H., Jim Elliff, Albert Mohler, Jr., and J.I. Packer. *The Glory of Christ*. Wheaton, Illinois: Crossway Books, 2002.

Bennett, Arthur, ed. *The Valley of Vision: A Collection of Puritan Prayers and Devotions*. Carlisle, Pennsylvania: The Banner of Truth Trust, 1989.

Dresser, Horatio W. *The Spirit of the New Thought: Essays and Addresses by Representative Authors and Leaders*. n.p.: Thomas Y. Crowell, 1917.

Jones, David W. and Russell S. Woodbridge, *Health, Wealth & Happiness, Has the Prosperity Gospel Overshadowed the Gospel of Christ?* Grand Rapids, Michigan: Kregel Publications, 2011.

Owen, John. *Meditations and Discourses on the Glory of Christ*. Chicago, Illinois: Moody Press, 1949.

Piper, John. *God's Passion for His Glory: Living the Vision of Jonathan Edwards*. Wheaton, Illinois: Crossway, 1998.

Vincent, Thomas, *The Shorter Catechism Explained from Scripture*. Carlisle, PA: The Banner of Truth Trust, 1980.

Spanish Sources

Azar, Aquiles. *Prosperados por la Palabra*. Ministerios Aquiles Azar, Santo Domingo: RD, 2016, Libro en formato PDF.

Barrientos, Marco. *¡Cree, todo es posible! La fe que mueve a Dios*. Pocket Book: Spanish Edition, Charisma House. Edición de Kindle.

Cruz, Camilo. *La Ley de la atracción: Mitos y Verdades sobre el Secreto más extraño del mundo* (Spanish Edition). Taller del Éxito. Edición de Kindle.

Harrison, Everett F., Geoffrey W. Bromiley, y Carl F. H. Henry. *Diccionario de Teología*. Grand Rapids, Michigan: Libros Desafío, 2006.

Osteen, Joel. *Su Mejor Vida Ahora: Siete pasos para vivir a su máximo potencial*. New York: Casa Creación, 2005.

Piper, John. *Los Deleites de Dios*. Miami, Florida: Editorial Vida, 2006.

Prosperidad Universal. "La ley de atracción—es el secreto—Prosperidad Universal." http://www.prosperidaduniversal.org/yo-soy-abundancia/ley-de-atraccion.

Christ Alone and the Fate of the Unreached

Culver, Robert Duncan. *Systematic Theology: Biblical and Historical*. Fearn, Tain, UK: Christian Focus, 2005.

Demarest, Bruce. *The Cross and Salvation: The Doctrine of Salvation*. Foundations of Evangelical Theology. Wheaton, Illinois: Crossway, 1997.

Doran, David M. *For the Sake of His Name: Challenging a New Generation for World Missions*. Allen Park, Michigan: Student Global Impact, 2002.

Erickson, Millard. "The Fate of Those Who Never Hear." *Bibliotheca Sacra* 152, January-March 1995.

Fackre, Gabriel. "Divine Perseverance." *What about Those Who Have Never Heard? Three Views on the Destiny of the Unevangelized*. Edited by John Sanders. Downers Grove, Illinois: Inter-Varsity Press, 1995.

Feinberg, J. S. "Theodicy." *Evangelical Dictionary of Theology*. Edited by Walter A. Elwell. Grand Rapids, Michigan: Baker, 1984.

Fleming, Kenneth C. "No Other Way, No Other Name." *Emmaus Journal* 4. Issue 2, Winter 1995.

Geisler, Norman L. *Systematic Theology* 1. Minneapolis, Minnesota: Bethany House, 2005.

Geivett, R. Douglas. "Is Jesus the Only Way?"*Jesus under Fire: Modern Scholarship Reinvents the Historical Jesus*. Edited by Michael J. Wilkins and James Porter Moreland. Grand Rapids, Michigan: Zondervan, 1995.

Hafemann, Scott. "Responses to Inclusivism: SNJT Forum." *The Southern Baptist Journal of Theology* 2, Issue 2, Summer 1998.

House, Paul R. "Biblical Theology and the Inclusivist Challenge." *The Southern Baptist Journal of Theology* 2, Issue 2, Summer 1998.

Lewis, C. S. *God in the Dock: Essays on Theology and Ethics*. Grand Rapids, Michigan: Eerdmans, 1970.

Lewis, C. S. *Mere Christianity*. New York: Macmillan, 1970.

MacArthur, John F., Jr. and Richard Mayhue, eds. *Biblical Doctrine: A Systematic Summary of Bible Truth*. Wheaton, Illinois: Crossway, forthcoming.

MacArthur, John F., Jr., ed. *The Inerrant Word: Biblical, Historical, Theological, and Pastoral Perspectives*. Wheaton, Illinois: Crossway, 2016.

Miles, Todd. *A God of Many Understandings? The Gospel and Theology of Religions*. Nashville, Tennessee: B&H Publishing, 2010.

Nash, Ronald H. "Restrictivism." *What about Those Who Have Never Heard? Three Views on the Destiny of the Unevangelized*. Edited by John Sanders. Downers Grove, Illinois: Inter-Varsity Press, 1995.

Pinnock, Clark H. *A Wideness in God's Mercy: The Finality of Jesus Christ in a World of Religions*. Grand Rapids, Michigan: Zondervan, 1992.

Pinnock, Clark H. "Overcoming Misgivings about Evangelical Inclusivism." *The Southern Baptist Journal of Theology* 2, Issue 2, Summer 1998.

Pinnock, Clark H. "Toward an Evangelical Theology of Religions." *Journal of the Evangelical Theological Society* 33/3, September 1990.

Piper, John. *Let the Nations be Glad!: The Supremacy of God in Missions*, 2nd ed. Grand Rapids, Michigan: Baker Academic, 2003.

Richard, Ramesh P. "Soteriological Inclusivism and Dispensationalism." *Bibliotheca Sacra* 151, January 1994.

Sanders, John. "Divine Providence and the Openness of God." *Perspectives on the Doctrine of God: 4 Views*. Edited by Bruce Ware. Nashville: Broadman & Holman Academic, 2008.

Sanders, John. "Introduction." *What about Those Who Have Never Heard? Three Views on the Destiny of the Unevangelized*. Edited by John Sanders. Downers Grove, Illinois: Inter-Varsity Press, 1995.

Tillich, Paul. *Christianity and the Encounter of World Religions*. New York: Columbia University Press, 1963.

CONTRIBUTORS

South Africa

Charlie Rampfumedzi serves as principal and lecturer at Christ Seminary in Polokwane, South Africa. After completing his B Juris (Law) at the University of Venda, he received his Diploma in Theology at Christ Seminary, as well as his BA (Honors in Theology) and MA (Theology) at the University of Pretoria. He is enrolled in the DMin program at The Master's Seminary. Charlie is married to Beauty, and they have three boys.

David Beakley serves as the senior pastor of Christ Baptist Church and the academic dean of Christ Seminary in Polokwane, South Africa. After earning a BA in math and business from Houston Baptist University and an MS in industrial engineering from Arizona State University, David spent twenty years in the electronics industry and also earned an MBA from the University of Notre Dame. In May of 1998, David met the Lord, got saved, and in January of 2000, subsequently went to The Master's Seminary (TMS) in Los Angeles. Since graduating from TMS in 2002, David has been serving as a lecturer and academic dean of Christ Seminary in Polokwane, South Africa. In 2014, David completed his PhD in Old Testament Studies from the University of Potchefstroom in South Africa. He has a wonderful bride of thirty-four years, Carol, and four children: Joshua, Jordan, Jason, and Jacob.

Italy

Massimo Mollica received his MDiv from The Master's Seminary in 2009 (ThM in progress). He currently serves as an adjunct faculty member for the Italian Theological Academy while working on evangelism and church planting in Genoa, Italy. Massimo and his wife Susanna have four children aged nine, eight, six, and six.

India

Samuel Williams received his BA in biblical studies from The Master's College and MDiv from The Master's Seminary. He is the dean of the Pastoral Training Seminary in Goa, India, and teaches preaching, Hebrew, and church history. Samuel and his wife Nicole live in Goa with their five children.

Ukraine

Igor Bodun received his MDiv at Irpin Biblical Seminary in Ukraine and his ThM from the European Bible Training Center in Berlin, Germany. He currently serves as professor of theology and preaching at Irpin Biblical Seminary. Also, he serves as senior pastor at First Baptist Church of Chernihiv, Ukraine. He and his wife Natalia have two daughters.

Czech Republic

Lance Roberts received his MDiv and DMin at The Master's Seminary, and has ministered in the Czech Republic since 2001. He currently serves as dean and professor of Bible and preaching at the Czech Bible Institute.

Marcus Denny received his MDiv at The Master's Seminary, and has ministered in the Czech Republic since 2009. He currently serves as a pastor of a church plant in Kladno as well as professor of Bible at the Czech Bible Institute.

Spain

Ruben Videira received his MDiv and ThM degrees at The Master's Seminary. He currently serves at Berea Seminary and

Evangelical Church of León, Spain. Ruben and his wife Jenn have three children: Oliver, Eden, and Caleb.

Mexico

Jim Dowdy is a graduate of Prairie Bible Institute (1975), and has served as a missionary for over forty years in Canada, the United States, and Mexico. He currently serves as a board member at Word of Grace Biblical Seminary in Mexico City and as a professor at its many extension schools throughout Mexico and Central America. He also works together with seminary graduates in the establishment of new congregations across the Valley of Mexico. He and his wife, Carolyn, have two children and nine grandchildren.

Singapore/China

Roger Ng, pastor of Grace Bible Fellowship and president of Grace Bible Seminary, received his MDiv degree from The Master's Seminary and is currently working on his DMin degree. Roger has been teaching in China for the past ten years. Roger and his wife have three sons ages twenty-three, twenty-one, and nineteen.

John Zheng, assistant pastor of Grace Bible Fellowship and professor of Grace Bible Seminary, received his MDiv and ThM degrees from The Master's Seminary. Born in China and raised in New York, John has been involved in the teaching ministry in East Asia for the past three years. John and his wife have two children ages five and three.

Andrew Cho, pastor of Beijing Chinese Church and professor of Grace Bible Seminary, received his MDiv degree from The Master's Seminary. Andrew was formerly a pastor in the United States. He and his wife have two girls, ages eleven and nine.

USA (Russian Language)

Alexey Kolomiytsev received his MDiv and ThM degrees at The Master's Seminary. Since 2002, he has served as pastor-teacher at

Word of Grace Bible Church in Battle Ground, Washington. Alexey and his wife Tanya are enjoying thirty-one years of marriage, praising the Lord for the privilege to serve Him.

Albania

Brad Lay serves as professor of hermeneutics, exegesis, Greek, and preaching at Southeastern Europe Theological Seminary. He received his MDiv at the Master's Seminary and has served in Albania in church planting and leadership training since 1998. He and his wife Julie have five children.

Henry Anderson is a current student at The Master's Seminary and works for The Master's Academy International. He has spent time in the Middle East and has great compassion toward Muslims. Henry is married to Allie.

Croatia

Miško Horvatek is serving as dean of Theological Biblical Academy in Krapina, Croatia. He received a Diploma in Theology at Evangelical and Bible Institute in Vienna, Austria, as well as a DD at Shepherds Theological Seminary in North Carolina and an MDiv from The Master's Seminary. Miško is married to Mira, and they have four children and eighteen grandchildren.

The Philippines

Vincent Greene serves as the dean of the Expository Preaching and Pastoral Ministry Program at The Expositor's Academy, located in the Philippines. He received an MDiv from The Master's Seminary and a ThM in preaching from Southeastern Baptist Theological Seminary. Vincent is married to Kimberly, and they have five children

Honduras

Robert Kensinger is a former family practice physician who received an MDiv from the Master's Seminary in 2007. He serves as professor of theology at the Seminary for Expository Preaching in Siguatepeque, Honduras. He and his wife, Sherry, have three grown children who know and serve the Lord: Daniel, Caleb, and Jaclyn.

Germany/Switzerland

Benedikt Peters is a member of the faculty of European Bible Training Center in Zurich, teaching systematic theology, homiletics and Bible survey. He received his Lic. Phil. in Hebrew and Greek language and literature at the University of Zurich. Benedikt is married to Helene, and they have four children and nine grandchildren.

USA (Spanish Language)

This essay was co-authored by the faculty of The Spanish Expositors Institute (IDEX), a TMAI training center located in Sun Valley, California. IDEX is committed to equipping Spanish-speakers in the United States and around the world for pastoral ministry, expository preaching, and biblical counseling.

Russia

Alexander Gurtaev received his MDiv in 2010 from Samara Center for Biblical Training in Samara, Russia, and his ThM in 2012 from The Master's Seminary. He currently serves as the director and an instructor at Samara Center for Biblical Training. He is also one of the pastors of Transfiguration Baptist Church in Samara. Alexander and his wife Irina have five children ages eleven, nine, five, three, and one.

ABOUT TMAI

MISSION

The Master's Academy International is a worldwide fellowship of training centers committed to fulfilling the Great Commission by training indigenous church leaders to be approved pastor-teachers, able to equip their churches to make biblically sound disciples.

TMAI is a registered nonprofit organization and provides financial support, as well as academic, financial and theological accountability to its member schools.

MINISTRY DISTINCTIVES

LONGEVITY National students are trained and equipped for a lifetime of ministry in their home country. TMAI's commitment to indigenous leadership means that ultimately, each training center will be entrusted to local leaders.

MATURITY Our training centers take seriously the call to equip pastor-teachers for the work of the ministry. TMAI grounds men in the Word of God and gives them the skills to powerfully exposit the Word and Shepherd the flock.

IMPACT Indigenous church leaders are fluent in the language, have an innate knowledge of their culture, and are intimately connected to the people to whom they minister. Ministry effectiveness is maximized from day one.

MULTIPLICATION By training one local pastor, we are strengthening an entire church congregation. With over 4,000 graduates to date, gospel witnesses are multiplied exponentially.

PRESENCE Our faculty live in the country where they minister. This allows them to thoroughly invest in the lives of their students, discipling them and their families as they apply what they've learned through ministry in the local church.

WAYS TO SUPPORT TMAI

PRAY for the faculty and students at our training centers.

SUBSCRIBE to our mailing list to receive field updates and missions insights at www.tmai.org

GIVE to the ministry at www.tmai.org/donate

PARTNER Churches can adopt a particular training center through our ambassador church program. Contact us at ambassador@tmai.org

CONTACT INFORMATION

Mailing Address	24307 Magic Mountain Parkway #540, VALENCIA, CA 91355
Office Address	13248 Roscoe Blvd, Sun Valley, CA 91352
Website	www.tmai.org
Email	info@tmai.org

ALBANIA
CROATIA
CZECH REPUBLIC
GERMANY
HONDURAS
INDIA
ITALY
MALAWI
MEXICO
PHILIPPINES
RUSSIA
SINGAPORE
SOUTH AFRICA
SPAIN
UKRAINE
USA

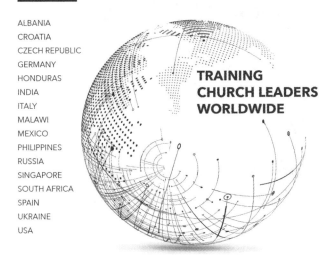

TRAINING CHURCH LEADERS WORLDWIDE

GLOBAL IMPLICATIONS
OF BIBLICAL DOCTRINE
Volume One

GOD'S
PERFECT WORD

THE IMPLICATIONS OF INERRANCY
FOR THE GLOBAL CHURCH

by faculty and graduates of
THE MASTER'S ACADEMY INTERNATIONAL

GENERAL EDITOR MARK TATLOCK
FOREWORD BY JOHN MACARTHUR

GOD'S PERFECT WORD
The Implications of Inerrancy for the Global Church
Global Implications of Biblical Doctrine: Volume 1 (2015)